The Second Seminole War and
the Limits of American Aggression

The
Second Seminole War

AND

the Limits of American Aggression

C. S. MONACO

Johns Hopkins University Press

Baltimore

© 2018 Johns Hopkins University Press
All rights reserved. Published 2018
Printed in the United States of America on acid-free paper

Johns Hopkins Paperback edition, 2019
2 4 6 8 9 7 5 3 1

Johns Hopkins University Press
2715 North Charles Street
Baltimore, Maryland 21218-4363
www.press.jhu.edu

*The Library of Congress has cataloged the hardcover edition of this book
as follows:*

Names: Monaco, C. S., 1950– author.
Title: The Second Seminole War and the limits of American aggression /
C. S. Monaco.
Description: Baltimore : Johns Hopkins University Press, 2018. |
Includes bibliographical references and index.
Identifiers: LCCN 2017025726 | ISBN 9781421424811 (hardcover : alk.
paper) | ISBN 9781421424828 (electronic) | ISBN 1421424819
(hardcover : alk. paper) | ISBN 1421424827 (electronic)
Subjects: LCSH: Seminole War, 2nd, 1835–1842.
Classification: LCC E83.835 .M66 2018 | DDC 973.5/7—dc23
LC record available at https://lccn.loc.gov/2017025726

A catalog record for this book is available from the British Library.

ISBN-13: 978-1-4214-3634-0
ISBN-10: 1-4214-3634-5

*Special discounts are available for bulk purchases of this book.
For more information, please contact Special Sales at 410-516-6936
or specialsales@press.jhu.edu.*

Johns Hopkins University Press uses environmentally friendly book
materials, including recycled text paper that is composed of at least
30 percent post-consumer waste, whenever possible.

For Rose

Contents

Illustrations

Acknowledgments

The idea for this book initially took shape fifteen years ago. But it was not until I grew familiar with the theoretical foundations of settler-colonial studies and its practical applications to the Second Seminole War that I felt prepared to actually proceed with this project. Fragments of text that I had collected for some time suddenly fell into place as part of a larger whole. I therefore owe an intellectual debt to the work of such scholars as Patrick Wolfe and Lorenzo Veracini, as well as an escalating number of other contributors to the field. Moreover, a new outlook emerged through my work as co-principal investigator of a historical and archaeological study of the opening conflicts of the war, a project sponsored by the American Battlefield Protection Program of the National Park Service. For two years I worked alongside archaeologist Gary Ellis and his team from Gulf Archaeology Research Institute while they dug and sifted through layers of soil, revealing the habitations and everyday artifacts of the long-forgotten participants of this unpopular and seemingly unending war. Among some unexpected sensory experiences, the still pungent odor of burned wood (from 180-year-old torched forts and houses) unearthed some eighteen inches underground came as a surprise. This experience evoked a sense of immediacy that seemed to transcend time itself and was of course certainly at odds with the typical archival environment that has marked a large part of my professional life. Aside from engendering a less esoteric, "down to earth" appreciation for the past, this episode convinced me of the necessity of employing an interdisciplinary approach to my research, a decision that is much in evidence in this book.

I am indebted to the help and advice of a host of archivists from all the repositories listed here. I would particularly like to thank the staff of the Gilcrease Museum in Tulsa, Oklahoma, for their research assistance and access to the diaries of Ethan Allen Hitchcock. Jim Cusick of the P. K. Yonge Library of Florida History at the University of Florida also went beyond the call of duty when he helped during a time when I was still recovering from a hospital stay. Such kindnesses are deeply appreciated and not easily forgotten. Both Patricia Wickman and Paul Backhouse read the entire manuscript, and their comments and suggestions helped steer me in the right direction on more than one occasion. It was extremely important to award equal attention to the Indigenous perspective, and both these individuals, as well as informal and all-too-brief meetings with several Seminole elders, aided greatly in this regard. The professionalism of the staff of Johns Hopkins University Press was exemplary, and the kind support of Elizabeth Demers helped make the entire effort as stress-free as one could possibly imagine. I also extend my thanks to the anonymous reviewer for the press. This individual's knowledgeable criticism and remarks clearly resulted in an improved manuscript. I thank the *Journal of Social History*, *American Indian Quarterly*, and the *Florida Historical Quarterly* for their permission to use versions of previous articles of mine here. I also send my heartfelt thanks to all and sundry—both friends and strangers—who have contributed their effort, not only in the production of this volume but in taking the time to discuss different aspects of the Second Seminole War throughout the years. I have gained much in informal talks with students, colleagues, and interested readers of all levels.

I additionally owe a great deal to my wife, Rose. She encouraged me in this multiyear endeavor and did so in virtually every conceivable way. After forty-three years of marriage, she remains the first person I consult while forging any book or article. Her intelligence and deep insight, including her skills as a copy editor, are gifts that any writer would value greatly. It is therefore with great love and affection that I dedicate this book to Rose.

*The Second Seminole War and
the Limits of American Aggression*

Introduction

The Second Seminole War (1835–42) was the boldest and most enduring armed struggle by eastern Indians against the forces of the United States. The initial battlefield successes of the Seminoles caused such apprehension that senior generals believed it would spark a pan-Indian rebellion, especially among thousands of newly displaced Indians who were forced west of the Mississippi River by the removal policies of President Andrew Jackson.[1] The presence of black warriors among the Seminoles was another heady component of the Florida war and struck a note of panic among southerners, who were hypervigilant against any sign of slave revolt. Once more, the specter of a united coalition—this time between Indians and blacks from throughout the country—appeared plausible (though nothing of this nature ever surfaced) and justified all efforts to quash the Seminole uprising, no matter the cost.[2] The victims of America's two original sins, that is, the brutal ethnic cleansing of Indians from their homelands and racialized slavery, loomed as combined forces of retributive justice, a fear that can be traced at least to the mid-eighteenth century.[3]

Furthermore, the war thoroughly stymied the capabilities of the US Army, and, for the first time in its brief history, the army garnered an ignominious reputation both at home and abroad. Incidents such as the capture of the Seminole war leader Osceola—the most renowned Indigenous figure of the antebellum period—while under a white flag of truce betrayed the code of honor that was so deeply instilled at the Military Academy at West Point and contradicted Euro-American cultural mores of gallantry and fair play. Among other seemingly endless assaults to the army's character and abilities, a military court of inquiry initiated by Andrew Jackson placed two of the country's preeminent generals, Winfield

Scott and Edmund P. Gaines, under harsh scrutiny for their botched operations in Florida. A plethora of bad decision making resulted in heated criticism by America's rapidly growing newspaper press and provided a potent political weapon to the administration's Whig opponents.

For a country accustomed to relatively brief and overwhelming victories over Native opponents dating back to the colonial era, the war proved particularly frustrating. Complicating this issue was the fact that the military campaign unfolded amid the liminal characteristics of the Florida peninsula, a subtropical wilderness that often took on an almost otherworldly reputation. This region has indeed been curiously susceptible to the imaginations of outsiders. The territory may have constituted a "howling wilderness," as one war veteran described it, but it also evoked equal parts revulsion and awe: "A glowing picture of hell and heaven."[4] Florida's incongruous nature, much like the Native people who inhabited it, cast it beyond genuine comprehension. Physicians from both the North and the South, for example, envisioned the territory as a land of dark and sinister swamps that continually emitted invisible and poisonous vapors, like some exotic engine of disease and death.[5] Vestiges of this enigmatic, outlier status have lingered to the present. Most historians, for example, have paid slight attention to this conflict, despite its lengthy and widespread impact.[6] Lack of martial success certainly aided in its later marginality, but there is little doubt that geography was also a factor. Florida's rather undistinguished Spanish colonial past, meager population, endemic diseases, and lack of economic development further placed it as a region apart from traditional southern sensibilities as well as the country as a whole. Aside from a single major study, *The History of the Second Seminole War*, written by John K. Mahon fifty years ago, no other academic historian before now has attempted a book-length analysis and virtually no one has looked beyond a strictly military viewpoint to examine how the entire nation was affected—an omission, as will be demonstrated, of startling dimensions.[7] The present volume is intended to fill the gap.

America certainly did not endure the seemingly endless Florida war, as it was called, in stoic indifference; instead, numerous social and political ramifications followed in its protracted wake. A dearth of military laurels, phenomenal costs— $40 million by one estimate, a figure that far exceeded the average annual budget of $33.7 million—rampant fraud, dejected morale, desertions, a high rate of officer resignations, as well the fact that the entire effort appeared to exclusively benefit southern interests were among the most vocal complaints within Congress and among the public at large.[8] The Jackson and Van Buren administrations misjudged the readiness and training of the approximately ten thousand regular army troops (the bulk of the nation's undersized standing army) and thirty thousand militiamen who served. Moreover, a succession of generals failed to accurately assess the leadership abilities and combat prowess of their adversaries. Another perilous factor was the army's unpreparedness for the natural hazards of this southernmost territory, which included a particularly lethal malarial strain. Fear of disease predominated soon after the army's arrival and necessitated regular troop withdrawals between late spring and fall, the so-called sickly season. These hiatuses left Seminoles ample opportunity to reoccupy much of the land that had been lost during the prior year's actions. They also could recover their strength, plan strategy, hunt, plant food crops, attend to their families, and, as one contemporary put it, "again be ready to deal death from their hiding places."[9] Despite most of the surviving Seminoles and their black auxiliaries being transported west by the end of the conflict, the setback to national esteem was palpable. The war dealt an unforeseen blow to Indian removal and clearly refuted deeply held presumptions of military and cultural superiority. On another level, in addition to being a violent clash between the US military and the Seminoles, the campaign can be seen as a contest between ecological forces and American expansionism. Swarms of malaria-infected mosquitoes (whose role in disease was then unknown), in combination with the indefatigable Seminole, proved to be the strongest deterrent to settler-colonialism yet experienced.

In order to present the war as comprehensively as possible, this book follows an interdisciplinary approach. One must not only place this protracted conflict within a military context but also engage the various environmental, medical, and social aspects of the war or its true significance and complexity would be lost. This work is thus divided into four sections that focus on a variety of subdisciplines. Part I, "Genesis of War," covers its origins: from tracing the development of the Seminoles as a distinct people and deciphering the often-misunderstood role that African Americans played among them to the problematic treaties that were imposed upon the Indian leadership and that formed the questionable legal foundation for the deportation process. Seminole cultural and spiritual identity was fundamentally linked to their continued presence in Florida, and the very thought of leaving it was anathema to those who saw themselves as the rightful guardians of the land and the creatures who dwelt there. With the passage of the Indian Removal Act (1830), however, the US government became focused on the indiscriminate expulsion of the eastern Indians to lands west of the Mississippi. But the treaties that were implemented in Florida, like most other Indian treaties, were so fraught with irregularities and fraud that even army officers regarded them with unveiled contempt. These accords may have endowed the mission of Native exclusion with the appearance of legality, but this one-sided and manifestly unjust process also set the stage for war.

Part II, "War of Indian Removal," centers on the principal military engagements and related peace overtures. Faced with their impending exile to the Arkansas Territory, the Seminole war council refused to surrender their reservation land and, contrary to the acquiescence of other, far larger southeastern tribes, resolved upon an aggressive war posture. The Seminole leadership planned a "total war" scenario that aimed to destroy all vestiges of white settler existence in the Florida interior. Implementation of this line of attack was done with such effectiveness that most of the inhabited portions of the peninsula, including major sugar plantations and mills, expansive livestock operations, and myriad farms, were annihilated along with virtually every small homestead and farmhouse—a swath of devastation that totaled $8.5 million in damages.[10] Army commanders were never able to mount an effective campaign against such a strategy. The near total annihilation of a column of 108 men under Major Francis L. Dade—the "Dade Massacre"—as well as the separate assassination of General Wiley Thompson, the superintendent of Seminole removal and a former congressman, on December 28, 1835, shocked the country and resulted in impassioned calls for the "extermination" of the Seminoles. The loss of Dade's command was entirely unexpected, and its emotional impact on the country would not be matched until Custer's notorious "Last Stand" forty years later. Given the unique topography of the Florida Territory and the tactical skills and resolve of the combined forces of the Seminoles, traditional military tactics were deficient in all respects. Under the command of Major General Thomas S. Jesup, however, the army resorted to acts of deception in order to apprehend as many of their foes as possible. The large, pitched battles that marked the first years of combat eventually ceased, and depleted Native forces implemented low-level, guerilla-style maneuvers instead. During the war's final stage, the army used "the persuasive power of gold" (large monetary incentives given to prominent chiefs and warriors) to lure their recalcitrant enemies to the West.[11] Finally, the government announced the end of hostilities only after a few hundred Seminoles were left in the most inaccessible region of the southern Everglades—the forebears of today's Seminole Tribe of Florida, the Miccosukee Tribe of Indians and, lastly, the Independent or Traditional Seminoles still living in various regions of southern Florida.

Although specifics concerning the health and mortality of Indigenous forces may never be known, documentation from the US Army has nevertheless provided valued insights into the war years. Even so, the state of medical care available to the troops and the weighty consequences of continued ill-health on the military's capabilities has been one of the least explored facets of this conflict. Part III, "Health, Medicine, and the Environment," thus examines this rarely mentioned topic as well as the effect of the environment on health and morale. Viewed within a biocultural perspective, malaria-infected mosquitoes were deadly in relation to the invading army while simultaneously shielding Native forces—most of whom benefited from resistance to local diseases due to their long exposure to such illnesses.[12] Insufficient diets, filthy living conditions, a strange "miasmatic" terrain, unremitting Indian attacks, mercury-laden medicines, as well as high temperatures and humidity all lowered the body's resistance to infection and also adversely affected the mental health of US troops. Despite a surfeit of difficulties, the Army Medical Department's usage of quinine sulphate offered definitive proof of its effectiveness under such conditions. Although it was never employed as a prophylactic, quinine was still the primary reason that many soldiers could return to duty after suffering from malaria. This achievement aided in the drug's proliferation among civilian doctors and also led to its usage during subsequent wars— an outcome of the Seminole war that has seldom been noted. By the end of the Florida war, the Medical Department seemingly held an unsurpassed competency, and publications from the surgeon general's office, as well as the department's new statistical orientation, led to the assumption that matters of health could be systematically surveyed and analyzed. This new "scientific" orientation promised to add a new level of dignity and authority to the medical profession as a whole. Conversely, the reputation of East Florida as a land of "darkness and shadows, where pestilence walketh at noonday," as an army surgeon summarized it, discouraged white settlers from migrating to the peninsula, and it remained the least inhabited region of the South until the mid-twentieth century, an outcome that reinforced the far-ranging sense of futility attached to the war effort.

Finally, part IV, "The War and 'The National Mind,'" explores another seldom acknowledged characteristic: the unprecedented role of the burgeoning newspaper press in framing political agendas directly related to the conflict—a development that the Whig Party used to full effect. The Whig construction of Osceola as "the fallen Prince and Hero of Florida" and the party's heated denunciation of his ignoble seizure exposed the Democratic administration as lacking a moral foundation and thus intrinsically unworthy of public office. Sensationalized accounts of Osceola reflected the idealized norms of antebellum society and had little to do with his actual persona. Alternatively, Democrats countered Whig embellishments with the equally forceful claim that Osceola was a savage and "inhuman butcher" of innocents.[13] Following massive newspaper coverage of Osceola's death while imprisoned, his reputation grew exponentially. His demise resulted in the creation of what one scholar has called a "consumable, controlled Euro-american image" that could be advanced for multiple purposes.[14] Whether as hero or red devil, Osceola's entry into the American mythos derived first and foremost from self-interest on the part of white society.

The success of such political "spin" inspired other groups to utilize the "sad and tender chords of the Indian story" for their own gain.[15] An especially notewor-thy example is the notorious "Bloodhound War" cry enacted by abolitionists. Despite the fact that bloodhounds only made a brief appearance in Florida— General Zachary Taylor once implemented a short-lived and ineffective exper-iment using a few tethered and muzzled dogs as trackers—abolitionists never-theless constructed the false claim that the army unleashed these animals to indiscriminately maul and kill Seminoles and blacks, a theme that gained inter-national condemnation.[16] It is thus hardly surprising that this same resonate theme was also employed by Whigs during the 1840 presidential campaign. The proven ease with which certain factions could manipulate events further inspired abolitionists to reframe the Florida war as a racial uplift narrative. Seminole lead-ership was unfortunately co-opted in this imaginative retelling that featured blacks as heroicized freedom fighters. This motif is best exemplified by Joshua Giddings's abolitionist tome, *The Exiles of Florida* (1858), a work still cited today, most often without caveat, by a small cohort of like-minded historians. The back-woods of territorial Florida, in other words, functioned as a convenient canvas on which to project a certain type of visionary politics, a circumstance that has fur-ther aided in the war's historical marginalization.

A NOTE ON SETTLER-COLONIALISM

The emergence of settler-colonial studies* as a distinct discipline has added much-desired clarity to the type of colonial endeavor that was undertaken in Florida and will thus be referenced throughout this book.[17] The field's transnational perspec-tive and analytical framework adds to its utility; the rudiments of settler-colonial-ism thereby become clearly recognizable no matter where this process happened to take root. Settler-colonialism not only pervaded the United States but extended to such countries as Australia, New Zealand, South Africa, and Canada as well. It differs from other colonial undertakings in its emphasis on intensive settlement and land appropriation in addition to the colonial administration of newly occu-pied regions. Unlike the British experience in India, for example, where the In-digenous population was used for their labor and Anglo-settlement was limited,

---

*I have chosen to hypthenate all variations of "settler-colonial" because this gives proper and consistent emphasis, I believe, to the term as a specific subset of colonialism.

the goal of settler-colonialism was to dispossess Native inhabitants from land that had been integral to their existence for millennia and to replace these people and their culture with a new settler society. Indeed, according to anthropologist Patrick Wolfe, a distinctive "logic of elimination" surfaces as settler-colonialism's most definitive characteristic, a situation rife with violence and callous disregard for human life.[18] The myriad colonial wars with Indigenes that arose throughout the world in fact bear a striking resemblance to one another. The long-lived Xhosa Wars (1779–1879) in South Africa in fact demonstrate a certain likeness to what has traditionally been defined as the First, Second, and Third Seminole Wars (1817–58), and featured many of the same traits, albeit on a larger scale: ruthless land seizures, dubious treaties, the large-scale collapse of Indigenous populations, and the intentional setting of rival Native forces against one another by colonial authorities.[19] Settlers inevitably viewed the original inhabitants in their midst as abject strangers, the unwanted and excluded "other," while exalting their own hypermasculine, frontier identity. Given such rank injustice, settler-colonial societies such as those that existed on the Florida frontier developed various psychological means of rendering this process not only as reasonable but just. This underlying and pernicious mind-set continues to thrive unrecognized into the present, requiring attentive scholars to undertake a "decolonizing" approach to history, intentionally stripping away the interpretative veneer or "legitimating illusions" that have protected the interests of settler states. The primary aim here, however, is not to create heroes or villains but to take a renewed look at the Florida war through a far more realistic interpretive lens. The mythic view of America as "a land where settlers won freedom from the wilderness," as one historian has phrased it, is but one of many rhetorical devices that omit the process of Native removal altogether in order to render a prideful frontier narrative.[20] The settlers' prime concern, of course, was never the wilderness per se but "freedom" from Indigenous people. Settler-colonialism was (and still remains) encompassed within the culture at large and thus affected the agenda of political parties, inspired works of art and literature, and was meticulously ingrained in the legal system. Merely to be thought of as a patriotic American also required an unquestioned adherence to the often-contradictory tenets of settler-colonialism.

Following this line of thought, mention of traditional terminology usually applied to the war is merited. The standard progression of three Seminole wars implies a continuity of purpose that may be misleading. As we shall see, the second and third of these wars were wars of attempted Indian removal and thus intrinsically linked to settler-colonialism, while the first campaign involved a relatively short-lived punitive assault across an international border. Seminole deportation and the wholesale resettlement of the frontier were never central concerns during Jackson's initial military expedition. The standard framing of three successive conflicts has nevertheless become so ingrained that it could prove counterproductive at this date to devise entirely new, albeit more detailed, terms. And so, I continue to refer to conventional phrasing in the expectation that the reader will easily discern the intrinsic differences.

The Florida wars have surely been a negligible topic in US history, a startling omission given the full range of circumstances mentioned here. If one additionally considers that the Second Seminole War was the last major conflict fought on American soil before the Civil War and also happened to exhaust the financial resources of the early republic during a time of prolonged economic downturn, such oversight becomes even more startling. This book is therefore dedicated to restoring renewed interest in an undervalued military and cultural phenomenon of far-ranging significance, a full appreciation of which should be judged vital to any thorough understanding of the Jacksonian era as well as the country's problematic relationship with Native people.

PART I

Genesis of the War

CHAPTER 1

Treaties and Reservations

Throughout December 1835, isolated ranchers and yeoman farmers in the remote East Florida interior (the region between the Suwannee and St. Johns Rivers) were caught in an escalating reversal of fortunes. They found they were powerless to fend off numerous Seminoles on horseback, now in full war paint and aided by black warriors, as they fired rifles, torched farms and homesteads, and confiscated livestock. Their war whoops eerily resembled howling wolves, a frightening chorus that, along with the smoke and the cries of livestock, punctuated the mayhem.[1] Surviving families fled in panic to the nearest pine-log stockades, while the disfigured remnants of their former lives littered the countryside: vestiges of furniture, books, personal papers, family heirlooms of all descriptions, and articles of clothing. Feathers from shredded bedding swirled in the wind, a more ethereal reminder of their losses.[2] The roughly two thousand "cracker" settlers who had built, beginning in the early 1820s, widely dispersed settlements in the "Alachua country" (Tierras de la Chua, under the Spanish) found themselves at the mercy of the same "savages" who had been the settlers' main source of contention for years.[3]

Despite its geographic isolation, the Alachua region had long been deemed the most bountiful in Florida, a distinction that dated to at least the late eighteenth century, when naturalist William Bartram praised the region. But this romanticized landscape of "Elysian fields and green plains," to quote Bartram, also held more tangible assets for its Native people.[4] Herds of prized cattle grazed here, especially in the lush Paynes Prairie area, and became a source of unprecedented wealth for the Alachua Seminoles.[5] Shortly after the United States gained jurisdiction of Florida (1821), Seminoles vacated the area for reservation lands, and

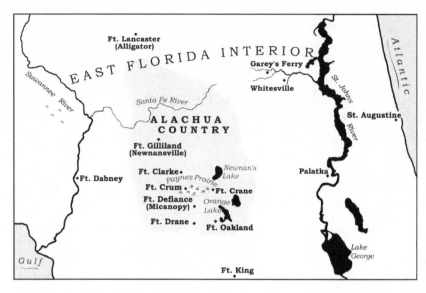

The towns and forts of the East Florida interior (circa 1835–36), scene of the opening of the war and the December uprising. Map by author.

an influx of settlers, mostly from nearby southern Georgia, arrived. These settlers, given their proximity to north-central Florida, were already acclimatized to this subtropical area and had acquired some immunity from the endemic strains of malaria that beset the territory, and so they benefited from the same disease resistance that typically favored Native people.[6] Cattle production thrived once more, and modest towns and hamlets such as Wacahoota, Hogtown, Spring Grove, Micanopy, Newnansville (the Alachua County seat), and myriad other enclaves comprised the nexus of settlement in one of the least accessible regions in the eastern United States—a key aspect of the war that has often been ignored.[7] Hence, from a Native perspective, the outbreak of war was not only a fight for self-determination but also an act of retributive justice. They had, after all, been forced to relinquish these same lands. Micanopy, the paramount chief during the outbreak of war, as well as prominent leaders such as Ote Emathla (Jumper), Abiaka (Sam Jones), Halpatter Tustenuggee (Alligator), Emathla (King Philip), Osceola (Powell), Coacoochee (Wild Cat), and Yaholoochee (Cloud) all recognized that the impending departure date of January 1836 that was imposed by the US government could no longer be postponed. Faced with no other option except deportation to the West, the Seminoles' initial move was to retake Alachua, a sacred ground and the location of much of their former prosperity, an act that possessed both symbolic and strategic value.

Aside from a few army officers in Florida, such as Brigadier General Duncan L. Clinch—commander of the small force that was expected to defend the territory and a career officer with decades of experience in the region—the vulnerability of both the interior settlements and the commercial sugar mills along the east coast went largely unacknowledged. A year before the deadline for Seminole removal, Clinch, who also owned the Lang Syne sugar plantation in Alachua, indeed feared insurrection. "The more I see of this Tribe of Indians," he warned the War Department, "the more fully am I convinced that they have not the least intention of fulfilling their treaty stipulations, unless compelled to do so by a stronger force than mere words."[8] Clinch was supported in his demands by John H. Eaton, the territorial governor, who urged Secretary of War Lewis Cass to send "such an imposing force as shall overawe resistance."[9] Despite such warnings, Cass denied Clinch all the troops that he requested and was emphatic that the general's seven-hundred-man force (actually 10 percent of the nation's miniscule standing army) was ample enough to remove six thousand Seminoles and their slaves to the Arkansas Territory—a demonstration not only of bureaucratic disconnect but of the gross insufficiency of the US Army.[10] The administration of Andrew Jackson presumed that the Seminoles were a spent force, a viewpoint reinforced by high-ranking territorial officials who often remarked that the once "noble race" had become "drunken, lazy and worthless."[11] The conditions of reservation life, created by the punitive terms of the Treaty of Moultrie Creek (1823), did in fact cause severe deprivation, but the Seminoles effectively concealed their intentions and planned their assaults a year in advance. Having placed Native people as debased "others," as is the proclivity of all settler-colonial societies, distant officials were thus predisposed to underestimate the resolve, military capability, and organizational skills of their opponents. Seminole leaders appear to have factored this predilection into their decision making and turned it to their advantage. Despite the desolation wrought during the first weeks of coordinated strikes, many whites still remained in a state of deep psychological denial and presumed that hostilities would end quickly. The initial term for drafting the Florida militia was a scant thirty days.[12]

RESERVATION LAND

A decade prior to the war, relations between non-Natives and Natives were very different. Before the actual signing of the Treaty of Moultrie Creek at an isolated location several miles south of St. Augustine, federal officials followed the advice of General Jackson and believed that only a robust military presence would, in the opinion of the commissioner, Colonel James Gadsden, "render them [Native

Americans] perfectly Subservient to the views of the Government."[13] Nothing less than the complete forfeiture of tribal land was acceptable. Aside from serving the interests of the federal government, land appropriation directly benefited the newly arrived farmers and herdsmen as well as an influential circle of elite planters.[14] Under Spanish dominion, the colony of La Florida (1513–1763) was primarily intended as a geopolitical foothold on the North American continent; large-scale colonization was never seriously considered, and the eastern part of the colony, with the military garrison at St. Augustine, functioned as a base to protect Spanish interests along the ocean trade routes in the region. The demise of the Catholic missions resulted in the relinquishment of the interior, and a modest number of colonial inhabitants restricted themselves to the areas surrounding St. Augustine and Pensacola. During the twenty-year British interregnum (1763–83), a series of indigo and rice plantations were established along the northeastern coastal region, what one historian has called "a brief but promising experiment in plantation-building based on African labor."[15] A few ill-conceived colonization attempts also unfolded in "the Infant Colony"; all met with failure as these ventures were beset with malarial fevers, remained under recurrent danger of Indian attack, and were otherwise ill-prepared for life on the peninsula.[16] The British trading firm of Panton, Leslie & Company had far-reaching influence among Seminoles, however. Company agents and stores on the frontier provided valued trade goods in exchange for deer skins and other items; in effect, licensed agents aided in spreading a culture of mercantilism among the Seminoles.[17] After the retrocession to the Spanish in 1783, the colony continued to produce a limited amount of rice, indigo, cotton, and sugar cane, and in addition it began exporting valuable hardwoods.[18] Like the British, Spanish officials acknowledged that the bulk of the peninsula remained under Seminole sovereignty, and agricultural ventures were restricted to a modest area east of the St. Johns River. With the assumption of US jurisdiction in 1821, however, an entirely new and ambitious agenda was implemented. Officials sought to remake this massive territory under a settler-colonial framework for the first time, quite an enormous undertaking. In order to establish undisputed dominion, the US government, unlike the Spanish and the British, was determined to rid the region of its Native people. "Territoriality," as Patrick Wolfe has emphasized, "is settler colonialism's specific, irreducible element"—a premise that is certainly applicable to Florida at this time.[19]

While Jackson served briefly as provisional Florida governor in 1821, he had yet to see the utility of treaties as a mechanism for Indian removal. His view of Native people under his authority, undoubtedly influenced by the presence of his former enemies, the Red Stick Creeks, was analogous to a vanquished and humiliated foreign enemy: as such, these persons could never be allowed autonomy. Hence Jackson refused any attempt at negotiation, a stance that he adhered to despite pressure to initiate some form of treaty. Formal accords would only endow Indians with an undeserved sense of authority, according to the governor, and would create rights where none should exist.[20] Following Jackson's departure, however, a congressional committee determined that the United States was bound by the terms of the prior Spanish cession (Adams-Onís Treaty, 1819), whereby former colonial "inhabitants," which included Indigenes, were to be recognized as citizens.[21] Territorial political appointees had no other choice but to proceed with a formal treaty that would not only put an official end to many years of hostilities but would be obligated, albeit reluctantly and very briefly, to recognize Native land rights. The central goal was the resettlement and containment of Seminoles on a territorial reservation. Relocation assured, at least in theory, that the expected influx of white settlers would be free from Native interference. Aside from dispossessing Seminoles of their land and villages (transforming them into refugees), reservations were intended to isolate them from settler communities, restrict mobility, and, as will be demonstrated, establish the basis for future subjugation.[22] Under immense pressure, Seminole chiefs from across the territory, under the leadership of Neamathla, yielded to Gadsden's demands to cede twenty-eight million acres of ancestral lands, much of it first-rate farming land, in exchange for four million acres of reservation holdings (the latter would increase slightly over time).[23]

By one conservative estimate, the former Native land was worth a staggering $35 million on the open market. The annual federal budget, in contrast, was a mere $16 million in 1823.[24] In return for this immense concession, Seminoles received a relative pittance—a $5,000 yearly annuity plus other token benefits—a situation that Gadsden, a personal friend of Jackson and a zealous advocate of removal, actually defended as quite liberal.[25] Only a minority of Seminoles in the panhandle who were considered friendly to the United States were allowed to retain their productive holdings in the Apalachicola River district. This faction was not immune to removal pressures, however, and in time they too were similarly compelled to move to the West. In contrast, the majority holdings of the main reservation were regarded as deficient for either hunting or agriculture and subsequently was thought to have slight tangible worth. Decades of aggression between the United States and the Seminoles, including the Patriot War (1812–1814), the First Seminole War (1817–18), and raids by Coweta Creeks (1821), which decimated Seminole and black villages following Jackson's appointment as governor, exacted a severe toll.[26] Seminoles realized they could no longer defy the dreaded general, also known as "Old Mad Jackson" by his Native adversaries;

capitulation remained the sole option.[27] Their strategy shifted from a defensive posture to that of accommodation, an approach often utilized by vulnerable minorities and that inevitably stems from a major imbalance in power.[28] The reservation may have been "the poorest and most miserable region I ever beheld," as "Old Hickory's" replacement William P. DuVal stated after a rare firsthand visit, but Seminoles valiantly tried to make the best of it.[29]

No sooner had they arrived at the reservation, the government began urging yet another move—this time to land west of the Mississippi River. But the mere thought was anathema to Native leaders. "The hardship we suffered . . . gave us pain enough—we do not wish to feel it again," stated Tuckose Emathla (John Hicks), the new tribal leader who replaced an increasingly defiant Neamathla, after a visit with President John Quincy Adams and his secretary of war in Washington, DC (1826).[30] Officials could not fathom why Seminoles would prefer their inadequate lands rather than move to an expansive region out west. Indeed, the government not only restricted Seminoles to the reservation but further circumscribed their movements by creating a vast buffer zone between their inland territory and Florida's extensive Atlantic and Gulf coastlines. Firm lines of demarcation had been drawn in the hope, as a petition from the Alachua settlers stated, that an inferior "species" of people would be confined to their own country so as not "to retard the prosperity of the Territory."[31] However, a few years after the treaty, Joseph M. White, Florida's congressional delegate, became livid about having Seminoles within the territory and demanded their expulsion. Writing to his Florida constituents from Washington, White conjured a variation of the Red Devil stereotype whereby he compared Seminoles to "an *incubus* that paralyzes all our moral and physical energies, preys upon the vitals of the Territory within, and prevents emigration from without."[32] Such hyperbole certainly suited the deep-seated animus of the frontier. But demonization of Native people was hardly new, as it harkened to the colonial era when, among other examples, evangelical preachers likened Indians to "infernal furies in human shape."[33] As settler dominion became inseparable from Euro-American identity, various means were used to objectify Indigenous people as nonhuman: both barbarous and unassimilable.[34]

The reservation lands stretched down the center of the peninsula and ranged from the area of present-day Ocala in the north to the Charlotte River in the south. Quite unlike the dense subtropical hardwood hammocks, lakes, and prairies that distinguished the Alachua district and other fertile regions, the bulk of the land consisted of a much dryer—and nutrient-poor—sandhill and scrub pine ecosystem as well as swampland.[35] "The land to which they are *legally banished*," wrote one contemporary, "is almost wholly unfit for cultivation."[36] Indeed, famine conditions predominated throughout the prewar years, despite sporadic government food assistance. In response to dire conditions, roving bands of Seminoles often headed north to Paynes Prairie, a twenty-thousand-acre expanse of grassy plain and freshwater marsh, and other regions where cattle and game were taken as food. Settlers had dramatically increased their cattle to roughly the same number that the Alachua Seminoles formerly managed at their peak: upward of ten thousand head grazed on this prairie alone.[37] Such superabundance became a natural lure for any starving and distressed population, most especially those who revered the region both as their rightful homeland and as sacred ground (land that was believed to harbor ancestral spirits), a state of affairs that greatly exacerbated tensions with settlers.[38] It had become quite obvious that Seminole cultural and spiritual identity was intrinsically linked to their continued presence in Florida. Even the poor land allotted them was not a sufficient reason to break a bond considered sacrosanct. "If a man has a bad looking woman for his wife, he loves to keep her," as Tuckose Emathla explained to officials who urged him to move again. "So it is with us, if we have a bad country we love to keep it."[39] Indigenous values stood in stark opposition to the binary, cost-benefit mind-set of white entrepreneurs. Above all else, Seminoles, like other Indigenous people, held a spiritual connection to the physical landscape.[40] This reverence, and the belief that Seminoles were the ethical custodians of the land, was reinforced from birth, when mothers ritually buried their newborns' umbilical cords in the soil beneath their dwellings. "Here our navel strings were first cut & the blood from them sunk into the earth & made the country dear to us," Tuckose Emathla further explained.[41] Moreover, ceremonies such as the Green Corn Festival focused on the power of sacred fire; the concept of ceremonial ground thus added to an already-heightened regard for the land. The burial places of the Seminole dead were yet another weighty dimension. "The graves of a community link the dead forever to the landscape," Seminole historian Susan A. Miller observes, "for the spirits of the deceased remain at or return to the site of burial."[42] In describing the Seminoles' reluctance to leave the country, a contemporary journalist quoted an unidentified Native source as saying that "the trees were as his body; their branches as his limbs; and the water of the land as his blood."[43] This sensibility is featured in the modern-day reflections of Anne Waters, a Seminole academic and philosopher: "As a child, my being Indian was being a Seminole. My family was not just Indian, but a people with a long and serious history in the Americas. To be Seminole was to still be a renegade, tergiversator, an insurgent presence in our own land. And to us that land was everything that we had been and were still. Always, it was about the land."[44] The physical environment, in other words, including the waters and

creatures that inhabited it, was deemed so fundamental that the thought of relin-
quishing it for a foreign land meant nothing less than a kind of symbolic death.[45]

Before the official transfer of Florida to the United States, Spanish colonial
governor José Coppinger (East Florida) privately assured Seminole leaders that
they would retain their land holdings. In a move that provoked rancor between
Seminoles and US authorities, Coppinger claimed that Spain had merely sold
that part of East Florida where *"the white man had cultivated with the plough and
the hoe."*[46] Since whites only farmed east of the St. Johns River (in the northern
part of the territory), Indians were misled into thinking that they still held dominion over most of the territory. "They therefore look upon us as robbers and oppres-
sors," General Thomas Jesup later informed the secretary of war during the height
of hostilities, "and have determined . . . to die on the ground rather than leave it."[47]
Therefore, according to Jesup, colonial officials deliberately exacerbated tensions
between Indigenes and the United States. Some Spanish officials did indeed retain bitter feelings toward the United States in response to the destruction, massive
financial damages, and loss of honor brought about by previous armed incursions,
such as Andrew Jackson's invasion during the First Seminole War. Moreover,
affronts against Coppinger (including the breaking and entering of his personal
residence in St. Augustine and the pilfering of his private papers by US officials
during the transition) exacerbated long-standing animosities. The outgoing Spanish administration therefore had adequate motivation to make the transition as
difficult as possible for the Americans. A policy of significant misinformation directed to the Seminoles became an easy form of payback.[48]

FRAUDULENT TREATIES

In accordance with the settler-colonial mentality of the Jackson era, dealings with
Native people stemmed from a rejectionist strategy that, first and foremost, aimed
to eliminate them from the land. Deceit and coercion, as we have already seen,
were pervasive. In a moment of candor on the floor of the US House of Representatives, Horace Everett of Vermont, addressing the opening of the Seminole war,
simply stated the obvious when he replied in the negative to his self-posed question "Is our quarrel just?" His initial reason, quite tellingly, was "the fact that our
treaties are, as they say, white men's treaties, made in *our* language, translated by
our interpreters, and by them [Seminoles] imperfectly *understood* and imperfectly
remembered." Another primary objection, according to Everett (an ardent Whig
opponent of Jacksonian Indian removal), was the unquestionable fact that "we
[Euro-Americans] are our own historians—we tell the whole story." Because of
these circumstances, he insisted that "in all questions of doubt, proper allowances

should be made in their [Seminoles'] favor."[49] In any legal contest between Native people and the government, the former, lacking attorneys or even highly acculturated tribal members, were defenseless.

The objective of removing the eastern Indians to the trans-Mississippi West initiated with President Thomas Jefferson, but this defining project was first implemented on a national scale by the Jackson administration.[50] Congressional passage of the Indian Removal Act (1830), even though by a narrow margin and after heated national debate, was a crucial victory for Jacksonians in that it endowed removal with the national imprimatur. Supporters, such as Secretary Cass, a former governor of the Michigan Territory, felt entitled to declare that it was "a solemn national declaration" and insisted that Indian removal was consistent with the highest Christian principles and thus due grave respect throughout the land.[51] Cass's rhetoric notwithstanding, an increasing number of modern scholars have likened the passage of the law to the enactment of a national policy of ethnic cleansing.[52] This pejorative clearly seems warranted given the horrifically brutal and often lethal measures that were carried out during this time and the racist motivations behind the designation of a colossal geologic barrier (i.e., the Mississippi River) between the "civilized" and the lesser "aboriginal race" as well as a series of forts that encircled the territory and functioned to keep these refugees in a state of financial dependence.[53] Be that as it may, a close reading of the law reveals that it did not sanction the unilateral revocation of treaties such as Moultrie Creek nor did it specifically allow for *forced* relocation—such inclusions would almost certainly have prevented the act from passing. Indeed, the law was constructed around the principle of a voluntary exchange of land, wherein original Native landholdings were, hypothetically at any rate, "traded" for new land in the West, with the allowance for appropriate financial inducements. As a result, the actual legal mechanism that was utilized in this program of mass expulsion and land appropriation centered on Indian treaties rather than on the removal act per se. By 1840, an estimated seventy thousand Native people were confined in the West. These were the survivors of brutal forced marches overseen by US troops. Traveling without adequate nourishment, clothing, or even shoes through the most challenging terrain, including extensive swamplands, onlookers reported wretched scenes of those who died by the wayside. Indians were further subjected to theft, merciless attacks, and constant harassment. "Reconciliation with the whites," a concerned citizen wrote in 1832 after witnessing starving "old women and young children [Choctaws] without any covering for their feet, legs, or body" drudging before his home, "could never exist in the bosom of any of those who passed here."[54] Forced migration resulted in the great suffering of innocents; yet, in government circles this ignominious chapter was cloaked in a bureaucratic language of paternalistic largesse and humanitarianism.[55]

Despite outward appearances that may have even appeared benign to some Euro-Americans, it is vital to consider that by this time Indian treaties were deemed by Jackson and his political associates as nothing more than temporary dealings that could be retracted in the future.[56] Moreover, in 1830 the House Committee on Indian Affairs asserted that reservations that were linked to the treaties were created solely because they were "expedient to the interests of the Government making them" and nothing more. "No respectable jurist," it was claimed, ever considered "that the right of the Indians to hold their reserved lands could be supported in the courts upon any other ground than the grant or permission of the sovereignty or State in which such lands lie."[57] The United States, in other words, reserved final judgment, and any tribal land claim, as opposed to individual ownership, was suspect. To compound their lack of proper legal standing, testimony from Native Americans was routinely excluded by the courts, and they were denied the rights of citizens.[58] Even in the exceptional case of the Cherokees, whose leadership had sufficient funds, English-language facility, and substantial cultural knowledge to draw upon, in the favorable Supreme Court decision in *Worcester v. Georgia* (1832) the state of Georgia refused to obey the court's finding of tribal sovereignty, and, as is well known, Jackson similarly ignored the verdict—a situation that ultimately led to the suffering of the Trail of Tears. Within this context, the position of Indigenous people as legal nonentities was unequivocal. Under Jackson and his successors, the very concept of an Indian treaty, other than serving as a fictive device to allow government claims of removal powers, was reduced to a cynical pretense. Indian treaties—ninety of which originated under Andrew Jackson—served as a legitimating illusion, a kind of sleight of hand that drew attention away from the country's core aggression toward Native people by focusing on complex accords that reinforced the appearance of benign legitimacy.[59] The power of this framework was considerable—even though these documents were signed (more often by an "x") by people who were uninformed as to the nature of US law and even the language that was being used. This facade was additionally secured by the solemn ratification by the US Senate. What was in essence state-sanctioned theft of a politically powerless underclass became obscured under a veil of legal decorum and high-toned rhetoric. As the French political philosopher and author Alexis de Tocqueville acerbically noted in regard to America's treatment of Indigenous people: "It is impossible to destroy men with more respect for the laws of humanity."[60] Even among those who recognized the injustice of Indian removal, the entire process was nevertheless perceived as inevitable. "The laws and habits of the white man, like the wash of the sea," concluded John Sprague, a contemporary chronicler of the Seminole war, "must and will efface the footstep of every Indian from the soil."[61] The war, Sprague aptly concluded, did not originate in "the vindication of any principle" but entirely rested on "the spirit of [financial] gain; the feverish passions of the multitude for settlements."[62]

Once this operative condition is recognized, charges of misconduct associated with the two legal accords that were intended to negate the Treaty of Moultrie Creek and also provided the legal rationale for war — the Treaty of Payne's Landing (1832) and the supplementary Treaty of Fort Gibson (1833) — should be treated with due diligence. Even so, John K. Mahon, in his influential and now quite dated *History of the Second Seminole War*, still regarded as the principal scholarly treatment of the war, treats accusations of government fraud with an element of suspicion.[63] Mahon was unpersuaded by documentary evidence that surfaced, among other sources, in the private diaries of Major Ethan Allen Hitchcock (the army's leading expert on Indian policy). Hitchcock was quite adamant in charging the Jackson administration with dishonest dealings and chicanery. His moral condemnation is especially significant when one considers that Hitchcock was a former commandant of cadets at West Point and held exceptional influence within the War Department, where he worked directly under two secretaries of war and also served three tours of duty in Florida. Even though Mahon admitted that "there is no reason . . . to suspect Hitchcock of perpetuating a fictitious [claim]," he further adds, rather inexplicably, that such a scenario was "not impossible."[64] The fact that Hitchcock relegated his opinions to his personal journal and never went public (and thus did not "perpetuate" any claim) is never placed into proper perspective. Mahon's final judgment concerning the treaties is highly ambiguous; ultimately, he states, all that remains is the white man's version of events versus the Indian's. Such a noncommittal stance by the war's historian of record is all the more puzzling, as it disregards another essential fact that Mahon acknowledged: the majority of officers in Florida also maintained that the treaties were "begot in fraud and brought forth in the blackest villainy," to quote an army captain.[65] Ironically, the fact that the Seminoles risked everything in order to defend *hearth and home*, to use a much-hallowed phrase of the time, and did so in opposition to the patently dishonest actions of the US government, was thoroughly in keeping with the ideals of the Early Republic. The war ironically brought Seminoles a great deal of respect, especially among the Whig-dominated officer corps.[66] Accusations of chicanery even found their way to the floor of the US Senate when Samuel L. Southard (Whig) of New Jersey, a senior statesman and former secretary of the navy, asserted that the Seminole war originated with sham treaties and that "all the blood and money expended were the results of that fraud."[67] This extraordinarily candid remark spawned sizable indignation from Jacksonians and the Democratic Party in general, who felt the country's honor had been unjustly impugned (in other words, that the illusion of legitimacy had been breached). Be that as it may, scholarship regarding the war continues to be influenced by Mahon's previous stance. Francis Paul Prucha's *American Indian Treaties: The History of a Political Anomaly*, for example, entirely sidesteps charges of fraud in regard to the Florida treaties and defers to Mahon's judgment.[68]

The Treaty of Payne's Landing was held during the first weeks of May 1832 at a remote setting along the Ocklawaha River. In an unusual arrangement, the commissioner—once again James Gadsden—bypassed the nearby Indian Agency at Fort King in favor of this even more isolated location. Moreover, there were no minutes or records of any kind taken during the proceedings, a fact that later drew suspicion, especially in light of the Seminoles' firm, decade-long refusal to move. Hitchcock was convinced that Gadsden had resorted to bribery and chicanery in order to acquire the necessary signatures and the supposed consent of the Seminoles. This allegation stemmed from a firsthand account by army captain Charles Thruston, who later heard Gadsden openly admit to his friend President Jackson during a meeting in Washington, DC, that "he never could have got the treaty through if he had not bribed the negro interpreter." According to Thruston—a West Point graduate (1814) who was also present during efforts to enforce the treaties in Florida—a black interpreter named Abraham (aka Abram) purposely misrepresented the stipulations "in such a manner as to leave the chiefs under the impression that they were to have the ultimate decision" on whether to move to the West.[69] This was "the simple unquestionable truth," as Hitchcock understood it. It also supports the Seminoles' version of events, as they maintained that the treaty stipulations were falsely presented to them.[70] The fact that a payment of $200 to Abraham, under the guise of just compensation, was written into the treaty at the time—plus other reports regarding his penchant for soliciting bribes in return for favorable influence with the Seminoles—adds further credence to this scenario.[71] Moreover, the Seminoles stated that they reluctantly agreed to affix their marks solely because of Gadsden's clamorous insistence and because they understood that they were only required to send representatives to the Arkansas Territory without further obligation. They were surely unaware that by signing they had just placed their reservation lands in great jeopardy. These holdings were, they still believed, a "sacred" pact.[72] Although the annuity paid to the Seminoles would last no more than twenty years, the Moultrie Creek treaty explicitly stated that their reservation lands "shall herein be allotted them," with no time limit attached.[73] Because there were no witnesses other than the participants, the Seminole version has carried little weight with certain historians. For whatever reason, the commonsense dictum of Representative Everett—"In all questions of doubt . . . ," and so forth—has often been ignored.

Payne's Landing was followed some months later by the supplemental treaty that was held at Fort Gibson (present-day eastern Oklahoma) during the winter of 1833. Fort Gibson served as the headquarters of the southwestern frontier and was the supply depot for the new Indian Territory. Article 1 of Payne's Landing stated that the "Seminole Indians relinquish to the United States all claim to the lands they at present occupy in the Territory of Florida, and agree to emigrate to the country assigned to the Creeks, west of the Mississippi river."[74] Judged simply on its face, this was a most improbable concession, had it actually been known to the Seminoles, as this would have placed them in close proximity and under the authority of a long-standing enemy who vigorously sought their annihilation while allied with General Jackson and who held a highly contentious claim to a number of their black slaves.[75] Indeed, the administration could hardly have devised a more distressing and demeaning scenario. In order to finalize the agreement at Payne's Landing, Seminole representatives were obligated to give their formal consent after they were physically present in the new territory. Hitchcock's informant on this particular accord was an unnamed officer at Fort Gibson who took part in the proceedings. The officer stated that a seven-member Seminole delegation did arrive under the supervision of federal Indian agent Major John Phagan and was offered a document to endorse, which specified their approval of the lands. "The Indians refused to sign," Hitchcock quoted his source, "saying that they had no authority to do it."[76] In a fit of pique, Phagan threatened to leave the Seminole delegates stranded alone in the territory during midwinter—1,100 miles from the Florida reservation—unless they affixed their marks, which they eventually did under duress on February 13, 1833.[77] This brazen misconduct is also corroborated by Jumper (Hotemathla), Micanopy's principal adviser, who was actually present: "The agents of the United States made us sign our hands to a paper."[78] Another leader, Charley Emathla, emphatically declared that "the white people forced us into the treaty."[79] Captain George A. McCall, who was stationed at Fort Gibson, related in his published memoirs how the Seminoles were "induced" to sign, although McCall was unwilling to go into further detail.[80] After reviewing the evidence, Lieutenant Woodbourne Potter, author of The War in Florida (1836), also reluctantly concluded that "they [Seminoles] were, indeed, forced into the measure."[81] No matter the method, it is obvious that both treaties

adhered to a familiar pattern that was applied elsewhere among Indigenous people. John F. Schermerhorn, one of three commissioners who oversaw the infamous
Cherokee removal treaty of New Echota (1835) and approved the Seminole
treaty at Fort Gibson, serves as a fitting example of the contemporary mind-set as
he once warned the Cherokees who dared remain east "that the screws would be
turned upon them till they would be ground into powder."[82] All things considered, it is apparent that the treaties with the Seminoles followed "the farcical,
fraudulent way that had been customary," as historian Annie Heloise Abel dryly
commented about the government's conduct at this time.[83]

Abundant evidence also arises in connection with the character of agent Phagan. Another Jackson appointee, Phagan was under investigation during this period for a variety of illegal activities, including embezzlement of Indian funds.
These charges originated from his earliest days while serving as the US Indian
agent in Florida. In 1832, matters were so far out of hand that congressional delegate White asked Secretary Cass to "order the agent and all his subordinate
agents out of the [Seminole] Nation," but White's appeal was disregarded.[84] Despite Phagan's ill-repute and his widespread standing as "totally unqualified, both
by education and morals," he was nevertheless deemed well suited for the purposes
of the Jackson administration.[85] A few months after his return from Fort Gibson,
Phagan was dismissed from office, a consequence of an independent investigation by Acting Governor James D. Westcott, who uncovered damning evidence
during a visit to the Seminole Agency.[86] Ultimately, as Sprague observed: "Such
conduct exasperated Indians. They were surrounded by crafty and designing
men, and subjected to the advice and control of an agent, who, not content with
wronging them . . . was carrying on ingenious schemes to defraud."[87] All things
considered, Hitchcock's insights vis-à-vis the injustices accorded the Seminoles
appears well founded. The fact that the new secretary of war John Bell offered
Hitchcock the influential post of commissioner of Indian Affairs a few years later
(which he declined), and then directed him to the Indian Territory to head a five-
month investigation into claims of extensive fraud against the Indians, which was
then turned into a damning report published by Congress, adds even more gravity
to his judgment.[88] No matter how devastating the conflict proved for both soldiers
and settlers, the Seminoles adhered, in Hitchcock's expert opinion, to the principles of just war. "The natives used every means to avoid a war," he recorded in his
diary, "but were forced into it by the tyranny of our government."[89]

The treaties that were imposed by the United States certainly stand as the most
obvious causative factor in what may be understood as the final and most forceful
struggle of the eastern Indians against US expansionism. As demonstrated, how-

ever, these accords functioned as powerful legitimating illusions that endowed the dubious national mission of Native expulsion from the east with the outward trappings of legality and benign paternalism. The government's goal of asserting dominion over the land was made easier by envisioning Indigenous people as degraded "others" whose essential rights could either be diminished or entirely refuted. The Indian Removal Act may have cast the process into motion, but Jackson's emphasis on treaties, along with enlisting a cohort of like-minded agents who were unencumbered by ethical qualms, was vital in completing the dual processes of removal and land confiscation. The reputation of the United States on the world stage nevertheless demanded that this large-scale deportation program, riddled though it was with corruption and callousness toward human rights, proceed as unobtrusively as possible; hence, overt violence and publicity was purposely avoided. The ferocity expressed during the Second Seminole War was not only a powerful rebuke by Seminoles to their imminent forced expulsion but was rife with the type of symbolism that favored the Indian cause (a factor, as will be later demonstrated, that the opposition Whig Party was quick to integrate into their political campaigning). The Florida war embodied the most prolonged counterattack against the hegemonic forces of settler-colonialism yet attempted in North America. This unparalleled uprising threatened to controvert Jackson's "solemn" mission of removal and thus had to be vigorously opposed by whatever means necessary, lest similar insurrections spread to other tribes across the continent.

CHAPTER 2

Seminoles, Slaves, and Maroons

The Seminoles may have held de facto sovereignty over most of La Florida while it was a Spanish colony and also during the years of British jurisdiction, but these Native people were not entirely alone. Two factions of African Americans, the slaves of Seminoles and a separate maroon or free-black contingent, inhabited the peninsula as well. Since blacks also formed an important ancillary force under the Seminoles during the opening phase of the Second Seminole War and have been the focus of various revisionist claims of late, most notably a provocative assertion by historian Larry Rivers that "black leaders made up the backbone" of this conflict, it is especially vital to define who these people were and, as much as can be determined, what the basis of their relationship consisted of.[1]

Given the scarcity of primary sources from both Seminoles and African Americans, and the often-contradictory nature of the historical record, fine scrutiny and caution is paramount. White observers, including army officers, settlers, and government officials, viewed all nonwhites with extreme prejudice, and so few statements can be accepted at face value alone. Rivers's claim that the war should be renamed the "Black/Indian Rebellion" notwithstanding, it is unambiguously clear that the army's strategic goal was the relocation of Florida's Indigenous people, including their slaves, to the Arkansas Territory, as the Indian Removal Act and treaties attest.[2] Opposing the army command were Seminole leaders who formulated strategy, employed the operational skills necessary to move against the US Army and militia, and, in addition to black warriors, followed through with tactical engagements. This is the standard view accepted by specialists in military history, from Mahon's *History of the Second Seminole War* to myriad articles and book chapters by the majority of scholars who have followed suit.[3] Even so, in order to make sense of the rather unusual relationship between Seminoles and blacks, their separate backgrounds should first be broached. In doing so, a great deal of needed historical context to the prewar years also surfaces.

ORIGINS

Many Native people who came to be known as the Seminoles can be traced to the various tribes that inhabited the uncharted Creek (Muscogee) territory of what is now Georgia and Alabama during the early eighteenth century. Contrary to most assumptions, this more northern region still remained a province of Spanish La Florida until Great Britain took possession of Florida in 1763 and redrew pre-existing political boundaries.[4] Two centuries earlier, beginning with Hernando De Soto's brutal expeditions, diseases such as smallpox, measles, and influenza decimated the Indigenous people of the lower Southeast; population collapse, intertribal conflict, and frequent migration resulted.[5] Some scholars believe that the formation of the Creek Confederacy was a consequence of the remaining Indigenous people being drawn together as a form of self-protection; others maintain that bonds of association predated De Soto.[6] In any case, additional pressure from the British and then later the United States gave rise to further relocation. Ahaya (aka Waccapuchasee, or "Cowkeeper"), the forebear of later Seminole leaders such as King Payne, Boleck (aka "Bowlegs"), and Micanopy, sought the advantages of an alliance with the British and in 1740 led a group of his Oconee Creek warriors to the aid of Georgia Colonial Governor James Ogelthorpe and his ill-fated siege of St. Augustine.[7] During this same timeframe, Ahaya, a warrior with a fierce reputation who boasted that he had slayed eighty-four Spaniards during his lifetime, founded the proto-Seminole town of Cuscowilla (present-day Micanopy) in the Alachua country.[8] He quickly took possession of the feral cattle left after the Spanish abandoned their *rancho* operations several decades earlier.[9] In addition, a "sister" town along the Suwannee River, near present-day Old Town, was under the leadership of the "White King." Both the Alachua and Suwannee River villages were bound by ceremonial and political ties and sustained a strong alliance throughout this period, much in the manner of the earlier Creek tradition.[10] Prior to Cuscowilla, a different Lower Creek band headed by the pro-Spanish Secoffee (Simpukasse), a son of the Creek *micco* (chief) Emperor Brim, established a village in the Red Hills district near present-day Tallahassee as well as a group of associated villages near Lake Miccosukee. (These "Miccosukees" later fought with the Seminoles during the war and eventually merged with them).[11] This time span (1716–63) has often been referred to as the *colonization* period of the Seminoles, a term employed by archaeologist Charles Fairbanks.[12] Coloniza-

La Floride, divisee en Floride et Caroline, 1749. Prior to 1763, large portions of present-day Georgia and Alabama were an integral part of the Spanish colony of La Florida. Rare Map Collection, University of South Florida.

tion, however, is both inaccurate and misleading. As we have seen, settler-colonialism refers to non-Native outsiders who occupy a region held by Indigenous people through domination and conquest, and force the removal of these inhabitants, taking their lands, in other words, the very situation that was imposed on the Seminoles. *Relocation* is a more precise term, as it reflects the movement of Native people from one part of La Florida to another, as they responded to the widespread disruption created by the hegemonic colonial powers of Britain, France, and Spain. Be that as it may, Creeks, Apalache, Yamassee, Yuchee, and, following the Creek War (1813–14), Upper Creek "Red Sticks" continued their movement toward the panhandle and peninsular regions of Florida.[13] Much of this land was part of the same longleaf pine, mixed forest, and savannah ecosystem that characterized the region as a whole and was an integral part of the traditional

Creek hunting grounds.[14] These Indigenes, who also included remnants of the Timucua and Apalache who survived the epidemics brought on by the Spanish, subsequently formed a new Seminole identity—a political act of independence that delineated themselves from all others.[15] Seminoles or "Seminolies," as the British first recorded the name in 1765, was the Native pronunciation of the Spanish *Cimaronnes*, which referred to a wild or free-spirited people.[16] Because this identification was first applied to Ahaya's Alachua tribe, it undoubtedly reflected the reputation of this noncolonized people. Not only were they antagonistic toward the Spanish—"the most bitter and formidable Indian enemies the Spaniards ever had," as William Bartram stated—but they severed themselves from Creek suzerainty as well. Bartram, steeped in Romanticism, also recounted the "terrible" appearance of these individuals: "the painted, fearless, uncontrolled and free Siminole [*sic*] . . . whose plumed head flashes lightning."[17]

In marked contrast, it should be noted that Euro-American settlers interpreted any type of movement by Indigenous people as intrinsically suspect. Settlers often branded Seminoles as outsiders or intruders, an instance of psychological inversion that served to bolster a sense of entitlement.[18] Unsettledness of any kind may have been construed as illegitimate, but ironically the settlers themselves were actually wanderers *par excellence* (i.e., until they staked their land claims on Native soil).[19] A congressional speech delivered during the war years by Florida Delegate David Levy illustrates the depth of self-delusion. Levy, an immigrant from the Danish Caribbean who spent the latter part of his youth in Norfolk, Virginia, scrupulously upheld settler dominance while expounding on his account of Seminole origins: "Stragglers from other tribes, from time to time, found their way to Florida, and by degrees increased the number of red inhabitants there: who from their wandering habits became known as Seminoles—which means wanderers."[20] The congressman, just as many of his constituents (the settler body politic), delegitimized Seminoles, branding them as criminal "vagabonds" from other tribes who lacked a valid identity. As illegal "trespassers," they had forfeited any right to live in the territory. Levy, invoking the patriarchal tone of white sovereignty, upheld the dubious notion that the only *genuine* "aboriginal inhabitants" had not only stayed fixed in one locality but were "long ago exterminated."[21] Implicit in his address was the supposition that white settlers, rather than Native Americans, were the legitimate heirs of these "original" inhabitants. Such a view was not unique to the Florida Territory, as settler societies throughout the world practiced similar methods of Indigenous exclusion. (In South Africa, for example, the conquering white Afrikaners similarly asserted their own nativism while defining Zulus as "immigrants" and "newcomers."[22]) No matter how incongruous, denial of Seminole indigeneity strengthened a fundamental principle: "By drawing different circles of inclusion and exclusion," social theorist Lorenzo Veracini observes, "the settler body politic establishes its [very] sovereignty."[23]

In addition to the realignment of Native people in Florida was an exodus of fugitive slaves, Gullahs who heralded from plantations in coastal Georgia and South Carolina, who ultimately gained protection once in the Spanish province. In a provocative gesture, the colonial government in La Florida actively sought runaway slaves—promising freedom—in the hope of utilizing this group, in addition to the Native people who lived in the interior, to help defend against the expansionist designs of Great Britain and later the United States. Some fugitives reached St. Augustine, where they formed a small but important free-black contingent.[24] Indeed, free-black militias as well as armed slaves became a vital part of a pragmatic defense strategy.[25] During the seventeenth century, Native people in the interior cooperated with Spanish officials and returned runaways who strayed into the interior. By the time of the Seminole emergence, however, such collaboration no longer existed (and by 1790, St. Augustine officials ceased offering sanctuary to runaways[26]). Just as the rest of the so-called Five Civilized Tribes, Seminoles adopted black slavery, but, as has often been noted, this system was more akin to vassalage than to the more rigid slavery regimen practiced elsewhere.[27] Seminoles purchased slaves directly from the Spanish, augmented their slaveholdings by raiding nearby plantations in Georgia and Florida, and certainly re-enslaved escapees.[28] Even so, some "refugee Negroes belonging to Indians & Citizens of this territory," explained an Anglo-Spanish contemporary, succeeded in forming maroon communities along the Gulf Coast region south of Tampa Bay.[29] Earlier, an important settlement at Prospect Bluff—not far from the mouth of the Apalachicola River—thrived as an autonomous maroon community but quickly dispersed after a combined attack by the US Army and Navy as well as by Creek Indians in July 1816. Led by Duncan Clinch (then a colonel), the mission destroyed much of the "Negro Fort," a British-built fortification situated on high ground above the river.[30] Thus ended what historian J. Leitch Wright Jr. defined as "the largest and most heavily armed Maroon community ever to appear in the Southeast."[31] Both cases of "willful self-extrication," as an anthropologist has described the phenomenon of maroonage, from a place of enslavement to enclaves of self-determination represent events of obvious historical import, no matter how brief or dire their ultimate ends.[32]

By the close of the Revolutionary War and the reinstatement of Spanish jurisdiction, the colonial tradition of black militias and drafting slaves as a fighting force increasingly alarmed white inhabitants of adjoining slave states.[33] Tales of Seminole prosperity also enticed settlers who looked upon these lands, particularly in Alachua, as ripe for the taking. As a result of an invasion by Georgia militia and US forces during the Patriot War, the colony's armed blacks, reinforced by black troops from Cuba, joined with Seminoles and their own black auxiliaries in the wilderness interior and ultimately repelled this incursion.[34] The coalition's effectiveness was aided by the services of a handful of multilingual slaves who acted as translators and cultural mediators between colonial officials and Native leaders such as Ahaya's immediate successors, King Payne and Bowlegs.[35] The conflict may have frustrated US advances, but it also resulted in the destruction of Native villages and the death of the influential Payne. Most survivors fled to more southern regions of the peninsula or westward toward the Suwannee River. A new village situated along this river, established by Bowlegs, served as the new seat of power for the Seminoles. Following the destruction at Prospect Bluff, several hundred black fighters and their families fled to Bowlegs Town, where they were allowed to settle in the immediate area. These men were well armed and retained the disciplined military training originally provided by the British and so augmented Bowlegs's armed struggle against the United States.[36] But their presence, along with Red Stick survivors of the Creek War, also caused alarm on the opposite side of the border. Jackson consequently led another invasion (the First Seminole War) and again aimed at the annihilation of Indigenous settlements and the smaller, affiliated black villages that ranged from the Florida panhandle to Bowlegs Town. Just as his half brother Payne before him, Bowlegs did not survive long after the invasion; many Seminoles simply withdrew to increasingly remote areas rather than fight superior forces.[37] Once more, surviving maroons were able to discover a sanctuary, this time in a region called Angola, south of Tampa Bay. In 1821, Spain formally transferred Florida to the United States. Jackson, now provisional governor, gave tacit approval to his former Coweta Creek allies in Georgia to destroy Red Stick refugee settlements along the Peace River in southwest Florida as well as the maroons in Angola.[38] Cowetas mounted a fierce surprise attack and captured about three hundred blacks, including Red Stick slaves, and forced them to Georgia, where they were re-enslaved. An estimated 250 maroons escaped by boat to Nassau, Bahamas; freedom, they realized, would only be possible under the British.[39] One year afterward, it was believed that a mere "80 refugee Negroes" still resided in the southern Tampa Bay region.[40] Maroons presented an existential threat to white authority, and the fact that they united with Native forces against the United States further compelled Jackson to entirely oust them from the peninsula. For decades, Seminoles, along with African Americans among them, experienced almost perpetual conflict. Now, as the United States assumed authority, Seminoles were even more vulnerable, as they had suffered major losses, including the deaths of senior leaders. What is more, the Spanish had not only abandoned the colony but had ceded Seminole lands to their foremost enemies. This was done despite reported assurances from the Spanish government, as General Jesup later recounted, that all of the country "beyond the line of cultivation belonged to the Indians."[41]

While the comparatively short-lived expedition in which Jackson invaded sovereign Spanish territory and endured weighty international censure in the process was in large part a reaction to the sizable armed maroon presence in Florida, the motivation for the Second Seminole War was altogether different. For one, maroons had ceased being a large presence. Even more fundamental, however, is that from the moment Euro-American settlers started to arrive at Pensacola and St. Augustine during the summer of 1821, and then sought the more fertile regions of the panhandle and the East Florida interior, the new US territory was primed for a contest over land. The dictates of settler-colonialism required that millions of acres that had existed for millennia as an Indigenous homeland be reconfigured as the exclusive domain of white settlers. From this point on, it actually made little or no difference if Florida's Native people were friends or foes. The territory may have been legally transferred by Spain to the United States, but true sovereignty (*dominium*), following Lockean precedent, could only be fulfilled after settlers took physical possession of the land.[42] This jurisdictional philosophy emphasized "improvement" to heretofore pristine and "neglected" land as an economic and moral necessity.[43] As proper cultivators of the soil, unlike the "Savage Race," the new inhabitants imagined themselves as acting according to God's commandments, as they would be engaged in subduing and replenishing the earth.[44] Certainly the presence of Seminole slaves caused heightened tensions, distrust, and paranoia, and resulted in a cohort of slave catchers who were continually on patrol. But from a broad policy perspective, the US government determined that it was far better that slaves depart with their Indian masters to the West if it resulted in the total exclusion of Native people. Settlers had only to wait for a national program of Indian removal to transform the territory into a settler haven, or so it was assumed.

SLAVES OR FREEPERSONS?

Ten months before the onset of the Seminole war, General Clinch voiced his concerns over the potential for a full-scale insurrection to the War Department. "The whole frontier may be laid waste by a combination of Indians, Indian negroes & the negroes on the plantations."[45] Clinch's warning was couched in the most vivid imagery he could muster. Indeed, the very existence of black slaves among any Indigenous population easily fueled suspicions by the southern elite that rebellion could ensue.[46] However, even the danger of an Indian-slave alliance failed to be taken seriously by the War Department. As the proprietor of two plantations—one in Camden County, Georgia, and the other in the Alachua district—Clinch understood the wisdom of keeping a diligent eye toward any sign of slave insurrection.[47] Indeed, this quality was considered essential to the survival of the entire social and economic order. The horrific excesses of the Haitian Revolution (1791–1804) and the revenge exacted on slaveholders in that Caribbean nation provided a story line that haunted the southern consciousness beginning from childhood.[48] Such apprehensions ran like a dark undercurrent throughout the South. "A slave population, coerced into obedience," wrote British author Fanny Kemble during her tenure as the mistress of a Georgia plantation, "is a threatening source of constant insecurity, and every southern woman to whom I have spoken on the subject, has admitted to me that they live in terror of their slaves."[49] The more recent Turner Rebellion (1831) in Virginia greatly reinforced this dread. While Clinch was certainly justified in his concerns, in other instances in the South hysterical imaginings of slave revolts often took hold of entire regions and resulted in extensive panic (a kind of *Negrophobia*, to use a term by Frantz Fanon).[50] The general, however, like most in the army, possessed a solid appreciation of power: the dispossession of any people from their lands was dependent on brute force, or the threat thereof, as well as the backing of a state infrastructure.[51] As the Florida Territory was wanting in both respects, trouble surely lay ahead.

Who, then, were the blacks that Clinch referred to? Did they in any way usurp Seminole authority or present an autonomous threat to the United States? These are certainly key questions that should be answered. But in order to proceed, one must first distinguish the nature of Seminole slavery, a task that is fraught with misunderstanding. It should be emphasized that African Americans who lived in the wilderness interior prior to the Seminole war faced the ever-present reality of Native dominion. In contrast to Prospect Bluff and the maroon settlements prior to the Coweta raids, situations that were actually closest to the ideal of black freedom, slaves in the interior were required to adapt to the cultural norms and governance of the Seminoles. Early white travelers into the interior (i.e., the "Seminole Nation") often marveled at the dress and manner of "Indian Negroes." During a journey through the region in 1822, Dr. William H. Simmons, a physician and poet as well as a fairly reliable observer, remarked that blacks "dress and live pretty much like the Indians."[52] He also estimated that of the four hundred blacks who lived in the region at that date, most were not fugitives or runaways, but slaves.

Their Native owners "were in the habit of purchasing slaves with cattle, when they were rich in that species of property." (Standard practice was to trade forty head of cattle for a single slave, but the size and value of the cattle corresponded to the size, age, and sex of the slave.)[53] Moreover, Simmons observed, while "Negroes . . . pursue pretty much the same mode of life as their owners, the latter do not, in any circumstance, imitate the conduct of blacks."[54] The dominant culture was thus Seminole, not African American.

Life in East Florida was set on a far different course after the United States gained formal acquisition of the territory. The relationship between the Seminoles and the influx of Euro-American settlers steadily grew more contentious, and the presence of Seminole slaves exacerbated affairs. Tribal groups from across the territory eventually moved within the confines of the central Florida reservation, and, of course, slaves went with them. Blacks who lived on the reservation did not roam far, as they were vulnerable to predatory groups of slave catchers. In 1829, Tuckose Emathla informed Gad Humphreys, the government Indian agent, that he had obeyed instructions and "sent away all the black people who had no masters [maroons]." But this Native leader vehemently protested that when Seminoles "bought a black man" in a legitimate transaction, duplicitous whites soon returned to steal the slave back, "so that we have no money and negroes too."[55] Territorial records abound in similar complaints of grand larceny. "It is well known that a great deal of our property, negroes, horses, cattle, etc. is now in the hands of the whites, and yet their laws give us no satisfaction," asserted Micanopy, the future paramount chief and the owner of one hundred slaves.[56] Despite such a scenario, there is little doubt that slavery, especially as practiced by the Seminoles in the Florida interior, was more lax than elsewhere in the South. Evidence is scarce, but it appears that no overseers were present to enforce strict regimens, and families were also allowed to live together and cultivate their fields—a situation not dissimilar to a type of slavery practiced by certain Creeks.[57] As we have seen, one of the roles of male slaves, following the example of Spanish colonials, was to serve as an ancillary fighting force in times of need. The entire slave community was also expected to produce a surplus of livestock and agricultural produce, with a portion set aside for their masters. Anthropologist Brent Weisman identified this system as a regional adaptation of the southern plantation regime, with farms producing a surplus of corn, rice, peanuts, and melons, as well as livestock.[58] Blacks performed the farm labor that Seminole men believed was unseemly and degrading. Hunting, an activity that was symbolically linked to war, along with the prestige that was awarded it, remained an overarching concern.[59] Black males who performed such women's work therefore reinforced traditional perceptions of black inferiority.[60] Indeed, the future war leader Osceola, after being denied the right to buy gunpowder before the outbreak of the Seminole war, replied in a tirade infused with the racialized views of the period: "Am I a Negro? . . . A slave? My skin is dark but not black. I am an Indian—a Seminole." By denying gunpowder, a frontier necessity, Osceola believed that the federal Indian agent had, in effect, demoted his position in the racial hierarchy, thereby "making him black" (slaves, of course, were prevented from purchasing guns or ammunition).[61] In another instance of the racialization of labor, among those few Seminoles who accepted work for hire among the whites, Simmons relates, all would abruptly depart, never to return, if other Indians happened upon the scene. They left quickly in the hope that they would avoid detection, fully realizing that they risked sharp ridicule and ostracism for performing the work of servile blacks.[62]

Before the cession to the United States, black men were additionally employed as cowhands in Alachua. This was especially evident during the height of the Seminoles' prosperity (1790–1812), a veritable golden age wherein Indians, as one observer noted, not only were "numerous, proud, and wealthy" but possessed "great numbers of cattle, horses, and slaves" in proximity to lush prairies.[63] Florida may have been a Spanish colony, but in reality Seminoles were entirely self-governing; indeed, the lucrative cattle industry they established in Alachua was theirs to do with as they liked.[64] Appropriating a crucial economic niche previously filled by affluent Spanish *rancheros*, Seminoles became the principal suppliers of beef to St. Augustine. Local ranchers along the east coast of Florida simply could not match the lower prices or the sheer quantity offered by the Seminoles.[65] As a result, Native people became a vital component in the regional market economy. The colonial government seldom interacted directly with the Alachua Indians, however, as officials sent free blacks and mulattoes into the interior to conduct business instead. Astute entrepreneurs, Seminoles also knew when to set Spanish offers for their valued livestock against American competitors if it resulted in fairer prices and more straightforward business dealings.[66] Simmons reported that Bowlegs alone "sold annually a thousand head of steers" and noted that Seminoles were once considered "the most wealthy of the American tribes."[67] Reflecting prosperity as well as enculturation, King Payne, Ahaya's successor, rejected the traditionalist norm and constructed an ample "European-style plantation house" that was stocked full of fine items acquired from Anglo-Spanish traders.[68]

As these cattle operations suggest, the labor that Native people demanded of their slaves during this period necessitated skills that were often self-directed. Slave management thus tended to be less regimented and oppressive than plantation slavery as a whole.[69] Bondage has typically been construed in dualistic terms, with the extremes of antebellum plantation slavery standing in stark opposition to the concept of absolute freedom. But Indigenous people, as Seminoles illustrate, practiced a highly variable and pragmatic approach to this institution.[70] Some degree of liberty within slavery, regardless of cultural context, was thus common and should not serve to diminish or deny the demeaning reality of being held as an item of property. Additionally, Seminole slavery was both permanent and heritable (unless terminated through manumission), and represented substantial wealth. "Even if black slaves had a somewhat easier and freer time among the Seminoles," historian William G. McLoughlin aptly observed, "they were still slaves, not equals."[71] It is within this simple premise that the present divergence of historical opinion centers.

Beginning in the 1930s, Kenneth W. Porter (1905–84) wrote a series of articles about relations between blacks and Native people that appeared in a number of peer reviewed journals including the *Journal of Negro History*. Porter, a white historian and committed socialist, advanced an empowering model of African Americans in the Florida wilds, a perspective that coincided with the emergence of the civil rights movement. "Not only were Seminole slaves not slaves in the usual sense of the word," Porter declared, "but they might claim to be the true rulers of the nation."[72] Possessed with scant evidence as well as considerable ethnocentric bias, Porter theorized that Indians were actually "perplexed" as to what to do with their slaves and so left them to their own devices—assumptions that portray the historian's naiveté and condescension vis-à-vis Native people. The lives of blacks among the Seminoles are also expressed in idyllic, essentialist terms, with the former supposedly possessing a superior stance "over the less sophisticated Indians."[73] Porter bypassed valuable, firsthand accounts from Seminole slave owners such as Micanopy, whom the author casually denigrated as "indolent and stupid," and relied instead on contemporary utterances from either white settlers or military officers.[74] The latter were personally (and often financially) invested in diminishing any sense of Indigenous entitlement. Porter also asserted that black leaders such as John Caesar actually seized the initiative from the St. Johns River branch of Seminoles during the war and deployed small bands to attack plantations when Native leaders supposedly opted to "do nothing" at the time. Such a claim, however, not only counters accepted history but is left entirely unsubstantiated.[75] It may be tempting to dismiss this work as a product of a biased, outmoded, and less rigorous scholarly approach, but this author's body of work—much of it written during the 1930s and 1940s—remains central to revisionist historians such as Larry Rivers and Canter Brown Jr., and is viewed as an important resource for many historians who have yet to question Porter's conclu-

Portrait of Micanopy by George Catlin. *Illustrations of the Manners, Customs, and Condition of the North American Indians* (London: Henry G. Bohn, 1845).

sions.[76] The author's often caricatured view of Native people is certainly at odds with his empowerment of blacks and amply demonstrates what political scientist Mahmood Mamdani has identified as America's retention of a settler-colonial consciousness. "If the *race question* marks the cutting edge of American reform," Mamdani observes, "the *native question* highlights the limits of that reform."[77]

A considerable amount of Porter's attention focused on a series of comments gleaned from the historical record, all of which posit a mysterious, almost spell-binding relationship that black slaves supposedly maintained over their Indian masters. As early as 1821, the newly appointed Indian agent Jean A. Penieres, as Porter noted, declared that blacks possessed an inexplicable power over the Indians "whom they in fact govern."[78] Penieres, a French émigré who fell ill with malaria soon after arriving in St. Augustine, was seriously impeded in forming any impression of the Native people he was expected to supervise (he died soon afterward).[79] What one can reasonably glean from his statements, however, is that the concept of black "rule" was already widespread among the white residents of East Florida, most of whom, it should be stressed, seldom risked a journey into the interior and had little to no direct contact with either Seminoles or their slaves. One of the more revealing accounts is from the commander of the army garrison at Tampa Bay who struck an apparently empathetic tone in 1828: "I really pity those Indians, and although Negroes are of little value to the Indians, being rather masters than slaves, still they view them as their property. So many claims are now made on them, that they begin to believe that it is the determination of the United States to take them all."[80] Thus, despite the assertions of property rights by Seminoles as well as their record of slave sales (e.g., thirty slaves were auctioned in St. Augustine in 1821), and even instances of manumission, the perceived social standing of these bondservants, according to the view of Euro-American outsiders, was as de facto sovereigns.[81] What circumstances could account for a position that so coolly denied reality and common logic? (If slaves were masters, then it surely followed that masters were slaves, a fairly nonsensical construct.) Amazingly, this very basic question has never been broached; indeed, certain incongruities appear to be accepted with ease. Historian Kevin Mulroy, for example, has asserted that black "control," coupled with their opposition to removal, "paved the way for the onset of the Second Seminole War," a far-ranging conclusion that not only averts the primacy of tribal governance and decision making but is startling for its dearth of substantive evidence.[82]

One explanation for the ideas expressed by white contemporaries may be found in the realm of southern social mores, especially those aimed at slaveholders who were judged remiss in their obligations as ultimate authority figures. Masters who were seen as exceedingly lax were routinely subject to public censure and scorn, as the absence of rigid discipline was thought to result in "villainy" or even outright revolt. As Genovese and others have noted, slaveowners as well as the public at large were hypervigilant in this regard, and any perceived weakening of authority was thought to be a major threat to the communal welfare.[83] Given that the Florida Territory was in the process of transitioning from an obscure Spanish colony into the southern fold—a cultural and political development of some magnitude—the mode of slavery practiced by Seminoles (including armed slaves

among them), though long accepted by colonial officials, would have been abhorred by newcomers.[84] Within the context of the new US territory, Seminoles
were perceived as ultimate strangers who had muddled societal boundaries that
should have reinforced the perception of safe hierarchies but instead produced
anxiety and fear.[85]

Second, Native slave ownership undermined a central tenet of settler-colonialism. Indians, given their supposedly wild and childlike natures (e.g., "the children of the forest"), were thought to be incapable of managing the land, let alone
slaves; hence, colonizers had an implicit and righteous duty to appropriate these
wasted resources.[86] "While the law furnishes to the Indians ample means of redress for the aggressions of Whitemen," a group of Florida slaveowners complained, "we are Constrained to look with patience, whilst they possess and enjoy
the property most justly and rightfully ours."[87] Native people were in essence regarded as quasi-phantoms who were never allowed a tangible identity; indeed,
they were only permitted those attributes that colonizers wished to project. Repudiation of slave ownership was just one aspect of a fairly elaborate psychological
process of denial and was an extension of the larger diminution of Seminole
cultural and political sovereignty in the Florida interior.[88] "An unbending logic
of exclusion," Veracini observes, indeed figures as the most consistent element
within settler narratives worldwide.[89] Any objective assessment of the role of African Americans within Seminole society would endow Native people with a degree
of autonomy and parity with whites that would contradict the core assumptions
of Jacksonian racial ideology and pose a vital threat to the settler-colonial state.

Third, most white southerners struggled to integrate two divergent themes regarding blacks on a daily basis: the latter were presumed to be indolent, cowardly,
and infantile while at the same time they could be suspected of harboring elaborate
and quite cunning schemes of liberation. As mentioned previously, the dread of
another Haitian Revolution loomed large in southern consciousness. Because Seminole slaves often carried arms and maintained, by most accounts, a swaggering,
nondeferential manner toward the whites they came in contact with—behavior
that would not have been tolerated anywhere else in the South—distrust and
paranoia ran rampant. Black males further tapped into this skewed perspective
by engaging in their warrior roles during the Florida war.[90] It is therefore histor-
ically imprudent, to say the least, to divorce contemporary remarks from the racial
prejudices of the day—biases that consistently warped and guided white settler
perceptions of both Indians and blacks alike—and to accept commentary without
examining context and motivation.

The stereotype of black males as a controlling, malevolent force came to the fore in contemporary publications about the war, especially those by southern authors. The few blacks who were designated as interpreters by the Seminoles and were familiar with Anglo-American ways were especially singled out for recrimination. Indeed, reactions to Abraham, an emancipated slave of Micanopy, illuminate the innate southern distrust of any astute African American male, self-taught as they may have been. M. M. Cohen, a militia officer who wrote the popular *Notices of Florida and the Campaigns* (1836) after returning to Charleston following his war service, thus portrayed Abraham's attentive but nevertheless deferential role as one of Micanopy's trusted aids as nothing less than a deceitful ruse. Affecting a continental literary style, Cohen concluded, very tongue in cheek, that this individual was actually a frontier version of "Cardinal De Retz" (another Charlestonian, Jacob Rhett Motte, snidely evoked "Talleyrand"), who was, after more serious reflection, thought to conceal "deep, dark and bloody purposes."[91] The presumption that blacks functioned as clandestine schemers who manipulated the supposedly lazy and dim-witted Indian revealed a complex and highly contradictory racist ideology that favored white Americans above everyone else.[92] In reality, Abraham, who was exceptional in that he was eventually adopted into the tribe and given clan membership, did indeed hold some influence, but ultimate authority resided with the Seminole war council.[93] Motte claimed that Abraham's supposed control "over his *imbecilic* master" resulted in his "entire sway over all the councils and actions of the Indians," but this scenario was merely the product of Motte's racialized imagination and undoubtedly reflected his intention to appeal to southern readers.[94] The supreme irony in all of this is that some modern authors have selectively taken one aspect of the devious and controlling black male stereotype, especially as presented by Cohen and Motte (minus the sarcasm), as proof of the genuine authority of African Americans while ignoring the racism and systematic distortion that undergirded such remarks.

INDIAN REMOVAL OR "NEGRO WAR"?

A single phrase by Major General Thomas Jesup—army quartermaster general, southern Democrat, slaveholder, and one of the commanders of the Florida war—has attained such attention by certain historians of late that one cannot reasonably approach the history of the war without first coming to terms with this problematic comment. The existence of approximately four hundred to five hundred slaves, including women and children, in addition to a much smaller maroon contingent, certainly created immense logistical and public relations problems during the war.[95] Military historians agree that a few hundred black males served an important supportive role under the Seminoles and were especially visible during the first two years of conflict. However, no tangible evidence exists that African Americans ever appropriated Native authority. Even so, Jesup's comment in which he casually described the war as "a negro, not an Indian war" has become the single most "authoritative" piece of evidence cited by a group of historians, beginning with Kenneth Porter, who have supported the claim of black sovereignty.[96] It also continues to influence a new generation of scholars as well.[97]

In order to understand Jesup's unusual phraseology, one obviously has to be willing to acknowledge the circumstances under which it was written. Quite remarkably, given the pervasive usage of this phrase, this basic task has never before been attempted. Nevertheless, on December 9, 1836, in a letter addressed to Georgia Governor William Schley, General Jesup confided that he was in desperate straits, as he purportedly had only a few hundred men at his disposal at the time. Despite sending previous letters, he had not yet received a reply to his pressing demands for a Georgia militia regiment and so remained vexed. In order to spark Schley's attention, Jesup—true to his liking for hyperbole—raised the ominous threat of slave insurrection, a subject sure to capture the vigorous attention of any southern governor. "This you may be assured is a negro, not an Indian war; and as such it is of the utmost importance to the South that it be instantly closed."[98] The general used virtually the same wording in another letter to the acting secretary of war as part of his effort to garner more troops and additional pay for soldiers.[99] The fact that both these missives were sent on the very day that Jesup learned that he had been appointed commander in Florida, with the memory of his predecessors' well-publicized failures presumably fresh in his mind, should not be ignored. Hence the motivations behind that day's communications was not, as historian Canter Brown Jr. has posited, to deliver a frank assessment to the nation's leaders regarding the actual circumstances of the war (such a weighty statement actually came later and, as will be shown, posited quite the opposite conclusion).[100] Rather, Jesup intended to prod otherwise reluctant officials, using the disturbing specter of slave revolt, to act upon his requests and was disconnected to any substantive line of argument.

Jesup, far more than any other general during the war, utilized a series of unconventional and highly provocative tactics; hyperbole was a critical part of his modus operandi. In order to gain a psychological edge over his Native adversaries, for example, Jesup once spread a false report—via black interpreters—that a band of Shawnee warriors he had enlisted would not only murder all the Seminole men they captured but also "take their hearts out and drink their blood, and make slaves of their women and children."[101] The Seminoles, however, failed to treat this rumor seriously (and nothing of the sort ever occurred). Moreover, after much-publicized peace negotiations with the Seminole leadership collapsed during the spring of 1837 and the promise of a concord vanished, Jesup was livid.[102] He wrote to his second-in-command that not only would it be "extreme folly to trust him [Micanopy] or any of the chiefs again" but decreed that only *extermination* would "rid the country of the Indians." As for the blacks, he flatly stated, "they should be hung up as they are taken."[103] The officer who received this letter did not act upon these instructions; presumably, he could intuit when his superior was merely venting sound and fury. Jesup is best known for his dishonorable capture of Osceola, an incident that sullied a time-honored tenet of war and drew national censure. Still hounded by criticism decades later, Jesup radically altered his account and claimed that it was Osceola who had actually disgraced the white flag by his supposed intention of capturing the formidable Castillo de San Marcos (Fort Marion) at St. Augustine.[104] Surely, here was a person who was unfettered by notions of chivalry and who also shaded the truth when the need arose. Yet determining which of Jesup's copious statements were written in earnest, simply "hot air," calculated overstatement or outright fabrication necessitates very fine scrutiny and consideration of the full range of his war correspondence. In fact, Jesup's letters to the War Department as well as his personal correspondence overwhelmingly posit Seminole authority and control.

A particularly telling incident that occurred midway through the war summarizes this position rather well. In a letter to Secretary of War Joel Poinsett, the general confided that experience had convinced him that the continued goal of the forced removal of Seminoles was utterly senseless. "By disease, capture, and battle the Seminoles and Miccasukeys [sic] including their negroes have lost since the commencement of the war, more than five hundred warriors—those that remain have lost all their property except their rifles, and are now fugitives, without a home." Jesup also believed that what was asked of the army was unprecedented in human history: "I, as well as my predecessors in command in Florida, have failed to catch and remove the Seminoles to Arkansas; but it should be remembered that we are the only commanders who have ever been required to go into an unexplored wilderness, catch Savages, and remove them to another wilderness. Search all history and another instance is not to be found."[105] Whether this action was as unprecedented as Jesup believed may be open to question, but the essential point is that he placed Native Americans, the proverbial "Savages," as the principal enemy—with blacks playing a supportive role—and that Jesup's as yet unfulfilled goal was the transportation of the Seminoles to the West.

Jesup revealed his core thinking vis-à-vis the war's origins in a candid letter directed to one of Poinsett's successors, William Wilkins, a few years after the war.[106] No longer under the stress of field command and writing from his office as quartermaster general in Washington, Jesup expounded on what he thought directly led to the violence. He highlighted the government's failure to make timely preparations for the Indian removal process and specifically singled out the newly appointed Indian agent, General Wiley Thompson, who Jesup disparaged as ill-suited to the job and who acted haughtily toward Native leaders. Moreover, "the constant interference with their negroes [by unscrupulous slave catchers and others]" as well as the "failure to have an adequate force in Florida to support the authority of the Chiefs who were in favor of emigration" was also judged detrimental. Jesup admitted that the Treaty of Payne's Landing "was far from being acceptable to the Indians" but in retrospect maintained that "with prudence and proper regard to their rights and feelings it [relocation] might have been executed without resort to War." The general did not allude to a "negro war" nor did he suggest that Seminole authority had at any time been appropriated or even questioned by blacks. Quite the opposite, Jesup believed the outbreak of war, while the result of blatant mismanagement by the United States, was entirely in the hands of Native leaders.[107]

Even though abundant evidence suggests that the "negro war" comment was used for calculated effect, we may never know what Jesup's intentions were with absolute certainty. Be that as it may, a far more crucial question remains: should historians privilege a single uncharacteristic remark over the content of treaties, executive commands, extensive legislative debate, countless documents relating to the war, and the expressed opinions of military historians? Social scientists routinely discard such statistical outliers or possibly place this data aside for future study. Historians typically do the same, albeit in a less structured manner. A brief phrase written by a certain general on his initial day of command that remains disconnected from any detailed explanation and also happens to contradict the established view of the war—as well as the positions of six other military commanders—hardly qualifies as compelling evidence of anything, other than the idiosyncratic.[108] Conversely, an imposing body of evidence exists, including a trove of official documents in the National Archives and newspaper reports from journalists on the scene (information that was fully utilized in writing this book), and that counter any notion of a "negro war." And if one happens to subscribe to a theory of a vast (and implausible) government cover-up, other sources, including a significant body of letters sent from soldiers in the field as well as their personal diaries and journals, none of which could possibly have been censored, confirm mainstream historical opinion.[109] Primary documents thus point to Indian removal and Indian leadership, with mention, of course, of blacks who fought alongside or who were either captured by or fled to the Seminoles during the war. All things considered, any lingering doubts that still exist will undoubtedly emanate from something other than purely historical reasoning.[110] Ultimately, the most obvious answer to the revisionism of Porter and his recent disciples is to step back from any single phrase and instead look at the totality of the conflict from beginning to end, a goal that happens to be a central focus of this book.

PART II

War of Indian Removal

CHAPTER 3

"It Came with the Suddenness
of the Whirlwind"

On April 21, 1835, more than 1,500 Seminoles gathered in numerous makeshift
camps surrounding the federal Indian Agency near Fort King.[1] The next day, the
principal chiefs were scheduled to meet with General Clinch and Wiley Thompson, the new superintendent of Seminole removal. Thompson was a Georgia
militia general and an influential US congressman who once served as chairman
of the House Military Affairs Committee. Secretary Cass decided that only an
individual of sufficient rank and authority could oversee the deportation process,
and so this newly created office, with its lofty annual salary of $2,000 per year,
displaced the usual position of Indian agent.[2] Thompson's tenure was especially
troublesome, however. His imperious and condescending manner was deemed
"altogether too grandiloquent" for the Seminoles, according to a journalist on
the scene, and his actions consistently exacerbated tensions, especially as the time
drew nearer to the intended departure.[3] The series of meetings between Thompson and Seminole leaders at Fort King grew increasingly one-sided. Despite the
trappings of a specially constructed "council house," it became apparent to all that
the United States never truly valued the thoughts and opinions of Native leaders
but only desired their expedient deportation west.

Clinch earlier received an invitation from the Seminoles to attend a war dance
on the evening of the twenty-first—certainly an odd request, given the circumstances. The ceremony was to be held at a remote location a few miles from the
Indian Agency at a place where Micanopy had set up an elaborate pavilion. This
overture undoubtedly caught Clinch by surprise, as it followed a strongly worded
reprimand from President Jackson that was read to the Seminole chiefs several
weeks before, wherein leaders were admonished for not abiding by the treaty stip-

ulations. Jackson threatened to use armed force if they refused to move.[4] Their cause was useless, he further declared, as the Florida reservation was scheduled to be "surveyed and sold and afterwards will be occupied by a white population."[5] The upcoming meeting was intended as a formal response to the president's weighty communique. But the dance ceremony was certainly not on anyone's official agenda and has, in fact, been missed by historians. James W. Simmons, a noted Whig journalist and brother of William H. Simmons, an author who wrote an early book about East Florida's territorial beginnings, was nevertheless on the scene—one of many proceedings that James Simmons reported on during this period.[6]

Although Clinch did not foresee anything threatening about such an affair, in retrospect one can easily deduce that any large communal ceremony dedicated to war should have sparked concern. As it turned out, this ritual invoked the ancient performative power of sacred dance, and what transpired was an unapologetic expression of Indianness. The symbolic imagery, which was centered on fire, featured a foreboding style of ritual chanting and drumming as well as the emotive power of moving, rhythmic bodies. Even for white observers such as Simmons, who was ignorant of the deeper meanings of the ritual, the dance clearly evoked death and war. The seemingly inchoate and "primitive" world of these Native people with their foreign cosmology and religious traditions must have offered little of practical value to the general, however, for he failed to attend. Even so, Clinch allowed ten of his men, mostly officers, to be present. Simmons also gained admittance and subsequently wrote an evocative impression of the night's activities.

After walking a few miles in pitch darkness, except for torchlights along the way, the journalist and his companions finally reached their destination: the "Governor's" quarters, where Micanopy presided over the mass of people in attendance. Simmons was taken aback by the beauty of the scene, composed of primeval forest and a beautiful meadow. One of Simmons's companions, an English recruit named John Bemrose, similarly noted the "Fairy Land" aspect of the scene.[7] Both also observed the foreboding mood; something they all expected as an "amusement" was eerily transformed by the sound of bloodcurdling war cries. "The ground under the trees (in the form of a circle) they had cleared up before we arrived," Simmons explained.

> [They] built a large fire in the center, towards which one of them suddenly
> darted, and, bowing low to it, commenced a sort of canter around the ring,
> followed by another, then another—each first doing the same reverence to the

fire—till nearly all the appointed number (some 40 or 50) had fallen into the dance—when the Queen of the evening, a very graceful, pretty looking Squaw (wife of one of the chiefs) decorated in all her finery—with a profusion (some dozen sets) of beads around her neck, and a world of tinkling shells (the small terrapin shell perforated, and filled with shot) glided from under a tree . . . and with her head held modestly down—and the tips of her fingers employed in spreading out her dress on either side broad as a turkey's tail!—glided into the now fiery and impetuous circle, that carried her round as the wind would the gossamer!—The movement of the dancers was graceful, though vehement and rapid—yet keeping time to the low sepulchral chant that accompanied it; while the hollow tramp of their feet, that sent its echoes far into the forest—the occasional and measured pause, followed by the supple bound!—and the significant glancing of the right arm, as if well pleased with its work of death—for it was expressive of that dark thought!—the glare of the flames shooting up almost to their faces, and giving to them an aspect scarcely of the earth!—their tall wild figures as they glanced against the torch light, and the thrilling hum as it arose slowly and heavily upon the night—all combined to furnish forth a sample of the Indian War Dance, which those who have once seen it are not likely to forget.[8]

The ceremony continued well after midnight when the author and his companions took their leave and returned to the agency. Later that morning, on the first day of the proceedings, Simmons was surprised to note that "the Chiefs came into Council, calm, cool, and clear—as if the dance, the dust, the heat, the whirl and the whiz of the preceding night, had neither taken vigor from limbs, nor dissipated for a moment one idea in connection with the business they had come upon."[9] Their mood, however, would change rapidly. Clinch made a great show of his ability to enforce the treaties by the military force under his command, and Thompson was equally adamant and confrontational. Micanopy was absent on the second day of deliberations, but after the other leading chiefs agreed with his position and once more refused to depart, reiterating that the treaties were coerced and meaningless, Thompson commanded all five—Micanopy, Jumper, Abiaka, Holata Micco, and Coe Hadjo—to be struck from "the council of the nation" and would thereafter be repudiated as chiefs by the government. Abiaka, a prominent Miccosukee chief and future war leader who was also a *hiliswa haya*, or medicine man, may have stamped his feet and clenched his teeth in anger, but he and the others refrained from issuing direct war threats.[10] To be sure, they had already set out on this path, but the spring season was not the proper time: crops had to be harvested in the fall, while an additional period was needed to remove their families from harm's way.[11] After Thompson's fit of temper, he managed to compel sixteen lesser-ranked chiefs and subchiefs to give their consent to the treaties by placing their marks on a legal document: an outcome that satisfied Clinch and ultimately Jackson himself.[12] Hence it was only after employing the "menace of force," as Representative Everett critically noted in Congress, that yet another dubious legal accord was "ratified."[13] No matter how the proceedings may have looked to outsiders in Washington, however, the time and place for the opening of hostilities were unfolding according to the Seminoles' own agenda. The war dance was all the warning most non-Natives would receive. The ceremony amounted to a vigorous, albeit nonverbal and highly symbolic, rebuke to Jackson's threats as well as an affirmation of Seminole nativism. The fact that its meaning went unnoted was proof of the wide chasm that existed between the US government and those Native leaders who no longer wished to yield to the demands of Old Mad Jackson.

Two months afterward, in June, Thompson ordered Osceola (Asin Yahola)—a charismatic young warrior, a descendent of Red Stick Creeks, and someone who would rise to tremendous notoriety during the war—to be placed in irons and held in the guardhouse jail after the superintendent objected to the latter's "insolent" manner. The exact reasons for the imprisonment remain unclear. Simmons, however, was certain that Osceola had the temerity to tell Thompson to his face, some months before the onset of hostilities, that it was *he* who should leave Florida—a threat, certainly, but one that should have generated some concern on Thompson's part. In any case, Osceola, though imprisoned for just one day and outwardly feigning compliance to Thompson's demands to leave for the West, was privately seething with anger after being treated in such a fashion.[14]

The Seminole war council, composed of elder warriors and shamans from a broad spectrum of clans, held firmly to their decision to fight for their right to remain in the territory.[15] The council's secretive plans depended on a high-risk strategy. While stopping the influx of settlers or defeating the United States in a conventional war may have appeared as impossibilities, the Seminoles nonetheless decided that their best option was to deliver an overpowering and far-ranging first strike throughout the peninsula. By pursuing such a robust strategy, the likes of which had never before been witnessed in the United States, they surely expected a new balance of power, no matter how transitory, to emerge in their favor. Perhaps their position would be strong enough to proceed with a peace overture and to extract the most valued concession: their right to remain unmolested in the territory. The scheme was nevertheless fraught with great risk, as it relied upon a scorched-earth approach that would cause massive economic loses and destroy virtually every homestead and plantation in East Florida. War would entail killing both civilians and soldiers, displace thousands of settlers, result in the release of several hundred plantation slaves (an event with profound national repercussions), and involve the theft of immense herds of livestock and the burning of fields and homesteads. This approach was essentially what historians of the Civil War have called a "hard war."[16] Just as General Sherman would later subject the civilian population of the South to the ravages of warfare, the Seminoles basically did the same in Florida three decades earlier. This path set the United States on a war footing and presented Seminoles with the likelihood of suffering massive casualties or even annihilation.

Retribution should also be considered as part of Seminole strategy. Seminoles had certainly not forgotten about the raids by US forces in the Alachua country during the winter of 1813 (the Patriot War), when torches were set to their towns and the black settlements by a joint force composed of the US Army and Tennessee Volunteers. During a three-week rampage, American troops systematically destroyed each abandoned village. A total of 386 dwelling houses were burned along with huts and any other conceivable personal item of worth.[17] Thousands of deer skins were either taken by soldiers or burned along with storehouses of corn. Shifting columns of smoke filled the air for miles as the site of Seminole prosperity throughout the Paynes Prairie region was largely left as scorched earth. Similar scenes of devastation followed in other regions of Florida during Jackson's First Seminole War and the brutal Coweta raids, events that had deeply affected every faction that now made up the war council. The time had clearly come for this oppressive power dynamic to be overturned.

Among the factors that favored the Seminole offensive was the ease with which they could gather intelligence regarding the army's actions in Florida. The number of newly arrived troops who either became incapacitated or died during the hot-weather months was surely noted as a major vulnerability, as Seminole and black warriors were decidedly less prone to the endemic strains of malaria and yellow fever (chapter 8). Furthermore, the Seminoles' highly mobile, asymmetric warfare, effective spy and communications networks, combined with intimate knowledge of some of the most diverse and challenging terrain in the South (most of it unmapped, with portions teeming with alligators, venomous snakes, and disease-carrying mosquitoes), including the location of food sources and drinking water, offered key advantages to any fighting force looking to survive a probable military onslaught. The Seminoles' familiarity and ease within this geographic domain offered remarkable assets in pursuing an asymmetric style of combat.

Another seldom noted advantage was the presence of open international borders (i.e., the Spanish colonial island of Cuba to the south and the British Bahamas to the east). Cuba, as will be shown, would be a consistent provider of vital arms and munitions, without which the war would have come to a rapid conclusion.[18] The Seminoles were additionally strengthened by their ethnic and religious identity and their adherence to the principles that first animated the Red Stick rebellion. The militant nativist movement that was generated in the early part of the century by the Shawnee war chief Tecumseh held special resonance—despite the military defeats inflicted by Jackson—and it was this transcendent struggle against the incursions of the white man, reinforced by the Seminoles' own prophets and spirit guides, that played a considerable role in solidifying and maintaining support for the war. The fact that the war council included veterans of these past conflicts, men who also happened to be exceptionally capable and resolute commanders, proved invaluable. During the opening of the war, the *National Intelligencer* admitted that these Native combatants demonstrated "a wary dissimulation, celerity of movement, courage in attacking, and a skill in retreating, subversive of all our military plans."[19] Historian Samuel Watson recently concluded that "Seminole command and control was better organized, in effect if not in structure, than that of the United States during the first six months of the war."[20] An apt admission, albeit one that has been very late in coming.

Tensions on the frontier escalated during the summer and fall of 1835. Despite the silence of the war council, some tribal members, according to settlers, no longer disguised "their contempt for the government and its laws" and were less restrained by the reservation boundaries.[21] Certain bands, especially the Miccosukees, boldly encamped within range of white settlements and butchered stolen livestock in plain sight. An incident erupted on Paynes Prairie in June that involved irate settlers and a group of Miccosukees who were caught in the act of cattle rustling. Two Indians endured brutal floggings with cattle whips and another was shot dead after coming to the aid of his companions. There were wounded individuals on both sides. News of the event spread very rapidly, and many settlers feared that such vigilantism could trigger all-out war.[22] Not long afterward, the terribly mutilated and lifeless body of an army mail carrier was found floating in a pond—an act that most saw as revenge for the Paynes Prairie incident. Clinch planned to mount a retaliatory strike on a group of Miccosukees who had assembled at a remote area called the Cove of the Withlacoochee—an impressive natural sanctuary and the intended Seminole stronghold for the upcoming war. The "Cove" was an immense 63,000-acre wetland within the reservation boundaries (see map on facing page). One contemporary observed that the region, located

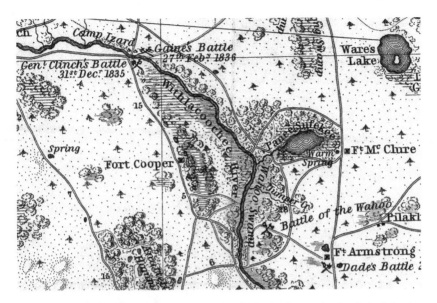

The Cove of the Withlacoochee, the area selected by the Seminoles for their defensive operations and scene of the first large-scale engagements of the war. This region includes the battles of Dade, Clinch, and Gaines as well as the Battle of Wahoo Swamp. Detail from *Map of the Seat of the War* (1839), Rare Map Collection, University of South Florida.

near the Withlacoochee River and which also included the smaller Wahoo Swamp, consisted of "a chain of lakes or ponds, communicating with each other by boggy sluices" and made up of "pine islands, Cyprus swamps, hammocks, bogs and ponds," but also noted that there was enough high ground for essential crops and cattle.[23] The secretary of war cautioned Clinch against any action until the pro-removal bloc had actually departed Florida.[24] Despite scattered incidents of violence, life in the interior continued more or less the same, although some settlers felt that something especially sinister was in the offing. (A few fortunate families who had befriended the Seminoles were in fact permitted advance warning and managed to escape before general hostilities commenced.[25])

Events began to rapidly escalate beginning on November 26. Charley (Chalo) Emathla, an Apalachee *micco* who was a leader among the proremoval group of Seminoles, was executed by Osceola. This action alerted Clinch and his officers that the antiremoval coalition headed by Micanopy was in control, regardless of events at the Indian Agency, and that war was imminent.[26] The Seminole council had previously ruled that anyone who relented to US demands to sell their livestock and accept removal would be subject to the death penalty—precisely the kind of severe, intratribal justice that was meted out during the earlier Red Stick War.[27] Charley Emathla unfortunately opted to defy this grave edict by taking an accommodationist stance; he agreed to removal and sold his cattle to officials at Fort King.[28] After Charley's execution, Osceola instructed that his body be left unburied along a road several miles from the fort. In a further symbolic gesture, he scattered the gold and silver coins that were received from the sale over the body and on the dirt road, and then barred anyone from touching the money, "as it was made of the red man's blood."[29] Now primed for war and infused with a militant spirit (with Osceola acting as tribal enforcer), the anti-accommodationist majority would not tolerate insubordination of such magnitude.[30]

Following this execution, most Seminoles quickly retreated from view, and white settlers were certainly justified in expecting more violence. About one hundred proremoval Seminoles led by Fuche Luste Hadjo (Black Dirt) fled to the safety of Fort Brooke, a Tampa Bay garrison manned by about 230 army regulars and militia.[31] (This fort had previously been designated as the port of departure for both the Seminoles and their slaves via vessels anchored on the bay.) As Clinch and others feared, the myriad Alachua settlements were soon under attack during the first week of December, a wave of destruction that "came with the suddenness of the whirlwind and the storm," as one resident phrased it.[32] "It is truly distressing to witness the panic and sufferings of the white frontier inhabitants," Clinch urgently wrote to the War Department. "Men, women and children are seen flying in every direction and leaving everything behind them save a few articles of clothing. Many families that were comfortable and independent in their circumstances are now reduced to want, their houses and their [farms] all having been plundered and burned by small bands of Indians, who have spread themselves through the country, taking advantage of their knowledge of the swamps and hammocks to conceal their operations. The first object of everyone was to remove their wives and children to a place of safety."[33] "Murderous & incendiary bands" of Seminoles now appeared fully united and in conjunction with their "negroes," Clinch observed, manifested "a determination to engage in War, murder and plunder."[34] Most Seminole slaves were by all accounts also opposed to moving from Florida, despite assurances that they would follow their Indian masters to the Arkansas Territory. As hostilities commenced, these skilled warriors became a conspicuous force, and their commitment to defy removal certainly boosted morale and added to the Seminoles' formidable fighting capability. Given the level of devastation that also rapidly extended to the Tampa Bay region, and the many hundreds who sought protection at the closest fortification, Clinch could not resist stating that if his original recommendations had been followed such wholesale destruction might have been avoided.[35] He similarly complained about the lack of officers, food and supplies, wagons, hospital tents, and so forth—all were requisitioned many months previously. Jackson was in no mood for self-recriminations, however. He sent word to Cass that Clinch should move his forces "into the Indian Towns, seize the women & children and inflict merited chastisement for these atrocious murders so unprovoked."[36] Whether Clinch actually received Jackson's missive is unknown, but to his credit he never pursued a policy of wanton slaughter.

The Alachua district was on high alert, with homesteads abandoned and many farms already consumed by fire, when Florida militia Colonel John Warren gathered 150 volunteers at Paynes Prairie on December 18 and sent a mounted detachment to defend a supply train that was heading south toward the now-barricaded village of Micanopy. Not long after Warren separated his main force from the wagons, Osceola led eighty warriors in an ambush of the train and took possession of its contents at a place called Black Point, along the prairie's southern rim. This was an elevated region of thick palmetto stands and dense hammocks that concealed the warriors quite effectively. Militia captain John McLemore, who witnessed the situation from afar, and despite being outnumbered more than two to one, led an abortive charge against the Seminoles in order to recover scarce supplies and ammunition. In the process, eight militiamen were killed and six wounded.[37] Compared to the scattered bands that were decimating the region, absconding with droves of horses and an estimated 25,000 head of cattle—seeming more intent on generating terror than engaging in indiscriminate slaughter—the concerted assault on the militia train represented a notable tactical escalation.[38] The shift from targeting domestic buildings and farms to coordinated, lethal attacks on armed troops became a milestone of sorts. What would later be dubbed a full-scale "war upon the whites" in the press had just been extended to the military—a forerunner to far larger events.[39] Despite its modest scale, the ambush at Black Point has been viewed as the first "military" engagement of the war. But its significance should certainly be seen in conjunction with the ongoing devastation of the settler enclaves in Alachua.

News of the December uprising had surely reached all the Florida garrisons by the time two companies under the command of Major Francis Dade proceeded on a one-hundred-mile march along a sandy, isolated road that connected Fort Brooke to the more northerly Fort King. These troops were intended to relieve the latter, severely undermanned garrison. Earlier, Clinch had depleted this post in order to man Fort Drane, the general's Lang Syne sugar plantation that had been hastily fortified by twelve-feet-high pine-log palisades. This move may have protected Clinch's financial investments, but it also made practical sense, as his plantation happened to be much closer to the Alachua settlements under attack. On the morning of December 28, Dade's column of 108 men, now about fifty miles from Fort King, continued through pine lands and dense hammocks, all the while oblivious to the warriors who were quietly monitoring their movements. As it happened, half the infantrymen in Dade's command were European nationals. Many were utter novices to the military and often joined on a drunken dare; some simply desired to escape financial or family difficulties. Within the army as a whole, a substantial portion of the more experienced sergeants were a hardened group of veterans from the Napoleonic wars who hardly knew a word of English.[40] No matter their background, they were now outfitted in US Army uniforms—sky-blue winter outfits that were offset by white crossbelts and topped off by black leather caps. Unfortunately, all the enlisted men and officers were proceeding into a precisely orchestrated ambush, an event that Alligator (Halpatter Tustenuggee), who was present at the scene, later recalled as part of a decisive blow that the war council had been preparing for some time. At the agreed-upon site, a few miles north of the Little Withlacoochee River, 180 warriors took up their positions on the west side of the road, directly across from a pond that impeded escape. Alligator's narrative provides an uncommon Native perspective. "Every warrior was protected by a tree, or secreted in the high palmettoes," Alligator noted.

> About nine o'clock in the morning the command approached. In advance, some distance, was an officer on a horse, who, Micanopy said, was the captain; he knew him personally; had been his friend in Tampa. [As] soon as *all* the soldiers were opposite, between us and the pond, perhaps twenty yards off, Jumper gave the whoop, Micanopy fired the first rifle, the signal agreed upon, when every Indian arose and fired, which laid upon the ground, dead, about half the white men. The [army] cannon was discharged several times, but the men who loaded it were shot down as soon as the smoke cleared away; the balls passed far over our heads. The soldiers shouted and whooped, and the officers shook their swords and swore. There was a little man, a great brave, who shook his sword at the soldiers and said "God-dam!" no rifle-ball could hit him.[41]

In time, however, the feisty Captain George W. Gardiner, a mere five feet, would in fact perish (there would only be three immediate survivors). Alligator's rendition differs significantly from an account by one of the army survivors, Private Ransom Clark. In his published version of the affair that would attract national attention, Clark noted that the cannon, loaded with six pounds of canister (loose rounds that would have scattered like a shotgun), caused significant harm and resulted in a Seminole retreat. This allowed those who were lucky to have evaded serious injury (perhaps thirty in number) enough time to erect a makeshift "triangular breastwork" by quickly felling some pine trees before the Seminoles returned to attack. Clark sustained severe wounds but evidently was alert enough to estimate that they had engaged the enemy for five hours.[42] Conversely, Alligator stated that their force did not retreat but only withdrew to their camp after they believed all had died during the initial devastating volleys. Some half-dozen soldiers, following this version of events, not only managed to survive but took up a defensive position behind a hastily assembled log structure. When Alligator was alerted to this, he returned to the scene with Jumper and about ten other warriors and successfully avoided cannon fire "by dodging behind the trees just as they applied the fire." By this time, the soldiers were out of ammunition, and as the cannon was their only weapon the situation was quite futile. It was only a matter of minutes before all were killed. "The firing had ceased and all was quiet" by about noon, Alligator recalled.[43] The Seminoles retired to their camp once again. But this time, they directed a number of their black forces to return to the battlefield in order to guarantee that all were indeed killed and not feigning death.

Regardless of which version rings true, what is most germane is the simple fact that Seminoles, long maligned as a conquered and dispirited people, planned and executed a resoundingly successful surprise attack on an unprepared detachment of the US Army while only claiming three dead and five wounded of their own.[44] Clark's inclusion of an especially gory scene of "butchery" and plunder that supposedly took place at the hands of up to fifty black warriors wielding axes and knives who had been set loose on the fallen—along with their "fiendish laughter"—perfectly suited the sensationalist style of journalism that was popular at the time and buttressed racialized fears of bloody rebellion.[45] The possibility surely arises that Clark may have exaggerated details even before he was forced to retire and provide for his family (still plagued by festering wounds) on the paltry disability pay of $8 per month. But once this version was published, its credibility was really beside the point.

Adding even more to their substantial tactical success that day, fifty-four-year-old Wiley Thompson, as well as several others in his entourage, was assassinated by Osceola and his band while taking an ill-advised stroll outside the gates of Fort King. The war council undoubtedly expected that the killing of such a high-ranking person, especially in tandem with the losses previously incurred, would cause even more of a furor and augment their goal of a crushing first strike—along with extracting a very high emotional toll. Reports of Thompson's death and scalping did indeed result in considerable shock and anger, and alerted Washington that Seminoles did not seem to dread US reprisals. If the events of December 28 were intended to provoke the army to retaliate quickly (and hastily), then, as we will see, this tactic was brilliantly conceived. Historians have typically accentuated the role that Osceola played in Thompson's death and emphasized his supposedly brooding and morbid quest for personal revenge, as if a dark character in a melodrama. Alligator stated, however, that Osceola was given the task of eliminating Thompson by the war council—partly as payback, to be sure, but a war assignment nevertheless.[46] Tactical and strategic planning on the part of the Seminoles has typically been ignored by historians of the war, and events have mostly been interpreted as mere random opportunities on the part of Native forces.[47] Mahon even asserted that the power of the Seminoles "did not come from organization, but from desperation."[48] Such an opinion grossly undervalues and misjudges the capability of an adversary that so thoroughly dominated the opening of the war. The Seminole leadership knew full well that the likelihood of a full military victory was nil; they simply made the best possible stand that they could muster and were undeterred by the possible consequences.

An integral part of the Seminole plan was to destroy the approximately two dozen sugar estates located along the east coast, from the area of St. Augustine down the coast to New Smyrna, and to inflict further financial damage by the release of hundreds of plantation slaves. Much in the manner of the earlier Alachua attacks, small bands, under the leadership of Emathla (King Philip) and his son Coacoochee (Wildcat), who many officers believed to be "the most dangerous chieftain in the field," began on Christmas Day and continued for the next month.[49] All sugar mills, cotton gins, plantation houses, slave quarters, crops, and an unknown number of settler homesteads were eventually burned and left in ruins. Although the fledgling sugar industry in Florida represented a small fraction of sugar production compared to Louisiana, for instance, these losses created an economic cataclysm in the territory as many mills, outfitted with the latest steam-powered technology, were heavily mortgaged and also employed hundreds of people.[50] Major sugar works such as Dunlawton, Bulowville, Dummet Grove, Rees Spring Grove, and Cruger-DePeyster were not only destroyed but their owners were left in fiscal shambles. Throughout the month of January, Coacoochee assumed a terrifying persona. His mere visage—wearing only a breechcloth and mounted on a stunning white horse, decked out in full war paint and having fastened the remnants of former lighthouse reflectors on his headdress, which presumably sent rays of sunlight in every direction—was fearsome enough to propel inexperienced militia into retreat.[51] Panic was further compounded when John Caesar, a black leader under Emathla's leadership, led his own war party and, among myriad acts of destruction, set fire to the elegant New Smyrna mansion and plantation of Judge David R. Dunham.[52]

The northeastern region was under the command of Joseph M. Hernandez, an elite planter and Spanish *Floridiano* (native Floridian) who previously headed the St. Augustine militia and was mustered into the army as a brigadier general on December 20.[53] Although Hernandez was by all accounts a capable commander, many in the ranks of the regional militia were substandard at best. George Ormand, a sergeant in the local "Mosquito Roarers" (Company B), freely admitted: "They were just an undisciplined rabble, under no command of their officers, and not a man had ever before seen a gun fired in anger."[54] Even so, militia forces were able to guard the transportation of several hundred slaves from some of the leading mills to Anastasia Island, east of St. Augustine, before the plantations were overrun.[55] But a great proportion of those who escaped, another observer wrote, "[were] carried off and sold outside the Territory" and never seen again. Some months later, additional escapees were openly sold in St. Augustine to newly arrived slave dealers, who were "hovering around like vultures after a favorite prey."[56] No doubt, small bands of armed blacks managed to survive on their own in the wilderness. Indeed, by the spring a war correspondent on assignment from an Annapolis newspaper noted that Coacoochee along with Abraham "were effecting to establish a junction with the negroes now under arms."[57] Three hundred to four hundred others, however, were taken by the Seminoles in January. While we can assume that many were eager to assist the war effort, others risked death by escaping back to the plantation region.[58] Jane Sheldon, a local eyewitness who questioned some of the plantation slaves who absconded from the Seminoles (only to return), reported that although they initially supported and abetted the uprising, they quickly became disenchanted, explaining that "they were glad enough to get away from the Indians, as they treated them very cruelly."[59] Adding credence to this claim, Emathla compelled three hundred plantation slaves, via the forceful oversight of "armed sentinels," to devote themselves to cultivating his crops, "whilst his warriors [were] marauding about the country."[60] Rumors continued to spread about how harshly the Seminoles treated former plantation slaves, even as far as killing young children who were sickly and unable to keep up.[61] According to the diary entries of Lieutenant Andrew A. Humphreys, Seminoles kept these blacks—quite unlike their own slaves—under the closest scrutiny and treated them in "the severest manner"; otherwise, he noted, they would "run to the whites" at the first opportunity. Moreover, the men were forced to fight by placing them on the front lines, where they had no other choice but to try to defend themselves.[62] Delegate Joseph White further declared in Congress that Seminoles had resorted to threatening "those slaves who would not operate with them" with transportation to Cuba, presumably to labor on the island's dreaded *ingenios* (sugar plantations).[63] Such a scenario was possible since Seminoles maintained strong ties to the island and relied on shipments of arms, ammunition, and food stuffs that arrived on-board the vessels of Cuban fisherman who plied the Gulf waters.[64]

On the day following the Dade ambush and the Thompson assassination, Clinch joined forces with the Florida militia, then under the command of Major General Richard K. Call, for an attack against Seminoles who had withdrawn into the Cove of the Withlacoochee. Both Clinch and Call, while informed of the brazen killing of the superintendent, were still unaware of the dire outcome of Major Dade's command (instead, the sound of distant cannon fire was interpreted as thunder). The need for prompt retaliation for the December uprising and for Thompson's murder was keenly felt, especially since the enlistment period for the militia would end on January 1. Because of the army's scarce knowledge of the terrain, Clinch relied on a small cadre of friendly Indians and "spies" (i.e., blacks who were familiar with the area).[65] On December 31, the joint command of 250 regular army and 500 volunteers pressed toward the enemy stronghold and stopped at a point on the Withlacoochee River where spies had assured them that they would find their adversaries—directly across the waterway.[66] Clinch faced two major problems: losing the militia the following day and finding a way to ford a section of the river that was both deep and possessed a strong current. Pressure from the War Department was another concern. It was quite clear that the army in Florida had to retaliate, using every means possible, against an enemy that was "spreading desolation over the whole land," as Call phrased it.[67] If they failed to respond forcefully, given the unprecedented magnitude of Seminole attacks, repercussions from Washington would have been formidable. One of Clinch's men, a strong swimmer, stripped off his clothes and succeeded in crossing the current, at which point he retrieved an abandoned dugout canoe on the opposite side. The general then made a fateful decision. He ordered his men to begin crossing aboard this single, small craft, five at a time—a feat that took two hours for just the army component to accomplish. Once on the other side, Clinch's detachment marched several hundred yards until they entered an oval-shaped clearing that was surrounded on all sides by a dense hammock. Inexplicably, with the militia yet to arrive, the men were permitted to stack their muskets, relax, and regroup at the clearing. It was exactly at the moment when they least expected an assault that Osceola, wearing a captured US Army jacket, gave the command for his 250 men (including thirty black warriors) to open fire. Immediate chaos ensued. "The suddenness of the thing," an observer wrote afterward, "conjoined to the terrible and bloodcurdling cry of the Indians, struck at once terror and some degree of panic among the soldiers."[68] But after several minutes, officers were finally able to gather and rally the men while under a hail of bullets. Lieutenant Colonel Alexander Fanning strained mightily to convince Clinch that their only chance of survival was to mount a bayonet charge toward the concealed enemy. But the general repeatedly denied this request and summarily ordered Fanning to return to his troops. Watching his men continue to fall and with tears in his eyes, Fanning frantically appealed once again. This time, the truth of the matter finally penetrated the general. Three charges followed, and while each resulted in large numbers of army wounded, this aggressive move caused the Seminoles to fall back, and it certainly prevented complete annihilation. About thirty volunteers managed to cross the river in time to provide an additional line of defense. From then on, the only recourse was withdrawal; with the support of the added militia, a line of fire was established that allowed the troops to extricate themselves. After an hour and fifteen minutes of concentrated firepower, a "peeling sound" that an observer compared to one thousand rifles fired simultaneously as well as "the unearthly war whoop from a thousand savage throats" resonated throughout the battlefield.[69] In addition to the large number of wounded, some inexperienced troops showed signs of shock. Even so, Clinch's men were able to return to the river bank, carrying a shocking total of fifty-nine wounded and four dead.[70] In a stroke of good fortune for the US military, Call managed to construct a makeshift bridge of logs that afforded easy withdrawal across the river—instead of the miserable prospects of a dugout canoe.[71] Hospital wagons were packed with the wounded on the return trip to Fort Drane. Soldiers were awestruck at the length "of the litters and wagons filled with the maimed," an assemblage that stretched almost a mile in length.[72] If there was any question who gained the advantage at the Withlacoochee, the number of Clinch's men who were taken out of action in such a fashion should serve as a good barometer.

Many newspapers, possessed only with Clinch's official version of events, hailed the general's performance. But the Battle of the Withlacoochee, as it became known, also stirred controversy. A firm line of contention arose between those who maligned the militia for not fully coming to the aid of the army regulars and others who extolled the heroism of Call and the Florida volunteers. Such discussions remain moot, however, as the case against the militia is not nearly as compelling as the evidence against Clinch. The fact that his command escaped Dade's tragic fate by the narrowest of margins was undeniable. The general's stunningly ill-conceived plan to risk everything on a single derelict canoe was, as his biographer had to admit, simply "the wrong decision."[73] Clinch, for all his

George Catlin's iconic portrait of Osceola. National Portrait Gallery, Washington, DC.

prescient understanding of the trouble that was brewing before the war, seriously misjudged the Seminoles' fighting ability after he found himself in the field. Most of his career had been spent in frontier isolation, and he lacked extensive experience in battle.[74] One can thus more easily understand how Clinch committed the most basic of errors by allowing his forces to become divided, therefore handing Osceola a sterling advantage. Historian Edwin C. McReynolds claimed (circa 1950s) that the canoe was placed as "bait."[75] If ever proven to be true, this would certainly seal Osceola's reputation as a tactician of astonishing merit.

Although outnumbered three to one, Seminole losses were light: three killed and five wounded, including a minor wound suffered by Osceola. In Sprague's version of the battle, the author describes a crucial turning point regarding the

Native leadership—an account that has been all but forgotten. Once again citing Alligator as his source, Sprague stated that during the end of the engagement, Micanopy learned that two of his slaves were among the dead and thereafter became terribly distraught. He let his emotions override his judgment and vehemently forbade any of his other slaves (a considerable number) from participating as warriors in the future, a stance that would have certainly hindered the war effort. From that time onward, the war council appears to have lost confidence in Micanopy. Since the beginning of hostilities, other leaders noted that Micanopy exhibited certain troubling characteristics. He continually vacillated and procrastinated, even during battle, infuriating other warriors and potentially risking lives in the process. On this occasion, however, Micanopy revealed that his personal interests superseded the welfare of his people and was thus dishonored. War was an intensely communal affair among the Seminoles; no one, no matter their rank, was exempt from the sacrifices that were required. Micanopy's hereditary civil authority was left uncontested, but he no longer participated, like his forebears Ahaya, King Payne, and Bowlegs, as a warrior-chief.[76]

CHAPTER 4

The United States Responds

Given the surprise nature of the December uprising, the isolation of the Florida Territory, and the sluggishness of news dissemination before the advent of the telegraph, notice of the upheaval did not become widely known on a national level until mid-January. Numerous and often conflicting details came to light all at once. Adding to this confusion, editors often crammed multiple stories, mostly taken from the letters of army or militia officers as well as affluent planters, into single voluminous pages. A shocked public therefore had to interpret early reports that possessed little or no coherence and were rife with rumor. In due course, however, certain papers such as the *New York Commercial Advertiser* (Whig) resolved on an editorial stance and surprisingly came out as sympathetic to the Seminole cause. "The Indians cannot be mad enough to hope for ultimate success but they seem to have resolved upon a war of extermination—to die fighting to the last, upon the graves of their fathers." The editor, William Leete Stone, an influential author and rare advocate for Native Americans, therefore chose to represent Seminoles in a compassionate and Romantic vein. "They have drawn the sword and cast away the scabbard, willing to perish, but determined not to perish unavenged."[1] The Romantic genre, as will be shown, would eventually be used as an effective political tool in the anti-Jacksonian arsenal throughout the war.

Such sentiments were entirely missing in the South, however, and those who claimed the moral high ground were mostly doing so on behalf of the soldiers who perished during what came to be known as "Dade's Massacre." The tragedy became a crucial element in rallying volunteer militias, largely from southern states—especially South Carolina, Georgia, Alabama, Tennessee, and Louisiana— and uniting them in a "gallant" fight against the Seminoles. The Mobile *Mercan-*

Departure of the Augusta [Ga.] Volunteers for Florida, 1836. Detail from a broadside commemorating the town of Augusta's militia participation in the Florida war. Similar scenes of military fervor were repeated throughout the South during the first months of the war. Augusta Museum of History.

tile Advertiser was incredulous after receiving news of the defeat, urged a merciless response, and included genocide as an option: "The Seminole Indians must be either exterminated totally, or . . . driven out beyond the boundaries of civilized life."[2] Hundreds of volunteers heeded such impassioned rhetoric and after various emotion-filled public meetings where citizen soldiers, some as young as fourteen and as old as seventy, swore to come to the aid of those who were "in urgent peril and extreme suffering" joined the regular troops assembled in ports such as Charleston, Savannah, and New Orleans.[3] "We anticipate victories and national renown," Tennessean Benjamin Franklin Baldwin freely admitted.[4] Some Charleston regiments—composed of the sons of gentry who had been raised, as M. M. Cohen confided, "most daintily by our dear mamas"—suddenly discovered that after entering Florida they no longer dreamt of Byron "but of Bacon and hard bread."[5] Youthful adventurism was indeed quelled soon after experiencing conditions in the peninsula.

When Major General Edmund P. Gaines, then stationed in Louisiana and in command of the US Army's Western Division, was informed of the uprising, he called up a force of Louisiana volunteers to accompany four hundred of his regulars via a small fleet of steamboats to Fort Brooke on Tampa Bay. The army's western and eastern departments extended equidistantly through the center of the Florida peninsula. Forts Brookes, King, and Drane, as well as the Key West garrison, were under his jurisdiction. Gaines's newly appointed adjutant, Captain Ethan A. Hitchcock, observed in his diary that the newspapers "are full of reports on the depredations and ferocity of the Indians"—accounts that filled the men with the righteousness of their cause.[6] Both officers and enlisted men were also familiar with Private Clark's horrific storyline and were appalled at the specter of rampaging blacks. To compound matters, ill-founded rumors circulated that the territorial capital of Tallahassee had been burned and left in ruins.[7] With a heightened sense of purpose, Gaines's command left New Orleans by sea on February 4 and arrived at Pensacola two days later. Here the general received a letter from Washington that alerted him that Major General Winfield Scott, Gaines's longtime rival, had been ordered by President Jackson to assume the Florida command, replacing Clinch. Gaines was expected to await further orders in New Orleans. Despite this knowledge, he was convinced that the situation was quickly deteriorating and thus warranted proceeding on his original course to Tampa, a decision that became a focus of a future court of inquiry.[8] While at Fort Brooke, Gaines placed Hitchcock as his acting inspector general, and so the latter helped organize the troops, volunteers, and "friendly Indians"—a combined force of about 1,100. They marched for Fort King on the 13th.[9] While Gaines did not relish meeting up with his nemesis in the backwoods, the humiliating loss of Dade's command and the immense destruction throughout the territory lured him into the interior, where he hoped to deliver a crushing strike against the intractable Seminoles.

The army followed the same road to Fort King that Major Dade took in December, halting only to burn several small, abandoned Seminole villages along the way. On the 20th, Gaines and his troops encountered the bodily remains of those who perished two months earlier. After so long a period, vultures and decomposition had reduced the corpses to skeletons, while uniforms were still relatively intact; everyone, Hitchcock observed, was found precisely where they had fallen in battle. "We buried them all," he wrote, "[and] honored with funeral rights [sic] the bodies of Major Dade & his command." To their surprise, valuable personal items were left untouched by their adversaries, making identification possible: Major Dade was known by a gold plug in one of his teeth, while others were identified by their private pistols, rings, breastpins, and so forth. At Hitchcock's suggestion, the single cannon in which Dade's soldiers had placed so much of their confidence was recovered and positioned vertically to honor the fallen.[10] Hitchcock's written account of this first battlefield reconnaissance, in which macabre details regarding the interment of the corpses proved especially powerful, not for its elegant language but rather for its plainspoken manner, appeared in newspapers the following month.[11] "There was a preciseness and truth in the picture of this field of the dead which was striking and appalling in the highest degree," an officer concluded after reading the report.[12] Compelling images of uniformed skeletons lying at their posts—still grasping arms—served as a kind of *tableau vivant* in which "specters of the miserably slain" offered an instructive meditation on duty and honor.[13] Hitchcock's unadorned verse then inspired a host of writers on the national scene, who attempted to deal with the war through the Romantic genre then held in high esteem.

After a burial ceremony that featured a solemn march and a funeral dirge by army musicians, Gaines continued onward and on the 22nd reached Fort King, a simple outpost enclosed by pine-log pickets.[14] Stories circulated that the highly secluded post had been overrun and decimated by Seminoles, so all were relieved to see the garrison still standing.[15] None of the men, Hitchcock noted, "had dared go a hundred yards from the pickets" after the death of Wiley Thompson and the others and had thus only recently heard of the loss of Dade's command.[16] Gaines had expected to find adequate rations for his men but was frustrated to learn that recent shipments from the quartermaster general's office had failed to arrive. With only two days' rations available for the men at Fort King and an additional seven days gathered at Fort Drane, as well as the fact that some militia volunteers had not eaten adequately for some time, the general faced a considerable problem. While at Fort King, Gaines was also told of General Scott's plans to encircle the Seminoles at the Withlacoochee with considerable force.[17] Despite this information, Gaines incautiously departed the fort on the 26th, three columns abreast, and headed directly for the scene of Clinch's last battle, requisitioning a cannon (a "six-pounder") before departing. The army reached the river the next day and paused at a place where low swampland predominated on top of the riverbanks. While examining a likely spot for fording, a modest contingent of Seminoles from the opposite side began a steady rifle barrage. The firing and yelling continued for more than a half hour; at the end of the encounter, one lay dead and eight were wounded.[18] Afterward, Gaines decided to encamp for the evening, during which time his Indian guides suggested heading for another site two miles downriver.[19] The general agreed, but as the column advanced along a circuitous route toward the river bank the next morning, they became enveloped by a dense live-oak hammock that was shrouded in Spanish moss—a likely ambush site. A heavy barrage of rifle and musket fire, aimed at the advance guard, erupted from a considerable force across the river.[20] Despite the initial confusion, the troops were instructed to break formation and "take to the trees" to find cover.[21] It was at this time that Lieutenant James F. Izard, the acting brigade major who had volunteered to lead an advance party across the river, suffered a grave head wound (dying after five days).

In the twenty-four hours since Gaines first reached the Withlacoochee, the Seminoles had adequate time to assemble a commanding presence from their base at the Cove. A total of 1,131 warriors led by Jumper, Alligator, and Osceola, including eighty blacks under Abraham, would shortly be united—numerically Gaines's equal.[22] When an additional contingent of warriors arrived and joined the main force on the opposite bank, the Seminoles unexpectedly stopped firing and a celebration took place. A tremendous war cry filled the battlefield as they began yelling in unison, repeating what sounded like a single enigmatic word: "Kirr-wowh!" This loud outburst reverberated off the water and filled the surrounding hammock area, rallying the warriors and leaving the troops astonished. The first syllable, as described by Lieutenant Henry Prince, was extremely shrill but then "glided down the octave," to be followed by an even louder and completely "guttural" sound.[23] War cries, or what poet Edmund Spenser once described as a "terrible yell and hubbub" that could somehow dislodge heaven and earth, were as ancient as humanity itself.[24] But for the US military in 1836, composed mostly of individuals who were unaccustomed to any large body of Indians, this united cry was a one-of-a-kind experience (some indeed believed it "hideous" as well). The surreal sound was so finely executed that it seemed to emanate "from one prodigious instrument."[25] Just as unexpectedly as it began, the chorus terminated with a feu de joie, or rifle salute. The battleground remained eerily silent for an hour, and then massive volleys erupted again and lasted until late afternoon. During this period, cannon fire, consisting of grape shot, was liberally directed at the Seminoles and surely took a heavy toll. A pause during the evening allowed the army to construct a log breastwork, "200 paces" in each direction and consisting of three logs stacked on top of each other—a fortification quickly dubbed Camp Izard.[26] Also that night, Gaines sent out ten mounted express riders to reach General Clinch. Six thousand rations were requested immediately from Fort Drane, in addition to ammunition and a wide assortment of axes, saws, and other tools. It was additionally proposed that Clinch cross the Withlacoochee and attack the enemy from the rear.[27] "I have now near me the principal force of the Seminole Indians and their black vassals and allies," Gaines wrote. He confidently asserted that quick action on Clinch's part would result in "the end of the war in the next ten days."[28] The general nevertheless ordered his command to go on half rations.[29]

At ten o'clock the following morning, the situation escalated. Seminoles succeeded in traversing the water undetected and proceeded to attack. As many as four hundred warriors fired at relatively close range for two hours — coming within two hundred yards of the camp — and eventually surrounded the breastwork. Warriors also lit the grass and underbrush on fire, hoping to flush soldiers from the barricade, but the wind direction abruptly changed and the blaze burned itself out. The end result of this "spirited and vigorous attack," as Gaines described it, was one killed and thirty-two wounded. Just as Clinch's last battle at the river, the number of dead was few compared to the wounded. In any case, a simple log barricade and a sudden shift in wind fortuitously prevented a full-scale calamity. This action by the Seminoles greatly flummoxed Gaines, and he admitted that he did not foresee "that the enemy would have the temerity to attack me in my position."[30] Instead of planning a counterattack, Gaines dug in deeper and ordered the breastwork to be reinforced. He regarded his position as much degraded from the previous day and wrote another letter to inform Clinch not to attempt a rear attack but to come directly to his aid.[31] The general was certain that launching a sortie against the Seminoles would be pointless. It would only scatter Native forces throughout the region, making it impossible to achieve anything militarily. As they were now surrounded, none of the troops would volunteer as express couriers. But after much cajoling (offering the ample inducement of $200), officers persuaded three of the remaining ten Indian guides to deliver vital communications to Fort Drane.[32]

Unknown to Gaines, General Scott, who was monitoring the situation from the fortified village of Picolata on the St. Johns River, continually denied his requests for relief (copies of Gaines's letters had been sent to him).[33] Scott refused to recognize Gaines's predicament and, officially at any rate, expected Gaines to withdraw to Fort Drane, where his men would be provided with emergency provisions. Because these communications became part of the public record, both generals were careful to uphold the appearance of propriety — even though they shared a history of deep personal rancor. Scott, who years earlier actually challenged Gaines to a duel over a dispute about who held the most senior rank, seemed oddly content to let his rival, as well as the men under his command, suffer.[34] Variations on such conduct were one of the unfortunate characteristics of the "Old Army," where the slightest perception of insult was often taken beyond all proportion and the vindictiveness and egotism of many senior officers was unbounded.[35] With some justification, Scott viewed Gaines as an interloper who had no right to conduct independent operations within his sphere of command. Gaines, intentionally or not, had indeed muddled and delayed Scott's campaign

to an infuriating degree. Both generals may have constituted the army's top echelon and earned heroic reputations dating to the War of 1812, but their mutual
antagonism only served to degrade the army's operations at a critical juncture.

With occasional lulls, including rainy downpours, Seminoles continued to fire
on Camp Izard for several days, keeping Gaines hemmed in. On March 5, the
shooting picked up considerably. Starting in the early morning, warriors used
the cover of fog and smoke to crawl near the barricades, fired at close range, and
then withdrew. Also that day, troops began slaughtering their horses for food.
"Horsehead soup," feigned a ravenous Lieutenant Prince, "is spoken of in some
praise."[36] Dogs soon followed. Details of these desperate measures would later
shock the country; the situation not only underscored the army's ineffectiveness
but painted a desperate picture of war that was utterly lacking in daring or gallantry. Indeed, many of Gaines's soldiers were in such pitiable condition that a
hospital steward remarked that "they represented living skeletons."[37] The remaining Indian scouts, believing that Gaines's position was hopeless, asked permission
to depart for Fort Brooke, but they were only allowed to travel to Fort Drane as
couriers.[38] Despite the incessant rifle fire that was directed on the camp, a significant change among the Seminoles began to emerge. That evening, the Indians
opened direct communications with Gaines's men. This decision was likely
spurred by the fact that the Seminoles knew that Clinch had taken matters into
his own hands and departed with five hundred men and was headed toward the
Withlacoochee. (Formal approval from Scott actually arrived the following day.)
The voice of a black interpreter, possibly Abraham, called out "in a very audible
and clear manner"[39] from the darkness of the woods and asserted that "the Indians had had fighting enough & wanted to come in, have a friendly talk & shake
hands."[40] In response to this astonishing pronouncement, Lieutenant Colonel
David Twiggs, Gaines's second-in-command, calmly informed this individual
that they would expect the Seminoles to arrive in the morning with a white flag.[41]
After such a prolonged siege, Gaines's command was in desperate straits: altogether, they had endured forty-six wounded and five killed, faced starvation, and
were nearly out of ammunition, being forced to load their cannon with debris and
refuse from their camp. Given the circumstances and as yet unaware of Clinch's
imminent arrival, it was assumed that the Seminole overture was a ruse, and thus
every man was on alert.[42]

On the morning of the 6th, contrary to expectations, three hundred armed
Seminoles peacefully converged at the rear of Camp Izard and kept a distance
of about five hundred yards. Five unarmed warriors, including Jumper, Osceola,
and Alligator, cautiously approached the camp holding a white flag and stopped

within two hundred yards, where they were met by an officer of the Louisiana Volunteers. According to an observer, Jumper conducted the talk through Abraham (serving as interpreter) "in a grave and respectful manner."[43] Initially, Jumper, a veteran of the Red Stick War who subsequently joined the Alachua Seminoles and later became Micanopy's "sense-bearer" or foremost adviser and spokesperson, merely declared they wanted the army to go away and refrain from crossing the river.[44] After this was related to Gaines, the general appointed Hitchcock to lead the parlay. Hitchcock initially delivered a stern message from his superior, informing the leaders that a large army, in all about five thousand, would soon be aimed at them. Differing from his official report of the affair, Hitchcock admitted in his diary that he "soothed them a little" by interjecting a note of empathy. He emphasized the merits of General Gaines, "his willingness to do them justice — the bleeding of his heart for their sufferings, &c."[45] (Despite his aggressive moves in Florida, Gaines had indeed gone on record as opposing Jackson's Indian removal policy.)[46] In contrast to the usual authoritarian posturing, Hitchcock actually conceded that "[t]hey [Seminoles] had suffered great wrong" but noted, adhering to the language of honor-bound societies, that if that was true, then they had surely "taken satisfaction."[47] Without explicitly stating the great damages that Native forces had inflicted upon the territory—where, as one recent arrival phrased it, "everything that industry and civilization had done was destroyed"—it was obvious that the magnitude of these loses had certainly served to expiate past wrongs.[48] Osceola, impressed by this sympathetic stance, said he was indeed "satisfied." Hitchcock set the tone for effective diplomacy while casually talking and sitting with these men on a single log amid an open field.[49] No mention was made of removal to the west. After a private conference that lasted several hours, Jumper and the others returned and spoke freely of their losses and stated "that blood enough had been shed—& they wished to put a stop to it." They claimed thirty fatalities during the battle. Still, before any binding agreement could be made, further consultation with Micanopy, who remained the final authority but was thirty miles distant, was required. Hitchcock similarly declared that neither he nor Gaines could authorize a peace treaty; that would be done by another commander who was arriving directly from the president himself. For the present, he gave assurances that Gaines would stop fighting as long as the Seminoles withdrew to the south side of the river, remained nonviolent, and agreed to attend a future "grand Council." Each of the war leaders gave their assent. At that precise moment, however, Clinch's advance guard arrived. Unaware of the situation that was unfolding, they began to fire, but the Seminoles remained beyond the range of their muskets and managed to flee unharmed.[50]

The reaction of Lieutenant Colonel Twiggs was unequivocal: "If it had not been for this unfortunate circumstance, everything would have been accomplished in the way of peace."[51] Despite the interruption, the Seminoles kept their word and maintained a ceasefire for three weeks. In no other battle during the Florida war were hostilities ended in such a manner, and certainly not when the Indians held such an overwhelming advantage. Despite its minimal presence in the historiography—Mahon, for example, simply stated that Seminoles ("like others of their race") were ill-equipped to carry on an extended siege and were more than willing to retire and fight another day—the Seminole peace overture drew intense scrutiny from the military court that was convened to examine Gaines's actions.[52] Jurists discussed possible motivations, noting that some of those questioned remained skeptical vis-à-vis Seminole intent (assuming a feint or ruse), while others thought the offer was legitimate, especially given the length of the negotiations and the fact that the Indians remained noncombative and even allowed troops to bathe in the river as well as fish for needed food.[53] The evidence indeed supports Gaines's subsequent claim that the Seminoles truly desired peace. Be that as it may, Gaines transferred command to Clinch on March 9 while at Camp Izard and resolved to leave the prosecution of the war entirely to Scott. Hitchcock accompanied Gaines to Fort Drane, where, after an icy reception by Scott, they continued by horseback to Tallahassee. (They proceeded on a journey toward the Mexican border, where they confronted a far different set of problems posed by General Santa Anna.[54]) Gaines, however, further complicated matters in Florida by boasting along the way that he had negotiated an end to all hostilities by forcing the Seminoles to sue for peace. Many newspapers published this announcement—the first of numerous, premature end-of-war declarations.

As can be expected, Scott was the least likely person to pursue a peace initiative linked in any way to his archrival, and so he continued his operations against the Seminoles. It is also doubtful that Jackson would have altered his rigid intention of complete Indian removal. Hence the unique opportunity presented at the Withlacoochee fell to naught and a lethal but potentially short war evolved into a costly and deadly multiyear conflict. The peace parley nevertheless offers key insight into the strategic mind-set of the Seminoles and confirms that although, as William L. Stone stated, they were certainly willing "to die fighting to the last," given the right circumstances they were also prepared to place weapons aside.[55] Moreover, Native leaders actually had good reason to assume that such a leading figure as Gaines would follow through on his promises. But Seminoles were surely not privy to the behind-the-scenes rivalry with Scott or the circumstances surrounding the change of commanders. Finally, while it is true that Gaines's actions were, as one officer recounted, "premature, ill-advised and ill-organized," and thus merited Jackson's ire, the superior position held by the Seminoles was not entirely the result of such bungling.[56] Seminoles had dominated the war through their own militant prowess. Without their unexpected success during three months of conflict, the peace talks, along with the notable concession of allowing them to remain in Florida, would surely never have been broached.

SCOTT'S COMMAND AND THE NEW SEMINOLE OFFENSIVE

In his role as the new commander, General Scott (aka Old Fuss and Feathers) gathered a combined force of five thousand men, both regular army and militia, to engage in a complex, three-pronged attack that would once again center on the Seminole stronghold on the Withlacoochee. At the outset, some proudly referred to this impressive assembly as Scott's "grand army," as it actually constituted the largest US battle force since the War of 1812.[57] Given such a considerable number of troops, many believed that their Native adversaries would not dare put up a fight. "It is the opinion of everyone," a Georgia militia captain boasted in a letter to his wife, "that they will surrender to this force without exchanging a single shot."[58] Whether this naive expectation was as universal as the captain believed is unknown. Scott nevertheless remained entirely confident in his position. In keeping with someone who expected an overwhelming victory over his Native adversaries—despite the fact that all others had failed—Scott's personal hubris resembled the manner of a rather haughty European aristocrat. (Scott, for example, had no difficulty comparing his later appearance before the court of inquiry to the humiliation suffered by the "Doge of Genoa," a historical personage who had to defend himself, as Scott put it, against "some imaginary offence imputed by Louis XIV."[59]) In addition to his own retinue, which included choice musicians outfitted in full regalia, three wagons were required to transport the general's personal collection of fine furniture and accoutrements, imported wines, fresh fruit, and myriad other comforts.[60] Such a display was, to say the least, peculiarly out of place amid the immense, semitropical wilderness that he found himself in. More importantly, Scott's rigid adherence to French-inspired military tactics would prove similarly unfitting.[61] His ambitions to form a grand army also forced troops to be suddenly diverted to serve in this new campaign. Hence the Atlantic coast garrisons from Maine to Georgia, already sparsely manned, were depleted even more. Worries actually surfaced that the nation was disturbingly susceptible to invasion.[62]

Scott divided the army into three divisions. The right wing was under the command of General Clinch and was projected to travel from Fort Drane and descend yet again to the Withlacoochee, where—it was anticipated—Seminoles would then be driven into the remaining two wings. The center wing at Fort Brooke was under the command of Colonel William Lindsay and was expected to march northward toward the Cove. Brigadier General Abraham Eustis, another veteran of the War of 1812, directed the left wing. Departing from Volusia on the upper St. Johns River, Eustis would lead his troops in a southwesterly direction and then take up a more northerly approach toward the Withlacoochee. Precise timing was essential, and without good lines of communication, such an elaborate scheme, even if attempted on the most level plane in Europe, would have been problematic. Each wing began their operations out of sync with the others, but the assumption that the Seminoles would not have been alert to all this activity and thus unable to take effective countermeasures, via their own methods of warfare, was at the center of Scott's conceptual failure. In actuality, the Seminoles dispersed from the Withlacoochee and other interior villages and enclaves, such as Peace Creek, Chocochatti, Okahumpka, and Peliklakaha, and hence easily evaded the ponderous, slow-moving army. Peliklakaha had recently been "the joint place of residence of the chief [Micanopy] and his slaves," according to James Gadsden, but this Native leader had ample time to withdraw and was never in danger.[63] Adding to Scott's problems was the fact that his forces were continually delayed by hundreds of heavily loaded supply wagons; thus, mule teams strained even more as they were forced to pass through the deep mud caused by torrential rains. Often without the benefit of maps, roads, trails, or bridges, troops regularly slogged through swamps in waist-high water. Small bands of Seminoles were free to attack the exposed flanks at will, and at the end the troops failed to encounter any large group. "The Indians," Sergeant Joel W. Jones wrote to his wife while in the field, "absolutely laughed at us" and mocked the army's incompetence.[64] Long before operations ceased, the senselessness of such a venture became clear throughout the ranks. "I am sick of the whole concern," Jones continued, "and if I live to get out of Florida, Uncle Sam shall not catch me in such a place again."[65] From the last week of March through April, the army lacked any accomplishment, and the goal of entrapping the Seminoles remained a chimera. By mid-April, the weather turned even hotter, and men began to fall ill by the hundreds from a combination of measles, malaria, and the ill-effects of drinking stagnant pond water.[66] Their only recompense was in knowing that the campaign was coming to a close for the approaching summer, and most expected to be transferred out of the territory by the end of April or, in the case of the militia, returned to their hometowns.

The campaign, according to the Washington *Globe*, brought Scott "the indignation of the South, universal dissatisfaction among the people and the chagrin of the president."[67] The Tallahassee *Floridian* was far less mannered: "Our Army in the late campaign can be compared to nothing but a prize ox, stung to death by hornets, without the ability to fly from, or catch his annoyers. . . . Our only hope is that General Scott has had enough of Glory, and will retire."[68] Unlike Scott, General Clinch did retire (or, more accurately, resigned) from the army after the campaign, despite being offered the Florida command yet again. In June, President Jackson, facing rising criticism of Secretary Cass, conveniently nominated him as the new ambassador to France.[69] Clinch's letters to Cass requesting more troops from a year earlier had circulated in the press, much to the secretary's embarrassment. In addition, the overall muddling of the war effort and the predominant feeling that the army had been "out-generaled" by the likes of Osceola caused many to assume that Cass's days in the Cabinet were numbered.[70] He indeed resigned his post in October. During the remainder of Scott's brief tenure, the general infuriated territorial residents by denigrating both the fighting skill of the militia and the valor of its citizens. In response, a throng of protestors in Tallahassee mounted an effigy of the imperious and ample-bodied Scott, replete with ornate uniform and golden epaulets, on a rail and then paraded it through the streets. In mock accompaniment with a tin pan band, "his mightiness" was set ablaze and went up in smoke—"much like his late brilliant campaign," noted a local editorialist.[71] In a letter to Jackson dated May 28, Congressional Delegate White demanded Scott's removal, stating that the general "has produced a state of feeling that forbids all harmony or concert with the local authorities, or the people of the country."[72] White was unaware that Scott had already left Florida the week before. Jackson had redirected the general to conduct the campaign against the Creeks, who, inspired by the Seminoles, began a smaller-scale uprising in Alabama. Because of Scott's scant knowledge of Indian warfare, he fared little better in that campaign than he did in Florida. Jackson then appointed Florida Governor Richard K. Call as the new commander. A close friend of the president, Call had previously served as Jackson's aide-de-camp during the Red Stick War. Aside from his own self-confident assertions that he was best suited to the task, Call hardly possessed the background to assume such responsibility.

In November, Scott and Gaines were forced to defend their actions during a military tribunal in Frederick, Maryland, a court that would never have been convened without the express orders of the president. Headed by the commander of the US Army, Major General Alexander Macomb, the proceedings were closely monitored by Jackson. Following a few months of intensive newspaper coverage that included full-length transcripts from the trial and with details of the court proceedings debated in Congress, the tribunal ultimately absolved the generals of any wrongdoing.[73] As far as the court was concerned, the result of Scott's campaign was solely the fault of "the insalubrity of the climate," insufficient time to operate before the onset of the sickly season, the imperviousness of the swamps and hammocks, a dearth of basic geographical information, and the problems of transporting supplies. Scott's war plan was quite startlingly adjudged "well-devised" despite the compelling testimony of officers who felt otherwise.[74] Gaines was similarly exonerated, and the issue of his aggressive pursuit of the Seminoles while Scott was in command was pointedly ignored. The court, however, gently chastised Gaines for not making a sortie against the enemy while at Camp Izard and additionally reprimanded him for indulging in excessive criticism of Scott during the trial (indeed, Gaines dared to compare his rival to Benedict Arnold).[75] Macomb was hardly inclined to impugn the generals, as this would only serve to degrade the army's own tenuous standing among the public. The most fervent Jacksonians abhorred the concept of a standing army and even the existence of the Military Academy at West Point. Both smacked of European elitism and monarchical authority, and were diametrically opposed to the deeply revered ideal of citizen militias. Guilty verdicts would therefore blacken the reputation of the service and foment additional distrust. There were other political considerations as well. Gaines, a native Virginian, had the solid backing of southerners, many of whom were horrified that such a heroic figure had been treated in such an inglorious manner. Scott also had southern origins, although he became a particular favorite of many northern Whigs and was against slavery. (Following a far more effective performance during the Mexican-American War [1846–47], Scott redeemed his reputation and became the Whig presidential candidate in 1852, losing to Franklin Pierce.) All things considered, Macomb and his colleagues obviously believed that their own professional interests as well as the army's would be best served with acquittal and that subjecting the defendants to the court proceeding was sufficient enough. Jackson felt otherwise. He rejected the decision and remanded the case back to the court. Knowing that the president's term was to end soon, Macomb cleverly delayed resubmission of the verdict until after Martin Van Buren assumed office in October 1837. Van Buren then confirmed the court's original finding.[76]

Scott's Florida operations reportedly cost the government a staggering $1.5 million during April alone.[77] Scott's original intentions notwithstanding, this extraordinarily costly campaign resulted in diminishing public confidence in the military and even brought the Napoleonic-centered training at West Point into question. (The war was a testing ground for many officers, most of whom by this time had graduated from the academy.) The failure additionally reinforced the mounting belief within the officer corps that the effort against the Seminoles was not worth the cost in lives and treasure, as it lacked both nobility of purpose and a cogent stratagem. Low morale, not surprisingly, became one of the army's most troublesome issues. And the cumulative effect of all the military downturns boosted the position of the Seminoles, who were, according to army intelligence, "highly elated with their successes."[78]

The army's withdrawal at the end of April created an opportunity for the Seminoles to regain momentum and to assume an offensive posture. Clinch had once estimated their total force to be "1,500 warriors, and 200 or 300 negroes."[79] Despite their comparatively small size, the Seminoles had proven to be an especially formidable, battle-hardened group whose leaders knew when and how to aggressively target their opponent's weaknesses. Hence the interior forts, all of which were understaffed and increasingly burdened with illness, were particularly susceptible to attack. Aside from their military function, garrisons additionally served as emergency shelters for hundreds of settler families who first sought refuge in December. These people had been reduced to pitiable conditions: mostly ill and malnourished, they struggled to survive in crude shacks and lean-tos.[80] Of course, army posts, even the most rudimentary and seemingly peripheral, also held particular symbolic power. Each represented the broad reach of federal authority and marked the degree to which the US government was invested in reasserting control and displacing Seminole autonomy on the frontier. Fort King and Fort Drane still remained, but these posts were now augmented by Fort Oakland, another converted sugar plantation, and Fort Defiance, the palisaded settler village of Micanopy that was taken over by the army during late spring.

Beginning in May, faced with a daunting number of sick troops at Fort King and the questionable significance of a post so far removed from the site of the Alachua settlements, the army decided to withdraw from this garrison.[81] This "retrograde movement" gave Native forces the initiative. After quickly occupying the abandoned fort, Osceola and the other leaders launched an unsuccessful assault on Fort Drane. Afterward, their attention focused on Fort Defiance. On May 20, Jumper launched a nighttime salvo at the fort as a ploy to release the slaves at the nearby plantation of former Indian agent Colonel Gad Humphreys.[82] A few weeks later, a far more serious confrontation ensued. On June 9, about 250 Indian and black warriors lead by Osceola (and possibly Jumper as well) gathered at a moderate distance from the Micanopy palisades in an effort to draw out the troops in a full-fledged engagement.[83] Despite being outnumbered (only seventy-five troops were fit for duty), Major Julius Heileman, commander of the remaining interior forts, decided to envelop the Seminoles in a classic pincer movement. Known as the Battle of Micanopy, this daytime engagement involved a charge by the dragoons, a surprise attack on the Seminoles' rear flank, and rounds of artillery that resulted in Native forces withdrawing into the safety of nearby Cuscowilla Hammock after an hour or so of intense fighting.[84] The Jackson administration did not delay in touting what they labeled as a victory, and official reports from the officers in command (Heileman died a few weeks later from malaria) were published in the *Globe* and then extensively reprinted in other papers.[85] Many believed this battle marked the first time during the war when the nation's troops — notably without the presence of imperious generals — truly exemplified their presumed superiority over their Native adversaries. "The repulse and defeat of the Indians at Micanopy," wrote an anonymous contributor to the influential *Army and Navy Chronicle*, "has partially dispelled the gloom that was pressing upon our arms in the south, and furnish Andrew Jackson with an opportunity . . . of dispersing the mead of praise upon the gallant and the brave."[86] In actuality, however, the fact that the Seminoles happened to withdraw hardly constituted a triumph in any tangible sense. Native forces fought opportunistically and were quite prepared to retire and fight another time under more advantageous conditions. In such encounters, they were simply under no compunction, romantic or otherwise, to hold the ground if it meant enduring increased casualties without any tangible benefit.

One of Heileman's last actions before his death was to order the abandonment and burning of Fort Oakland, the large, barricaded plantation of Clinch's brother-in-law John H. McIntosh.[87] This was done in an effort to consolidate the army's steadily dwindling resources. Moreover, the few officers who remained healthy were constantly rotated among the posts, and unremitting Seminole raids were beginning to take a stark psychological toll — there was simply little or no time to recover. In combination with an unknown "pestilence" that had reached epidemic proportions, some indeed lost hope that they would ever return home alive.[88] Because many officers originated from New England, newspapers as far as Maine, drawing upon letters from men in the field, grew intimately familiar with these distant Florida garrisons, referring to Forts Drane and Defiance as "grave yards."[89] Given these bleak and ever-worsening conditions, the order to begin evacuation of Fort Drane was inevitable. Many rejoiced at the news that Colonel Ichabod Crane, headquartered in St. Augustine, finally recognized this necessity toward the end of June. During the next few weeks, convoys arrived at Fort Drane with wagons to transport the sick and wounded to the general hospital in St. Augustine.[90] On the morning of July 19, the fort's commanding officer ordered an escort of sixty-two dragoons and foot artillery to accompany twenty-two supply wagons to Fort Defiance. One mile from Micanopy, at a point where the road curved east around a pond, several rifle shots were discharged by the Seminoles, fatally wounding a private. Dragoons immediately rode in the direction of the pond but found no one. The wagons continued unopposed for three-quarters of a mile but were again attacked, this time by a large body of Seminoles. The initial rifle shots thus proved to be a feint, as Native forces actually laid in ambush within a forested area just a quarter mile from the fort. The convoy was pinned down by a heavy barrage of rifle fire until two companies of dragoons arrived from the fort. Inspired by this display of force, the dragoons that were guarding the wagon train mounted a charge and drove the Seminoles back into the hammock. This affair, called the Battle of Welika Pond (although it was clearly a second Battle of Micanopy), once more served the interests of the administration, as it featured courageous action by the dragoons and resulted in the Seminoles retiring to the safety of a nearby hammock.[91] Taking into account the pervasive ill-health at the Micanopy garrison at the time, it is plausible that the Seminoles could have easily returned at a later date and overtaken the fort had they so desired. It had nevertheless become very clear that the army could no longer sustain themselves in the area, and the destiny of Fort Defiance would shortly follow the same trajectory as Forts King, Drane, and Oakland. Persistent attacks merely accelerated the inevitable. On August 24, Fort Defiance—the last remaining army post in the Alachua region—was put to the torch in order to deny Seminoles any possible material advantage. (The fort would be rebuilt the following year and renamed Fort Micanopy.) The troops, in addition to the remaining town residents and a contingent of settler refugees, then made their way unmolested to Garey's Ferry, where an extensive supply depot had been built alongside a tributary of the St. Johns River.

By the end of summer, the US military was yet again required to explain why the peninsular interior still remained under the control of Native adversaries. The past actions of Scott and Cass became the most obvious targets.[92] But the army's core problems were much greater than the questionable decisions of either of these individuals. Not only did the army as an institution consistently misjudge the competence of their foes, still maintaining an ill-deserved sense of supremacy, but commanders failed to adopt the tactical flexibility needed to cope with the unique characteristics of the Florida peninsula. In addition to the Seminoles' superior knowledge and usage of the terrain, their mode of warfare, which included constant raids, ambushes, and expedient withdrawals, proved decisive in driving the US Army from the interior. Furthermore, all soldiers faced diseases that proliferated during hot weather, illnesses for which the army medical corps possessed no cures. The sickness and debility that afflicted US troops through the spring and fall of 1836, and which was decisive in the abandonment and destruction of the forts, was an initial indication of another potent (and invisible) enemy that was to plague the remainder of the conflict.

CHAPTER 5

"Sacrifice of National Honor"

The US Army demonstrably failed to meet its objectives throughout the first year of the Seminole war. One contributing cause was the fact that the Military Academy at West Point eschewed any mention of Indian wars in the curriculum — newly graduated officers were consequently ill-prepared for this type of conflict. The dismal outcome in Florida should have indicated that change was needed, but as the maxims of Napoleonic warfare were judged central to success, failures were instead attributed to other causes.

It should be noted that the leaders of the new professional army that emerged during the early nineteenth century looked to the fabled armies of Europe in an effort to establish legitimacy and respect among other nations. Scores of officers, including Winfield Scott, traveled to the continent after the conclusion of the War of 1812, where they observed the military firsthand and consulted with leading generals.[1] Colonel Sylvanus Thayer, the academy superintendent (1817–33) most responsible for its newfound orientation, had in fact visited the Ecole Polytechnique, the renowned French military academy, and subsequently sought to recreate the curriculum and disciplinary environment at West Point.[2] Cadets were expected to emerge as "scientific" soldiers and so were immersed in engineering, mathematics, science, and European-style military strategy and tactics.[3] As most texts were in French, instruction also stressed proficiency in that language. Amid all these organizational developments and the rush toward respectability in the eyes of the world, the nation's extensive record of Indian wars was ignored. Considering the fact that the Indian Removal Act had reinforced a settler-colonial trajectory, this Eurocentric orientation would become a major stumbling block.[4]

The weakness of such a course was indeed touched upon in testimony during the court of inquiry by Colonel James Gadsden, the same calculating individual who had overseen the Seminole treaties. Contrary to the court's findings, Gadsden, a non-academy-trained officer, attributed Scott's failing to his basic misunderstanding of "the character of the contest" and the latter's mistaken notion that a single battle would bring the war to an end. Because guerilla warfare predominated during these operations and Indians fired from concealed positions, the tactics and strategy favored at West Point were destined to flounder in the Florida backwoods. Gadsden — true to his southern settler-colonial origins — advocated treating Seminoles as wild predators and not as a rival army. "Our true game, therefore, would not [be] to move in masses, but in parties of sufficient strength, thus multiplying the chances of flushing the enemy and of keeping him at bay . . . until reinforced by one or the other hunting parties." Gadsden conceded that his suggestion of tracking Indians as if partaking in a "hunting party" — though a staple of the frontier — "was not supported in the army generally."[5] For those indoctrinated in the methods of the military academy, such ideas were anathema.

Gadsden's suggested tactics (aka "bush-whack fighting") followed the same path as his powerful mentor, Andrew Jackson.[6] As we have seen, Jackson often resorted to excessively brutal and devious means during his campaigns against southeastern Indians, violated international boundaries, and felt free to set one Indigenous faction against the other if it meant ultimate triumph. In comparison, West Point instructors, many of whom were northerners who did not hold their southern brethren in much esteem, looked to the ideals of the European Enlightenment for inspiration and even encouraged ethical distinctions between just and unjust wars.[7] White flags of truce remained inviolable, verbal commitments were strictly upheld, and formal treaties were similarly sacrosanct. Moreover, academy graduates were far more likely to accept Hitchcock's premise that Native people were part of "the great human family" and not mere savages to be exploited.[8] As a result, many officers privately criticized the war as the height of dishonor and were deeply distressed by the Florida campaign. Ethical concerns regarding Indigenous people had indeed broadened significantly, and many officers had accepted a path of moral nobility, as Aristotle phrased it, and chose to direct their behavior based on the highest principles.[9] After spending time in the territory, a visiting war correspondent for the New York *Herald* was careful to emphasize that "[t]he officers themselves are disgusted with the service, and take no pride in conquering men for whose wrongs they sympathize, and against whom they feel no hatred."[10] Many thought the war was based on an ignoble foundation (i.e.,

Gadsden's coerced treaties). Hence, following the reasoning of Emmerich de Vattel's *The Law of Nations* (1758), a required text at the academy, Seminoles possessed the natural right to defend their homeland and way of life.[11] "I've tried every argument to still my conscience," Lieutenant Nathaniel Hunter confessed in his Florida journal, "but this restless imp will not be quiet." "Have God and justice no claims upon you prior and paramount to a government that incites you to a commission of a crime? Will no compunctions deter you from wringing your hands in innocent blood, even though it may be the command of a superior officer? Enforce a treaty, a compact begat in fraud and brought forth in the blackest villainy. . . . Is not every act of the Indians sanctioned by the practice of civilized nations?"[12] Such painful soul-searching, of course, was not shared by every officer. Future Civil War general William T. Sherman—a young second lieutenant who was taking part in his first battlefield experience—quickly realized the limits of orthodox tactics and eagerly confided to his future fiancée that the Seminole war represented the "kind of warfare that every young officer should be acquainted with."[13] Be that as it may, Hunter's reaction may have been closest to the norm and was so prevalent that this kind of personal torment contributed to a high rate of resignations (103 company officers resigned their commissions in 1836 alone), a circumstance that left the army at an even greater disadvantage.[14] In contrast, officers of the southern states' militias were generally unencumbered by similar ethical quandaries regarding the Seminoles.

Conversely, Seminole leaders successfully employed a wide range of innovative techniques, including nighttime attacks, lengthy sieges, and even amphibious assaults—sophisticated tactics that necessitated high-level planning and organization.[15] When engaged in pitched battles, according to a recent archaeological study, "the Seminole employed excellent use of key terrain elements in staging before the battle, mounting an aggressive frontal assault, and then retiring in order to minimize losses."[16] Native forces were placed with precision and with the intention of concentrating firepower and diminishing opportunities for flanking by the enemy. They further excelled at exploiting natural obstacles in order to hinder horse and infantry units. And, in contrast to the low morale of the army, most Seminoles still regarded their cause as sacred and inviolate, despite the severe toll that it continued to take on the tribe as a whole. The "Great Spirit" had given the country to the Seminoles as a revered trust, as the young chief Halleck Hadjo explained. Such a trust was not easily yielded.[17] Overall, Native forces retained distinct advantages over the US military, and most contemporary observers, caught up by ethnocentric biases and nationalist fervor, seemed incapable of admitting why this was so.[18]

CALL'S MISFORTUNES AND THE RISE OF JESUP

Governor Richard K. Call, now the army commander in Florida, had harbored ambitious plans to conduct a summer campaign, despite the known risks to health. His ideas for the summer of 1836 had to be delayed, however, until the required militia troops arrived in mid-September. In a variation of Scott's three-pronged attack, Call envisioned multiple columns converging yet again at the Cove of the Withlacoochee, this time with about 2,500 troops—a combination of Tennessee and Florida militia, Creek auxiliaries, and the regular army.[19] This scheme met the approval of both the president and Major General Thomas Jesup. The latter had been transferred from his post as quartermaster general in Washington to assume Scott's former command against the Creeks in Alabama and now headed the Army of the South. Call had been assured of the cooperation of the US Navy as well. His interaction with Commodore Alexander J. Dallas, commander of the West India Squadron in Pensacola, was less than cordial, how-ever. The governor's expectations that a robust naval presence along the Gulf Coast would prevent Seminoles from continuing to exchange captive plantation slaves for vital munitions via Cuban boatmen was thwarted by apparent indifference.[20]

Call's plans were fraught with difficulties from the outset. For one, the gover-nor was stricken with malaria but continued despite his illness. Poor planning, accidents, and bad fortune prevented supply depots from being established within the allotted time frame. These depots—one each at Volusia, Fort Brooke, and the Suwannee and Withlacoochee Rivers—were supposed to have solved the persis-tent problems of inadequate rations and dwindling supplies of ammunition. Call was furious that Colonel Crane ordered the destruction of Fort Defiance without his permission, as Call had planned on utilizing this centrally located garrison as another vital depot. Despite these circumstances, the governor spent the first two weeks of October in an unproductive attempt to engage the Seminoles with about half the number of his expected troops. Confronted with near starvation of his men and the loss of hundreds of horses caused by a lack of forage, Call was com-pelled to return to Camp Drane on October 17 (the abandoned fort had been burned by Seminoles, but the army nevertheless continued to use the same site). When Jackson was informed of these events, his support for his friend began to quickly evaporate, and Call was subsequently relieved of command by the acting secretary of war Benjamin F. Butler. Because of Call's long absences in the wilder-ness interior, these orders were not actually conveyed to him for another month, and so he unwittingly continued with his campaign.

On November 17 and 18, Call directed his energies toward a secluded Seminole sanctuary located on elevated, dry ground within the Wahoo Swamp. Several abandoned villages were destroyed, including a place called "Negro Town," which consisted of numerous log cabin dwellings. A series of mounted charges by the Tennessee volunteers succeeded in driving back the Seminoles and resulted in very high Native losses—exceeding one hundred (from an estimated total of six hundred to seven hundred).[21] On the 21st, a much larger force of 1,500 troops, divided into regulars, militia, and Creeks, revisited the same location, where they again engaged the Seminoles. Call's men opened fire and then charged their adversaries, causing them to fall back and disperse farther into the swamp. The attackers soon lost track of the Seminoles, however, and wound up scattered amid the maze-like marshes and bogs, "the most gloomy and dismal [place] that the imagination can conceive," an officer afterward declared. It was further thought that such a dark, humid, and foreboding environment abounded in noxious vapors (miasma), adding yet another level of anxiety.[22] After much confusion, a detachment of Creek auxiliaries chanced upon a stream of water about thirty feet wide, where they encountered a large Seminole contingent on the opposite side. The Seminoles, hidden by a dense thicket, took up a defensive stand and began a heavy volley of rifle fire, while other warriors waited in ambush on their left and right flanks. Fire was quickly returned by the Creeks, and eventually a total of three hundred of Call's men took part in this action. Major David Moniac, an enculturated Creek who became the first Native American graduate of West Point, was killed instantly after attempting to cross the stream, dissuading any others from making a similar move.[23] In his subsequent analysis of this day's combat, Lieutenant John Phelps, a recent academy graduate, remarked on how the Seminoles utilized the natural features of the swamp to their maximum advantage as they employed tactics analogous to "modern systems of defense." The stream itself functioned as a type of "entrenchment," Phelps observed, as the waterway was "filled with latent Cyprus knees, almost as pointed and dreadful as the stakes of war pits." Horses therefore risked impalement if ridden into the water. "Numerous vines interwoven with the underbrush, together with quagmires, formed such entanglements and impediments as the most harassed body of infantry might wish to protect them from the attacks of a pursuing cavalry. The strategy that led to the choice of this point, and the tactic displayed in its defense reflect much credit upon the skill of the Seminoles."[24] The importance of the Seminole position was revealed by the ferocity of the rifle fire and the presence of prominent leaders such as Yaholoochee (Cloud) and Osuchee (Cooper), whose voices could be identified as they yelled out commands over the din. Unknown to the army was the fact that these 420 warriors, along with a reputed 200 blacks, were actually defending their own nearby settlement with its large contingent of women, children, and elders.[25] The battle continued to midafternoon with the Seminoles holding firm. As this standoff failed to produce tangible results, the army, malnourished and additionally weakened by continual stress, declined to risk a water crossing and instead gathered their dead and wounded and returned to camp.[26] Some younger warriors followed the retreating soldiers, taunting them and firing their rifles in a show of victory. Despite this bravado, their forces had endured tremendous losses. Indeed, the several days' encounter at Wahoo Swamp represented one of the largest Native death tolls during the war. Be that as it may, Call's men proceeded eastward on an arduous sixty-mile trek to Volusia—a less-than-stirring ending to what was named the Battle of Wahoo Swamp. Even though this series of engagements represented the most aggressive foray into the Seminole stronghold ever attempted, Call's command—composed of many who were eager to redeem the army's reputation—was nevertheless unprepared to sustain the hardships of such a challenging enterprise. Despite having invaded a previously untouched Native sanctuary and wreaking very substantial blows, Call was still without the type of traditional battlefield triumph that he promised the president. Jackson was dissatisfied that his old friend had not pursued the enemy further because of his embarrassing "want of supplies" and that the war continued in a succession of "blunders and misfortune."[27]

On December 9, one year after the commencement of the war, leadership of the army's beleaguered campaign shifted for the fourth time. General Jesup now took over the helm of the nation's most publicly scrutinized and controversial military command, a position beset by ineptitude, oversized egos, and an unsettling turnover rate. Despite the odds, Jesup expressed confidence in his abilities to turn the tide. Self-assurance was one of the general's most conspicuous assets, dating from the start of his career in 1808. Without any prior military experience, Jesup was commissioned a second lieutenant based on the recommendations of a prominent friend.[28] His rise through the ranks was swift. From the outset, he was determined to distinguish himself from "the crowd of ignorance & stupidity with which [the] army abounds."[29] Jesup excelled in organizational ability and leadership, and in ten years was promoted to brigadier general. His accomplishments while quartermaster general were recognized in 1828 when he was breveted to major general. Jesup's time in Florida, in dramatic contrast, was marked by extensive controversy, most notably the seizure of Osceola. Given Jesup's reported abilities and subsequent fall from grace in the public eye, his character may at first seem rather contradictory. Lieutenant Phelps, who served under Jesup, privately sought to come to terms with this very issue. The general's lengthy residence and professional standing in Washington, DC, had tainted his judgment, or so Phelps believed. And thus, any adherence to "fine principles" that was deemed so necessary to the career of an officer had been destroyed by the culture of "intrigue and machination" that predominated in the nation's capital.[30] This was doubtless true to a certain extent, but the primary cause of Jesup's failings to adhere to the academy standard was his settler-colonial orientation. As a slaveholder and southern stalwart as well as a friend of Jackson's, Jesup could not allow ethical qualms or self-doubts to interfere with the dual objectives of ethnic cleansing and land appropriation. Jesup blithely encapsulated this winner-take-all mind-set one year after his appointment: "The Indians are already driven from more than fifteen million acres of land, worth twenty millions of dollars," he reported to the new secretary of war Joel Poinsett. "And in less than a month we shall drive them off from five to ten millions of acres more."[31] The general was accomplishing exactly what was expected. Land acquisition, devoid of any ethical judgment, was emphasized to delineate "progress," and the violence and loss of life that made such a massive land grab possible was left unstated. As far as Native people were concerned, notions of "God and justice" had slight relevance.[32]

On the initial day of Jesup's command, the general was anxious to resolve the overall shortage of men. He was left with 450 regulars, 250 marines, 350 volunteers from Alabama, and the Creek regiment. An unspecified illness predominated among all the troops, and so Jesup was unable to fully garrison the few forts that remained in East Florida.[33] In contrast to Commodore Dallas's strained relations with Governor Call, Dallas was now eager to aid Jesup in whatever way he could. The commodore reduced the crews onboard his fleet and sent sixty sailors to help man Fort Brooke. Additional sailors were directed to Fort Foster on the Hillsborough River (twenty-one miles northeast of Tampa), Fort Clinch (twelve miles north of the mouth of the Withlacoochee), and Camp Drane.[34] What is more, Jesup wrote letters to various state governors in an appeal for militia and included his now-famous "negro war" line to help spur now-reluctant southerners to assist with the war. Jesup admitted to Secretary Butler that the term of service in Florida was so arduous "that not a man whose term of service expires will re-enlist."[35]

By mid-January 1837, the US Sixth Infantry and four companies of Georgia mounted militia arrived in Florida. Augmenting Jesup's command, Colonel Archibald Henderson, commandant of the Marine Corps, served as commander of the Second Brigade, and draftees from the South Carolina and Alabama militias were also expected. Following a reconnaissance mission in the Cove, Jesup's scouts discovered that the Seminoles had dispersed and relocated with their families well to the southeast—at the headwaters of the Ocklawaha River and in the

Lake Tohopekaliga region (south of present-day Orlando). Jesup modified his original intention of forming a single unified force and adopted ideas similar to Gadsden's, such as the use of small-scale "hunting parties." In addition, Jesup also benefited from the supply lines and depots that had been established. The vigor of fresh troops and the relatively healthy winter conditions also aided his operations. Seminoles, by comparison, lacked reinforcements, and the warriors who remained were often the wounded or physically exhausted survivors of an entire year of unremitting combat. Because the army consistently employed cannons loaded with grapeshot, the number of Native casualties undoubtedly outnumbered the army's, although precise figures may never surface. If one factors the Seminoles' relatively small population, each death—including the men, women, and children who died either directly or indirectly from combat—produced a highly disproportionate impact within their community. Still, the tenacity of the war spirit was so strong that the wives of warriors who died freely distributed their spouse's gunpowder and lead to those men who promised to use it in war.[36] When Jesup assumed command, the Seminoles had just suffered considerable fatalities at Wahoo Swamp and had been forced to flee from their settlements (along with their productive farmlands), circumstances that exacerbated feelings of grief and misery.

Jesup was convinced—at least in his letters to the War Department—that his primary difficulty was not in fighting the enemy but in *finding* them.[37] In preparation for this pursuit, the general ordered the prompt construction of additional wooden forts and supply depots. Following his new practice of employing small scouting parties, on January 24 a detachment of fifty Creek Indians, led by a black guide and supervised by two army officers, happened upon a trail that directly led to several huts on the periphery of Lake Apopka. Instead of reporting this finding to the brigade commander, Lieutenant Colonel Caulfield, or even waiting for their own officers, the Creeks proceeded to attack all those they found. They killed and scalped Osuchee, who was recuperating from wounds he received at Wahoo Swamp, as well as members of his extended family, including the chief's teenage son. When the officers caught up with the Creeks, they immediately halted what could have been a larger bloodbath; nine Seminole women and children as well as eight blacks were subsequently made prisoners.[38] Osuchee was an important figure not only because he was Micanopy's brother-in-law but because he served, according to the army, as "the immediate commander of the negroes."[39] His death was thus deemed a significant loss. Adding to the Seminoles' decreasing fortunes, a week earlier the black leader John Caesar was killed along with several others by the Florida militia south of St. Augustine.[40]

Marching without detailed maps and mostly in complete ignorance of the country, Jesup had originally intended for his 1,300 troops to reach the area of the Great Cypress Swamp after his initial departure from Fort Armstrong (recently erected near the site of the Dade ambush). After spending days of constant backtracking in the desperate hope of discovering a trail, on January 29 Jesup was amazed to find that his army was, entirely by chance, not only in the right location but in a superior position vis-à-vis a large body of Seminoles. This stroke of luck also allowed his men to confiscate hundreds of cattle, a move that deprived their adversaries of a valued food source without having to fire a shot.[41] The day before, Jesup had sent a black prisoner by the name of Ben ahead of the army in an effort to contact Jumper and the rest of the hostile leaders and entice them with a peace overture.[42] Weeks earlier, Jesup had been advised, via reports from prisoners who had just been captured, of Micanopy's apparent willingness to pursue a ceasefire. Even though the disposition of the rest of the Seminole leaders was still unknown, Jesup trusted that Micanopy's position as principal chief would guarantee a permanent agreement. To most everyone's surprise, Ben, now carrying a white flag from the Seminoles, returned to Jesup's camp the next evening. Although he failed to contact either Jumper or Micanopy directly, Ben was able to convince Abraham to set up a meeting with the ranking chiefs, despite the prevalent mood of distrust among them.

On February 2, according to the observations of Major Thomas Childs, Abraham, cognizant that his wife and children had been captured the previous week during an encounter with the army at Hatchelustee Creek, arrived on two separate occasions, but the chiefs failed to show. Abraham later confided to Childs that he had to confront his own misgivings caused by various ill-omens that appeared before him along the way to the army camp. When a lone wolf abruptly stopped in front of him and began to howl in broad daylight, a scene he had never before witnessed, he became convinced that it augured ill-tidings and that the whites intended to harm him — "Maybe it is a trick. Maybe they want to kill me," he thought.[43] (Wolves were often harbingers of the future as well as the manifestations of shape-shifters within Seminole culture.[44]) While Abraham may have secretly acted as a paid agent of the United States in the past, his core predicament was even more complicated than the Seminoles themselves. Lacking a formal education and surrounded by manipulative whites who would not hesitate to re-enslave him and his family, Abraham still inhabited a natural world that was informed by spirits and omens. In retrospect, his internal dilemma recalls sociologist W. E. B. Du Bois's classic concept of "double consciousness," where black survival necessitated a certain psychosocial splitting. As a black man living within the parameters of Seminole society, Abraham offers another expression of Du Bois's thesis: an enactment of "two warring ideals in one black body, whose dogged strength alone keeps it from being torn asunder."[45] In this case, any splitting became an even more unwieldy three-way contest: a black man living as Sounaffee Tustenuggee (Abraham's Indian name) in a Seminole society that was in the process of being dismantled and vanquished by white settler-colonialism.[46]

The episode of the wolf notwithstanding, Abraham eventually mustered his courage and helped arrange a meeting for February 3, but at a locale well outside of Jesup's camp. Jumper and Alligator, "along with four or five inferior Chiefs"— Osceola being notably absent—reluctantly decided to meet the general and his staff, but only after they were safely "positioned on the opposite side of a deep morass," as Childs phrased it, thereby assuring that they could not be taken prisoner through treachery.[47] Though this precondition clearly indicated the heightened level of Seminole distrust, enough was said to convince Native leaders of Jesup's sincerity. All promised to meet again in fifteen days at Fort Dade (located on the Withlacoochee), and just as importantly the chiefs consented to an armistice until that time. Like the previous Camp Izard accord, it was clear that Micanopy's consent was needed, but since he was many miles away, this would have to occur at a later date. According to Childs, Jumper's appearance was troubling; while an impressive six feet tall and in his midfifties, he was nevertheless "poorly dressed, and very dirty." It was reported that Jumper had nearly lost his entire command at Wahoo Swamp. Many weeks of living on the run had taken a toll, and he also appeared ill.[48]

The Seminole chiefs, after weeks of hesitation and postponement, finally arrived in sufficient numbers at Fort Dade on March 6 to constitute what Jesup believed was a binding capitulation of the Seminole Nation. Although Micanopy was absent, Jumper, Cloud, and Holatoochee (Micanopy's nephew and heir apparent) assigned their marks at Micanopy's behest, thereby consenting to move to the Arkansas Territory. What is more, they agreed to withdraw south of the Hillsborough River until the time of their departure from Tampa Bay. In return, the United States was expected to provide food for all the Seminoles, beginning from the time they arrived at the vicinity of Fort Brooke and for an additional year after relocating to the West. Jesup had agreed that the "Seminoles, and their allies, who come in and emigrate west, shall be secure in their lives and property . . . their negroes, their bona fide property, shall accompany them to the West."[49] Great pains were thus made to assure the Seminoles that their slaves would be allowed to accompany them unmolested. (This provision would ultimately cause much confusion and disagreement over who indeed qualified as "bona fide property" and was bitterly contested by the elite planters.) In order to compel the Seminoles to abide by the stipulations, hostages, including Micanopy himself, were to be held by the army.[50]

On March 18, Micanopy arrived at Fort Dade to place his mark on the capitulation agreement. "I found myself in the presence of a man," Childs wrote, "of about forty years of age" who, while he may not have been the intellectual equal of his top aides, nevertheless possessed the "appearance of a man of authority—of one accustomed to command and to be obeyed."[51] Unlike Jumper, who was likely suffering from pneumonia, Micanopy was still relatively healthy and had the resources to keep his attire in order, even under the most stressful circumstances.[52] "A handsome, bright-colored fancy handkerchief was tied around his head, with peculiar gracefulness; a hunting-shirt, of blue and white cotton encased his very corpulent body; red leggings, handsomely beaded, covered his legs."[53] The success of the new accord was obviously contingent on Micanopy's reputed sway with the different factions of the war coalition. In answer to Jesup's question: "What authority or power has Micanopy to compel the Indians to come in?" Alligator, acting as Micanopy's spokesman, responded with the air of a practiced diplomat: "Micanopy is the mother and father of this little spot of earth; [*with a circular gesture*] of the trees and everything that grows. We have had a straight talk—he does not wish to turn it. When we meet again, it will be on the same line. With other people, some of the young men wish to have something to say; but with us, it is different: when the Governor speaks, all must obey [Micanopy is called "the Governor"]."[54] As we have seen, Jesup's predecessors continually underrated the resolve and military capability of the Seminole coalition. In his desire to put a quick end to the war, Jesup unwittingly fell into this same pattern. Regardless of what Alligator claimed, the life and death contest that had transpired for so long was not easily forfeited by the likes of Abiaka and the Miccosukees—with whom Osceola was closely associated. Their absence in the proceedings, as well as King Philip's and Coacoochee's, should have alerted Jesup that something was amiss. The full range and complexity of the army's adversaries would normally have dictated a warranted skepticism. To be sure, the other leaders gave their verbal assents following the capitulation and even began to assemble a token number of their tribesmen near Fort Mellon (present-day Sanford) on the edge of Lake Monroe, but this distant group was never central to negotiations.[55]

The national press did not wait long before announcing, often in bold type (a rarity at the time), Jesup's apparent achievement. In fact, by the third week of February, the New York *Commercial Advertiser* confirmed a story that was making headway throughout the country, "that all may be assured that *the war has been terminated.*"[56] What is more, this news was followed by the seemingly authoritative claim that Osceola had surrendered with his warriors. "The great Chief formed his men into a line—leaned against a tree—and [then] . . . gave up his rifle, with all the grace of a fallen hero."[57] The fact that such implausible fiction was taken as a legitimate story would certainly not have been possible without extensive public angst over the war and a concomitant willingness to suspend disbelief— as if wishful thinking alone could alter the course of events. "A strange *dreamishness,*" a Florida newspaper remarked, had indeed made its appearance in the country.[58] (Later retractions conceded that "Osceola, the *Invincible*" had never surrendered, and Jesup's official report also put an end to this speculation.[59]) The unresolved matter of Osceola, however, underscores the exceptional manner in which Jesup trusted in the finality of the treaty. The anxiety of this period was additionally marked by the fact that Jackson's court of inquiry had begun to cast a deeply humiliating light on some of the country's most eminent personages as well as the army itself, uncovering the basic fragility of America's heroic pantheon. Furthermore, the long-held legitimizing myth of "superior intellectual ability and sagacity" over Native people was left in tatters.[60] The ensuing sense of collective shame was addressed by William Cullen Bryant's New York *Evening Post,* the foremost Democratic Party organ in the Northeast, in an editorial that could at last proclaim that Jesup "had covered himself in glory" and that the stain on the nation's honor would be removed. "One of our generals, at least will not be brought into Court Martial for not doing his duty. What Clinch, Gaines and Scott, under fair auspices, could have accomplished, Gen. Jesup has been enabled to perform. The stain which has blotted our national escutcheon, that of permitting a band of savages to burn our habitations, and destroy our citizens with impunity, is at last wiped off."[61] From the southern democratic perspective, the eminent *Richmond Enquirer,* edited by the influential Thomas Ritchie, similarly rejoiced and noted that "the last days of the [Jackson] administration will be cheered by the knowledge that the Seminoles have been subdued; that the only Indian tribe which could give us any sort of difficulty, is beaten; and that under his auspices, all the States on the East of the Mississippi, will be delivered from the presence of all the Indian tribes."[62] Yet Florida was still not ready for such "deliverance." Difficulties first emerged at Fort Mellon when Native leaders ignored calls for their people to leave and to begin assembling at a camp arranged for them eight miles south of Tampa. Jesup even threatened to engage bloodhounds to round up any recalcitrant holdouts and let it be known that he would not hesitate to hang them when captured.[63] On the evening of June 2, while a fleet of twenty-six vessels at Tampa Bay were anchored and ready to transport the Seminoles west, a band of two hundred armed warriors under the command of Abiaka and Osceola surrounded and then abducted Micanopy, Jumper, and Cloud, and, as Jesup reported, "hurried them off to the swamps of the interior."[64] Hundreds of their followers, under threat of violence, immediately followed and left the camp deserted. The previous day, a high-placed Creek informant had cautioned Jesup that an attempt would be made to either seize or kill the leaders who had capitulated, but the Creek spies who should have monitored the situation at the camp failed to arrive, and the abductions went unnoted for twelve hours.[65] Jesup found himself in an exceedingly grim and awkward situation. Not only had the prowar faction grabbed control and appointed Abiaka as the principal chief, an event that Jesup never considered as a possibility, but the summer season prevented the army from making a retaliatory response. Aside from having to deal with the disappointment of the nation, the caustic remarks of the press, and the loss of faith in his command, Jesup's first year in command had effectively given the most belligerent of his Native adversaries a much-needed respite as well as food at governmental expense. He nonetheless maintained, at least in his letters to Poinsett, that the majority of Seminoles "felt themselves beaten and were tired of the war," notwithstanding numerous reports to the contrary.[66]

In order to save the government any further embarrassment, Jesup initially offered to resign. General Macomb refused this request and because the usual interference of the president was no longer a major factor (Jackson having left office), Jesup eventually resolved to retain command—primarily from a desire to redeem his reputation.[67] During the next few months, Gaines and Scott each attempted to replace Jesup, but the secretary backed Jesup over the others.[68] (Jesup undoubtedly retained the behind-the-scenes support of Jackson.) Reports that claimed the general "was much depressed in spirits" began to circulate.[69] Regardless of the truth of this comment, Jesup certainly manifested a newfound bitterness toward his Native adversaries and became much more disposed to use deadly means to achieve his goals. "I understand these people now, and know how to treat them," he admitted to one of his subordinates in a very grave manner. "The Miccasukeys . . . and Indian negroes must be exterminated before the Seminoles, proper, can be removed."[70] (On other occasions, he advocated that all Seminoles should be killed instead of transported west.) Jesup also made the point to his superiors in Washington that if the war was to be renewed, then whoever was in command "should be unrestricted as to means."[71] He advocated that the standard treatment of Native people as formal enemies of war, which entailed certain reciprocal obligations, should be ended straightaway. Despite Jesup's ready inclination to partake in genocidal retribution, the Van Buren administration was unwilling to pay the political price for such an extreme course. Alternatively, as we shall see, the tenor of the war changed dramatically, and whatever notions of ethical behavior that still remained on the battlefield would be stifled amid Jesup's new-found cynicism. Two years after the December uprising and following the army's unfulfilled efforts to remove Native people from the peninsula, treatment of Seminoles would become even more compromised.

Among other outcomes, the abduction of Micanopy and his entourage happened to leave Abraham in an extremely vulnerable situation. Jesup initially had him placed under guard but eventually decided to employ him as a guide and interpreter for future operations, using the welfare of his family and the threat of death as incentives to cooperate. "I have promised Abraham the freedom of his family if he be faithful to us; and I shall certainly hang him if he be not faithful."[72] Jesup's spies had also conveyed that the new Seminole leadership wanted Abraham killed for his proremoval advocacy, and the general used this information to additionally sway his loyalties.[73] Jesup then renewed attention toward all the blacks who were associated with the Seminoles. By the fall of 1837, increasing numbers of former plantation slaves who had either been captured by or willingly joined Native forces began to make their way to the various army posts or to troops in the field. Life had grown increasingly difficult, and they often told of harsh treatment and deprivations—to such a degree that they judged re-enslavement as preferable. Early in 1838, Jesup decided to exploit this discontent by offering amnesty and freedom to each black who came in willingly. More, indeed, actually surrendered—a scenario that caused a furor among white slaveowners who denied the right of the government to arbitrarily award any slave their freedom.[74] Moreover, Jesup instigated a perplexing method to deprive Seminoles of their own slaves as well as the ex-plantation slaves in their midst. He permitted militia as well as army regulars to capture blacks in exchange for a monetary award, and he also allowed Creeks an $8,000 bounty for those they had already absconded with. By attaching a bounty, Jesup intended "to induce the Creek Indians to take alive, and not destroy the negroes of citizens who had been captured by the Seminoles."[75] Of course, implementing a policy of freedom made no sense as long as there were individuals seeking a bounty for these same persons. The number who freely turned themselves in was thus curtailed. Re-enslavement remained the only option for approximately one hundred blacks who could be identified as former plantation slaves, regardless of Jesup's promises. Despite the confusion and the very impropriety of the US Army being engaged in slave dealing, a charge that would later stir abolitionist outrage, Jesup actually honored his previous agreement with Micanopy and transported the Seminole blacks to the Arkansas Territory.[76] This was done entirely from a sense of utility; the safe transfer of Seminole slaves would give Jesup an advantage in his goal of Seminole removal. The focus on separating these men, women, and children from the Indians in Florida resulted in such a drastic reduction of their numbers that by mid-1838, blacks no longer constituted a significant segment among the remaining Seminoles (five hundred were transported west).[77]

Secretary Poinsett may have agreed to free Jesup's hand so he could employ extraordinary means to end the war, but neither he nor the Van Buren administration was prepared for the kind of heated rebuke that was to follow. The forfeiture of the traditional military code of honor would elicit significant outrage on the national scene. The seizure of Osceola best illustrates this state of affairs; yet it is vital to consider that this was not an isolated incident but resulted from a series of aggressive encounters with the Seminole leadership, some of which were entirely Machiavellian in character. During the first week of September 1837, a slave of King Philip, tired of the privations of wartime life, escaped from the wilderness along with his wife and sought the safety of St. Augustine. This individual, likely under the threat of hanging, then guided an army detachment under the command of General Joseph Hernandez to the site of Philip's encampment. On the evening of September 8 near the ruins of the Dunlawton Sugar Plantation, thirty miles south of St. Augustine, Hernandez surrounded Philip's camp and easily captured him. In the jaundiced view of Jacob R. Motte, an army surgeon who was on the scene, "there were also a number of women and children captured; the former miserable, blackened, haggard and shriveled [smoke-dried and half-clad devils]; the latter, ugly little nudities."[78] Philip, as Motte interpreted the event, "was naked as he was born, except the breech-cloth, and covered in most unkingly dirt." He had just been catapulted to the ground by an officer on horseback. Although others described Philip as calm and intelligent, Motte only perceived a "sternness in this chief's dark eye,—which black as a thundercloud and emitting flashes like its lightning,—plainly told his spirit was unquelled."[79] Among the prisoners was a Yuchee Indian by the name of Tomoka John, who, after supposedly being offered a share of future plunder, guided the army directly to another isolated camp about six miles distant, the abode of important Yuchee leaders. The next day, Hernandez's men once again engaged in a surprise capture; Yuchee Billy, a war chief in the northeastern region, and his brother Jack joined Philip as prisoners.

While in confinement at Fort Marion (aka the Castillo de San Marcos, the formidable Spanish-built fortress in St. Augustine) and with Jesup's approval, Philip sent a messenger to meet his son Coacoochee, urging him to come in and talk. Coacoochee did indeed approach St. Augustine under a white flag, accompanied by Philip's brother Blue Snake. Jesup used this opportunity to deliver a threat to Coacoochee: as his father and other members of his family were in army custody, their lives would be endangered if he failed to obey Jesup's orders. Coacoochee agreed to depart on a mission to request that Osceola come in to meet with General Hernandez and, fearing for the lives of his family, further consented to return as Jesup's prisoner.[80] Regardless of the obvious risks and the warnings of others, on October 20 Osceola accepted this invitation and sent a messenger to Hernandez to confirm a site for a parley. The agreed-upon spot was one mile from Fort Peyton, a newly built wooden fortification on Moultrie Creek.[81] According to the observations of Nathan Jarvis, another (slightly less biased) army physician, the following day Hernandez met Osceola at his camp, which "we discern'd at a short distance by a white flag flying."[82] (Jesup had earlier supplied the Seminoles with a quantity of white cloth to be used expressly for such purposes.) Following a round of polite handshakes and a short talk, Hernandez, acting under orders from Jesup, gave a prearranged signal and had Osceola's party quickly surrounded by 250 men. In this manner, the famed warrior, along with his compatriot, Coe Hadjo, was captured without a shot being fired. Jarvis reported that both men were allowed to ride on horseback toward St. Augustine, but Osceola, neatly attired in a blue calico shirt, red leggings, and an ornate shawl wrapped around his head, nevertheless "appeared to be unwell." He had, in fact, been ill from malaria for some time. Upon his arrival in town, the entire populace turned out to gaze at the celebrated warrior as he rode slowly toward the Castillo under armed guards. Once locked in a cell, Jesup allowed Osceola to send a messenger to bring in his two wives and children, as well as the blacks who were part of his band.[83]

In a comparatively short period of time, Jesup's irregular tactics resulted in an impressive tally: Philip, Coachoochee, Osceola, Coe Hadjo, Holata Tustenuggee, Miccopotokee, Yuchee Billy, and Jack, as well as eighty-one warriors.[84] The unseemliness of Osceola's capture, however, tainted Jesup's reputation and alienated him from much of the officer corps. The employment of "a new code of morals," as the Boston *Atlas* lamented, transgressed the nation's sense of integrity and fairness.[85] An editorialist in Albany, New York, similarly stated that it would have been better that "Florida be given up to the aborigines to the end of time, than that their expulsion should be purchased at such a sacrifice of national honor."[86] To be sure, much of this indignation was political posturing; even so, the furor that resulted actually stemmed from a conflict over core values within the American psyche, particularly as it regarded the military. Jesup's actions were antithetical to the ideals of gallantry and moral forthrightness, and threatened the country's sense of exceptionalism; indeed, the general was compelled to defend his behavior to the US Senate. The sense of shame was so pervasive that Jesup addressed this issue in an open letter to his own troops. "The character and qualities of the American soldier," he assured them, had not suffered by his actions. "Whatever difference of opinion may exist as to the measures of the commander," he wrote, "the pen of history, guided by the hand of justice, will not fail to assign the officers and troops of his command a high place among the champions of their country's rights and honor."[87] Despite such posturing as well as a subsequent vote of confidence by the Senate—inspired by the profuse oratory of Senator Thomas Hart Benton (Missouri), who never faltered to portray Osceola as a barbarous Red Devil—constant, heartrending descriptions of the capture, imprisonment, and early death of the nation's most renowned Native hero made any overt justification appear as callous artifice to many Americans and reinforced the persistent Whig Party charge of the moral bankruptcy of Jacksonians.[88]

CHAPTER 6

The Last Pitched Battles

During the summer of 1837, John Ross, the principal chief of the Cherokee Nation, was approached by an agent of Secretary Poinsett, Colonel John H. Sherburne, who requested that the Cherokees act as mediators in an effort to finally resolve the war in Florida. In return for a successful outcome, Sherburne intimated that the government would allow the Cherokees favorable treatment in the future. He eventually promised that "an amicable adjustment" would be made to their impending removal terms, regardless of the result.[1] Though at first very hesitant, Ross eventually accepted this proposal and assigned a four-person delegation to meet with Seminole leaders and deliver a written appeal by Ross to trust "in the magnanimity and justice of the American people."[2] In a well-crafted testimonial, Ross confided to the Seminoles that he had been personally "assured by the secretary of war that you shall be liberally compensated for any losses or injuries you may have sustained by the injustice of your white brethren." Ross also pledged that

> [i]f your people desire peace, and would lay aside your warlike attitude, and come in . . . a treaty of peace would be negotiated with you, under the authority of the president of the United States, and that a veil shall be thrown over everything that has taken place during the war, so that they may be covered and never remembered or revenged. That you . . . and all others, who may have been considered as principal actors in the conflict, shall be received into equal favor and protection, with all the Seminoles in the treaty of peace.[3]

Despite General Jesup's manifest indifference toward the Cherokee delegates after their arrival in November, the mediators, outfitted in traditional dress, succeeded in establishing friendly discussions with Micanopy and other leaders at a council house that was newly built at Fowl Creek, a site about fifty miles from Fort Mellon.[4] Although historians have long recognized the events that took place, full context has suffered. Poinsett, for example, declined to honor the promises made in his name and, far from making life easier, the secretary soon unleashed the Cherokee removal process and the subsequent Trail of Tears.[5] Regarding the Seminoles, Jesup decided to use the goodwill that emanated from the visiting delegation as an opportunity to again transgress the rules of war. On this occasion, Micanopy was joined at Fort Mellon by Yaholoochee and other tribal members. "We are all of the opinion," noted an officer on the scene, "that Micanopy was in all he promised sincere."[6] Stirred by the reading of Ross's benevolent address, Micanopy initially entered discussions in a buoyant and expectant mood, and attempted to fashion a peace agreement while "the white scarf of peace" wafted in the breeze.[7] According to Sherburne, the inclusion of an ordained Baptist minister, Reverend Jesse Bushyhead, a Cherokee, as one of the mediators was done under the assumption that "Micanopy and some of the principal warriors were of the Baptist persuasion."[8] Whether this unlikely claim was true or not, Micanopy was entirely pleased with the Cherokees. On December 14, however, after Abiaka refused to travel to a meeting at Fort Mellon, Jesup dashed all hopes for peace and ordered guards to seize Micanopy and his party—ignoring all the assurances he had previously given. The Seminoles noted that the proceedings were awry long before Jesup's true intentions came to the surface. The general grew increasingly imperious and ill-tempered, and refused to recognize any treaty but the one he originally brokered with Micanopy. In the end, as armed guards led both Micanopy and Yaholoochee below the deck of a steamboat that stood ready to transport them to St. Augustine, white observers noted that while both men accepted this betrayal calmly, their eyes nevertheless welled up with tears.[9] Poinsett's supposed reconciliation thus proved to be a cynical ruse intended to manipulate one Native faction into acting as unwitting pawns—all under the pretext of a humanitarian gesture.

Ross wrote a series of letters to Poinsett in vigorous objection. "I do hereby most solemnly protest against this unprecedented violation of that sacred rule which has ever been recognized by every nation, civilized and uncivilized, of treating with all due respect those who had ever presented themselves under a flag of truce before their enemy, for the purpose of proposing the termination of warfare."[10] On the same date (January 2), Jesup sent Poinsett a warning of what he believed to be Ross's true (allegedly nefarious) intentions. Based on dubious hearsay, he claimed that Ross, if given the financial resources available from the government for the former Cherokee lands, would then "rally the Indian force west of the Mississippi, as well as the black force within the Southern States and the Territory of Florida against the United States."[11] Such a bold and unsubstantiated assertion, other than highlighting Jesup's intense paranoia regarding Native people and blacks, countered everything that was known about Ross. All the same, Jesup obviously trusted that Poinsett would be willing to entertain such a charge.

Whether this allegation played any tangible role is unknown, but the secretary did ignore Ross's letters, and within a few months the chief joined the forced march to the Arkansas Territory, whereby, as one historian phrased it, four thousand to five thousand of his fellow Cherokees "rode, walked, sickened and died" on the way west.[12] Ross made the error of trusting that his literate and enculturated lifestyle, his advocacy of republicanism, and his nonviolent resistance to removal, along with his authority as a tribal advocate in Washington, DC, would have at least earned some degree of reciprocity. According to Poinsett's thinking, however, all Native people were forever destined to live inferior lives, fixed in a barbarous state. Ross may have benefited from his mixed-white ancestry, but, as Poinsett deemed it, "the pure and unmixed races" of Indians of North and South America were more animal than human. In a treatise published in his native Charleston, the secretary drew upon his extensive travels abroad and utilized a pseudoscientific tone to account for the differences between roaming, hostile tribes and peaceful, agriculturally based Native Americans by comparing them to "the untamed wolf and the domestic house dog." Moreover, just as many of his contemporaries, Poinsett concluded that Indigenous people as a whole were doomed to obliteration, regardless of their way of life.[13] Ross's true subaltern fate was sealed regardless of outward enculturation.

Once Native people were dehumanized and relegated as "others," shorn of the higher qualities presumed to be intrinsic to Euro-Americans, the government's settler-colonial enforcers could more easily proceed with the lethal means at their disposal. The "systematic negation of the other person and a furious determination to deny the other person all attributes of humanity," as theorist Frantz Fanon summarized colonial societies, gave rise to a profound degree of emotional detachment on the part of the colonizer.[14] An equally blind eye could also be turned toward any internal detractors. In reaction to the ill-treatment of the Seminoles and Cherokee mediators, Virginia Congressman Henry A. Wise (Whig) may have declared on the House floor that these actions stood "as a dark monument, a lasting opprobrium on our national character," but any appeal to "generous feelings" would be discounted as naive and hypocritical by Democratic opponents.[15] After all, "in order to carry out their own doctrine with consistency," a Jacksonian replied in a rare moment of candor, "[congressional critics] must resign all the soil they now possess" and return the land in their home states to their former Native populations—a thought that, of course, could never be entertained, even among the government's most passionate critics.[16] Whether they admitted it or not, each citizen shared in the ignominious legacy of Indian exclusion and land seizure that long preceded Andrew Jackson.

BATTLES OF OKEECHOBEE AND LOXAHATCHEE

By the time Jesup entrapped Micanopy and Yaholoochee at Fort Mellon, he had already assembled the largest army yet to serve in the Florida Territory. Nine thousand men, half of whom were militia volunteers from the South (augmented by companies from Washington, DC, Pennsylvania, New York, and Missouri), were now under Jesup's authority. Their numbers dwarfed Scott's erstwhile grand army. (As there were a meager 7,130 men in the entire US Army and more than half [4,000] had been directed to the Florida campaign, Congress shortly increased the enlisted force to 11,800.[17]) "Gathered from every quarter of the Union [the assembled force] embraced men of almost every grade and character, and from every rank in life," as an anonymous enlisted man, a teenager at the time, described the situation. The financial Panic of 1837 aided in recruitment, despite the war's growing ill-repute. "The difficulties attendant to [the economic downturn], had driven to the army many who in vain sought employment in their usual pursuits, and some who wished to drown amid its dissipations the memory of their misfortunes." Many foreigners happened to be deserters from the British regiments in Canada. According to this particular informant, the "best" soldiers— "though the worst men" in terms of accepted morals—were veterans of past European wars who had fought in almost every battlefield on the continent. Exposure to bloodshed and violence, however, had only "hardened their hearts and rendered them familiar with every species of vice."[18] But officers were hardly paragons of virtue either, and fully half of the enlisted men, as Private Bartholomew Lynch ventured to estimate while at Fort Mellon, would privately welcome news that any of their officers had fallen in battle, no matter how bravely—a fact that Lynch attributed to "the unnecessary tyranny" and brutal physical abuse that officers were expected to wield over the men.[19]

Despite Jesup's penchant for organization and Poinsett's desire to provide all that the general required, the commander experienced the same logistical problems that beset his predecessors. Jesup realized that his ever-expanding and costly demands for matériel, which ranged from rubber pontoon bridges and specially designed shallow-draft boats to standard wagons and coffee rations, were at the mercy of citizen contractors who did not always meet deadlines and often delivered shoddy goods (including spoiled food and broken-down horses and mules).[20] Opportunities to profit from the war effort were intentionally spread across the nation and awarded to the administration's Democratic supporters and home states, often without regard to business acumen or trustworthiness. Jesup also came to embrace the same tactics that had proven so fruitless in previous campaigns, and after filling his ranks to such a high degree he employed a plan of attack that again relied on large, converging columns. On this occasion, the general hoped to drive the Seminoles into the Everglades, using a northern column under the command of Colonel Zachary Taylor.[21] Jesup assumed that his combined forces could then finish off his adversaries amid this vast and foreboding region.

As we have seen, Seminoles had endured severe losses that included the deaths or capture of some of their most effective and esteemed leaders. Even so, Abiaka (glibly dubbed "Sam Jones" by whites, after a character in a popular tune) was an enormously determined and charismatic opponent.[22] As war chief, *hilíswa haya*, and a member of the elite Panther clan, Abiaka, in his midfifties, was reputed to possess "magical" war powers that were both deadly and unfathomable to outsiders.[23] Seminoles moreover exalted in the news of Coacoochee's escape from the Castillo. On the evening of November 29, about the same time as the Cherokee mediation, Coacoochee and Juan Cavallo (John Horse), a mestizo of mixed Indian and black heritage, along with sixteen other warriors and two women, managed to climb fifteen feet above the floor of their cell and, after removing an iron bar from a small opening, climbed out and glided down the steep exterior walls using a length of makeshift rope.[24] Historian Patricia Wickman has doubted the veracity of this narrative, noting that such an escape would have been physically impossible, given the narrow, eight-inch-wide opening.[25] Whether by physical prowess, bribery, the drunkenness of the guards, or, as Seminole folklore has it, mystic incantations and potions to reduce the size of their bodies—the key point was that this audacious escape actually succeeded.

On December 13, during the end of the Cherokee mediation, one of the delegates unexpectedly met a young warrior after returning from an unsuccessful meeting with Abiaka. Speaking in a confidential tone, the warrior relayed that Coacoochee's escape had rekindled the war spirit among them and that regardless of the conciliatory attitude of Micanopy and Yaholoochee, a significant portion of Seminoles were preparing for combat.[26] All the escaped prisoners relayed Jesup's treachery and the harsh treatment they endured—details that, according to army intelligence, "changed the intentions of the Indians as to surrendering [and] their pacific dispositions to that of the most deadly hostility."[27] The projected battlefield, located on the northern rim of Lake Okeechobee, was being meticulously readied for a confrontation with Taylor's column of 1,032 men, a force that had been steadily advancing southward along the banks of the Kissimmee River.[28] During the course of several weeks, Seminoles carefully lured Taylor to their intended battle site; they consciously pulled away from any engagement without firing their rifles and headed toward Lake Okeechobee, leaving visible tracks in their wake. On the evening of December 19—in a highly unforeseen development— Jumper, suffering from a protracted illness and weary of war, finally became reconciled to departing Florida and thus surrendered to Taylor, along with sixty-three of his followers. Micanopy's former sense-bearer died four months later at the army barracks in New Orleans while on the journey to the Indian Territory.[29]

The Seminoles who assembled at Lake Okeechobee—a meager 380 warriors—were led by Jumper's friends and allies: Coacoochee, Alligator, and Abiaka. They resolved to make a stand within an area of giant cypress trees that bordered the vast lake.[30] On this occasion, Native forces would fight without the able support of many of their black compatriots, a direct consequence of Jesup's policy of enticing and capturing this group.

After Taylor approached the region on Christmas Day, he discovered that his men would have to negotiate three-quarters of a mile of swamp water, three feet deep, an area that also abounded in sawgrass—a tall, ubiquitous sedge plant with razor-sharp, serrated edges—in order to engage the enemy. Acutely aware of the army's superior numbers and their stores of weaponry, Seminoles tried to bolster the odds in their favor. A swath of sawgrass was cut down to provide a more inviting corridor for their approaching adversaries—a move that concentrated the army as tightly as possible and that provided a clear line of sight. If permitted to enter this area, horses would have sunk hopelessly into the soft muck bottom. Consequently, Taylor banned mounted men from the battle, thereby eliminating one of the Seminole's most dreaded adversaries. The dark muck was of such consistency that, as one soldier complained, "[e]very step took you above your knees in mud."[31] The elevated area amid the cypress trees additionally afforded Seminoles a distinct advantage. Despite the site's impressive assets—officers noted that their enemy was posted in the strongest position that they had ever encountered— Seminoles were still outnumbered by an imposing concentration of fresh troops.[32] The best they could reasonably expect was to strike a blow to army morale by obstructing their progress and inflicting large casualties. In doing so, they would send a robust message that the Seminoles were far from being a spent force. Canoes were consequently readied on the banks of the lake, and well-designed escape routes were planned in advance.

As it happened, Taylor chose a conservative and rather unimaginative course of action. He accepted the tactical limitations that were imposed upon him without any attempt to circumvent matters and thus refused to outflank the enemy, use artillery, or enlist any element of surprise—no matter how meager. He thus engaged the Seminoles on their own terms.[33] About half past noon, he placed six hundred men in motion; all labored amid the mud, water, and sawgrass in an ungainly and slow-moving frontal attack. Taylor directed one of the least experienced groups under his command, 132 volunteers from Missouri, a cohort that had suffered disproportionately from illness upon arriving in Florida, to take up the front line.[34] One hundred seventy-five men of the Sixth Infantry followed behind them, keeping a margin of forty yards. About the same number from the Fourth Infantry took up a third line, maintaining an equal distance. Finally, Taylor placed two hundred of the First Infantry regiment at the rear as a reserve force. As soon as the front line approached within eighty to one hundred yards of the cypress hammock, the Seminoles "commenced a most furious attack."[35] Rifle fire erupted from a multitude of concealed positions, from behind trees and underbrush as well as from snipers skillfully camouflaged with Spanish moss from atop giant cypresses—locations that proved especially effective. The Missourians managed to briefly return fire, but with no visible targets they soon became hopelessly pinned down and saw no other recourse but to squat down in the water close to the sawgrass. The Sixth Infantry opened fire, subjecting the volunteer force to intense crossfire in the process. Before the battle, Taylor had instructed the volunteers to fall back behind the regulars if they could not hold the line. Following the loss of their commander, Colonel Richard Gentry, as well as many of their number in the first few minutes, some volunteers broke formation and withdrew from the action entirely—an issue that became hotly contested after the battle.[36] The infantry nevertheless remained and "not only stood firm," as Taylor later reported, but "continued to advance."[37] Away from the line of fire, according to Alligator's recollection, Otulkee Thlocco, a medicine man also known as the Prophet, sought to inspire warriors with courage by performing ritual singing and dancing.[38] Whether stirred by these spiritual invocations or not, a group of warriors charged the army on three different occasions and turned back after inflicting heavy casualties—a highly unusual move. Dogged perseverance and an unexpected rush by the Fourth Infantry allowed Taylor's regulars to eventually reach the hammock area. This show of force on the elevated ground deprived warriors of the time needed to reload their weapons, and after two and a half hours of some of the heaviest fighting of the war, Native leaders deemed it prudent to enact their withdrawal plans. In a gory spectacle, some men of Taylor's First Infantry, a unit that was never integral to the day's fighting, grew intent on exacting revenge and "scalped, bayonetted & cut off the ears" of the bodies of eight Seminoles who remained on the hammock floor—a detail that was understandably kept from official reports.[39]

Seminoles lost about a dozen men and fourteen were wounded, but the army, as one would presume, suffered far more severely: 26 fatalities and 112 wounded. "The fatality among the officers in the command," Sprague observed, "was enough to shake the firmest troops."[40] Taylor's force indeed suffered the largest loss of any battle during the war. In light of such a skewed outcome, the colonel's later claim of "victory" in his formal report that was published in the *Globe* may seem problematic. In fact, initial newspaper accounts—based solely on the disproportionate number of casualties—such as an article in the New Orleans *Daily Picayune*, described the engagement as "one of the most disastrous battles that has yet been fought in Florida."[41] To be sure, the battle stands as a prime example of Seminole tactical brilliance. The achievement is all the more impressive in that it took place after years of fighting, the loss of hundreds of warriors, the fragmentation of Native leadership, and the numerical advantage of the US Army, a force that was now well supplied by rations and other essentials. Even so, the politically astute Taylor managed to turn the general perception of this engagement from a pyrrhic victory at best into an unqualified triumph. Far more attuned to the public relations value of battlefield narratives than his predecessors, he conveyed a sweeping sense of hard-fought triumph in his published report. Cognizant of the battle's value as propaganda and the leeway he held in framing it for public consumption, Taylor adjudged that "the enemy was completely routed, and driven in every direction."[42] Yet again, the Seminole proclivity for leaving the field to engage another day was portrayed as certain proof of victory. More precisely, however, symbols drawn in the sand that were intentionally left behind and then interpreted by Abraham (functioning as an army scout) made it known to all that the Seminoles had not given up but intended to fight to the death.[43]

The Battle of Lake Okeechobee heroicized Taylor and lifted public opinion during a continual low ebb that had been dominated by Jesup's discreditable tactics, dampened by Jackson's prolonged antagonism toward army leaders and by the perceived weakness of the military since the commencement of the war. According to one of Taylor's biographers, the colonel's tenure during the war earned him two distinctions: "One was promotion by brevet to brigadier general, and the other, based on his personal bravery in advancing through the Okeechobee swamp with his men, was the bestowal of the nickname Old Rough and Ready."[44] In reality, however, it is doubtful that Taylor actually slogged through the mud at Lake

Okeechobee. What is more, the sobriquet originated before the Florida campaign and derived from his plainspoken and often gruff manner, his avoidance of pomp and ceremony, and his willingness to endure the general privations of war along with his men (the antithesis of Scott).[45] In any case, the battle thrust Taylor on the national scene and served as a foundation for his later rise both within the military and the political arena, eventually ascending to the presidency following the Mexican-American War.

Taylor's battle report was not entirely free from controversy. As noted, his reproach of the Missouri volunteers, who he declared "mostly broke [ranks] and . . . retired across the swamp to their baggage and horses," was taken as an unjust affront to the character and reputation of the entire state of Missouri.[46] Among other repercussions, this remark, which may have overstated the number of those who "broke," triggered the special ire of Senator Benton, who criticized the colonel's choice of "exposing citizens [not professional soldiers] to the fate of a forlorn hope."[47] With some justification, Benton argued that these men were only placed on the front line as bodies to draw enemy fire. This episode opened up a larger national discourse regarding the role of the militia and the steadily increasing presence of a professional army. Benton's complaints against Taylor abruptly exposed the internal prejudices of the army against citizen soldiers. The volunteers subsequently noted that "from the first moment of our joining the army till we left it," they experienced continual "manifestations of their contempt and dislike toward us."[48] By all accounts, Taylor likewise treated them shabbily and, with very slight cause, severely berated their commanding officer, Colonel Gentry, on at least two occasions. While Benton's power in the senate was substantial, Taylor had influential political supporters of his own, such as Kentucky Senator John J. Crittenden (Whig), whose wife was Taylor's cousin. This, in addition to the Van Buren administration's ardent support for the colonel's actions, was enough to offset whatever ill-will Benton may have desired to cast in his direction. In order to mollify the unfolding furor, Taylor edited his previous remarks in a later version of his report and described the volunteers as falling back behind the regulars as they were expected to do.[49] But the assault to honor had already taken place, an indignity that was so profoundly felt—the Florida war represented the first time that the Missouri militia had been called into battle—that state legislators assailed Taylor for what they felt was perfidious conduct and formed a special committee to undertake a lengthy, formal investigation.[50] The final resolution declared that Taylor "had wantonly misrepresented the conduct of men who gallantly sustained him in battle" and was hence "unworthy of a commission in the Army of the United

States."[51] Even if President Van Buren had actually read this missive, it is clear that nothing came of it.

In the meantime, Jesup's other columns were engaged in a futile effort to deliver an overwhelming blow to the Seminoles. Taylor had suffered so many casualties that his force was effectively placed out of action for the next month, and a significant amount of time was spent transporting the wounded to the army's general hospital at Tampa Bay.[52] Despite the apparent success at Okeechobee, the feeling within the army at large was not of elation; rather, a sense of despondency appears to have overtaken many. Three weeks after the engagement, Lieutenant Colonel William S. Foster, the officer who led the Fourth Infantry in the decisive charge at Okeechobee, perceived only trouble ahead for himself and his men. In a sardonic mood, he wrote to his wife that "a Great Army of about 5,000 men" under the command of "Major General Jesup, the Brig. General (Eustis) and the brave & accomplished Colonel (Twiggs)" were nowhere to be found when Foster and Taylor had first advanced toward the Kissimmee River. Having missed the rendezvous, they should have at least assembled on the east side of the Okeechobee. Yet again, according to Foster, Jesup and the others failed to show. Hence, as he perceived events, "803 men of all kinds present, 360 of whom only fired a musket, met fought & defeated the whole of the hostile Indians, fought the battle in which this grand Army was to be engaged." Taylor's force traveled twice as far in the wilderness interior—and in half the time as well. Jesup, Eustis, and Twiggs were thus "well matched," Foster noted derisively, as each was devoid of the "*sacred fire*" necessary in war.[53] (If, in fact, only 360 men engaged the Seminoles—contrary to Taylor's report—the casualty rate would have been even more calamitous.) In consequence of the situation in Florida, Foster fully expected that death awaited him, and he urged his wife, Betty, to be prepared for his demise and to console their children.[54] Foster nonetheless grew more accepting of the circumstances in which he found himself. After serving three winter campaigns in Florida without serious injury—the longest stretch of any field officer—he was transferred out of the territory and briefly joined his family. Ironically, while visiting New Orleans, he contracted yellow fever and died shortly thereafter, not a year after his gloomy premonitions.

By mid-January, the various columns that Foster had expected earlier were more or less in place, and Jesup was confident that he had the remaining Seminoles surrounded. On January 24, while in a section of the Everglades known as the Alpatiokee Swamp (east of Lake Okeechobee and west of the newly built Fort Jupiter on the Atlantic coast), Jesup learned from an Indian prisoner that he was only a half hour's march from a Seminole encampment.[55] The general ordered fourteen hundred men consisting of dragoons, artillery, Tennessee volunteers, and thirty-five Delaware Indians to proceed to the site straightaway, where they arrived between 11 a.m. and noon.[56] Though still winter, the weather was noted as "excessively hot." The peculiar, almost otherworldly characteristics of the Everglades (known as Payhayokee, or "grassy water") as well as the region's susceptibility to miasmatic illness led one soldier to hazard that "it would be safer to make a campaign in Africa than in this region of the country."[57] Another wrote to his hometown newspaper in Vermont and compared their situation to De Soto's "exploits."[58] No white man, it was safely assumed, had ever set foot in this tropical wilderness zone. To be sure, the Seminoles—commanded on this occasion by Tuskegee, a high-ranking chief and brother of the deceased Osuchee (Cooper)—inhabited a seemingly impregnable hammock surrounded by cypress swamp.[59] According to an officer on the scene, the Indians had implemented many of the same sophisticated defense measures that had proven so effective at Okeechobee: "They had holes morticed in the trees, pickets set up, and palmettoes set up so as to cover them and form blinds." As in the previous battle, Native forces "had cleared away the hammock on the side that Jesup attacked them," a ploy that exposed attackers while obscuring the positions of the Indians.[60] The mud, sawgrass, and cypress knees caused the dragoons to dismount and charge on foot, greatly diminishing their effectiveness. As the fighting progressed, Jesup unleashed a flurry of Congreve rockets into the thickets. Even more substantially, both a cannon and a howitzer loaded with grapeshot and standard shells pounded the site and forced the Seminoles to retreat to another area that was purposively separated by a deep stream about ninety feet wide. It was here, as one soldier noted, that "the Indian rifle balls flew thick and fast," preventing some troops from advancing.[61] After Jesup dismounted, paused at the edge of the water, and turned to instruct his men, a bullet struck him in the face, shattering his glasses and inflicting a severe flesh wound on his left cheek.[62] Shortly afterward, the Seminoles successfully evacuated the smoke-filled area amid the tremendous cacophony of shouting, rocketry, cannon blasts, and musket and rifle fire, leaving the army with seven dead and thirty-one wounded. By Tuskegee's adroit maneuvering, an estimated one hundred warriors were able to skillfully fend off a highly armed and invigorated force fourteen times their number, while allowing their women, children, and elders to escape unharmed—a phenomenal feat that has never been sufficiently noted by historians.[63]

Foster, who was located about twenty miles away at the time, was dismissive of what was soon called the Battle of Loxahatchee and privately noted that the so-called battle accomplished nothing and only added to the frustration of "the wise heads who conduct this miserable war."[64] Jesup complained that the battle was "productive of no results" and merely resulted in dispersing the enemy.[65] The engagement, which lasted an hour and a half, was nevertheless the last pitched battle of the entire war. One-third of the troops were left barefooted, and most uniforms were literally torn to shreds.[66] The spines that were present along the leaf stalks of saw palmettoes and the needle-shaped prickles on the edges of sawgrass not only entirely wrecked shoes and clothing but caused deep skin lacerations that were prone to fester.[67] Following the same public relations stratagem as the Battle of Okeechobee, the army again claimed an unqualified victory. On this occasion, however, their overwhelming advantage in numbers was never featured in reports. It is possible that Seminole losses were extensive, but evidence is still lacking; in any case, Native forces afterward adopted a very different tactical response to the army's incursions. They dispersed throughout the region, congregated only in small numbers, and refrained from attacking even the smallest army detachments—at least for the short term. Their scattering into the Everglades, with its seemingly boundless grassy savannahs, occasional "islands" of high ground amid immense expanses of water—an environment that produced a disorienting sense of tedium for the troops—left Jesup with an awkward problem. Lacking guides who were even marginally familiar with this unmapped region, the possibility arose that he would never be able to detect his enemies. A few weeks earlier, Jesup proudly declared to Poinsett that "[w]hilst a warrior lives we shall have him to fight."[68] Now it was uncertain whether he could find warriors at all. Based on this rapid adaptation by Native forces, the general did not hesitate to inform his superiors that the conflict could not be terminated within the expected timeframe.[69]

JESUP'S SOLUTION

Despite the favorable publicity generated by the Everglades campaign, Jesup entered a different phase regarding his strategic options. For all the thousands of armed men at his disposal, as well as a plethora of supply depots, wagon trains, hospitals and medical personnel, boats of all descriptions, masses of civilian teamsters, mechanics and laborers, and a cordon of forts stretching across the peninsula— from the Indian River inlet on the east coast to Tampa Bay on the Gulf—Jesup's expectation for closing the war by the spring proved just as illusory as the most sanguinary hopes of his far less provisioned predecessors.[70] On February 11, Jesup wrote a surprisingly candid letter to Poinsett in which he laid out a proposal for what he thought was the only practical solution to terminating the campaign.[71] He knew for some time that the Seminoles would gladly relinquish hostilities if they were simply allowed a section of land in Florida to claim as their own. Because Jesup deemed the Everglades as entirely worthless and "a place not fit for the white man," the equivalent of a vast wasteland or desert, he committed a type of settler-colonial heresy by suggesting that the remaining Seminoles should simply be permitted to live in this portion of the territory in the short term.[72] Any respite would prove beneficial for the government, he reasoned, as the Seminoles' eventual removal—at some unspecified future date—would be facilitated by the fact that they could then be gathered far more easily, as they would have returned to a more domestic lifestyle and thus could be taken off guard. Straining to qualify his proposal within a settler-colonial perspective, Jesup posited that the war had been premature in the first place. The number of Florida settlers, according to the general, had not yet reached sufficient numbers to warrant the expulsion of the Native people. Unstated was the impressive achievement by the Seminoles at Loxahatchee, an event that convinced Jesup of the pointlessness of continuing the army's aggressive posture. (Moreover, the pain and trauma of his disfiguring facial wound may have also sent unsettling intimations of his own mortality.[73]) He deemed this correspondence of such immediate import that he ordered his aid-de-camp to deliver the letter directly to Secretary Poinsett in Washington.

In the meantime, Jesup unexpectedly confronted Tuskegee and his fellow chief, Halleck Hadjo, in the Everglades, but instead of pursuing military action, Jesup proposed peace—a decision that was approved by others among his principal officers, such as Eustis and Twiggs, but nevertheless piqued many in the junior ranks.[74] (Promotion came far more readily to those who claimed courageous action in battle.) Additional negotiations resulted in a "council" that was planned for the third week of February at Jesup's headquarters at Fort Jupiter, a post located on the banks of the Loxahatchee River and a few miles from the Atlantic. Top commanders, including Colonel Taylor, were expected to attend. According to a vivid journal entry by Lieutenant Phelps, the officers had assembled at the fort, "appearing like men who were likely to be humbugged."[75] Jesup may have held out a peace offering to the Seminoles, but he stressed that they would only be authorized to stay in the territory if Van Buren himself assented to Jesup's request. Women and children were also expected to arrive, and indeed everyone, about four hundred in number, encamped within a mile or so of the fort; all were told to ready themselves for the final decision of the chief executive. As news from Washington had not yet arrived, the status of the Seminoles remained tentative. Tuskegee and Halleck Hadjo nonetheless treated the matter of the council with all the stately formality they could muster and tried to imbue the meeting with peaceful intent.[76]

Despite serious misgivings from the officers, at 10 a.m. the chiefs appeared as planned but, as Phelps put it, "in a new and peculiar manner." "My attention was first attracted to their white flags as they were marshalling at some distance from the camp." After some yelling, Phelps noticed that a formal procession was under way. Stationed before and immediately behind a white-flag bearer were "two negroes each bearing the wing of a heron upon a stick," who were followed by some dozen individuals who each carried a single white feather on a pole.[77] Another observer, surgeon Jacob Motte, noted that Tuskegee, Halleck Hadjo, and others were dressed in all the trappings of "Indian finery" and led a procession of about one hundred Indians and blacks, plus a retinue of women and children.[78] Proceeding in a double line, the pageant was punctuated by the eerie timbre of a lone drummer and the distinctive rhythm of a "rattle-box."[79] Once within the wooden fort, the Seminoles stopped several times and took part in what Motte described as "a peculiar shrill whoop . . . commenced by their chief and taken up in chorus by the rest."[80] Having arrived at Jesup's tent, and after a brief, celebratory "peace dance," the official proceedings began.

After attendees took turns smoking from a calumet pipe, the council began with the oratory of a woman of very advanced years and of obvious authority, perhaps a clan elder, who, as Motte described the scene, pointed to the warriors who were now seated in the general's tent and declared that "[t]hey were all her children; that she was tired of the war; that her warriors were slain; her villages burnt; her little ones perishing by the road side; that the great spirit frowned upon his red children; that the star of her nation had set in blood." Most of all, she desired "that the hatchet be buried forever, between her children, and her white brethren.[81] After the elder's sorrowfully moving address, other Seminole leaders admitted that while their "heads and hearts" yearned for peace, it also became clear during this and subsequent meetings that the majority also desperately wanted to stay in Florida, even if it meant living in the Everglades.[82] Jesup, sensing the Seminole's desire to remain, ended the council for the day. In subsequent meetings and after being repeatedly pressed by Jesup, Tuskegee eventually agreed to abide by the president's decision but evidently kept this commitment from Halleck Hadjo, who remained opposed at this date.[83] And so, as the weeks passed, it was not at all clear what would actually transpire if Washington rejected the general's proposal. But a vocal contingent of junior officers was firmly opposed to these proceedings. One lieutenant, for example, openly professed that the general was "a disgrace to the army, [and] the most fickle, inconsistent man that ever lived."[84]

On March 6, still without word from the War Department, the inventor and gun manufacturer Samuel Colt arrived at the fort and relieved some of the tedium that was beginning to prevail by demonstrating his newly designed repeating rifle before an on-site committee. "Eight discharges could be made in less than one minute," Phelps remarked incredulously, and the accuracy of firing was equal to any other firearm.[85] The Seminoles were similarly enthralled. Previously, each side in the war had by necessity factored the time it took to load a single shot with their rifles and muskets—a delay that had a direct bearing on battlefield decisions. Lieutenant Colonel William S. Harney, who led the Second Dragoons, was sufficiently impressed to immediately order fifty rifles (at the extraordinary price of $125 per firearm) and afterward set out with an equal number of handpicked men, plus another fifty who were armed with standard carbines in an attempt to capture Abiaka. This elusive character, along with an estimated one hundred warriors, was reported to be in the extreme southern peninsula—a region that Abiaka and the Miccosukee bands had long been familiar with.[86]

The government's decision finally arrived on March 17. Several days earlier, Jesup had informally learned from friends that although Poinsett appeared receptive to such an arrangement, "the southern members [of the Cabinet] will generally oppose it; and the President will probably disapprove of it."[87] Hence Poinsett's subsequent rejection was not entirely a surprise. The government indeed staunchly refused to grant Seminoles any portion of the territory and insisted on their transportation, stating that national policy dictated that all tribes, without exception, were to move to the land reserved for them across the Mississippi.[88] The secretary cited the Treaty of Payne's Landing as the "law of the land" and therefore the "[c]onstitutional duty of the President requires that he should cause it to be executed."[89] A pointed reference was also made to the fact that the War Department had expected that the campaign would have successfully concluded due to the "extensive means" placed at Jesup's disposal. The general had thus been placed on notice and the administration, by implication, neither appreciated Jesup's plan nor the publicity that it garnered in the newspapers, as it led many to erroneously presume that peace was in the offing.

After the Indians failed to show up at Fort Jupiter on March 20 as directed—apparently, they had correctly deduced an unfavorable decision—Jesup believed he had no other choice but to instruct Colonel Twiggs to assemble his troops and round up the entire Seminole camp the next morning. This surprise maneuver, enacted at sunrise, was accomplished with such efficiency that the overwhelming majority were captured and placed under guard without violence. With obvious pride, Jesup informed Poinsett that he had secured 513 men, women, and children—151 of whom were warriors.[90] Jesup additionally reminded the War

Department that he had previously taken a contingent of 159 blacks who had been living with this Seminole band and sent them to Tampa for transportation west. The general, no doubt having prepared for this moment, actually carried out the largest capture of the war and did so without any fighting.[91]

Contrary to those who criticized Jesup for his inconsistency, a closer look at his original proposal and his subsequent actions reveals that he remained remarkably wedded to a very singular tactic. From the moment he first discovered the benefits of disallowing privileges normally accorded to enemy combatants, such as violating flags of truce, he became even more persuaded of the value of deception. His proposal to Washington never anticipated the long-term presence of Seminoles in southern Florida; rather, he sought to entice them into a state of complacency, with peace "councils" and the encouragement of settling with their families. As Jesup made clear to Governor Call by mid-March, "[t]he Indians can only be collected by peaceable means." In lieu of force, he continued, "they should be allowed to concentrate, and commence their cultivation of their crops for the season, and when entirely off their guard, they should be suddenly and promptly attacked—they can be conquered in no other way."[92] This deceitful ruse, not unlike the fraudulent treaty-making process that preceded it, hence remained at the center of Jesup's plans. He learned, based on the negative press generated by his earlier seizure of Osceola, that if he at least retained the facade of honorable "peace talks," he could not only bypass criticism but increase the number of captives. Entire bands could be apprehended along with their leaders. In the case of Tuskegee and Halleck Hadjo, events had merely escalated.

Jesup's presumptions notwithstanding, many of the remaining Native forces did not remain long in isolation. The presence of so many troops in the southern peninsula created an opportunity for some Seminoles to evade the army columns and to proceed north undetected. Small-scale but deadly attacks erupted in portions of the territory that had not seen fighting since the beginning of the war and included Middle Florida (the Tallahassee region), which greatly alarmed the white citizenry. Even so, some Indigenous leaders who played key roles during the opening of the war eventually succumbed to the constant stress of armed conflict, the loss of loved ones, and the added physical and emotional trauma that was placed on survivors who had to deal with life amid the territory's most inaccessible swamps and marshes, which included constant and severe food shortages. During the first week of April, Alligator responded favorably to a meeting with his former compatriots in arms, Abraham and Holatoochee, both sent by Jesup, and consented to surrender along with eighty-eight of his people. Bearing in mind the army's seemingly never-ending pursuits, Alligator simply could not see any reason to carry on the fight. The mestizo Juan Cavallo also accompanied this group, along with twenty-seven blacks—all in all, a most noteworthy capitulation.[93]

As far as the War Department was concerned, Jesup's overall tenure in Florida was seen as productive; even so, there was an increasing list of annoyances to deal with. The continuance of hostilities, the furor that resulted from both the Osceola affair and the Cherokee mediators, the outcry of Floridians who remonstrated against the very idea of leaving Seminoles (even for the shortest interval) in South Florida, and congressional opposition to the profligate level of military spending all left Van Buren's political opponents with a heady advantage on the national front. Moreover, Jesup's conduct exacerbated doubts concerning white dominion over Native people and, given the dearth of any genuinely epic battle (Okeechobee notwithstanding) and the general's reliance on unprincipled ploys and tricks, did little to restore faith in the nation's military prowess. In his defense, the general claimed that 2,400 Seminole and blacks had either been captured or voluntarily surrendered and further noted that of this total, more than seven hundred were warriors.[94] Indeed, when such a tally is viewed solely through the lens of Indian removal, Jesup plainly surpassed all of his predecessors. Despite the string of controversies that erupted on his watch, the general was genuinely taken aback by his curt dismissal in April. Without forewarning, the arrival of General Order No. 7 (dated April 10) served as the government's sole method of notifying him of the termination of his command—an act, as the general interpreted it, of "the deepest censure."[95] On May 15, 1838, he relinquished command to Zachary Taylor, newly promoted to brigadier general, and in doing so a major phase of the war came to a close. Jesup resumed his duties as the army's chief supply officer, joined his wife and children, and, despite his weakened reputation, once more presided as a Washington powerbroker. Soon afterward, however, he began a vigorous and protracted public defense of his controversial command—an ongoing stance that continued to his final days.

CHAPTER 7

"Never-Ending, Still-Beginning War"

Zachary Taylor assumed command during a period when the administration was under strain by an increasingly irate and uncompliant Congress. Legislators attempted to stem the spiraling expenditures of an Indian war whose overall duration and surfeit of blunders testified to military incompetence and excessive spending on a grand scale. It had become, as the *National Intelligencer* observed, paraphrasing Edmund Burke, "'a bleeding artery of profusion' which threatened to exhaust the Treasury."[1] The country's ongoing economic downturn certainly exacerbated tensions. Neither the Euro-American myth of an exceptional, demigod-like Native leader, as in the case of Osceola, nor the supposed "control" of manipulative blacks could explain why the war effort continued unabated, especially after both these overwrought themes had been eliminated. Although greatly reduced in numbers, Seminoles continued to baffle military operations and "the never-ending, still-beginning war," as a popular phrase had it, created a pervasive malaise that sapped army morale.[2] After so many years of conflict, the military lacked an effective strategy and yearned for a commander who could at least deliver consistent leadership. Alternatively, a new option began to surface outside the purview of the secretary of war, one that eschewed force in favor of simple expediency. The *Political Arena* (Fredericksburg, VA), a Whig newspaper, convinced that the Seminoles could never be removed otherwise, asserted that only "soft words and the persuasive force of gold [would] induce them to migrate."[3] Monetary compensation may have been anathema to the aggressive posture of Jacksonian true believers, yet it was an alternative that would in time gain reluctant acceptance and could easily be justified simply by acknowledging the length of the war and its costs.[4]

With the advent of Taylor's appointment, expectations were high that he would accomplish much more in Florida than his predecessors.[5] Still, as the general bluntly confided to Governor Call during the summer of 1838, the command was "neither asked for nor desired." Taylor knew full well that his professional reputation would not be advanced during such a campaign, even if he did manage to end the war. He may have claimed that he would pursue his responsibilities to the utmost, but Taylor also expressed that he would be far happier to relinquish command "to anyone the Government may think proper to Supersede me."[6] This was hardly the kind of attitude that was destined to inspire or win campaigns. Had Poinsett spent time interviewing Taylor before assigning him command, he would have discovered that he shared many of the same conclusions that Jesup had and that both men were convinced that pursuing Seminoles in the hope of engaging them in battle was senseless. Indeed, Taylor sent a strong reminder to the War Department that "[a]ll we can do is get in sight of the Indians, and when they choose to elude us, we have never been able, in a single instance, to overtake them."[7]

In a major break with his predecessors, however, Taylor placed settlers at the epicenter of governmental and military concern. Indeed, as he advised the War Department, "the war can only be brought to a close by protecting the actual settlers and encouraging others to emigrate to Florida."[8] Furthermore, he agreed with the governor's proposal that urged the formation of military/settler "colonies," especially since the application of brute military force, which included the latest technology in cannons and rocketry, had failed.[9] The territory may have been vividly transformed by Jesup's command — indeed, a network of interconnected trails led to a plethora of new wooden forts (seventy in total), scattered throughout the peninsula. But Taylor differed markedly from Jesup by the latter's distrust and disdain of Florida settlers, an attitude that also permeated much of the army.[10] Instead, Taylor followed a pattern long established in his native Kentucky as well as other "frontier" (Indigenous) regions in the Old Southwest and concluded that pioneer farmers and ranchers, while formerly a missing component in the army's plans, were vital to success. (It should be noted that before the advent of settler-colonial studies, historian Richard Maxwell Brown identified this general pattern as the "homestead ethic," a set of values and behaviors whose origins preceded the revolution and exalted a fierce, manly independence and self-sufficiency in the backcountry.[11]) Taylor therefore proposed dividing north central Florida, the previous settler enclave, into a series of uniform, twenty-mile square military districts, each consisting of at least one central garrison fortified by a blockhouse, composed of infantry and dragoons, and linked together by a network of roads and bridges. The army would then be better able to defend those who returned to rebuild their settlements, especially in the Alachua region. With its hammocks and verdant prairies, this area was still considered "the most beautiful and fertile portion of Florida," as Sprague once declared, despite the constant warfare.[12] Rather than assign settlers as a militia force that would serve alongside the army, Taylor was determined that they should only return to till the soil and otherwise carry on as they did before the Seminole insurgence. Self-interest, it was assumed, would drive settlers to defend their own homesteads, an option that seemed viable given the reduced number of Seminoles.[13]

Even so, the difference between what had taken place in other, more northern areas and the reality of this southernmost territory, with its distinct regional variations, was profound. Aside from the relatively modest number of "cracker" families from bordering states, there was never a population comparable to what occurred in Kentucky, a land of rich valleys and temperate climate, or similar locales. Moreover, longtime Floridians could easily recall the yellow fever epidemics in the former Spanish provincial capital of Pensacola after an influx of newcomers arrived following the territory's transference to the United States.[14] This was a period of frightening death tolls that certainly did not inspire further immigration. It was the rare outsider who was willing to jeopardize his own life, as well as his family's, by moving to such a region, an area that also harbored hostile Indians. But any frank admission of settler limitations would have defied centuries of proven experience elsewhere and refuted the racist presumption of white superiority that was so integral to the Jacksonian era.

Representative Caleb Cushing (Massachusetts), future US attorney general, thus felt compelled to defend the tenants of settler-colonialism in a rather grandiose and lengthy address during a debate over war appropriations in the House of Representatives. In a speech fraught with contradictions—made even more so as he struggled to fit settler hegemony into a Christian context—Cushing framed the entirety of Indian removal, "from the first day of our intercourse with them to the present," as a process that should not be subjected to normal conceptions of morality. "Was it better, in the general sum of good," he asked rhetorically, "that millions of Christians, or that thousands of Pagans, should occupy America? That the land should be suffered to remain as a lair of wild beasts . . . or that it should be filled with cultivated men?" "Our thronged cities, our cultivated fields, our edifices, ships, commerce, canals, railways, the marks of our prosperity and the monuments of civilization which meet the eye on all hands, bespeak the presence and the power of a great people. But the primitive lords of the soil are humble dependents on our annual bounty, mutilated, scattered, extinct, melted away in our path like a snowflake, devoured as the dew before the morning sun. The land once theirs is ours. The empire of our civilization is, by right or wrong, honestly or dishonestly, established indestructibly throughout the New World."[15]

In the case of East Florida, according to Cushing, this same (and necessarily amoral) advancement continued. But in a gross exception to the rule, Native removal had been plagued with innumerable difficulties. Seminoles simply did not melt away like "snowflakes" before "a great people." It was not just the country's honor, the memory of the army and militia men "who perished in the pestilential swamps," or the national treasure that was most at stake, he insisted. And neither was the fact that "the whole army of the United States [was] thrown into distraction, and half dissolved by the contentions of rank, the competitions of service, the criminations and recriminations that have sprung up in such rank abundance, like some noxious growth of the tropics, out of the soil of East Florida." Rather, in the congressman's estimation, the most severe consequence of the military's unsuccessful campaign was the risk of kindling similar flames of armed revolt among all the tribes transported to the West. "God forbid," he implored members of the House, "that such a calamity should descend upon our beloved country."[16]

Hence, despite the prevailing tedium and dissatisfaction, many believed that the war's completion was of such high magnitude that failure risked dismantling the mask of invulnerability and white privilege; as a result, the entire social and economic order might collapse like a house of cards. A pan-Indian rebellion would surely end in unthinkable horrors and, as Jesup also suspected, open the door for slave revolt. As the nation's treatment of all Native people (as well as blacks) was based on human subjugation on a grand scale, psychological elements of guilt, repression, and paranoia were doubtless at play. It is thus quite significant that Taylor, a Whig, revived the comforting, time-worn ethic of settler sovereignty in his war plans. Indeed, the folk iconography of the simple and venerable frontier settler, the valued tiller of the soil, set against his proverbial log cabin dwelling in the woods—although under major threat in Florida—would nevertheless become the most evocative image in the upcoming presidential campaign of 1840.

In addition to the issue of settlers, Taylor also looked at the breakdown of the army hierarchy as another prime reason for the protracted nature of the war. Specifically, he regarded the long-standing shortage of officers, including an insufficient number of "Medical Gentlemen" (physicians), as conclusive evidence for a host of maladies. Indeed, Taylor confided to Surgeon General Thomas Lawson that if an investigation was ever conducted by Congress into the reasons for the unresolved nature of the conflict, "many will have cause to blush for the Army, as it will be seen that one of the principal causes has been the difficulty to get officers to serve here in every department."[17] The dearth of line and staff officers, he predicted, would in due course result in the operational collapse of the entire campaign, a state of affairs that could only be corrected by a thorough reorganization by the War Department.

Instead of withdrawing troops from the territory for the summer, Taylor intended to defy convention by retaining this force to man the posts, although active operations were still suspended. He estimated that there were only "400 to 500 warriors dispersed in small parties" throughout the entire peninsula.[18] Even so, Taylor did not launch any large movements or participate in a major campaign during his first year of command. The War Department's approval for constructing the proposed military districts did not arrive until February 1839.[19] (Taylor later reduced the dimensions to eighteen square miles.) Even before this formal authorization, the construction of posts centered in the north central peninsula had already commenced. By mid-December, Taylor assured Governor Call that no other section of the country "was ever so well guarded as Alachua County" and only awaited the former white inhabitants to reoccupy the land.[20] It was, in essence, an occupation zone; yet Taylor failed to recognize that a minimum number of seasoned colonists was needed immediately if this scheme had any chance of working. Moreover, his assumption that twenty or twenty-five men stationed at each garrison would be sufficient to afford ample protection to settlers was unrealistic given the large wilderness tracts within each square. Adding yet another obstacle, all pioneers would be expected to erect pine-log stockades to protect their cabins and homesteads—a major detail not at all reassuring to those already wary of Seminole attacks.[21] Still lacking thorough knowledge of the territory, Taylor also presumed there were districts in the interior "sufficiently healthy to justify their permanent occupation during the summer."[22] Circumstances would later demonstrate how mistaken this conjecture was. In any case, none of the large-scale sugar planters, the majority of whom were left in financial shambles, planned to return, and no one had a clear idea of how many yeoman farmers remained or intended to start anew. (It is worth stating, however, that if such a broad defensive perimeter had been installed before the commencement of hostilities—fully manned and provisioned, together with armed settlers in place—it would have been a formidable presence. But that moment had long passed.)

The switch to a defensive posture and Taylor's reluctance to enlist the territorial militia as an active force did not sit well with white Floridians. The majority simply wished to expel the remaining Seminoles as rapidly as possible. An "inextinguishable fire of hate," as an anonymous letter writer phrased it, permeated the feelings of many whites. Deaths and injuries to family members as well as the destruction of their homes, crops, livestock, and entire savings brought about a new level of antipathy toward Native people. Although the initial carnage would have been far worse if it was not for Osceola's mediating influence (see chapter 10), blood had indeed been spilled, and an indeterminate number of settlers, including women and children, perished under horrific circumstances. The resulting mental trauma was profound, and the lives of many survivors were shattered. Hence the sympathetic stance of the Whig Party toward the Seminoles simply exacerbated preexisting hatred. Compassionate rhetoric was not only roundly denounced, but in more literate circles such remarks were relegated to "the canting sentiment of a false philanthropy" that was further viewed as circumventing "the holier and more sacred rights due our own race."[23] White inhabitants of all social ranks and political persuasions were united in furthering their own survival and looked upon Native people with the kind of ethnic and racial abhorrence that often surfaces in war. Accordingly, they constantly pressured the government to rid the territory "of the evil by which we are oppressed."[24]

Taylor began his command with fewer than two thousand regular troops and several hundred militiamen.[25] Most of Jesup's former force had been transferred out of the territory to oversee Cherokee removal, and concern for reining in costs also dominated in Washington. During the summer and fall of 1838, Taylor did not have an adequate number of men to mount any large campaign, even if he so desired, and Seminoles were again dispersed throughout the peninsula. A small band of "runaway" Creeks attacked and killed settlers in the Okefenokee Swamp region of southern Georgia, and similar tragedies occurred in the Tallahassee area, setting off fears of resurgence. Yet nothing of any far-reaching import surfaced, as most Seminoles remained hidden at this date. Taylor explained to his superiors in Washington that because of the nature of the country, "concealment is found to be more efficacious than opposition, and they [Seminoles] leave the climate to fight their battles, which certainly has proven more destructive to our troops than the rifle or scalping-knife"—a reference to rampant endemic disease.[26] In the meantime, topographical engineers began to survey the military districts, and after the start of cold weather Taylor ordered several unproductive forays into regions such as the Withlacoochee, Ocklawaha, St. Johns River, and Lake Okeechobee.

In January 1839, Senator Benton, apparently inspired by Taylor's efforts at reinvigorating a settler presence, introduced Senate Bill 160, "a bill to provide for the armed occupation of that part of Florida which is now overrun and infested by marauding bands of hostile Indians," an ambitious proposal that aimed to provide free land as well as material and financial support for prospective settlers.[27] "Armed occupation, with land to the occupant," Benton claimed, "is the true way of settling and holding a conquered country."[28] Benton may have irritated political opponents by his long-winded speeches and pronounced nasal twang, but he was still able to charm his supporters by his "flights of imaginative eloquence."[29] Any trace of lucidness, however, was often preempted by a type of magical thinking when it came to his much-venerated settlers. Benton's settlement hopes, for example, went against accepted wisdom, as most regarded any move into the interior as extremely dangerous. Indeed, as the senator's political opponent Henry Clay observed, it would be virtually impossible to recruit men "to enter a Country which has been the seat of War," no matter how much the government offered by way of financial inducements.[30] Benton's zealotry, however, was unbounded. He imbued scenes of settler domesticity with such gendered authority and homespun sentiment that he assumed that the combination of the settler's "implements of husbandry" along with "weapons of war" would be enough to repel Seminoles, as if these physical manifestations of white sovereignty possessed a kind of power to stupefy and compel Native people to withdraw on their own accord. "The heart of the Indian sickens when he hears the crowing of the cock, the barking of the dog, the sound of the axe and the crack of the rifle. They are the true evidences of the dominion of the white man; these are the proof that the owner has come, and means to stay; and then they feel it is time to go. . . . It is the settler alone, the armed settler, whose presence announces the dominion—the permanent dominion—of the white man."[31]

Seeking historical justification for this patriarchal fantasy (a vision seemingly devoid of women), Benton further claimed that this was the identical course followed ever since "the children of Israel entered the promised land," and it was similarly invoked during the Roman Empire and still continued in America. It was, after all, the preferred method whereby all the original colonies as well as such comparatively recent states as Kentucky and Tennessee were settled. The senator, however, faced congressional opposition from southerners who represented the interests of elite planters and wealthy speculators who bristled at the idea of giving away prime land to humble pioneers.[32] Indeed, Congress was unwilling to pass this measure until the end of the war when settlers became even more of a priority under a Whig administration.

MACOMB'S TREATY

Beginning in February 1839, leading congressmen attempted to persuade the administration to try another peace overture. Earlier state and congressional elections had established the mounting strength of the Whig Party, and new political coalitions resulted in an altered Congress, a body that was no longer as pliant, in terms of the war, as it was in the past.[33] In fact, both chambers approved a sum of $5,000 to cover expenses associated with this peace proposal. Information had reached Congress via Representative Everett that "if negotiations were entered into, the [Seminole] remnant now there would be content to retire within an ascertained line [in Florida]," a development that was strikingly similar to Jesup's earlier proposal.[34] The amount of money may have been small compared to the increasing war expenses, but the legislative intent was quite clear, and Van Buren was obligated to respond.[35] Under considerable pressure, Poinsett, in turn, appointed Major General Macomb to proceed to Florida to undertake this peace gambit. The general was a most improbable choice, however. For one, he had no prior experience with either the Seminoles or the Florida Territory. Second, he had spent the previous decade far from the field and in an exclusively administrative capacity as general-in-chief of the army. And lastly, this assignment would place the life of this chief executive in imminent danger, a needless risk given that any number of experienced individuals could have easily filled such a role. It may have been assumed that the remaining Seminoles, all living under dire conditions, would be suitably overawed by the presence of such an august individual, outfitted in an elaborate, full-dress uniform and accompanied by an imposing retinue—just as the country's most humble white citizens would be expected to act. The uniform of a major general was certainly extravagant: a cocked hat with ribbons, tassels, large yellow swan feathers, a brimstone vest (lemon-yellow), silk undergarments, blue and brimstone coat, golden epaulettes, sky-blue sash, and fine trousers, boots, gloves, and a sword knot—the very definition of an "eminent man."[36] But subsequent events would prove that no matter how grand the costume, appearances alone could not offset the bad faith consistently enacted by the army leadership and that deceitful ploys and artifice had created a surfeit of animosity. In any case, on April 5 Macomb arrived at Garey's Ferry (Black Creek) in East Florida—despite its stark isolation, the setting of the main army depot in the territory—in what may have seemed like an epic journey into the heart of darkness. (At this point, Macomb made a special effort to reassure Taylor that he would not interfere with his military authority.) Macomb was prepared to offer a major concession to the Seminoles: they could remain in Florida, below the Peace River in the west and the Kissimmee River and Lake Okeechobee in the east, if they agreed to suspend hostilities and remain only in the territory's southernmost region.[37] This offer followed Jesup's rationale in that the agreement was only conceived as temporary—a crucial point nonetheless kept hidden from the Seminoles. This approach also concurred with congressional leaders who saw no reason that the Indians could not provisionally inhabit a portion of the least desirable land, most of which would remain unsettled by whites for decades.[38] But this assignment was met with skepticism by officers in the field who not only thought it pointless but feared that events could go terribly wrong in any number of unanticipated ways.[39] Had not Jesup already muddied the waters and betrayed any preexisting trust by his treatment of Osceola, Micanopy, Cloud, Tuskegee, and others? The one-sided nature of communications between Washington and commanders in the field had perhaps reached its nadir—and was at least comparable to the start of the war—as government expectations did not match the reality on the ground. Still, Taylor did his best to facilitate what many deemed a fool's errand. He immediately ordered runners, consisting of friendly Indians, to spread word about a conference to be held with Macomb on May 1 at Fort King, with special mention given to the favorable terms. A contingent of recently captured Seminoles were similarly enlisted "to talk to those now in the swamps," and Macomb instructed Lieutenant Colonel Harney, then at Fort Mellon, to spur interest.[40]

After traveling by horseback to Fort King along with an armed escort and cognizant of the danger he faced—he had been warned that the Indians "would destroy anyone that might approach them with a flag"—Macomb encamped outside the fort and awaited news from the Seminoles (none of whom had yet showed).[41] On May 2, Taylor arrived with several of his senior staff in order to meet with Macomb. Such was the abysmal state of communications between the Florida command and the War Department that Taylor was entirely convinced that Macomb's true purpose was to replace him. Hence for this and other reasons, he asked to be relieved of command.[42] He cited several concerns, including a lack of cooperation from the Florida governor, the hostility of the territorial militia, the lack of a sufficient number of officers, and the continued outcry from the Missourians, who felt impugned. Taylor believed that only a court of inquiry could clear his name.[43] In a formal reply written three days later, Macomb assured Taylor that he had no other intention but to arrange a peaceful solution and then return to Washington. Furthermore, in a bid to forestall any additional uncertainty, he affirmed that a great injustice would be done to the service if Taylor were to resign and that no one else in the army could possibly match his exemplary contributions.[44] Macomb then forwarded this request to Poinsett.

At first, the Seminoles were justifiably wary of meeting with Macomb and spent time observing his camp from afar. Following repeated urging by the black interpreter Sandy and others hired by the army, on May 9 the first group of eight leaders arrived carrying a white flag and rode briskly toward the fort. In the lead was Halleck Tustenuggee, a youthful looking Miccosukee war chief, accompanied by other ranking warriors. Sprague, who was on the scene as Macomb's aide-de-camp, observed that they looked "miserably poor" and only had "ragged buckskin shirts to cover their nakedness." Though these men impressed observers by their self-possession and dignity, they still appeared, according to Sprague, as the most "wicked and demon-like set of savages" he had ever witnessed.[45] And so the tendency to relegate their foes—disheveled and battle weary as they were—beyond the realm of humanity continued, despite the fact that Sprague was personally sympathetic to the plight of the Seminoles and recognized the injustices they had suffered.[46]

Even in the face of the army's long and dubious record, this initial group appeared satisfied that Macomb could be trusted. Abiaka, much in keeping with his past conduct, pleaded illness and did not travel to Fort King; neither did Coacoochee or such rising figures as Tiger Tail and Holatta Micco (Billy Bowlegs). Despite these significant absences, the Indians eventually persuaded the general via their translators that Chitto Tustenuggee—who arrived at Fort King to head the Native delegation on May 17—had replaced Abiaka as the chief of all the Seminoles and that his word alone was sufficient. The fact that Chitto arrived with Harney seemed to add credibility to this claim. Unwilling to jeopardize the proceedings, Macomb accepted this abrupt transition, and the conference took place the following day with military fanfare, a finely orchestrated charade that included speeches that professed the government's outstanding intentions. Macomb nonetheless followed precedent by withholding the government's actual plans for Seminole removal.[47] Consequently, Native leaders were misled into thinking they had just won the most important concession of the war.

All the officers were now outfitted in dress uniforms, a rarity in the territory, and an elite brass band played a medley of martial music in close proximity to the improvised, circular "council house" that was erected. Macomb also had $1,000 to disburse as he saw fit, a sum that underscored the ritual smoking of the peace pipe as well as the hardy handshakes and whisky that was liberally offered. The scene was surely a welcome respite from a war footing, no matter how transitory. Such formality, in contrast, failed to assuage the hunger of the Seminole women and children who arrived and were in such a decrepit state that they covered themselves with old forage bags that had been collected in the vicinity of abandoned army posts.[48]

Macomb decided against any written agreement that would serve as a legal document, a departure from protocol that, given the withholding of information, would have been deemed a necessity. Native leaders gave their word to abide by the treaty, and two days before the council adjourned on May 21, Macomb was so entirely convinced of their sincerity and commitment that he issued a general order that declared the end of the war.[49]

The national press took the news with a bit more caution than they had with earlier claims, but the Fort King conference became a major story nonetheless. Conversely, Macomb's return to Washington lacked the grand ovations and laurels usually reserved for ending wars. In contrast, the reaction of Floridians was unequivocal in their rejection of Macomb's terms. The possibility that settlers would remain in proximity to "the murderers of our wives and children, and incendiaries, who, besides the destruction of our lives, have wasted our homes," declared an angry letter from the settlers of Alachua and Columbia Counties, would be "supposing something passing strange."[50] The fact that this situation would be temporary did not assuage feelings. It was further claimed that Chitto Tustenuggee was never recognized as the paramount chief and that Macomb had been duped. Chitto's underlying concern, according to one observer, was to recover his children and other relatives who were held prisoner at Garey's Ferry (a request that Macomb obliged). The same writer asserted that Chitto had spoken ill of the army and whites in general. After the conference, it was further claimed, he even spat on the silver peace medal that was conferred upon him by Macomb.[51] Whether the latter detail was true or was a fictional detail used to convey the anger and betrayal felt by many white Floridians may never be known. Having said this, any sense of righteous ire was not the exclusive purview of whites; feelings of hatred and revenge are, of course, reciprocal during wartime. By July, a letter from Poinsett that claimed that the treaty would "enable me to remove the Indians from the territory much sooner than can be done by force" was widely published in newspapers.[52] There can be little doubt, therefore, that literate Indian allies, including black interpreters and even Cuban arms suppliers, readily conveyed news of Macomb's deceit directly to the Seminoles.[53] Needless to say, gross underestimation of the intelligence-gathering capability of the army's adversaries was consistent throughout the war.

Abiaka, despite claims to the contrary, retained his position as war chief throughout this period, and thus Chitto was merely following orders by carrying out this ruse. Abiaka's initial reaction to Macomb's proposal was that it seemed too good to be true. After reports from the conference arrived, however, Abiaka's skepticism abated. Arriving at Fort Lauderdale under a white flag on June 22, this leader, who an officer described as "a tall, spare, old man, with locks as white as the crane feathers he wore in his girdle," gave his formal assent to the treaty.[54] To be sure, the thought of remaining in the southern part of the territory without any pressure to move west would have been judged a victory of historic dimensions. No matter how outwardly genial Abiaka may have seemed, however, he nevertheless adhered to an ultranativist worldview that regarded treachery with stringent contempt. It was clearly a matter of time before news of the government's actual objectives would arouse forceful retaliation.

Under the stipulations of the treaty, the army was required to establish a trading post along the edge of the Caloosahatchee River (the Sanibel Island region of southwest Florida). By midsummer this store, located near present-day Cape Coral, was up and running and had its own civilian proprietor and staff. A small detachment of twenty-six dragoons under the command of Lieutenant Colonel Harney was located less than a half mile away.[55] The store was in operation, and life progressed without incident; in fact, Indians arrived at Harney's camp every day to exchange friendly talks and, in a buoyant mood, continued to trade items with the sutler.[56] Any semblance to normality was soon to end, however. On the evening of July 23, Harney returned to camp after a day spent hunting wild boars and retired early to his tent—located about sixty yards from his men.[57] At dawn, an intense flurry of rifle fire, strident war whoops, and the frightening screams of wounded men reverberated throughout the encampment. Unprepared for an attack—the sergeant on duty neglected to order an armed sentinel—Harney, clad in night shirt and underdrawers, saw no other choice but to run to the river to save his life. Both he and another man located a canoe moored on the river and, despite the massive turmoil surrounding them, were able to safely drift unnoticed toward the mouth of the Caloosahatchee.[58] About eight other men also managed a similar escape by jumping onboard a sloop. The next day, Harney returned to inspect the carnage. Eighteen men were either captured or killed, and of the eleven that were found on the ground, most were terribly mutilated.[59] Several thousand dollars of merchandise, silver coins, liquor, gunpowder, and a large assortment of provisions and personal items were stolen as well as a quantity of Harney's prized Colt rifles.[60] It was discovered that a force of 160 Indians, divided into two groups, simultaneously attacked the trading post and the camp.

Blame fell squarely on the so-called Spanish Indians. This group was an enigmatic band of former Creeks who arrived in this highly secluded area sometime during the Spanish period and perhaps intermingled with the remaining native Calusa, although this latter claim has been disputed.[61] Later on, Spanish fishermen as well as runaway blacks and other "desperadoes" resided and married among them, and they established a tradition of living in small ranchos, or fishing villages of thatched huts, selling their dried, salted fish in Cuba, for which there was much demand.[62] Their leader during the raid was a chief named Chakaika. But Seminoles were also well represented and included Billy Bowlegs and Hospetarke, an individual who was related by marriage to the Spanish Indians and so was well positioned to influence their chief. While much evidence is lacking, the

Spanish Indians likely supplied arms and ammunition to the Seminoles via their Cuban connections but had, until this episode, refrained from fighting. What is more, the inclusion of Bowlegs and Hospetarke signified direct involvement by the Seminole war council. Indeed, a firsthand account by Sampson, a black interpreter who was present during the attack, confirmed that the raid was put into action by "a decree of the council, Sam Jones [Abiaka] and the Prophet [Otulkee Thlocco]."[63] The primary goal was to kill Harney and others who had been singled out for retribution (Harney had followed Macomb's instructions and thus implemented the government's subterfuge in his talks with Abiaka). This officer was exceedingly lucky, as two of those captured endured prolonged torture. One of these was Sandy, the same individual who had urged Seminole leaders to attend the conference but failed to warn them of the army's perfidious intent. He was tied to a pine tree and had numerous wooden splinters hammered into his body and then was lit on fire, while torches were also positioned at his feet. "In this way," Sampson recalled two years after the event, "it was five or six hours before he died."[64] Lingering and grisly torture (the pain of which can hardly be imagined) was rare among the Seminoles and was seldom reported while Micanopy was leader. Even so, this type of torment had ancient origins among the eastern Indians as a whole and was not only an expression of anger and retribution but also functioned to preserve order and power during wartime—warning others of the most dire consequences for any act of betrayal.[65] Sampson, it should be said, was saved only through the unwavering intervention of Billy Bowlegs but remained under close scrutiny throughout his capture.

Afterward, Abiaka feigned complete ignorance of this attack and then cast blame on the Spanish Indians as well as Sandy and Sampson for allegedly stirring up suspicions about Macomb.[66] Newspaper editors, as can be imagined, filled their columns with the cruelest details of what became known as Harney's Massacre, an episode that was portrayed as a hideous example of Indian barbarism. Unmentioned, of course, was any indication of government treachery vis-à-vis the most fundamental question of the war. Many blamed the army for incompetence instead. A correspondent for the *National Gazette* (Philadelphia) summarized the general mood rather well: "Thus has ended that precious and greatest of all humbugs—the 'Macomb Treaty'—entered into with a few vagabonds and a chief of whom nobody ever heard of."[67]

WAR CONTINUES

Following the killings at Caloosahatchee, Seminoles throughout the territory went on the offensive. On this occasion, they attacked in very small parties and focused on any returning settlers. Violence also continued in the Tallahassee region, which created heated denunciations from the territorial council and governor. In addition, because the troops did not entirely withdraw for the sickly season, the summer of 1839 was exceptionally unhealthy. The previous practice of abandoning posts for the summer had been costly for the army. These garrisons were inevitably burned by Native forces, which then required reconstruction of the posts when the army returned for the winter campaigns. But remaining during the hot months degraded the health of the troops. An unidentified officer at Fort Lauderdale summarized this moribund situation in a letter to the *Army and Navy Chronicle*: "We have nearly all been sick here already. . . . I believe I should have a greater chance for my life were a mill-stone tied around my neck, and I thrown into the sea, than to remain here this summer."[68] Taylor alerted the War Department that he expected a greatly accelerated rate of illness. He also reminded Poinsett that he had yet to hear back concerning his request for relief of his Florida command, adding that he would remain, if deemed necessary, but no longer than the upcoming winter season.[69] As events unfolded, a full-fledged epidemic took hold by November; malaria (aka "bilious fever") not only resulted in the deaths of highly valued officers and enlisted men but left Taylor very sick as well.[70] He was confined to bed for two weeks at his Tampa headquarters, where he was attended to by his wife and son-in-law (a physician).[71] Taylor's condition improved by December, the intended start of the winter campaign, but the epidemic had sickened an unprecedented 90 percent of his force.[72] Still, the general tried to make the best of the situation and, with only a limited number of available men, attempted to clear middle Florida of hostile Seminoles—a goal that was only a partial success. On February 26, 1840, having wrapped up most of his operations, Taylor reapplied to be relieved (Poinsett denied his first request) and expressed the hope that he could leave the territory by May 1.[73] Always a most reluctant commander, Taylor was finally granted his wish on April 22, 1840. Still weakened from his encounter with malaria, he took three weeks to put his affairs in order and then gratefully left the scene of what was for him an interminable series of frustrations.

Taylor was replaced by sixty-seven-year-old Walker K. Armistead, a brevet brigadier general who had already served intermittently in Florida. The least known of the Florida commanders, Armistead had been chief engineer of the army, served in other senior engineering posts, and then transferred to the Third Artillery before service in Florida. After acting as Jesup's second-in-command, Armistead spent time on court martial duty before he was called once more to Florida as commander, a post that he would hold for one year.

Several days after he assumed command and desirous of making his own mark on the war, Armistead wrote to Washington and stated his dissatisfaction with Taylor's system of military squares, which he saw as only affording the Seminoles a "confident security" that they would never be actively pursued.[74] Such a policy created dissatisfaction among officers and enlisted men, Armistead insisted, all of whom were anxious for more active duty. The commander wanted to strike a surprise blow against his adversaries before the full onset of summer and, unlike Taylor, was quite willing to utilize local militia in his plans.[75] Fort King was assigned as command headquarters (replacing Fort Brooke); its interior location allowed closer proximity to Native adversaries. Nine hundred troops were assembled at the fort and were then separated into nine separate divisions, each consisting of one hundred men. These divisions were then expected to operate independently.[76] If the men failed to engage the enemy, Armistead reckoned that he would at least have the satisfaction of destroying Seminole villages as well as their verdant crops. By the middle of summer, five hundred cultivated acres had been cut down and many villages were destroyed, along with "every species of property" in such former bastions as Wahoo Swamp, Big Swamp, Chocochatti, and the Oklawaha region. This caused angry reprisals from Coacoochee and others, who sought revenge through an escalation of deadly skirmishes and ambuscades.[77] In response to the few chiefs who were interested in coming in of their own accord, Armistead requested that Poinsett send $50,000 in gold or silver coins, as only "bribery," he contended, would assure that the Seminoles would fulfill their promises.[78]

The War Department decided on a novel concept for reassigning military responsibility in the territory, one that was influenced in part by Taylor's squares and past conflict with the territorial government. Fort King would serve as a geographical marker: the region north of this post was designated as the entire concern of the state militia, and the half that remained below was under the army's purview. As a result, white Floridians would have only themselves to blame for any mishaps, as the southern peninsula was devoid of any substantial settler presence. Furthermore, Armistead quickly set into place some major structural changes. He moved the army's general depot from Garey's Ferry to Palatka, a far more accessible location on the St. Johns River.[79] Similarly, he ordered the general hospital at Tampa to be broken up and all facilities transferred north to Cedar Key, although a clear rationale for this move was never stated.[80]

Much like Jesup, Armistead did not hesitate to enact a peace overture; in this case, a meeting was planned for two of the remaining principal leaders: Halleck Tustenuggee and Tiger Tail (Thlocklo Tustenuggee). The two men came in to Fort King in October, along with their warriors, but after weeks of seemingly fruitful negotiations all the assembled Seminoles inexplicably fled in the early morning hours on November 15, leaving Armistead bitter and disillusioned.[81] To compound his frustration, illness predominated among the troops, and the general could no longer mount a large campaign. Nevertheless, in a quickly worded general order he not only alerted his men that the armistice had ended and that operations had resumed, but in case "the enemy appear hereafter with the white flag, they are to be made prisoners."[82]

Two days before the break up of these negotiations, a letter from Poinsett arrived that not only granted the use of monetary incentives but again offered Seminoles an opportunity to remain in the lower part of the peninsula. The general was permitted to make a truce, allowing Seminoles who refused to emigrate to temporarily reside in the south, keeping to a boundary from just below Tampa in the west to New Smyrna on the east coast—a far larger area than Macomb's previous offer.[83] While sending out peace feelers, Armistead simultaneously enacted hostile actions elsewhere in the territory, contradictory movements that provoked the Seminoles and magnified mistrust. The general clearly failed to reconcile his personal feelings with orders from Washington. Moreover, he was now unwilling to use money as an incentive and failed to present Seminoles with an option to reside in south Florida.[84] It was at this moment that Ethan A. Hitchcock, now a major, returned to Florida and took up his post among Armistead's senior staff at Fort King. In his diary, Hitchcock termed the general's actions *abominable*, an assessment that only intensified over time. "If it were not that lives are at stake, I should look upon the whole thing as a farce."[85] Hitchcock also viewed Armistead as jeopardizing future communications with the enemy by imprisoning Seminoles who peacefully approached under a white flag. "No extremity of Savage War," he wrote, could justify such a violation.[86] What is more, instead of heeding the advice of his regimental field officers, Armistead appeared muddled and "puerile," and shielded himself behind a coterie of junior officers who were opposed to any peaceful advances.[87]

Throughout December and January, Hitchcock wrote letters to Poinsett and others in the War Department as well as to his friend and family relation Congressman John Bell (Whig), head of the Indian Affairs Committee and former Speaker of the House, and outlined Armistead's strange orders and overall confusion.[88] To rectify this situation, he suggested that the general be relieved of command and replaced by Colonel William J. Worth, who was also stationed at Fort King.[89] Worth was chosen not out of friendship—they, in fact, disliked each other—but because Hitchcock believed that the colonel, despite his "pride & conceit," had the determination to swiftly end the war.[90] Also during this period, Harney devoted his energies to exacting revenge for his humiliation at the Caloosa-hatchee. He assembled a commando-like band of fit soldiers who eschewed uniforms, donned Native guise, and, with the aid of a black guide who was intimately familiar with the region, pursued Chaikaka's Spanish Indians in the Everglades until the chief was caught in a surprise operation and killed.[91] Armistead permitted Harney to execute male Seminole captives by summarily hanging them—an especially abhorrent form of death that transgressed the core spiritual beliefs of the Seminoles. Harney nevertheless performed these executions with apparent gusto.[92] Instead of censure, Harney received the approbation of the president, a promotion, as well as ebullient praise in the press. Newly appointed Florida governor Robert R. Reid declared that "the severest means are the best means" and became incensed at the military's critics, mocking their "gentle strains of humanity and brotherly love."[93]

Following William Henry Harrison's election as president, Bell was appointed secretary of war and Hitchcock was summoned to Washington posthaste. He declined the position of commissioner of Indian Affairs that Bell offered him and instead was retained in the War Department as the secretary's principal war adviser. After much deliberation, Bell accepted Hitchcock's assessment of the Florida command and asked him to draft letters directing Armistead to step down and assigning command to Worth. Hitchcock further recommended that the colonel be given free range and then enticed with a brevet promotion to brigadier general if he proved successful in forging peace. Though he found fault in Worth's hasty disposition, Hitchcock was nevertheless impressed with his energy and determination. Besides, Worth had previously expressed full agreement with Hitchcock's views. The change of command was rapidly approved by the army leadership, with special commendation directed at Hitchcock for his selfless and "noble" choice, and implemented in May.[94] These behind-the-scenes events, though missed by historians, offer substantial insights into the direction of the war during its later years and, additionally, places Hitchcock as a significant player in the decision-making process.

One of the Whigs' prime political weapons was to lambast Van Buren for the exorbitant cost of the war—"millions on millions have been uselessly sunk in the swamps of Florida," decreed Horace Greeley's Log Cabin, the Whigs' major political organ during the 1840 campaign.[95] Henceforth, renewed exertions, short of increasing military action, were made to terminate the war. By the spring of 1841, active operations had been replaced by efforts to lure the principal chiefs with offers of money so they would come in with their people and be transported west—a tactic apparently approved by Hitchcock. These awards ranged from the astonishing sum of $8,000 for the notorious Coacoochee—who also agreed to recruit others to submit to removal—to several thousand for lesser-ranked chiefs. Lieutenant William T. Sherman privately remarked that this method of "buying them up" actually produced significant results and that the outgoing Armistead, as Sherman phrased it, "learned wisdom by the experience."[96]

Worth's tenure also continued for about a year, far longer than Hitchcock ever anticipated. Instead of implementing diplomatic moves, Worth decided to apply more conventional ideas, mostly in reaction to newly amplified measures by the Seminole leadership that created turmoil throughout the most populated portions of the territory.[97] The colonel therefore picked up where his predecessor left off—adopting aggressive moves during the summer months. (In the meantime, Hitchcock headed west to investigate massive fraud perpetrated by government suppliers who delivered spoiled food to the Seminoles and other tribes who had been transported to Indian Territory.[98]) Acting on his own initiative, Worth decided to refocus on the Cove of the Withlacoochee. Three separate columns entered the Cove, where they eventually demolished the camps of Tiger Tail, Halleck Tustenuggee, and others. Predictably, and in less than a month, nearly a quarter of Worth's five thousand men took ill and were confined in hospitals, presumably sickened by malaria.[99] At the same time, the colonel complied with congressional directives to reduce expenditures and thus dramatically curtailed the number of civilian contractors throughout the territory. He also encouraged the return of settlers, providing them with arms and ammunition, and, whenever possible, the full use of abandoned military garrisons.[100] The Everglades was also subject to multiple incursions. Between February and April 1842, US Navy lieutenant John McLaughlin led the so-called mosquito fleet, composed of specially built flat-bottom boats as well as canoes that penetrated the massive swamp region. While McLaughlin's forces never encountered Abiaka, the naval presence, which also included army troops, sent a robust message to the Seminoles that they could no longer remain in safe isolation. In doing so, a distinctive type of riverine warfare developed that had never before been attempted by the navy.[101]

DENOUEMENT

By February 1842, Worth decided that any continuation of the war would be futile, especially in light of the fact that only an estimated two hundred or three hundred Seminoles, including families, still endured in small bands. Three months later, Winfield Scott, who was appointed general-in-chief following the death of Macomb, consented to Worth's proposal, and the newly appointed secretary of war John C. Spencer ordered that hostilities be brought to a close.[102] Despite these developments, Hitchcock, now working directly under Spencer, felt betrayed by the confidence he initially placed in Worth. Indeed, the colonel failed to deliver on his promise of a diplomatic resolution and aggressively pursued the Seminoles instead. Thus, he succeeded, in Hitchcock's view, in needlessly extending the conflict at an excessive cost in lives and money.[103] Hitchcock was not alone in his reproach. Captain John McCall, while dutifully following Worth's orders in Florida, nevertheless adjudged any aggressive movement as "worse than useless" because it appeared to negate any promise of a peace overture.[104]

On May 12, President John Tyler presumed there were only 240 Seminoles left in the entire territory (the actual number was perhaps twice that), with no more than eighty warriors, and so the military would be redirected from a war footing to protecting settlers.[105] In response to the administration's claims, South Carolina senator William C. Preston (Whig) dryly observed, with ample justification, "that this was about the fortieth time that they had been told that the Florida war had ended."[106] Yet he had to admit that in this instance there was little question that hostilities had finally concluded. Without any formal agreement with Abiaka, Worth declared the end of hostilities and spread word among those Seminoles who had outlasted the war and refused remuneration that they would have to restrict themselves to the area formally delineated in Macomb's treaty. On August 14, the war was officially closed, and Worth, per Hitchcock's original proposal (and much to his personal chagrin), was promoted to brigadier general.

In retrospect, Armistead's and Worth's reinvigorated campaigns, in combination with the policy of providing large sums of money, helped spur even the most intractable of Native leaders into accepting removal and resulted in considerably fewer Seminoles in the territory—even while extending the conflict. Even so, Abiaka, Otulkee Thlocco, and Billy Bowlegs kept themselves secluded in the south, despite the fact that Worth made it known that Abiaka could personally expect up to $10,000—an undreamed-of fortune, especially within a frontier context.[107] In August, the commander tried to formalize the cessation of hostilities as best he could, holding conferences at Fort Brooke, which Billy Bowlegs attended, as well as Cedar Key, where Tiger Tail gave his assent—although his hesitance to carry out these commitments eventually led to his forced capture and deportation (like Jumper, he also died while in transit to Indian Territory).[108] None of the other remaining leaders, most notably Abiaka, signed or consented to a peace agreement.[109]

On August 15, Worth devised a way to bolster what would otherwise have been a rather hollow declaration of the war's end. An elaborate memorial, replete with monodies to the dead, pyramid monuments, military bands, and somber dirges, was held on the grounds of the army barracks in St. Augustine. Prior to this event, the remains of 165 bodies were exhumed from their battlefield graves in the interior, reverently covered, and placed on a train of wagons that transported them to the more "civilized" locale of the former provincial capital.[110] The remains included sixty of the seventy-four officers and surgeons who perished, plus all of Dade's command and those "several non-commissioned officers and privates who fell under peculiar circumstances of gallantry and conduct."[111] There was never any intention to reinter each enlisted man who perished, and so the total represented a fraction of those still left in unmarked graves. Yet the transference of these bodies from the frontier to a permanent military memorial was unparalleled in the army and thus rife with symbolic import. Not only did it serve to bolster nineteenth-century notions of a good death, endowing the fallen with heroic virtue, but this rite of remembrance seemed to assure that future war dead would similarly benefit.[112] Moreover, the reception of these remains in St. Augustine was itself deemed redemptive. "Gathered by their companions . . . to rest amid the habitations of man and civilized life," this innovation was judged by both political parties as altogether just and proper.[113] "The melancholy wail of music was heard in the distance," as the *Niles' National Register* described the scene. "The bright glitter of arms was seen glancing among the deep green of the wood, and the wagons covered with the stars and stripes, containing all that was of the honored dead, moved slowly onward. It was indeed a brilliant, a melancholy spectacle."[114] Rounds of musketry were fired each half hour from every army post in the territory.[115] Symbols of grieving, of nationalism, and of commemoration all coalesced in an attempt to place a tangible end to a lengthy and contentious struggle. The country had often raised "a cry of horror," as the *North American Review* attested, and endured years of humiliation while wasting "the life-blood of the nation" in an apparently futile cause.[116] The proceedings not only promised to add a sense of finality, but an unlikely social obligation had been forged, one that linked war's aftermath with those who "were immolated on the altar of their country," as a presiding minister put it.[117] Standard glorification of either the war itself or a single military champion was bypassed—heroism was instead awarded collectively, a conceptual shift that has evaded scholars who have looked to the Civil War for comparable innovation. (Three pyramid monuments—five feet in height, crafted of local coquina stone and originally finished in plain white stucco—stood atop the underground burial vaults and can still be seen today in St. Augustine.)

The army gradually retired their operations and numerous wooden forts were either left to decay or the building materials and contents freely given to white settlers who utilized the lumber, iron nails, and other resources for their own

Army soldiers pay homage to the Second Seminole War dead in St. Augustine, FL (circa 1890s). Private collection of the author.

purposes. But Taylor's ambitious plan for a settler-colonial resurgence was doomed as soon as Armistead entered the scene. Indeed, for reasons that will be demonstrated later, the Florida Territory was never destined to follow the Kentuckian or Tennessean model. And so, the complex network of trails that connected the farthest outposts with the military command, as well as the former battlegrounds, reverted to wilderness. In addition, a cohort of thieves, vagabonds, and other dangerous "ruff, scuff of civilization" prowled the interior and further aggravated the lives of those settlers who remained.[118]

Following so many years of conflict, the territory's Native inhabitants had almost been completely vanquished. Only a portion of the most intractable warriors and their families remained, and by doing so they managed to fulfill a longstanding prophecy. For many years, medicine men and various "prophets" had consistently foretold that Native people would ultimately find peaceful refuge within the southern tip of Florida, called *ichi bolan,* or "the nose of the deer."[119] Hence, Abiaka had relentlessly focused on what he believed to be their final sanctuary.[120] Despite the terrible losses endured, he must have surely been relieved to witness even the slightest fulfillment of this vision. The seed of cultural renewal had been planted. In this respect, Abiaka became heir to Tecumseh's quest for a place of refuge and revitalization to be founded east of the Mississippi. From this perspective, their severe reduction in numbers and the deaths or removal of honored chiefs, shamans, warriors, elders, spouses, children, and other loved ones as well as the forfeiture of sacred sites could at least be viewed with the knowledge that Seminoles had retained a foothold in the peninsula and by doing so defied the most prominent military force on the continent.

PART III

Health, Medicine, and the Environment

CHAPTER 8

Malarial Sword and Shield

As has been demonstrated, an immense sense of disillusionment as well as fear and anguish regarding the war extended far beyond the actual battlefields. From the start of hostilities, graphic correspondence that depicted grim scenes of death and infirmity were sent home from officers in the field and inspired newspapers to describe the wilderness posts as plague-stricken graveyards, a state of affairs that seriously impeded morale and made a lasting impression on the national scene.[1] To be sure, endemic disease, malnutrition, mental trauma, and other facets of ill-health have always beleaguered armies and have accounted for far more deaths than casualties in battle. Hence of the 1,466 recorded fatalities among the regular army during the war, 1,138 were noncombat related—most of which were caused by disease.[2] Among the much smaller naval force, there were sixty-nine deaths. Once again, the majority died from illness. (Comprehensive records regarding the thirty thousand militiamen were not kept, and there is even less known about the Seminoles.) When one considers that there were rarely more than several thousand troops stationed in Florida at any one time, such figures gain new perspective.[3] Even so, scholars of the war have traditionally emphasized human determination and agency, and so issues of health, largely detached from humanity's control during the first half of the nineteenth century, have been virtually ignored.

This section posits that malaria and other diseases affected the course and conduct of the war to a level heretofore unrecognized. Summer fevers, as we have seen, were dreaded to such an extent that the risk of illness far outweighed the considerable threat posed by Native forces and necessitated troop withdrawals during each sickly season (between May and September)—a convention that was only ignored toward the latter half of the war.[4] This on-again, off-again approach stalled any sense of momentum and prolonged an already lengthy conflict. As will be shown, malaria epidemics also impeded subsequent white settlement of the territory—the primary object of the war. The various strains of malaria had a synergistic effect on other illnesses; individuals may have survived infection only to succumb to further illnesses due to anemia and immune suppression. The overall impact was thus far worse than any single malady or the mortality from malaria alone.[5] Moreover, psychological trauma surfaced as a significant problem among soldiers, another neglected topic that adds needed clarity to the war years. On a far broader level, in addition to being a violent clash between the US military and Native forces, the Second Seminole War should also be understood as a contest between ecological forces and Jacksonian expansionism. In addition to the obvious fighting ability of the Seminoles, one also has to factor the heretofore obscure role of anopheline mosquitoes and the transmission of a virulent strain of malaria known today as *Plasmodium falciparum*, as well as other forms such as *P. vivax* and *P. malariae*, in any discussion of this conflict.

Malaria began to be treated during the war with high doses of quinine sulphate in 1839, the first large-scale use of such amounts by the US Army.[6] The efficacy of this practice had been established five years earlier by the French army in Algeria, and news of this development appeared in American medical journals.[7] Afterward, the surgeon general's office—noting the experiment's encouraging results—claimed this drug regimen "would revolutionize the treatment of fever in this country."[8] Until this time, there was considerable apprehension regarding any use of quinine, even in the raw form known as cinchona or Peruvian bark, and its use was not universally accepted by standard authorities.[9] Quinine did not cure malaria but rather suppressed disease symptoms and prevented paroxysms (severe chills and fever). This drug emerged as the army's single most effective medication, despite the fact that its usefulness as a preventative was still unknown.

In addition to malaria, the prevalence of diarrhea, dysentery, cholera, and hepatitis were also noted, and there were periodic outbreaks of yellow fever within port towns such as Pensacola, Key West, and St. Augustine.[10] The health of many soldiers who died of serious illnesses was often compromised by foul drinking water, poor diet, and lack of personal hygiene as well as outbreaks of measles and mumps, which often ran rampant in cramped frontier outposts. Young men who hailed from rural northern villages or farms were most susceptible to illness, as they had been totally isolated from the viruses and parasitic protozoa that pervaded the South. Sickness was so prevalent that officers were routinely furloughed to the North in the hope that they would recover from myriad indispositions before returning to the theater of war. Indeed, an extraordinary 108 officers were on medical leave by 1841, absences that added even more to a profound leadership gap.[11]

Seminole fatalities, including black warriors among them, may never be determined. Yet as far as overall health was concerned, these fighters had a substantial edge. Not only did they benefit from a distinct resistance and tolerance to mosquitoborne illness (which may have included a genetic or heritable component, especially among blacks who benefited from sickle cell trait), but they were acclimatized to heat and humidity, could live off the land, and could draw upon their own farm-grown produce during periods of relative calm.[12] They also relied on Indigenous remedies that undoubtedly afforded relief from a variety of conditions. Compared to US troops, many of whom were either recent foreign immigrants recruited in the North or, to quote General Jesup, "the dissipated [alcoholic] laborers of the cities," Native forces held a distinct advantage.[13] One soldier, a recent Irish immigrant, was so convinced of the Seminoles' physical superiority that he noted in his diary that "they have no lame, no blind, no asthmatic or consumptive people" and further deemed the warriors he observed as "the finest shaped men existing."[14] The enemy inexplicably breathed the same air and experienced the same miasmatic swamps but thrived nevertheless. As environmental historian J. R. McNeill has aptly noted, the role of anopheline mosquitoes in similar military engagements throughout the world should be envisioned as a metaphorical sword and shield. Viewed within a biocultural perspective, these insects were lethal in relation to the invading army while simultaneously shielding Indigenes from sustained attack.[15]

Given a lack of data concerning the various states' militias and a similar absence of evidence regarding the illnesses and mortality of Native combatants, this section necessarily centers on the experiences of the US Army, an institution that fortunately kept a modicum of records during its tenure in the Florida Territory.

"HEROIC" MEDICINE

The territory's reputation as an unhealthy destination was established long before the outbreak of the war. At the time of the previous British administration during the eighteenth century, malarial fevers were a major problem that afflicted soldiers, slaves, settlers, plantation managers, and colonial governors alike.[16] This situation restricted colonization and justified leaving most of the peninsula to the Seminoles. Dying or suffering from disease was likewise a grim reality during centuries of Spanish dominion. Ironically, according to medical historian Gerald N. Grob, malaria was most likely introduced into the region by the Spanish in the sixteenth century.[17] Irrespective of the origins of this disease, individuals from elsewhere in the Spanish empire considered the prospect of serving in the army in La Florida with trepidation, fearing sickness and Indian depredations, a situation that dramatically curtailed enlistment.[18] This same sense of anxiety and prevailing dread, mostly aimed at the unidentified forces that struck down newcomers with special intensity, also manifested itself during the war. Army physicians, like their earlier colonial counterparts, were unprepared when faced with the region's virulent diseases.

Physicians and the general public alike interpreted physical ailments through the peculiar perspective of early nineteenth-century medicine. It was thought, for example, that diseases originated from decaying matter (pythogenesis) and were then transmitted to people by a noxious, invisible vapor called miasma.[19] Antebellum-era doctors relied on an antiquated system of ideas and associations that was actively traced to Hippocrates (400 BCE). For instance, the ancient axiom of sustaining a balance of the four humors—blood, phlegm, black bile, and yellow bile—was a mainstay of medical training. Empirical evidence frequently proved secondary to deeply entrenched theories and speculations, and a dense, esoteric medical language obscured the profession's actual dearth of knowledge and also kept the uninitiated at bay. The supposed effects of geography and the weather on individual health held a prime position among doctors and laypersons. One's physical constitution was thought to be under threat by any number of environmental stresses as well as the consequences of personal behavior. Health therefore demanded humoral equilibrium and moral constancy; excesses of any kind had to be avoided—a construct that was certainly antithetical to actual wartime experience.[20] Germ theory and other breakthroughs associated with modern medicine remained decades in the future, so the actual root causes of disease was still an enigma—although theories and causal assumptions proliferated. Certain army surgeons in Florida, such as Joseph J. B. Wright, who rose to distinction during the Civil War, had become acutely aware that "speculations and not facts" garnered much of the profession's time and energy.[21] In most cases, the best that doctors could do was to attend to symptoms. In the United States, a particularly aggressive form of "heroic medicine," pioneered by Dr. Benjamin Rush (1746–1813), became the standard during the Florida war, just as it had been during the War of 1812. The practice of bloodletting, purges, blistering, cupping, enemas, and the liberal administration of such substances as calomel (a mercury-laden purgative) reflected Rush's dogma. "The physician's most potent weapon," according to historian Charles E. Rosenberg, was his ability "to 'regulate the secretions'—to extract blood, to promote the perspiration, urination or defecation which attested to his having helped the body regain its customary equilibrium."[22] Any notion of allowing the body to heal itself was fervently rejected, as was any cautious or exclusively palliative approach.[23] Doctors who attended to soldiers during the Florida campaign and who left written records revealed a consummate zeal and faith-based devotion to Rush's methodology—an orientation that would fall out of favor by the Civil War.[24] Of course, by following conventional practice, which included the application of highly toxic substances, these physicians often exacerbated the condition of patients already seriously ill. So convinced were they of the efficacy of their methods, however, that bad outcomes were routinely attributed to other factors.

Medical science was generally regarded as deeply engulfed "in cloud-like obscurity," to quote a leading medical journal, and those who attended the most reputable medical schools yearned to see the profession rise in equal stature to the physical sciences.[25] Widespread lack of training as well as aptitude was reflected in the high failure rate among applicants who sought a career in the army medical corps.[26] But those who passed their oral examinations and were then admitted were well-read and possessed a sufficient level of education to qualify as officers and gentlemen. Many persons with inferior schooling and little or no medical background could also claim to be physicians, as licensing requirements were nil, and so the army actually engaged in one of the few selective processes at the time. Jacksonian ideology, it must be stressed, denounced elitism in any form, and there was popular resistance against a professionalized, self-interested medical class.[27] (Given the actual paltry state of medicine, such antagonism was not entirely undeserved.) Even though army surgeons may have constituted an elite group within their profession at this date, they still could not claim much economic or cultural significance. Doctors, for example, may have held commissions in the army and were considered staff officers, yet they did not possess actual military rank and, similar to chaplains, existed outside the official hierarchy (a situation that was corrected in 1847). Toward the end of the war, surgeons' uniforms were redesigned to include an aiguillette, an ornamental braided cord, derided by Surgeon General Thomas Lawson as an insulting "piece of tinsel on one shoulder." This "demi-military dress," as Lawson phrased it, was an affront to those who were undergoing significant hazards in Florida and assumed ultimate responsibility in matters of life and death. After some struggle, Lawson succeeded in persuading the War Office to assign standard gold epaulets to physicians—a much-coveted "badge of distinction" that provided a substantive morale boost to those under Lawson's command.[28]

While medicine differed little from previous wars, East Florida, especially during the opening of the campaign, presented logistical difficulties that had never been encountered before. As the least accessible region along the eastern seaboard, without roads, towns, or ports of any consequence—other than the small, former provincial capital of St. Augustine—army hospital facilities were less extensive than the War of 1812. Indeed, surgeons in Florida, many of whom became ill themselves, were continually rotated among numerous, temporary wooden forts that were often without medical facilities of any kind and had a reputation for filthy conditions.[29] If a garrison happened to have a small infirmary or post hospital, they were basically log cabins with puncheon floors (split logs with the flat side facing upward).[30] Doctors who attended to patients in such circumstances were described by one contemporary as constantly "pressing the pulse of languid sickness" and breathing in "the pestiferous exhalations" of crowded wards.[31] General hospitals, however, were established on a different scale. Geared toward the sickest patients, they were typically positioned near the Atlantic or Gulf Coasts, as sea breezes were judged far superior to the "miasmatic" air of the interior forts. Far larger than the typical two-room post facility, the dimensions of the general hospital at Cedar Key, for example, were 160 by 30 feet—a size that could accommodate more than one hundred patients when necessary.[32] In addition, there were general hospitals at St. Augustine, Picolata on the St. Johns River, and Tampa Bay, where an additional facility on Mullet Key at the mouth of the bay was used as a convalescent hospital and featured sea-bathing for those who were ambulatory.[33] A female nursing corps had yet to evolve, and so male stewards, following standard practice, served directly under doctors. These enlisted men were literate enough to read prescriptions and were judged sufficiently astute to administer medications, perform bloodletting, clean and dress wounds, prepare surgical instruments, and monitor patients, and were expected to become familiar with basic anatomy and Latinate terms—all accomplished by on-the-job training. Male nurses and attendants were all under the authority of stewards.[34]

Hospital care was primitive, to be sure, even when judged within the standards of the day. As far as food was concerned, however, patient meals exceeded the quality of regular rations, which were normally quite deficient. The latter often consisted of hardtack (biscuits that were routinely infested with insects), pickled beef or pork, and black coffee and sugar—all transported to the backwoods at exorbitant cost.[35] In contrast, general hospitals had their own cooking staff and access to fresh seafood and game, and maintained vegetable gardens.[36] Herbs such as chamomile were regular staples, and the ill, when not subjected to an enforced diet of gruel, could also expect fresh bread, tea, and chocolate.[37] As one might expect, morphine and tincture of opium (laudanum) were administered to ease pain, and despite the fact that germ theory was nonexistent, distilled spirits, diluted with water, was effectively used to cleanse infected wounds. Prior to the introduction of large quantities of quinine sulphate midway through the war, physicians prescribed finely ground Peruvian bark, mixed with wine or brandy, for fever patients to drink. But this concoction was exceedingly bitter and difficult to swallow, and because the medicinal properties of raw bark fluctuated widely its actual potency was problematic.[38] As also occurred during previous wars, limb amputation—a high-risk procedure that was endured without anesthesia or antiseptic technique—was ubiquitous. The specter of gangrene convinced most doctors to forego more cautious approaches, and given the absence of family members or other patient advocates, the decisions of surgeons were final.[39]

Patients who suffered from chronic physical ailments in Florida were placed in an altogether different category. Those who failed to respond to treatment at the general hospitals were evacuated by ship to facilities at Fort Monroe, Virginia, and either Fort Hamilton or Fort Columbus hospitals at New York Harbor. In 1841, 129 new Florida invalids arrived at the latter facility during June and July alone, despite warnings of overcrowding.[40] Joseph P. Russell, the physician in charge at Fort Columbus, previously appealed to the War Department to transfer all future patients to more convenient southern posts, such as Fort Moultrie, South Carolina, where the climate was judged to be far more amenable to recovery. Russell noted that the influx from Florida was often subjected to constant drenching by bilge water during rough winter sea voyages as well as being left unattended in cabin hammocks—with some forced to wallow in their own waste. These invalids were in such a vile and decrepit state upon arrival that Russell worried they would not only adversely affect morale at the fort but also frighten off potential recruits and deter anyone from considering assignment to Florida. His plea was only partially heeded. In response, Secretary Poinsett ordered patients to be retained in the Florida hospitals during the winter and then transported to the North in the spring.[41]

The fact that poor health lingered even after treatment with quinine obviously reflected the severity of malarial infection. But any duration longer than a few weeks suggests that *P. falciparum* may not have been involved. The most likely culprit in this instance was *P. vivax*, generally considered a less pernicious variety, although recent research has placed this broad assumption into question. *Vivax* parasites cause multiple attacks, since these organisms stay dormant in the liver for up to two years after being bitten by a female *Anopheles* mosquito, while *falciparum* malaria causes a single, often severe attack within a few weeks and does not reoccur if the person is spared reinfection.[42] Significantly, Russell described a group of sixteen Florida survivors at Fort Columbus as "old soldiers," men who had reenlisted ten or more times previously—suggesting that they may have been over fifty years old.[43] Because it is also known that venereal disease, including syphilis, was present among patients at this facility, such infections coupled with advanced age would place this cohort at much higher odds of becoming gravely ill or dying from *P. vivax*. The incidence of morbidity and death due to malaria increased with each decade of life (within nonimmune populations), and bad outcomes were even more likely when nutrition was poor.[44]

An additional and seldom mentioned strain on army resources was the precarious situation of several thousand white settlers. Forced to flee their homes during the outbreak of war, they naturally sought the protection of fortified villages or army posts. Garey's Ferry (Black Creek) and the interior villages of Newnansville and Micanopy, both surrounded by log stockades, were among the primary destinations. Because refugees faced certain starvation, the federal government directed the army to provide rations to survivors. This subsistence steadily increased from ten thousand to thirty thousand rations per month by 1837.[45] Those tasked with distributing provisions tended to view this responsibility as an unfair burden, the equivalent of an additional army to feed. In time, "the Suffering Inhabitants of Florida," as they were officially called, became near pariahs in the eyes of the army. The situation at Garey's Ferry was particularly grim. Extended families of ten or more persons, having lost their homes, possessions, and livelihoods, had no other recourse but to take shelter in makeshift huts and crude lean-tos. Illness flourished under these overcrowded and unsanitary conditions, and constant exposure to the elements further lessened disease resistance. In addition to malarial fevers, measles and cholera also predominated.[46] Upward of eight hundred refugees, two-thirds of whom were sick, ultimately converged among the numerous ramshackle huts along the sandy banks of Black Creek—undoubtedly a prolific mosquito breeding ground.[47] Ninety died during a six-week span in the summer of 1836.[48] Desperation thus created one of the largest, albeit chronically ill and destitute, communities in East Florida during the first years of the war.[49]

Malaria was unquestionably the most far-ranging and potentially lethal illness that all individuals faced during this period. Although deadly outbreaks of yellow fever periodically affected the populations of port towns such as St. Augustine, Pensacola, and Apalachicola, most of the army was fortunately spared. Unlike malaria, yellow fever was transmitted by the *Aedes aegypti* mosquito, a species whose restricted flight range kept it from infesting the remote interior regions of the peninsula. As the yellow fever arbovirus was not endemic to North America, transmission was only possible via infected crew members or passengers who had been in regions such as the Caribbean and arrived onboard ships that docked in Florida ports. Infected persons then unwittingly spread the virus to the local *Aedes aegypti* mosquito population, at which point it often caused considerable devastation, especially among newly arrived persons with no prior immunity.[50] Because the bulk of the US military was spread across the uninhabited portions of the Florida peninsula during most of the year, troops were spared mass fatalities from this particularly lethal virus.[51]

"THE MISERY OF SOLDIERING": MENTAL TRAUMA

One of the best contemporary sources regarding everyday life during the Florida war is the journal of John Bemrose, a former pharmacist's apprentice from England who served as an army hospital steward during the opening of the war. Bemrose was stationed at Fort Drane during the harrowing summer of 1836 and recorded his impressions in a straightforward and unaffected manner. While working at a makeshift field hospital, the steward found himself amid a terrible outbreak of "country fever," undoubtedly *P. falciparum.* "I can truly say that the scene around me was an awful sight, such as few can imagine," Bemrose later wrote. "Is it my turn next? we used to think." Shortly thereafter, Bemrose indeed became stricken with fever at a time when many were dying within days of contracting malaria. Placed in a ward with up to twenty of the worst cases, he experienced an episode of delirium in which he believed that a troop of dragoons had suddenly become engulfed in "a flame of fire." After regaining his senses, Bemrose found that seven of his comrades were lying dead in the same room. "At first we suffered much," he confided much later. "But as the misery around us became an hourly companion always before us, we gradually became harder and [lost] feeling. Such constant association blunted the finer qualities of our nature. Alas! It is so, and perhaps wisely ordained, for were it otherwise no strength of body or mind could bear up. All would become either idiotical or insane."[52] The psychological strain of serving in the war was thus greatly compounded by the prevalence of a particularly lethal form of malaria. Such infections caused delirium, depression, cognitive deficits, and lethargy, and were an insidious and seldom acknowledged problem as it countered cultural expectations of unwavering strength and heroism under fire. Some men dealt with this illness, as well as the anxiety of battle, simply by staying intoxicated. During the Battle of Micanopy, for example, a lieutenant observed a drunken enlisted man pointlessly "marching up and down in bravado until some redskin put a bullet in him," although the soldier escaped serious wounds.[53] Other men, however, were susceptible to severe mental breakdowns and needed to be physically restrained. Bemrose recalled a peculiar case of a young soldier who became so gripped with fear during an Indian attack at Fort Drane, especially when the jarring sound of war whoops was at its highest, that "he became quite a maniac" and after being tied to the hospital floor and given forced enemas died soon after of mysterious causes.[54] Afterward, Bemrose assigned this case as "death from fright," although another more plausible explanation would be falciparum malaria. Psychosis and delirium frequently resulted from falciparum, and mortality was very high.[55] And, of course, the army's own treatment regimen, which included painful blisters to the head, almost certainly hastened this person's demise.

Some may have appeared less outwardly affected but were depressed nevertheless. During the same period, Colonel John F. Lane, an officer still in his twenties who complained of "great distress in his head," suddenly placed the hilt of his sword on the ground while he was alone in his tent and calmly ran the point through the corner of his eye into the brain, killing him instantly. Since Lane was considered one of the army's rising young stars, news of his death traveled widely. A surgeon who was attached to Lane's regiment remarked that he had acted strangely for several days and that he was in an agitated state. Moreover, "[h]is face was flushed, gestures rapid, voice stridulous and eyes restless."[56] His fellow officers assigned the cause of death to "a fit of insanity produced by brain fever"; any taint of moral failing was therefore diminished.[57] (In contrast, according to the harsher view of Andrew Jackson, Lane had merely acted "rashly and without orders" in his previous movements against the enemy and in consequence to his inability of "finding and defeating" Osceola surmised that humiliation alone had driven him to the act.[58]) In addition to Lane's passing, Lieutenant Thompson Wheelock, another West Point graduate who had gained a gallant reputation that summer, also committed suicide. Soon after returning to his quarters at Fort Defiance, Wheelock used a pistol to fatally shoot himself through the mouth. Like Lane, Wheelock also exhibited peculiar behavior, and, in addition to fever, he actually began talking incoherently before his final act.[59] Given the symptoms described, as well as the fact that both incidents occurred during a raging malaria epidemic, one can easily surmise that neurological complications from malaria were almost certainly a major factor in both cases and that combat stress exacerbated the situation.

Individuals who happened to survive their initial bout with this disease frequently discovered that their mental and physical abilities had been drastically reduced—a circumstance that could understandably lead to depression. This may have been the case with Captain William S. Maitland, who "in a fit of derangement," as the newspapers reported it, threw himself from the stern of a boat and drowned while arriving on medical leave at Charleston Harbor.[60] Maitland had survived both the aforementioned epidemic and the Battle of Welika Pond, and was subsequently wounded at Wahoo Swamp but ironically ended his life just when his much-sought-after leave was under way. Far more common than suicide, however, were furlough requests from officers who suffered repeated malarial infections and desired nothing more than to depart Florida. Captain R. B. Lee, who earned accolades during the Seminole offensive, explained his condition to General Jesup in terms the general was doubtlessly most familiar: "I was taken sick last August in the interior, and have been more or less indisposed ever since that time, being constantly subjected to attacks of intermittent fever."[61] As a result of these repeated bouts, Lee pessimistically assumed that his once-robust constitution had been irreparably broken and that he would never recover his health.

Often in tandem with the effects of malaria, post-traumatic stress disorder was, of course, also present. PTSD was certainly not recognized as a specific diagnosis, but the ill-effects of war on soldiers' psyches had been recognized for millennia.[62] Early nineteenth-century doctors referred to such concepts now known as dissociation, depression, hyperarousal, social anxiety, and other states currently associated with PTSD by other names. Nostalgia, melancholy, phrenitis (aka "phrensy"), monomania, and delirium were terms that were used in connection with the mental debilities of soldiers, as well as the ubiquitous and stunningly ill-defined "brain fever."[63] The latter was believed to be caused by an immense shock to the nervous system, which could result, in the worst instances, in sudden death or suicide. The diagnosis of brain fever, it should be noted, was not necessarily linked to an actual elevated body temperature, and so its determination was primarily subjective. Because a truly psychological perspective did not emerge until World War I, traumatic symptoms were interpreted as having physiological underpinnings—thus the necessity for aggressive intervention in the case of Bemrose's "maniac," treatment that included cathartics and blisters "to bring the excitement to the surface."[64] This regimen, it should be said, was actually the preferred treatment for "brain inflammation" and not mania per se. In classic mania, following the authoritative claims of Benjamin Rush, bleeding was the only accepted course.[65] Rush had convinced most of his colleagues in the United States that the root of all madness resided in the blood vessels of the brain; thus, only bleeding could correct this imbalance.[66] The aim in all cases was to place the body back into physical equilibrium, a task much easier said than done.

At this date, there was no uniform system of care that was directed at the severely disturbed or those labeled "lunatics," and no government facilities yet existed for mentally ill soldiers. There were, however, private mental hospitals that cared for the well-to-do, most of which followed the benevolent "moral treatment" course of therapy that was in vogue, kindness and rest being essential features. Carefully organized environments that stressed cultural activities, reading, handicrafts, fresh air, and physical exercise were thought to be just as central to patient well-being as medical intervention.[67] The poor, alternatively, were more often chained in basements or placed in similarly horrendous circumstances in jails, almshouses, or in state asylums.[68]

In Florida, troubled individuals who nonetheless remained quiet and nondisruptive were likely to be assigned to noncombat duty. A diagnosis of mania (or "raving madness") was the only mental disqualification recognized by the army, but as yet no records have surfaced that could account for the number determined to be afflicted.[69] More common are personal accounts of men who succeeded in overcoming severe trauma but nevertheless remained depressed. After enduring five months of illness, one officer admitted that not only was he "a wreck in mind and body" but that his future aspirations were greatly reduced—a state of mind exacerbated by his "conscientious scruples" and deep moral questioning of the war itself.[70] Those who survived their term of duty and returned home were left to their own devices. Many exhibited "shattered constitutions" and embittered feelings, and, as one congressman noted, "retired from the gaze of him whose diadem they had saved."[71] The mind could easily shift into a dissociative state during battle, but such conditions could also linger long afterward. Responsibility for the social withdrawal of veterans was often attributed to the failure of communities to meet basic social obligations. Similar to what later occurred during Vietnam, veterans did not always receive the requisite hero's welcome and ritual celebration—a situation likely exacerbated by antiwar rhetoric.[72] As the Florida war coincided with the emergence of mass-circulation newspapers, ethically based arguments that placed Native people as innocent victims of Jackson's expansionist policies struck a chord with an increasingly literate public. The noble savage motif then employed by popular authors served as a model for Whig journalists and resulted, among other things, in an almost cult-like celebration of the Seminole war leader Osceola and thus deepened any preexisting disillusionment.[73]

The seemingly unending barrage of Whig criticism weighed heavily upon those indoctrinated to uphold the highest ethical code, and many saw themselves as "stigmatized."[74] Young officers especially felt that their profession no longer merited a feeling of respect by the country as a whole.[75] Regional affiliations also came into play, as northerners tended to view the war as only benefiting southern interests. Be that as it may, despite a dearth of official records related to psycho-

logical trauma in Florida, one can extrapolate based on a high incidence of desertions among enlisted men (16 percent per month in 1842), an unprecedented
number of officer resignations (two hundred resigned between 1835 and 1837),
the rampant problem of alcoholic excess, reports of self-inflicted injuries, attempted
suicide, and other observations by contemporary diarists and conclude that most
soldiers were, at the very least, deeply unhappy with their lot.[76] "Depressed morale"
was indeed recognized as a leading symptom during the war by the office of the
surgeon general.[77]

Malaria has ceased being a major threat in the United States, and so the
magnitude of the physical suffering that this disease once left in its wake may not
be readily appreciated. As it happened, the Florida war became one of America's
most ill-fated and disease-afflicted military campaigns. When the presence of malaria is combined with inadequate diets, dirty and overcrowded living conditions,
unfamiliar and "poisonous" terrain, continual stress from Indian attacks, and heat
and humidity, then one is better able to appreciate the toll on the human psyche
as well as the body's resistance to infection. Wars are won by the vigorous and
able-bodied, and because of the extremely harsh conditions of daily life it became
obvious that manly courage alone was of slight value, a conviction that eroded
any lingering notions of martial gallantry. Furthermore, medical treatment itself
became a major source of misery. "The terrible character" of medicine during the
early nineteenth century, as one physician recollected during the 1870s, caused
patients to be "tormented continuously . . . by unutterable nausea of the stomach,
the torments of physic, the suffering from blisters, and the terrible thirst [from
mercury-laden medicines] which cried to heaven for relief."[78] Mercury poisoning
resulted in loss of teeth, severe bone lesions, and liver damage, and patients were
routinely left in filthy bed clothing, unwashed and foul smelling. This period has
quite rightfully been compared to the last vestiges of the medical dark ages — a
standard of care that may seem almost incomprehensible to modern sensibilities.

Although the use of quinine sulphate grew exponentially during the war, its
effectiveness was limited, as it was never employed as a prophylactic. Even so,
quinine was the primary reason that some soldiers were able to return to duty following an attack of malaria. Without this single drug, an already-bleak outcome in
Florida would have been even worse. Even so, its usage presented negative reactions as well. Large amounts of quinine (up to three times the modern dosage)
often reached toxic levels, causing what was called cinchonism: noted as ringing
in the ears, blurred vision, nausea, diarrhea, and even sudden death triggered by
anaphylactic shock. Despite such incidents, army physicians remained elated by

quinine's overall success. Word of this achievement aided in the drug's proliferation among both civilian doctors and the general population, and led to its use during the Mexican-American War.[79]

Military historians have often concluded that the army failed to retain much institutional memory of the Florida war; consequently, it has been assumed, this protracted campaign had little or no practical effect on later engagements. As in subsequent guerilla-style conflicts, such as the Philippine Insurrection (1899–1903) and Vietnam (1965–73), the army tended to overlook rather than learn from its involvement with irregular warfare.[80] (To what degree the Florida war influenced individual decision making, such as Winfield Scott's prescient avoidance of the malarial lowlands soon after his invasion of Mexico, may never be known with certainty.) Be that as it may, within the Army Medical Department at least, the war paradoxically resulted in a more efficient organization. Unlike the War of 1812, the department had been placed on a permanent footing; as a result, a fixed chain of command helped avoid the internal squabbles and supply shortages that plagued earlier campaigns and did so in the face of daunting challenges. Despite the actual abysmal state of health and medicine in the territory, by the close of the war the Medical Department's organizational structure possessed an unmatched competence. Widely noted publications from the surgeon general's office, particularly those that dealt with the efficacy of quinine sulphate as well as a plethora of statistical evidence, reinforced the view that matters of health were quantifiable—a task best done by the government. This new "scientific" orientation, according to the American Medical Association, promised to add a new level of dignity and authority to the profession as a whole.[81] Moreover, governmental reliance on the empirical observations of army physicians, the selective testing of candidates for appointment in the service, and the improved standing of surgeons as staff officers constituted notable first steps toward the eventual professionalization and consolidation of power of medical practitioners in the United States.

CHAPTER 9

Land of Darkness and Shadows

Throughout the war, the connection between landscape and illness became so intertwined that it seemed as if the military had taken on nature itself, with all the pessimism and futility that such a view necessarily evoked. John Reynolds, a Democratic congressman from Illinois, sadly concluded: "Our troops in Florida were compelled to overcome enemies to which the Indian force was insignificant, and even contemptible. They were forced to war against the elements, the swamps, hammocks, and sickness of the country, and in the summer were constrained to yield the field to malignant disease against which human power cannot contend. . . . The puny power of man must yield to the laws of nature. No matter if the man be the greatest of his race, and has command over the greatest military nation that ever existed, as was the case with Bonaparte; yet he cannot war with success against the laws of Heaven."[1] The emotional strain of contending with such immutable and supreme laws—in addition to fighting Native adversaries who appeared to become one with the natural world—was severe indeed. As Major James D. Elderkin, a veteran of the Second Seminole War, the Mexican-American War, and the Civil War, observed in retrospect: "Of all my experiences of hardships in three wars that which I experienced in Florida was the worst."[2] Elderkin described a heightened anxiety in which each step into the region's dense hammock areas was reckoned to be his last; the enemy hid unseen in thickets, entirely camouflaged, and waited for the best moment to shoot and kill. The Seminoles' native land had been turned into a weapon of war. The realities of guerilla combat, what Elderkin called "those terrible times of savage warfare," could prove overwhelming for untrained soldiers who found themselves in an unfamiliar wilderness that was itself deemed extremely maliferous. The very sounds one heard throughout the day and night could not be trusted, for a single passing bird call or wolf cry could in actuality be a signal from the enemy "to join in an onslaught that would end in a massacre or death-struggle of extermination for one side or another."[3] In effect, Elderkin differentiated between the emotional *terrors* of an unseen but deadly foe, as was often the case in Florida, and the all-too-visible *horrors* of conventional warfare.[4] While the mass carnage of the Civil War, for example, may easily conjure images of traumatized soldiers, less obvious is the abject terror induced by an all-pervasive, concealed enemy who was seemingly at one with nature—a scenario that especially predominated during the latter half of the war.

Since dominion over the land was the primary impetus at work in the years before and during the Seminole war, it is essential to come to terms with this landscape. Unlike the scenes of other Indian conflicts in America, such as the western plains or the desert southwest, Florida has presented a more challenging task. As has been shown, the territory contained many regions that differed substantially from one another. But, of course, whatever ecological features that may have flourished during the early nineteenth century may not have survived into the present. Currently, for example, the Alachua district is devoid of the old growth forests that were once a major distinguishing feature. Yet the canopies of the former lowland hammocks were once so profuse that even the midday sun failed to penetrate. Hammocks also contained thick underbrush, composed of "scrubs, shrubs, vines, and parasites of all kinds," which resulted in a "matted mass, impervious to the eye"—a natural refuge for Seminoles and their black allies throughout the war.[5] These ecosystems differed substantially, however, from the more open and dryer pine barrens that also pervaded the north central region. Like much of the eastern United States, the Florida interior has undergone massive ecological transformation.[6] While ancient woodlands have mostly disappeared, some protected areas such as Paynes Prairie still remain; its current manifestation as a wildlife preserve, however, has dramatically altered over time. The massive flocks of exotic birds mentioned by William Bartram no longer blot the horizon (hundreds of thousands of birds in Florida perished annually during the late nineteenth century, along with their eggs and nestlings, as their feathers headed to milliners worldwide) and certain predators, like the once-ubiquitous black wolf, are extinct.[7] Urban growth, excessive hunting, years of timber harvesting, and modern farming techniques have inalterably transfigured the region.[8] In short, the land the original settlers yearned to "subdue" has born the ultimate fruit, so to speak, of this very impulse. As a result, effort must be made to envision the contested terrain, or the real context will be missed. The mise-en-scène, in other words, has to be imagined for the war years.

The frontier abounded with exotic fauna that most newcomers had never encountered: wolves, panthers, alligators, large snakes, and myriad insects. What is more, misty and foreboding swamplands, moss-covered hammocks, and other terrain were judged through antebellum sensibilities and thus considered vile and repugnant, further intensifying fears. Since medicine and folklore linked outside forces to all manner of deleterious effects—geography, climate, bodies of water—even the wind and seasons of the year were conceived as directly affecting personal health (and thus the flow and actions of the humors).[9] As a result, mind and body were fundamentally linked to the physical environment.[10] Not even the simple act of breathing was taken for granted, given the abundance of invisible miasma, "where every breeze is charged with the minister of death," as a young militia officer confided in his diary.[11] The environment was considered so unhealthy that army physicians were convinced that even those who were lucky enough to escape illness could not entirely avoid its deleterious effects. A leading doctor once warned the surgeon general that symptoms would afflict anyone in such a situation: interrupted sleep, poor appetite, slow-healing wounds, and general malaise. "The system will be attacked from time to time by the offshoots of the diseases preying on others around him, though he will not be sick . . . but the whole constitution seems in some degree to labour under the influence of malaria."[12]

Most soldiers were complete strangers to such a dangerous, alien environment, and, consequently, even the most innocuous moment, if given a minimum of imagination and an excess of boredom, could take on weighty overtones. The monotonous drone of frogs and alligators during the night could sound ominous, especially when many weeks went by without any fighting or even the slightest sign of Indians. This cacophony seemed "to re-echo from one extremity of the territory to the other," an officer wrote from Fort Lauderdale, "seemingly saying 'this is our dominion, not man's.'"[13] Over half of the Florida Territory at this date consisted of wetlands; so outsiders were hard-pressed to understand why this land would be worth fighting for at all.[14] The terrain could be easily dismissed as both uninhabitable and unproductive, a terra incognita best left to alligators. This interpretation was entirely antithetical to the army's Seminole adversaries, who were so physically and spiritually attuned to the natural environment that they often compared their own bodies to the trees, their limbs as branches and "the water of the land" as their lifeblood.[15] With this in mind and accepting the fact that malaria disproportionately affected the army, one can still appreciate that much of the soldiers' misery was self-induced—an unintended product of their cultural upbringing and a deep societal prejudice against any true "howling" wilderness, a predilection that can be actually traced to the ancient Greeks and Romans.[16] And since all soldiers had to additionally contend with the genuine possibility of dying, this final emotional burden became even weightier. Indeed, many were quite shaken at the prospect of being buried and forgotten under such supremely forlorn circumstances. Clearly, the state of medicine had not advanced enough to offer solace or hope for the seriously ill, so a few looked to a dark, poetic fatalism that flourished during this era. "The arrows of Death are already in the quiver," noted a Tennessee militia officer as he witnessed many of his hometown acquaintances fall ill and die soon after reaching the peninsula. "The bow of the archer is bent—and it is truly an awful reflection to think how many poor fellows must inevitably fall beneath the fatal stroke!"[17]

Remarks from senior army officers are often notable for their denigration of the entire territory and stood in stark contrast to the settler community, who viewed the same landscape, prior to the war, as a kind of Promised Land—ripe for conquest. General Jesup adjudged the territory as fit only for Indians: "Even if the wilderness we are traversing could be inhabited by the white man (which is not the fact) . . . would the [war] be worth the cost?"[18] His informed opinion was that it was not. Subtropical forests and wetlands were considered to be unlike any other place in the South. Hammocks were so impenetrable, another ranking officer complained, "that an Indian who gets perhaps ten feet in them is not to be seen afterwards, and cannot be overtaken."[19] Special note was often given to the fact that General Jackson halted at the Suwannee River during the First Seminole War; supposedly an acknowledgment of the futility of venturing into the dreaded region.[20] Faced with "unmitigated suffering and privation, without the least possible expectation of fame or glory," General Scott once suggested that a bounty of 160 acres be offered to each man who enlisted, but stipulated that this should not be Florida land: "that would be a fraud."[21] Officers who were compelled to officially defend the conduct of the war failed to mention fertile regions such as the Alachua and Tallahassee regions; the year-round growing season; the once-prolific stocks of cattle, horses, and hogs; or techniques such as "girdling," whereby settlers had begun transforming hammocks into farmland and where abundant crops grew with little effort.[22] The army leadership's negative assessment (as well as their blatant omissions) can therefore be seen as central to a simple defensive rationale: if the land was not only insurmountable but truly valueless, then the war itself was entirely misplaced—and thus all failures could be more easily absolved.[23]

It should come as no surprise that the military's disparagement of the region was matched by an equally dismissive attitude toward the settler community as well. The abilities and courage of local militia volunteers were frequently maligned. And, as John Sprague paraphrased Zachary Taylor, Floridians had become corrupted by "the great amount of money" that circulated as a result of the war. Thus, according to this perspective, any effort to end hostilities was expected to be subverted by these "dependents and plunderers upon the government."[24] Furthermore, army personnel could not fathom why anyone would choose to live in such a remote and unforgiving backwoods environment, and, as is usually the case, the poorer and more uneducated the settler, the more liable they were to mockery. Poor whites or "crackers" from the piney woods were especially subject to contempt. Conversely, the prevalent settler outlook viewed the army, particularly foreign recruits who heralded from a host of European countries, as the exogenous "other." The motivations of outsiders, unlike the presumed righteousness of the settler collective, were thus highly suspect.[25] These "good for nothing . . . scourings of other countries," as one Newnansville resident complained, were nothing more than "brandy-drinking" sluggards.[26] Indeed, drunken raids by US soldiers on local homesteads resulted in major losses of property and intensified mutual antipathy. Settler marginalization continued into the twentieth century and also managed to infiltrate Florida historiography. This tendency was the converse of the hyper-romanticizing of settlers that typically marked other regions of the North American–Spanish borderlands, especially Texas.[27] For Texans at least, settlers were not the banditti who were so despised by Spanish colonial officials but heroes in a righteous quest.[28]

Perhaps no other army officer personified Reynolds's description of the Florida campaign as a futile "war against the elements" than Lieutenant Colonel Harney. Although Harney's aggressive maneuvers in the Everglades and his adoption of guerrilla-style tactics are well known and even admired by some, his scorched-earth policy toward the land itself (as well as the animals that dwelt there) has only recently come to light. In the spring of 1839, Lieutenant John Phelps was stationed at a remote camp near Fort Lauderdale and, as usual, detailed his daily experiences in his personal journal. Phelps was unique for an academy-trained officer in that he never dreaded or maligned the wilderness; rather, he was often deeply moved by the intrinsic beauty of his surroundings and spent time reflecting on the flora and fauna of the countryside. It was thus with much distress that he described the ruinous behavior of Harney and the members of his dragoon company while they spent their idle time in various nihilistic pursuits. "The country is burning wherever Col. Harney's men have set their feet," he wrote in

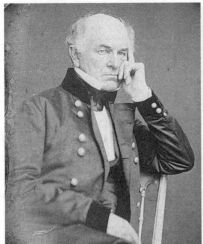

A study of opposites: Ethan A. Hitchcock and William S. Harney, both seen here as major generals during the Civil War. Prints and Photographs Division, Library of Congress.

great agitation. All wildlife, including bald eagles, became their indiscriminate prey, "so that this Eden where animals delighted in full confidence, is now desolate, filled with smoke, and resembling those regions the first view of which so astonished Lucifer." For no other reason than pursuing destruction for its own sake, Harney appeared to relish these pointless exercises of warring against the elements, leaving Phelps barely able to contain his revulsion. "Hail! Horrors! Hail! and thy profoundest hell. Prepare to receive thy new possessor."[29] One week later, Phelps's estimation fell to even lower depths when he witnessed the colonel "amusing himself" as he stood by two porpoises that he had lassoed by the tail and left stranded on the beach. After killing one animal and cutting it up into pieces, "he threatened the other with the same fate," as if to prolong and relish the torture.[30] Such sadistic acts are reminiscent of the conduct of psychopaths. Confirmation of this actually arrived five years earlier, when Harney escaped mob justice and the hangman's noose in St. Louis after disturbing details surfaced regarding his murder of a slave woman named Hannah—a person who Harney had just "inherited" as part of his wife's dowry. Harney whipped her so severely and for such a prolonged period of time (allegedly for losing a set of keys) that she died after the third day of continued thrashing that left her entire body horrifically mutilated. This revolting episode was well documented but never became part of Harney's military record, despite its widespread infamy in St. Louis and publication in the abolitionist press.[31] When one considers that Harney, a nonacademy appointee, earned the dubious distinction of becoming the first officer to hang Seminole prisoners and then, some fifteen years later, established another cruel benchmark by taking part in the mass slaughter of Sioux Indians, without regard to gender, age, or fighting status, then a long-term pattern becomes apparent.[32] In addition, allegations circulated during the Florida war that claimed the colonel had raped Indian girls at night and then summarily hung them the next day.[33] It is no wonder that Ethan Hitchcock, after being awarded the rank of brigadier general, chose to resign his commission rather than be placed under Harney's command in the western plains—"a man," he wrote in 1855, "without education, intelligence, or humanity" who nevertheless found his niche in the US Army.[34]

A NEW EL DORADO?

As has been demonstrated, when the war drew to an end the final exultant step in settler-colonialism—that is, an influx of industrious settlers—had yet to take place. But without a significant body of pioneers, the very purpose of Indian removal and thus the war itself would be fatally undermined.[35] Sensitive to the need for encouraging settlers, most Florida newspapers, fearing dire economic consequences if the truth regarding the high incidence of disease was made public, intentionally minimized or entirely omitted any indication of deadly epidemics.[36] Benton's efforts on behalf of settler-colonialism came to fruition via passage of the Armed Occupation Act, legislation that offered 160 acres of land located in the nonsurveyed portions of East Florida to persons willing to build homesteads, farm, and defend their property in return. Settlers were required to act as a paramilitary force to keep the remnant of Seminoles at bay and were also obligated to reside on the land for five years before being awarded title. By the fall of 1842, newspapers began to report that new arrivals had begun crossing into the territory to seek their fortunes. Promoters such as Florida congressional delegate David Levy characterized the territory as a veritable land of dreams. "To the wealthy planter," Levy wrote in the *National Intelligencer*, "Florida is eminently inviting. . . . But to the poor and the moderate in circumstances, it is, beyond comparison, the paradise of earth."[37] In his self-appointed role as territorial booster, Levy also quoted at length from a report issued by the office of Surgeon General Lawson that asserted that "no extraordinary mortality has been experienced in Florida."[38] In fact, he claimed, the health of soldiers in the territory differed very little from any other region in the United States. Lawson fixed the mortality rate from all causes during the first four years of the war at a meager 6.1 percent—an incredible assertion given that the actual figure, as is well known today, was (at the very least) 14 percent.[39]

Whether Lawson's statistics were intentionally skewed or the result of human error is, of course, difficult to prove. His interpretation certainly appeared to vindicate the government's settlement plans, but these conclusions did not go unchallenged. Indeed, they sparked a national debate featured in a series of articles published over a seven-month period in the *National Intelligencer* in 1843.[40] These columns highlighted the divergent views of two anonymous doctors. The first, "A Physician," was a St. Augustine doctor in private practice who upheld the surgeon general's sanguine assertions and declared that malaria in Florida was actually of a much milder form than any other state or territory in the union.[41] (Actually the opposite was true. The most lethal form of malaria, *P. falciparum*, was more prevalent in subtropical and tropical regions such as Florida, where temperature, rainfall, and relative humidity were high.[42]) As a member of the local business community, this doctor evidently felt considerable pressure to quash doubts concerning health risks and to extoll the region's supposed healthfulness instead. Alternatively, "Physician Second," an anonymous army surgeon with extensive experience during the war, took vigorous exception to these dubious claims and utilized testimonials from army doctors and regular officers as well as the surgeon general's own statistics to refute what he believed were extremely dangerous and potentially deadly distortions. In the end, this individual quite deftly defended his position and even paraphrased bible verses in order to bolster his conviction that "East Florida (and all Florida) will be what it has always been, a 'land of darkness and shadows, where pestilence walketh at noonday.'"[43]

The publicity that ensued presented a rare challenge to efforts to remake Florida's miasma-laden image into a kind of earthly paradise. At the same time, stories began to circulate concerning the calamitous outcome of new arrivals. A small Jacksonville newspaper, showing a rare determination to report the truth, recounted an especially grim scene: "Crops overgrown with weeds, and lost to all use; one-half of their families dead and broken down — dispirited in heart and feelings" and "sorry in soul" to have ever immigrated.[44] "This is no fancy picture," responded "Physician Second" in the *National Intelligencer*. "It is the language of reality."[45] The Baltimore *Sun* also carried the same disquieting news. "Disease and death have been busy with their brute creation — horses, cattle, [and] hogs have fallen victims. Many settlers, who are able, are deserting the country and returning to their former homes, while those who are unable to get away are recruiting themselves for another summer's conflict with their terrible enemy, the fever."[46] The number of men, women, and children who either perished or who fled the territory will perhaps never be known. Ironically, anopheline mosquitoes, particularly the *quadrimaculatus* species, preferred to breed in stagnant pools of freshwater that were heated by direct sunlight, and so their numbers actually increased by the clearing of trees, the digging of wells, the planting of crops, and other activities that were part and parcel of settler life.[47] Scientists now realize that epidemics are inevitable whenever a group of nonimmune persons enter a region where malaria is endemic—a situation that can evolve into one of the most deadly forces in nature.[48] News of these catastrophic circumstances was overshadowed, however, by the sheer quantity of accounts that attempted to remake the region into a "New El Dorado," as one headline claimed.[49] Despite this marketing campaign, in the end only between 2,000 and 2,500 settlers—an estimate that includes entire families—were motivated to stake their claims under the terms of the Armed Occupation Act, far short of the expected infusion of 10,000 newcomers.[50] To be sure, arrivals from nearby Georgia and from other portions of the territory, such as Middle Florida, were better able to endure endemic diseases. But despite reckless professions from national figures and the considerable temptation of free land, outsiders still harbored a basic distrust of this region. By 1853, a St. Augustine newspaper lamented that Florida was "shunned by settlers in search of a home," and that only 98,000 people, nearly half of whom were slaves, inhabited an immense territory of thirty-eight million acres. In fact, Florida remained the least populated southern state until the mid-twentieth century.[51]

Aside from Lawson's problematic claims, scant evidence has surfaced from this period that could shed more light on the diseases of the Florida war. Lawson actually continued his one-sided campaign on behalf of the area's "salubrious" qualities as late as 1855, when he wrote a letter in wholehearted support of now Senator David Levy Yulee's construction of a transpeninsular railroad, an ambitious project that would connect the east coast of Florida with the Gulf of Mexico.[52] Data gathered during the 1870 US census, however, presented a hitherto overlooked finding. Mortality tables demonstrated that Florida actually led all other states in the proportion of malaria deaths to its population—the exact opposite of Lawson's blithe hypothesis.[53] This alarming fact certainly not dissuade the state of Florida from insisting, in a pamphlet distributed to lure settlers, that "the incoming settler may rely upon it that he is no more liable to suffer from fever in Florida than in any other section of the country," and that malaria only presented in "the very mildest forms."[54] The next census of 1880 nevertheless listed malarial fever as the foremost cause of death in the state.[55] Physicians during the early twentieth century, now cognizant of the etiology and transmission of malaria, determined that 50 percent of Florida's inhabitants were infected with this disease—causing severe, multigenerational health issues. In some areas, estimates rose as high as 80 percent, comparable to certain countries in present-day sub-Saharan Africa.[56]

Malaria also presented a grave threat to pregnant women, causing spontaneous abortions and also disproportionately affected children's health. In demographic terms, the disease is responsible for dramatic declines in population.[57] An uncommon investigation into the types of malaria prevalent in the South that was conducted during the 1930s, a period when this illness was still endemic in Florida, demonstrated that P. *falciparum* was the most lethal strain (responsible for 40 percent of deaths), followed by P. *vivax* (21 percent), and P. *malariae* (2.5 percent), with the remainder listed as unspecified.[58] These figures confirm that *vivax* was far more deadly than commonly assumed and also verifies that both *falciparum* and *vivax* malaria were well established. This same study also pointed out that north central Florida in particular was one of the most lethal areas in the South. In 1934, for example, the mortality rate of 67 deaths per 100,000 was only equaled by the coastal regions of South Carolina.[59] (Such a figure would place these districts as some of the worst in the world by current criteria.) Not until the 1950s did malaria cease being a substantial health hazard, a breakthrough that happened to coincide with Florida's population boom.[60] This advance was made possible by extensive usage of the pesticide DDT post–World War II and following previous decades of organized "mosquito warfare" that resulted in the draining or filling in of wetlands, the application of thin layers of either kerosene or oil on standing freshwater ponds and marshes, and the introduction of a minnow species (*Gambusia affinis*) that fed on mosquito larvae.[61]

Given the prevalence of this debilitating disease during the war years, it was perhaps unavoidable that a uniform military strategy never emerged and that many perceived the conflict as both honorless and futile. Merely surviving their allotted time in Florida and escaping illness and a painful death was often deemed victory enough for both officers and enlisted men.[62] Malaria not only adversely affected the operational and strategic plans of military commanders but prohibited the government from adequately populating the territory. Newspapers may have remained eager to promote fanciful depictions for public consumption, but word of mouth from war veterans, including thousands of militia members from throughout the United States, as well as the ill-fated settlers who managed to return to their home states undoubtedly interjected a far more sobering reality.[63] America's privileged sense of Manifest Destiny was indeed diminished by Florida's failure to fully transform into an agrarian settler state during the nineteenth century. Malaria surfaced as a potent microbial sword and abruptly halted national ambitions to remake a region "that reeked with the steam of ten thousand swamps," to quote a prominent medical journal, into a settler paradise.[64]

PART IV

The War and "The National Mind"

CHAPTER 10

Osceola as Settler-Colonial Icon

To those who wish to obtain a perfect idea of the "head and heart"
of the Seminoles, we would refer them to Mr. Catlin's gallery.
Oceola breathes upon his canvas. It is the happiest likeness I have
ever seen. His spirit has joined its brethren in the land of the
shadows. His inglorious capture will descend to future ages.

Morning Herald (New York, NY), February 23, 1838

The struggle against the Seminoles and the controversies that ensued made a lasting impression on the American psyche and created a significant opening for partisan political advantage. Perhaps no better example exists of this far-reaching influence than the press's divergent treatment of Osceola. His capture and untimely death while in prison at Fort Moultrie created a wave of sympathy that was quite extraordinary, especially given that he was actually among the country's most resolute foes. Even so, for many Euro-Americans, Osceola—a name derived from the Muscogee (Creek and Seminole) *asse yahola*, or "black drink singer"—stood as the virtual embodiment of a tragic hero and hence anything that could detract from this stature was deemed particularly repugnant.[1] A host of writers and journalists placed him amid a pantheon of Native American champions that included Black Hawk, King Philip (Metacom), Pontiac, and Tecumseh—figures who appeared to fulfill the ideal of the wise, stoic, and noble red man, a stereotype popularized by author James Fenimore Cooper. Osceola was even compared to Napoleon by an admiring "scribbling fraternity."[2] But for many others, particularly frontier Democrats, Osceola's demise was judged a fitting end for a thoroughly disreputable character, "the most inhuman butcher of men, women and children."[3] Whether the warrior's capture and death elicited staunch approval or anger reflected one's political and regional affiliations. Thomas Hart Benton, as one might surmise, was unequivocal in his contempt for Osceola, who he judged as a coldblooded killer of innocents.[4] But the artist and chronicler of the American Indian, George Catlin, a Whig and native Pennsylvanian who spent time at Fort Moultrie while on commission to paint the famed warrior's portrait, perceived things differently. As Catlin expressed himself in a widely circulated article, Osceola was nothing less than "the fallen Prince and Hero of Florida."[5]

This chapter explores the meaning behind America's oddly divergent response to Osceola. Historians, such as biographer Patricia R. Wickman, have largely bypassed the ambiguities of Osceola's public persona in an effort to arrive at a more accurate rendition of his life story.[6] The perspective of this chapter, however, takes an opposite path. Journalistic embellishments certainly pose special problems, yet the language used to frame the debates that centered on the war nevertheless reveals larger historical processes. Scholars have long demonstrated the subtle power of *media framing*, a term used to describe "the context or narrative theme through which the story is told," to influence public opinion.[7] Previous studies of the war, however, have not benefited from such a perspective. It should thus be stressed that this extended conflict coincided with two major developments on the national scene: (1) the emergence of the Whigs as a second party, one whose prime goal was directed at defeating Jacksonian opponents, and (2) the parallel rise of mass-circulation, penny newspapers in major northeastern cities, most of which held strong political allegiances and depended on sensationalism to advance stories and increase profits.[8] For the first time, journalists began to be regarded as key players in swaying public opinion; newspaper editors in large metropolitan areas suddenly vied with elected officials as power brokers.[9] By 1840, there were fourteen hundred newspapers in the United States, and the combined annual production of newspapers and periodicals nearly tripled compared to the previous decade. News dissemination was augmented by the fact that articles were often picked up and reprinted by other papers as part of a national exchange system that flourished before the telegraph.[10] Moreover, the Washington *Globe*, the democratic administration's newspaper of record, increased its power and influence by a far-ranging association of state and county newspapers. Articles reinforced party doctrine, and during the Florida war presented the military campaign in as patriotic a light as possible—which included accentuating Seminole "outrages." Indeed, the war era served as a testing ground, especially for the nascent Whig Party, for political marketing and image making on a scale never before seen. Osceola's contradictory persona as both hero and red devil was a direct result of this early convergence of mass media and partisan politics—the birth of mass culture in the United States.

Typically, there was an urban versus frontier sectional divide in journalistic narratives regarding the Seminole campaign, with the most vehement criticism of the war emanating from northeastern Whig papers and a distinct antipathy toward Indigenes that centered in the southern and western frontier regions. Such distinctions have been lost in previous studies such as John Coward's *The Newspaper Indian* (1999) as well as standard histories of the Second Seminole War, most of which ignore the frontier democratic perspective altogether and suggest that the view of the media toward Osceola was exclusively sympathetic.[11] In a struggle to gain political leverage, the newly emergent Whig Party cast itself as a moral exemplar, vastly superior to "the moral malaria of Jacksonism," as a leading congressman phrased it in a House debate.[12] The Romantic idiom proved quite useful in this regard, and, among other charges, Whigs accused Democrats of being reckless war mongers who mistreated the proverbial *children of the forest*. The theme of an Indian "prince" who rose to prominence only to be dishonorably captured and tragically cut down by the party of Andrew Jackson became a most effective weapon in the Whig arsenal. Even after the Whig candidate for president, William Henry Harrison, an old Indian fighter who personally supported the war in Florida, entered the equation, a variation of this same stance continued to great effect during the presidential campaign (see chapter 11). Since the war continued for two more years under the new Whig administration, the party's outwardly sympathetic stance toward the Seminoles ultimately proved to be a form of political stagecraft that was devoid of genuine conviction, a premise that will be made clearer in the course of this chapter.

To be sure, representations of Native people as either idealized primitives or brutal savages had a long history in North America, a bifurcated view that can be traced to the ideas of such eighteenth-century philosophers as Thomas Hobbes and Jean-Jacques Rousseau. But it was not until the Florida war that political parties actually drew a line across this conceptual divide in the hope that their differing orientations would boost electoral odds. The dual concept of the good and bad Indian was no longer exclusively relegated to philosophical musings or seen as an element to add excitement and romance to an adventure yarn but was consciously employed in the rough-and-tumble world of "modern" politics. Romanticism became the de facto framework for the Whigs, while many Democrats focused on the savage motif. Ironically, both genres, as Patrick Wolfe has observed, would eventually be used throughout the colonial world as reinforced settler-colonial hegemony—although this concept may not at all be apparent at first glance. Romanticism helped sustain a legitimating illusion, a diversion that drew national attention away from the country's core aggression toward Indigenous people by focusing on highly idealized literary and artistic creations. Similar to the treaty-making process, the power of such an illusory framework derived from its capacity to define the terms of debate without the citizenry being cognizant of any overt manipulation or misrepresentation while at the same time reinforcing Euro-American moral authority.[13]

The persuasive formula devised by the Whigs certainly did not follow in the exact tradition of Rousseau, despite superficial similarities. Whig journalists, for example, were peculiarly ambivalent toward Seminoles. They often referred to the Indians' presumed extinction (attributing the Seminoles' tragic end to their own doing), compared them to dangerous and irrational beasts, and despite allusions to classical beauty and physical prowess (in the case of Osceola) still characterized Native people as intrinsically inferior and untrustworthy. In contrast, the savage framing used by Democrats may at first seem infinitely more straightforward. Hyperinflated reports of Seminole "atrocities" were intended to provoke moral outrage and sustained a foundation for the settler-colonial "logic of elimination" by appeals to retributive justice.[14] In this respect, most Democrats followed more directly in the footsteps of Hobbes, who envisioned "the savage people" of America as living in "a brutish manner," devoid of laws and living lives that only promised violent death.[15] Once again, however, a distinct duality surfaced. The Democratic elite in metropolitan areas such as New York City and Charleston also shared a strong affinity toward the Romantic movement and so evoked Osceola's tragic heroism while still advancing the tenants of Indian removal. Despite regional variations and contradictions, the frames of both parties strongly resonated within the culture at large and thus demonstrated high potential for influencing the electorate.

One's physical proximity to either cities or the frontier therefore proved as vital as party affiliation in the selection of media frames. While Democratic readers could rely on the *Globe* to consistently render the actions of the Seminoles under a vicious rubric, the activities of the Tammany Society in New York City, named for Lenni-Lenape leader Temane or "Tammany," developed a different orientation. Tammany Hall was the nexus of Democratic power in the city and had too long been invested in the noble Indian motif to abruptly shift its orientation during the Florida war. Since its founding as a fraternal organization in the eighteenth century, members had exhibited a peculiar pseudo-Indigenous posturing. Their council chamber was known as the Great Wigwam, elected leaders were "grand sachems," the rank and file were "braves," and there were thirteen "tribes" based on the original colonies.[16]

Emblems of Native legitimacy, bereft of any taint of savagery, were therefore embraced even while the wholesale purging of Indians from their lands was taking place. Such co-optation endowed the dominate culture with its own pseudo-Indigenous character.[17] Issues such as Native land title and duplicitous treaties became blurred when aggressive newcomers inverted the standard paradigm and incorporated a partially "Indianized" identity.[18] There was a significant psychological process that took place: in the act of assuming Native identities, a recent theorist has observed, "indigenous people are transferred away."[19] This selective appropriation, a form of "self-othering," served another symbolic function, as American citizens could accentuate their difference from European society, and in doing so they helped define a unique national mythos.[20] Unlike frontier Democrats, who consistently drew upon the savage cliché, the Tammany faction actually praised Osceola's heroic standing as a military leader while still remaining faithful to the war effort. The Romantic frame, with all its literary allusions and pretensions, simply held more cultural resonance in the city. This seeming paradox actually reinforces the idea that both genres were merely two sides of the same sword (as far as their relation to Native people was concerned). Ultimately, Whigs never adopted a truly humanitarian stance toward the Seminoles but merely "touched the sad and tender chords of the Indian story" for their own advantage.[21]

The celebrity that was bestowed upon Osceola was, of course, an imaginary exercise based entirely on nineteenth-century European American sensibilities. Writers often alluded to classical Greek and Roman literature in their homages to Osceola, and so there was certainly no equivalence within the traditional worldview of the Seminoles. Moreover, the concept of a unitary military hero was antithetical to Florida's Native people. As Wickman has emphasized, "White Americans have only a limited frame of reference for the force of the horizontal power structure that exists in the Maskókî [Muscogee] world."[22] As we have seen, Seminole war leaders consulted and acted together during large operations and served as lone commanders only during small-scale raids. Hence Osceola, an individual who may have gained the title of *tustenuggee thlacco* (big warrior) but lacked hereditary chiefly authority, was not a "general" in the full Western sense of the word and as the press often referred to him. Osceola's base of support among the Seminoles—who were, after all, a loose association of tribes that were drawn together by the exigencies of war—was indeed never as substantial as is commonly supposed.[23] The remarkable volume of literary efforts devoted to this war leader, Romantic paeans to singular heroic deeds, including poems and elaborate narratives, were surreal exercises that were seldom tethered to reality. Political aspirations, not facts, were the motive force behind the entire process. Osceola's celebrity (or infamy, as the case may be) became a form of kitsch directed at the masses, formulaic and excessive in sentiment: the mirror image of the antebellum literary and press culture that created it.[24]

THE MYTH BEGINS

The fact that Osceola's reputation survived the negative reaction that followed his assassination of Wiley Thompson at the beginning of the war testifies to the overriding need of Whigs to utilize a Native American leader as a strong symbolic counterweight to Andrew Jackson's policies. Senator Benton thus felt compelled to reinforce the idea of Osceola's aberrant cruelty. Indeed, Thompson's body had been riddled with bullets, he had been scalped "as far as the hair extended" (a practice also indulged in by settlers and soldiers), and his skull had been brutally beaten in. The general's companions suffered similar fates. "All this was done in open day light within 250 yards of Camp King," a journalist wrote incredulously at the time.[25] As this gruesome episode took place on the same day as the loss of Dade's command, both incidents magnified white America's general sense of shock and anger. The *National Intelligencer* assumed not only that "Thompson fell a victim to his misplaced confidence in the sincerity of Indian faith" but that all the devastation wrought by the Florida war arose "from the same source."[26] Shortly thereafter, however, Osceola (aka "Powell" at the time, a reference to his long-absent British trader father, William Powell) seemingly performed the impossible by his success against generals Clinch and Gaines at the Withlacoochee, and in both instances the US Army and militia were fortunate to survive the encounter. After the aborted efforts of Scott's "grand army," Seminole forces—which the press mistakenly assumed was under Osceola's exclusive command—regained control of a region revered both as their rightful homeland and as "consecrated ground."[27] Confronted with a disillusioned officer corps and aware of the increasing influence of the press, the military was extremely hesitant to reveal its dire position to the public.[28] In confidence, General Eustis nevertheless warned Secretary Cass that their adversaries were "gorged with blood & flushed with success."[29] The settler-colonial framework of a bounded geographical and physical space, especially as it applied to the confines of the once-famine-stricken Seminole reservation, had in effect been inverted after the war's first year and thus presented a kind of threat that had never been imagined.

Within a vast amount of press coverage that was devoted to the Florida war—numerous editorials, official battlefield accounts from the War Department, reports from the field by a select number of war correspondents, as well as myriad letter writers—Osceola emerged as a distinct mythic hero. James W. Simmons's

"Recollections of the Late Campaign in Florida" (1836) offered one of the first critical, personal accounts of the war. Early in the war, as we have seen, Simmons was sent by a New York City newspaper to report on Scott's campaign. The reporter's disparaging assessment of the war reinforced the party line, as did his seemingly sympathetic treatment of the Seminoles. Simmons suggested that the treaties imposed upon their adversaries were a sham and that the enforcement of "this attempted fraud upon the Seminole nation" violated the country's core principles.[30] He also manifested a particular fascination with Osceola, to the exclusion of all other leaders.

Drawing upon an encounter with Osceola in the months just prior to the war, the author provided a level of intimate commentary regarding his appearance and mannerisms that would have been deemed beyond the bounds of propriety if applied to any white male contemporary. Steeped in the Romantic idiom, Simmons helped forge a literary form of journalism that would later flourish during the Civil War. He also aided, along with Catlin and many others, in creating a mythos regarding Osceola that eventually permeated antebellum culture, a sociocultural construct that may have been used to counter Jacksonian policies but was also invested in the tenets of settler-colonialism. Irrespective of the degree to which some highly educated whites awarded certain Native figures with gallant virtue, most still perceived Indigenous people as fated to extinction and thus innately tragic, a peculiar aspect of the American character that Alexis de Tocqueville noted as "cold selfishness"—a ready acceptance and anticipation of the demise of Indians.[31] Indeed, Simmons managed to weave a sense of predestined gloom throughout his portrayal of Osceola, whose face was judged "eminently worthy of Raphael" and whose nose "was Grecian, perfect!" The eyes nevertheless denoted something tragic. "The prevailing tone was that of profound melancholy, which rendered his smile the most wildly beautiful we had ever beheld. The eye, shaded by long, dark lashes, appeared to sleep as within a shroud, but it was a shroud of thoughts, which you could not doubt had for their subject the sad fortunes of his race, hundreds of whom were there around him, reminding him by their presence of their impending doom—if, indeed, he could ever forget this—for did not the wing of that cloudy destiny which hovered over *them*, throw, too, its cold shadow upon *him*?"[32] Emotions clearly alternated between adulation and pity, but Simmons also gave free vent to fear—a journalistic propensity that would stop soon after Osceola's death. But even as this Native leader was imagined as fearlessly "snatching the laurel from the brows of [Winfield] Scott," there were facets of his heroic physiognomy that still remained troubling. The mere "play of his arms," for example, was judged analogous to "that ease and energy of animals accustomed to

spring at their prey." Simmons's perspective not only claimed a degree of clairvoy-
ance but was almost microscopic in detail. "The speck of froth, white as the flaked
snow, yet wrathful," that gathered at each corner of Osceola's mouth was the result,
it was imagined, of a "tremulous motion about the lips" that signified the "vexed
spirit within." "It was but the faint breath from the whirlwind of that stormy soul
that played upon them, and gave to them their nearly audible vibration—they
seemed as if they panted but to curse or kill!" Even the simple act of laughing and
smiling, instead of prompting feelings of common humanity, was taken as men-
acing. "There is something wild and scarcely natural in the laugh of an Indian;
and we never felt less inclined to trust him, than when he—*laughed!*"[33] (Any
laughter, of course, may have involved mockery toward whites, which would have
undermined colonial power.[34]) Despite elaborate efforts to render "the physical
man" to the public, the author—ostensibly favorably predisposed toward the
Seminoles—lapsed into a web of contradictions. Indigenes, even in the guise of
Osceola and despite rhapsodies of Greco-Roman aesthetics and battlefield glory,
had not only proven unknowable but inherently dangerous as well. Osceola's core
humanity and physicality were constantly beset by a narrative that relegated the
war leader to the arena of a soon-to-be-extinct predatory species.[35] Clearly, at this
time at any rate, his persona had not yet been transformed into the embodiment
of the "good" Indian.

Another contemporary treatment of Osceola emerged in M. M. Cohen's popular war reminiscence, *Notices of Florida and the Campaigns* (1836).[36] Cohen's
rendering also followed the same pattern of invading the personal sphere. (Historians have drawn a parallel between this tendency and the dramatic elements of
black-face minstrelsy during the same period.[37]) In *Notices of Florida*, the author
emphasized the warrior's "white" characteristics much more than his Whig contemporaries. (Journalists often referred to Osceola's mixed parentage and referenced his white father.) "When conversing on topics agreeable to him, his countenance manifests more the disposition of the white than of the red man."[38] Among
various attributes, the warrior's sense of exhilaration appeared to surpass all others.
Like Simmons, particular notice was also awarded the warrior's "tremulous" lips
(the result of emotions that "seem ever boiling within him"). There are obvious
homoerotic overtones, albeit strategically offset by the hypermasculine framework of sports and fitness: "For years past, [Osceola] has enjoyed the reputation
of being the best ball player and hunter, and the most expert at running, wrestling
and all active exercises. At such times, or when naked, his figure whence all su-
perfluous flesh is worn down, exhibits the most beautiful development of muscle
and power."[39] Cohen used the trope of Native physicality and oneness with nature

to create a near-Adonis in reader's minds. In the process, Indians were subjected to a white-defined manhood, a standard that appeared to exclude most Native males. They became, as historian Jeffrey D. Mason phrased it, "the unwitting . . . objects of the European gaze." Such perceptions, Mason continues, essentially made the case "that they should embrace their own luxuriously melancholy demise."[40] While Cohen relied on classical imagery in describing Osceola, he departed from the Romantic genre in more visibly ascribing sinister attributes. The author even likened Osceola to the character of Cassius in Shakespeare's *Julius Caesar*.[41] While Cassius certainly possessed a certain nobility of mind, he was also a devious schemer who served as a co-conspirator in Caesar's gory murder. As an educated Charlestonian, Cohen could not refrain from anchoring his prose in a fashionable, high-toned style, but as a southern Democrat he could not ignore or forgive the Seminole leader's killing of General Thompson. In the final analysis, Cohen believed, Osceola was simply like all other Indians, with revenge always "heading their bloody code."[42]

Compared to a convoluted style of writing that strained to camouflage Euro-American prejudices under a romanticized mantle, the approach of most Democrats, particularly from frontier regions, was noted by their espousal of a savage motif that was unadulterated by romantic pretensions.[43] "They [Seminoles] have the human form," as Democratic congressional delegate David Levy asserted on the House floor, "but nothing of the human heart. Horror and detestation should follow the thought of them. If they cannot be emigrated, they should be exterminated."[44] As posited, however, the essential difference between the two positions was actually slight. For southern Whigs such as US representative Joseph R. Underwood (Kentucky), the value of Florida land, in a similar stance to army generals such as Scott and Jesup, was thought to be second rate and thus not worth the price in lives and treasure to be extracted in war. Instead, the administration should have allowed "these Indians to spend their existence, and to dwindle into nothing, in the land where God had placed them." Given that the eventual demise of the "red man" was a forgone conclusion, the "white race . . . could have acquired the territory inch by inch, as it was wanted."[45] The final outcome, Indian removal and sovereignty over the land, thus remained constant.

Osceola's stature as the Seminoles' single most outstanding military leader was based on a view held by army officers, most of whom were ill-informed as to how their adversaries actually conducted their internal affairs. The army's prestige also improved in direct proportion to any magnification of the Seminoles' fighting abilities. Consciously or not, the rise of an exceptionally talented and charismatic Indian war leader also aided a disillusioned public to better comprehend the army's substantial losses. "This Powell is a perfect magician," claimed a correspondent for the mass-circulation New York *Herald*. "With 1500 men, at the most . . . he keeps every port in Florida in dread of an attack; cuts off all the communications; and threatens to eat up some six thousand regulars, volunteers, and militia, with their seven Generals."[46] Osceola was, of course, never in sole authority, and this exaggerated portrayal also omitted the decisive power of the war council. Yet, during the war's first year, most journalists, regardless of political affiliation, credited virtually every skirmish or battle to Osceola alone. This happened even during occasions such as the defeat of Major Dade, when Osceola was not even in the vicinity. Although never the "Master Spirit of the Seminole Nation," as he was variously identified in the press, Osceola was nevertheless a masterful tactician and was included in the top echelon of war leaders.[47] His appearance alongside Jumper and Alligator during the peace negotiations at the Camp Izard battlefield is clear evidence of his high standing. It is also worth noting that several months afterward—during the Battle of Micanopy—a concealed officer secretly observed Osceola directing the movements of his warriors in conjunction with another unnamed leader (possibly Jumper)—both held this joint command post from an elevated vantage point in the rear.[48] The horizontal power structure of the Maskókî was thus in full view. Moreover, all Seminole war leaders employed a range of innovative tactics. Nighttime assaults, long-term sieges, and even amphibious attacks were utilized—tactics that necessitated high-level planning, discipline, and precise timing.[49]

In addition to Osceola's talents in rallying his forces as an effective fighting unit was his heretofore unacknowledged resolve in curbing enemy casualties. According to an anonymous member of the Cherokee delegation who visited Osceola while he was still held at the Castillo in St. Augustine: "He is everything but savage, having punished his warriors in many instances for their barbarity. He has done much toward mitigating the evils of Indian warfare, by his powerful influence over his men; and had it not been for his talents and personal influence, the citizens of Florida would have suffered much worse."[50] Despite this Native author's strikingly Euro-American tone, this assertion clarifies why the settler population in the interior was never subjected to wholesale slaughter, an option that was plainly open to them.[51] Osceola thus appears to have followed the earlier stricture of Tecumseh, that Native people should abandon the custom of killing women and children in wartime.[52] While whites were indeed wounded, killed, and even tortured, the absence of mass carnage among the settler community certainly adds credence to this assumption.[53] As the editor of the *Pensacola Gazette* astutely remarked, the lack of wholesale killing "could not have arisen for want of opportunity."[54] This point of view is reinforced by the fact that the prewar census in the East Florida interior numbered 2,200 inhabitants.[55] Since the official tally of settlers who received federal food rations totaled about 1,800 by the end of the war (with a preponderance of widows and children), one can surmise that there was never the kind of annihilation that was so often emphasized by the Democratic press.[56] Food assistance, of course, did not include wealthy planters or others who left the territory entirely. Alternatively, whether the absence of mass casualties was Osceola's choice alone is most unlikely.

CAPTURE AND DEATH

General Jesup's public statements predicted that the Florida campaign would soon end following Osceola's imprisonment. Some newspapers agreed and proclaimed that the army had finally "drawn the fangs from the reptile, so that he can no longer bite."[57] As events unfolded, however, this assumption proved how little Jesup actually knew his enemy. His reckless decision to abandon the rules of war in order to capture Osceola went awry in almost every conceivable way. For one, it provided precisely the kind of material that Whig Party organs relished, for it centered on a presumed moral failing of immense proportions and, among other inadequacies, cast the Democratic administration as lacking fundamental decency. Amid escalating national indignation, Osceola was transferred by steamboat to South Carolina, where he and other Seminole leaders were imprisoned at Fort Moultrie, located directly across from Fort Sumter in Charleston Harbor. Attesting to the heightened level of newspaper coverage, large crowds gathered outside the garrison, waiting for a chance to glimpse the celebrity prisoner. "You have no idea of the curiosity raging here," an incredulous young army officer wrote to his father. "Old & young & more especially female throng the place from morning until night."[58] Several months prior to his seizure, Osceola had been ill, reportedly from malaria, and his health deteriorated even more while in prison.[59] Despite these circumstances, a weakened Osceola allowed himself to be taken to a window where he politely nodded to the masses of curious onlookers, as if a visiting head of state. He even agreed to meet with Catlin and then consented to sit for his portrait—the artist's written impressions of this encounter were then circulated in the press. "His face is certainly one of the most expressive I have ever seen," he noted. "Those who listen to his griefs as I have done, will see the sternness of a Roman, and in his agony a beautiful statue of Vengeance." As Simmons before him, Catlin decided that the "fallen Prince" was culpable in his own ruin. "He has a mind of a wonderful construction, calculated to fortify and yet destroy itself—a lurking cunning, capable of gilding with the warmth and glowing pleasantness of sunshine the whirling tempest that is raging in his soul, and even in his mirth and childishness destroying him."[60] By the end of January 1838, Osceola's condition became critical as he began to suffer from "violent quinsy": a throat infection that threatened suffocation. An account of his medical condition written by Frederick Weedon, the army physician in charge, was widely published and assumed a clinical tone that was intended to reassure the reading public that the warrior was offered a high level of care. (In a macabre twist, Weedon later decapitated his patient after death, ostensibly for phrenological study. A subsequent effort to exhibit the preserved head in New York City was quashed by mounting outrage.[61]) Osceola's traditional healer, who was also in attendance, refused the white man's medicine, and so physicians were obliged to leave the dying man alone.[62]

The war leader's final hours were portrayed in several different guises on the national scene. Whigs often emphasized the pain and anguish of the fallen warrior. The *New York Star* reported, in excruciating detail, the agony of Osceola's last moments: "the eye rolling in wild frenzy . . . the chest heaving in like the ocean billows; the throat laboring in the last death struggle of the deep gurgling rattle . . . ."[63] Minute details of pain and anguish took on an almost titillating aspect, a characteristic of a "culture of sensibility" that became a vital component of sensational journalism.[64] In contrast, the *National Banner and Nashville Whig* stressed another facet of this sensibility: the sentimentalization of womanhood. Hence the final caresses of Osceola's wife in prison were utilized to depict a rare moment of universal compassion. "The power of woman mastered the keen remembrances of the Indian's ills, and the voice of his faithful wife, as her arms supported his head and wiped from his brow the death damps, fell gratefully and soothingly upon the ebbing senses of the captive."[65] Poised amid great suffering, resigned to his fate, and attended to by a devoted wife, Osceola's deathbed scene became linked to American domesticity. (Other reports correctly noted that Osceola actually had two wives who were both present.) This melodrama also embodied the type of forbearance that was so prized within antebellum Christianity's death-embracing ethos; it effectively brought the dying man into an emotional community wherein sins were forgiven and remembrance of heroic deeds could be passed on to later generations.[66] Indeed, Osceola's cultural apotheosis was actually bestowed in conjunction with his demise. Only after "his spirit had joined its brethren in the land of the shadows," as the New York *Herald* phrased it, could a martyred Osceola (or rather white Americans' conception of the man) be fully embraced and incorporated into the national consciousness.[67] "Had we the power," declared another Whig paper, "we would send his name down to posterity in characters of light."[68] Such an encomium reflected a tendency of the party to merge the spheres of government and religion, but in this case such expressions also served a singular political utility.[69] The capture and horrid death of this noble champion was laid squarely on the shoulders of the Democratic administration. Given the importance of Romanticism among the elite establishment and the culture at large—beginning in the previous century, for example, there was a profusion of poetry that exclusively dealt with the theme of the noble "dying Indian"— any appeal framed within this genre became quite formidable.[70]

A few months after Osceola's passing, Tammany Hall exhibited a newly completed portrait of the war leader (albeit one not painted by Catlin) that was mounted in a splendid gilt frame and open to public view.[71] In effect, this portrait, as well as the celebrated likeness by Catlin, served as an *exemplum virtutis*: a hero whose noble conduct in battle was allowed broader emblematic significance within the culture at large. On another level, these portraits also functioned as a type of death mask, albeit rendered under a Euro-American aesthetic, which underscored the eventual demise of the "noble" Indian. Catlin admitted that although he believed Indians were fated to extinction, his portraits would still enable them "to live again on the canvas," albeit frozen in time and cut off from the future.[72] Such memorialization was facilitated by Osceola's exceptional "physiognomy and form," which was judged, according to some observers, as attributable to his mixed ancestry and thus inherently superior to "the mere Florida Indian," who were—correctly or not—thought to be "of a darker hue and coarser features, analogous to the African."[73] Since the high Romantic style was primarily a creation of urban environments that were far from the frontier, the prominence of these portraits in such cities as New York should come as no surprise.[74]

The death of Osceola evolved into one of the top news stories of 1838. One outcome of this notoriety was the appearance of carefully crafted public imagery that was marketed for a variety of self-serving intentions.[75] Proprietors of sailing vessels and steamboats of all descriptions along the eastern seaboard rechristened their ships *Osceola* in an attempt to evoke power and resiliency in the face of nature. The name was awarded to race horses and circus ponies alike, and various towns and counties, looking to brand themselves with a certain cachet, also took it as their own.[76] Parents chose the name for sons as well as daughters, and Osceola also served as a pseudonym among numerous editorialists. (Naming, it should be noted, implies entitlement, and name appropriation, as theorist Lorenzo Veracini observes, became "a powerful dispossessory tool" among settler-colonial societies.)[77] Among fashionable New Yorkers, the popularity of Catlin's portrait inspired young men to model themselves after "the perfect beau ideal of an Indian prince" by growing long locks of hair that draped over the ears "a la Powell."[78] In keeping with popular sentiment and the Whig Party's appeal among the cultured class, poets of varying skill penned effusive paeans to the Seminole warrior, a phenomenon that increased Osceola's symbolic value.[79] But if "the eagle soul of the chief had pass'd," as poet Alfred Billings Street declared, the memory of "the tomahawk's lightning stroke" still persisted.[80] No matter how grandiloquent the form, however, uneasy contradictions were also apparent. Whig Party operatives may have conceded that the Seminoles—indeed all Native people—had been "inhumanly persecuted," but this truism did not preclude an insistence on the Native Other's supposed intellectual inferiority or intrinsic barbarism. On more than one occasion, and despite the party's self-image as social and humanitarian reformers, certain journalists noted the absolute necessity of white dominion over Indians, although configured within a paternalistic guise.[81]

Van Buren supporters deployed their own editorial repertoire and countered idealized portrayals as well as the "hundred times told story" of Osceola's capture by accentuating a red devil caricature.[82] "Let those who weep for the sufferings of the Seminoles—whose pens are exerted in [sic] behalf of their virtues—but examine into the treacherous character of these Indians," exclaimed one editorialist.[83] Osceola's death, however, proved to be a potent obstacle to overcome for Democratic operatives. "To die," states religious scholar Ronald L. Grimes, "is not to become powerless, but to become powerful in a fixed mode."[84] Images of death were thus conjured of defenseless young mothers, widows, and orphans falling under the blows of Seminole tomahawks, which reeked, it was invariably stated, of the blood of innocent children. Articles falsely claimed that the Indians were never awarded safe conduct under any flag of truce, and scorn was leveled at those who dared impugn Jesup's honor or to criticize the military—labeling any reproach as "anti-American."[85] When a Whig politician in rural northeastern Ohio bestowed the name of Osceola upon his son, he drew fire from Democrats, who sensed an opening for ridicule. The local Democratic paper was incredulous: "Will you vote for Mr. Bliss, who has named his first born son after the most inhuman butcher of *men, women, and children* that ever disgraced the figure of the human frame?"[86] Moreover, it was believed that only a hypermasculine demeanor, settler-colonialism's sine qua non, could stand up to savagery. Literary homages to Osceola were deemed "sickly and old-maidish," according to Benton. The senator further asserted that the war leader was "effeminate" in both appearance and character, a type of personal attack that was not uncommon within the adversarial politics of the day.[87] Benton was indeed the most prominent proponent of a steady and "manly" course of action against the Seminoles and detested what he perceived as milk-soppishness and "pseudo-philanthropy."[88] His Senate speeches, first published in the *Globe* newspaper and then distributed nationally, not only denounced the mawkishness of Whig organs but identified Osceola as the principal symbol in a false crusade on behalf of the "imaginary wrongs to Indians."[89] It was simply the "perversity of party spirit"—as Benton saw it—that had turned Osceola into a hero-patriot, a claim that actually contained an element of truth.

Given the absence of written primary sources from Seminoles and the fact that the conflicting imagery connected with Osceola became so enmeshed with nineteenth-century sentiment, a true-to-life rendition of the man may never be possible. Beyond his intelligent and purposeful command, athletic prowess, charismatic personality, and desire to limit enemy casualties, more can be said about what he was *not* than what was fundamentally known about him. Significantly, the press honed in on Micanopy as Osceola's diametric opposite and thus became a convenient dramatic foil. Micanopy was quite often denigrated and termed *indolent* and *imbecilic* by the military; his supposedly "stupid countenance, full fat face, and short neck" placed this chief, and by extension the majority of Native people, as grossly inferior.[90] Only rarely did any correspondent depart from this caricature. Indeed, when a positive impression of this leader suited the interests of the military, it was suddenly asserted that "Micanopy was not the fat old fool we thought him." Far from being weak and debauched, the chief was now esteemed as "exercising *regal* powers" when he signed Jesup's treaty of capitulation. His demeanor was "respectable . . . comporting with his rank," and the chief further "evinced good judgment" during his public speaking.[91] This remarkable transformation reinforced Jesup's desire to add a level of legitimacy to the treaty. Such facile image manipulation was aided by the basic fact that Indigenous people were never allowed a firm identity within white culture. Indians, declared the eminent *North American Review*, may be "surveyed and observed," but much like phantoms they could never be truly comprehended or "explained."[92] Even the abolitionist Frederick Douglass pursued this dubious framework in order to gain advantage. He claimed that unlike blacks who also suffered abuse but still embraced American civilization, "the Indian wraps himself in gloom, and proudly glories in isolation—he retreats before the onward march of civilization."[93] Once relegated to such a peripheral status, a variety of writers and journalists were free to create their own contradictory impressions.

Given the ascendance of the newspaper press during the Florida war, highly stylized representations of Osceola not only functioned as self-serving illusions but were powerful icons in their own right—a type of mascot, if you will. Aside from being obvious appropriations of Indianness, mascots are in essence commodities to be rendered in whatever way the "owner" wishes; control can thus be fully asserted, albeit metaphorically, by the dominant colonial power.[94] Indeed, Osceola's demise resulted in the creation of what one scholar has called a "consumable, controlled Euroamerican image" that could be advanced for multiple purposes.[95] Whether as hero or red devil, the war leader's entrée into the American mythos derived first and foremost from self-interest on the part of the settler-state. Seminole warriors may have dominated the battlefields during the war's opening, but the country's burgeoning media proved to be a formidable foe in its own right. By creating and then controlling the image of a wunderkind "demi-savage" who possessed a blend of white settler and Indigenous characteristics, journalists either emphasized the tragic (yet inescapable) consequences of white dominion or stressed monstrous attributes that justified calls for outright extermination. "So much for the mind's sorcery," James Simmons aptly remarked. "It is *that* that colors all our objects—giving to them their power to curse, or bless!"[96] In the case of Indian removal, the end result of this convenient "sorcery" was the same; only the mode of operation and aesthetics differed. By enlisting the noble-but-doomed stereotype, Whigs indirectly supported Indian removal by casting Native extinction as inevitable. This entire process was similar to a theatrical melodrama whose primary aim was to buttress settler supremacy and, in the case of Whigs, to assuage any lingering guilt.[97] The manipulated image of Osceola may have been elevated into the realm of heroes among a portion of the populace, but Native people as a whole, and Seminoles in particular, would never be allowed to enter this exclusive pantheon.

Osceola was buried with military honors just outside the entrance to Fort Moultrie. Since settler-colonialism's effusive imagery still resonates today, some effort is required to depart from the legitimating illusion that has dominated Osceola's story for so long and to assess the interment objectively. The warrior's decapitated remains, by any measure a deeply humiliating desecration, were left under armed guard by the very entity that had resorted to deception in order to imprison him. Placed just outside the looming fortress walls and later encompassed by a Victorian-style, cast-iron fence, the gravesite can be interpreted as a veritable reservation in miniature. Army garrisons, especially those as substantial as this fort, are sites of immense symbolic power. In addition to extensive armaments, each fortification represented the broad reach of federal authority and the dominance of eastern establishment values. They also marked the degree to which the United States was invested in affirming its sovereignty and in displacing Indigenous autonomy. While ostensibly given a place of honor, the land where Osceola's body was placed occupied the physical margins between the fortress and the environs of Charleston, and in a state detached from the very Florida wilderness in which he wished to be ultimately returned. His remains were effectively placed in perpetual confinement. Military burial and the presence of uniformed guards, the custodians of power, symbolized the colonial norm: the radical transformation of a former Native space into a region of white cultural and geopolitical authority. (Indeed, it can be said that the entire nation was built on the graves of Native people.) Hence a potent framing was maintained even in Osceola's burial tableau, a state of affairs that encapsulated the power relations intrinsic to settler-colonialism.[98]

The antebellum imagery that was linked to Osceola has certainly endured to the present day. The Whig framing that was crafted almost two centuries ago has long supplanted its savage counterpart to dominate the present. From the onset, media depictions of Osceola were chimeras devised to reinforce racial hierarchies and state power. His public image was entirely shaped by whatever white society felt compelled to project—while alive, he was powerless to interject his own voice into the fray. The contentious framing that dominated political discourse for most of the war proved startlingly successful as propaganda. Unfortunately, these cultural artifacts of the past will continue to obscure the country's history of violence and moral failures toward Native Americans unless particular attention is paid to their illusory and misleading influence. A process of "decolonization" and renewed scrutiny becomes essential.

CHAPTER 11

Bloodhounds, Abolitionists, and Freedom Fighters

Oh, military glory!—when
  Thou'rt so degraded, that "BLOODHOUNDS"
Can win more "glory," than the MEN
  Who fight upon our battle grounds.
Our soldiers—tho' they may have much
  Of high-born chivalry and pride,
Cannot feel very proud, with such
  Rivals for glory by their side.

New York Whig (1840)[1]

Whig proficiency in manipulating public opinion via the print media grew even more enterprising during the 1840 presidential campaign. Nothing, it seemed, was too "humbug" to be off-limits. Savvy political handlers, buoyed by a startling absence of accountability and a tolerance for the surreal, co-opted the rustic log cabin and hard cider motifs more typically linked to Jacksonians in a brazen attempt to anoint their candidate, William Henry Harrison (a privileged son of Virginia gentry), as a modest man of the people. Such an "Omnibus of Lies"—as Democrats referred to this strategy—certainly aided Whigs, in addition to a distressing economic downturn, to capture the White House.[2] Far less known is the fact that the Florida war also became a vital component within this campaign and again centered on moral outrage regarding treatment of the Seminoles.

Beginning in February 1840 and continuing for months afterward, cries of "Bloodhound War" resonated across the nation's newspapers. This referred to the horrific claim that the army had unleashed brutal packs of bloodhounds, procured from slavers in Cuba, to track down and eviscerate the Seminoles and their black allies in a last-ditch effort to turn the tide of war. At the time, the word "bloodhound" had become synonymous with aberrant cruelty against blacks and Indigenous people, as this particular breed, or a close relative, had actually been used against rebellious slaves in Haiti and Jamaica, and prior to that against Native people during the Spanish invasion of the New World.[3] The abolitionist press, convinced that these animals were being used to kill and maim, was first to publish the story. Whigs quickly followed suit, as they recognized an opportunity to further erode the image of Democrats. A narrative of abject cruelty and indifference to life drew national and international condemnation and resulted in responses from both houses of Congress as well as Secretary of War Joel Poinsett.[4] In Canada, "nine tenths" of the newspapers, according to the *New York Spectator*, used the story to deprecate the United States at a time when tensions over a potential border war with Great Britain were at an unprecedented level.[5] The public became so agitated by the ignominious reputation that the country was gaining that a correspondent for the *National Gazette* (Philadelphia) felt compelled to reassure readers that "[i]t was never designed to use them [bloodhounds] for eating Indians."[6]

Despite the hue and cry, the army under Zachary Taylor never intended to fully "let slip the dogs of war," as military detractors were fond of charging.[7] General Jesup initially brought up the subject of bloodhounds to then-governor Call following Jesup's disappointment at Loxahatchee two years earlier. In his correspondence to the governor, Jesup cited the "success" of the Earl of Balcarres with these animals during the Second Maroon War in Jamaica (1795–96) in order to justify their use.[8] (He, unfortunately, neglected to mention King George III's abhorrence, as well as the political outrage that resulted from engaging such "improper weapons."[9]) Call, supported by the territorial legislature and apparently oblivious to any political ramifications that might ensue, initiated the process of procuring the animals, but by the time they arrived in January 1840, both Call and Jesup were no longer in command. The current governor, Robert R. Reid, may have been supportive of such a scheme, but Taylor was careful to keep his distance (despite a prior interest in using bloodhounds for tracking purposes only). As a result, Taylor only consented to briefly test a small number of muzzled and tethered hounds, part of a larger group originally procured in Cuba by Floridians. But after these animals proved to be "of no service whatever," the army's tentative involvement ended. In fact, the dogs were so inept that many doubted whether they were actual bloodhounds and concluded that the Floridians had been duped.[10] Each of the thirty-three hounds cost the territory $150, a bill that Taylor refused to reimburse, as he ultimately returned the animals back to the territory.[11] (Remarkably, no one drew any connection between the Cuban arms suppliers and the hounds that were delivered to the territory. Yet the possibility exists that the selection of such unusually ineffective dogs may have been intentional.)

Such vital distinctions were seldom to be found in the press, however. Instead, an alternate reality took over—similar to the media manipulation of Osceola—and highly impassioned outcries, exemplified by 162 congressional petitions signed by 8,000 citizens, emanated from those who sincerely believed that frenzied packs of bloodhounds would soon eviscerate all the Seminoles.[12] Fortunately, such an appalling scenario never unfolded; although, if the matter had been left to territorial officials and not the army, matters may well have descended into quite a different outcome. In any case, news of the bloodhounds made a strong national impression as the public immediately perceived such brutality was beyond the pale of human decency.[13] In March, Nathaniel Southard, a member of the executive board of the American Anti-Slavery Society, published a lithograph in New York City that appeared to encapsulate the shock and horror of the situation.[14] As the Garrisonian *Liberator* (Boston) phrased it: "This picture conveys to the heart, through the medium of the eye, a horrid conception of what is likely to take place at any moment in the slave-cursed, blood-reeking territory of Florida." Southard conjured a scene that lacked any veracity. The *Liberator* nevertheless described the artist's imagined charge of an unnamed military commander against the Seminoles—with bloodhounds taking the lead and "fastening their fangs in the flesh of the miserable natives"—not as an imaginative rendering "but [as] a dreadful reality."[15] Moreover, the use of bloodhounds was interpreted as "the refinement of diabolism, and the war itself as atrocious and sanguinary as any to be found in history."[16]

This same theme was integrated, via scathing editorials and mocking political cartoons, into the presidential campaign of 1840. Whigs condemned the Van Buren administration for its "deep and indelible disgrace" as well as cowardice for employing dogs to do the work of soldiers, all the while bolstering the Whig Party as the only choice left for voters who still held their moral principles intact.[17] When images of horror gradually subsided, Whigs effectively transitioned into sarcasm and mockery, taking their lead from John Quincy Adams, who asked Poinsett, tongue in cheek, if army pensions would extend to the dogs and their offspring.[18] From then on, writers indulged in low-brow humor and often assigned fictitious rank to individual hounds (e.g., "Captain Towzer"), along with political cartoons picturing officers reclining in luxury in their tents while ornately uniformed blood-

"The Secretary of War presenting a stand of colours to the 1st Regiment of Republican Bloodhounds (1840)." A Whig cartoon lithograph (by Henry Robinson) mocking Secretary of War Joel Poinsett and *Globe* editor Francis Blair for their defense of using bloodhounds, albeit in a limited capacity, during the war. Prints and Photographs Division, Library of Congress.

hounds lined up on parade and went about the actual business of soldiering.[19] Of all the problems that General Taylor may have imagined for himself as he assumed command, this episode must surely have been the least expected and certainly the most bizarre. Even so, such satirical efforts followed a long tradition initially established in England (although most of the artwork lacked the same level of sophistication). Yet these early attempts testified to the growing technical proficiency of printing and the ascendance of political marketing in the United States.[20] The bloodhound theme had reached such proportions and was so thoroughly identified with Van Buren that James Gordon Bennett's irreverent New York *Herald* proclaimed that "[t]he country is now panting to turn out the 'bloodhounds' and to turn in the 'Old Granny' [a disparaging term for Harrison coined by Democrats]—then we'll have such laws as the public good requires—but not till then."[21]

The identification of abolitionists with the oppression of the Seminoles may at first appear enlightened, but upon closer inspection one can discern a disquieting pattern that developed a distinctive narrative that has actually endured to the present. Far from placing the persecution and removal of Native people on the same level as the subjugation of blacks, the Florida war—the complexities of which were seldom presented with any accuracy—served as a useful backdrop to set a storyline of black superiority over the lowlier "savage warriors."[22] In an obvious display of wishful thinking, activists imagined Florida as a haven for a steady torrent of newly escaped slaves from throughout the South, the full magnitude of which was allegedly kept hidden from public view via an unnamed cabal of slaveowners. The Seminoles' unprecedented ability to ward off the army's impressive forces was instead attributed to former slaves who, it was declared, had suddenly acquired "a fearful knowledge of their physical and martial strength," as an article in the *Liberator* attested.[23] What else could explain how a small band of Seminoles could "resist the whole effort of the American armies . . . bathe the whole of our extended frontier in blood . . . immolate hundreds of brave soldiers, and gallant and chivalric volunteers on the altar of their deadly vengeance[?]" Moreover, it was posited, how could the Indians have procured food for themselves and their families while undertaking such an effort? This phenomenon, the *Liberator* concluded, could only have been possible through the extensive assistance of "hundreds of renegade and self-emancipated negroes," a mass of fugitive slaves from neighboring states who allegedly used "the covert of war to escape from their masters" and found independence in Florida. Actual Seminole authority and agency was thus replaced by a black freedom–fighter motif. Abolitionists had in effect followed the same formula enacted by the Whigs and reframed the war to suit their own purposes. The fact that Jesup had already deported most of the Seminoles' black warriors, along with their families, to the West was omitted altogether. As the "Bloodhound War" demonstrated, calm deliberation and reason proved antithetical to the amplified passions of a grand moral crusade. Similar to Florida settlers, although with far different motives in mind, abolitionists unwittingly adopted a settler-colonial mind-set simply by presuming that blacks entirely dominated the affairs of Seminoles.

Paradoxically, even though the most liberal in society may have espoused the antislavery cause, the majority had yet to transcend the deep-seated prejudices imposed on Indigenes. When given the opportunity, the Seminoles' exceptional struggle against the US military was easily co-opted on behalf of another persecuted minority. Authentic history, in other words, was sidelined as part of a process that was seemingly immune to scrutiny. Native American identity was so peripheral to society that white activists felt free to refashion the Florida war if it meant that their immediate goals were better served.

JOSHUA R. GIDDINGS: "FACT AND FANCY"

African American dominion over the Seminoles was exactly the view held by Representative Joshua R. Giddings, a radical abolitionist from Ohio's Western Reserve region, a vital component of the northern evangelical Bible Belt and an antislavery stronghold. While he was certainly one of the most divisive figures in Congress, Giddings was nevertheless quite popular with his constituents and held his seat for twenty-one years (1838–59). Although Giddings emerged as a substantial critic of the Florida war shortly after he was first elected, he honed his vision of a black-freedom struggle to new heights in the years prior to the Civil War with the publication of *The Exiles of Florida* (1858), a lengthy revisionist history of the war. The author selected historical quotes out of context and ignored a host of contradictory evidence in order to make his case that the actual (and supposedly hidden) reason behind the war was to sustain slavery. Giddings dismissed the notion of an Indian war and instead portrayed the conflict as a struggle for black liberation, with Seminoles playing an ancillary role at best. While purporting to be history, the book was well grounded in the persuasive techniques of abolitionist propaganda. Yet Giddings's work is still cited and revered by some modern scholars as well as a growing cohort of avocational historians who unfortunately look to it as a revered primary source and font of inspiration. Some explanation is thus needed in order to come to terms with its continued sway.

Giddings, a one-time member of the Whig, Free-Soil, and Republican Parties, openly supported slave insurrection and therefore belonged to the most militant branch of abolitionism. He justified any wholesale massacres that might ensue simply as divine retribution—a belligerent posture that opposed the peaceful "moral suasion" approach of the antislavery majority.[24] In fact, he shared a distinct revolutionary ethos with such militants as Gerrit Smith, Frederick Douglass, and John Brown.[25] By the 1850s, violence was increasingly seen as a legitimate option by a faction who rejected pacifism because of its perceived inability to affect meaningful change. Josiah Wedgwood's eighteenth-century British abolitionist slogan "Am I not a Man and a Brother?" was indelibly linked with an image of a chained black man kneeling in supplication before the world, a tactic of mass persuasion that was deemed a terrible anachronism by radical abolitionists on the other side of the Atlantic. Instead, they sought to refashion the Byronic freedom-fighter archetype then in literary vogue under a more "American" guise and so began to identify their struggle with the romanticized image of the *savage warrior* (arguably, America's first black power movement.)[26] As John Stauffer, a noted scholar of abolitionism, has observed about this group: "Their revolutionary ethos was closely linked to their embrace of the symbolic Indian, their understanding of manhood, their sacred visions of America, and their acceptance of savage means to fight slavery."[27]

Giddings and his colleagues may have integrated a partly "Indianized" identity for enslaved blacks in their speeches and writings, but in doing so they also felt compelled to cast blacks as superior to Indigenes—similar to the white penchant for assuming pseudo-Indian identities to augment political power (e.g., the Tammany Society's *grand sachem*). A conscious decision was made to promote black pride and racial strength and to differentiate African Americans from the supposedly lowlier Native American. Once having learned the virtue of violent rebellion, it was theorized that blacks would then earn the true respect of the nation and go on to become productive citizens, analogous to the earlier experience of white settlers who once tamed the northeastern wilderness. "The Indian dies under the flashing glance of the Anglo-Saxon," Douglass claimed in an 1854 speech. "Not so the Negro; civilization cannot kill him. He accepts it—becomes a part of it."[28] Awaiting blacks after their longed-for liberation, according to Douglass and his cohorts, was well-earned assimilation into society, the antithesis of the isolation and anticipated extinction of Native people. Of course, most of these individuals had little or no contact with Indians and instead relied on their own romanticized versions of the past to provide the framework for this revolutionary social-engineering scheme. These reformers were nevertheless convinced that the institution would disintegrate as soon as slaves embraced active rebellion—a conviction that directly followed the "regeneration through violence" frontier mythos that historian Richard Slotkin has previously identified.[29] When blacks became endowed with the proper settler virtues of rugged individuality and heroism, their successful transition into society was more assured, or so they believed.[30]

It is thus not unexpected that Giddings garnered his greatest inspiration from the Florida war, an outlook that was given full expression in *Exiles of Florida*. By the time of its publication, Giddings had already declared that he looked forward to the day when every slave would wage "a war of extermination against his master."[31] *Exiles* was thus a literary extension of his personal crusade. Since this tome was written well after the war by someone who had never been to Florida or witnessed any events firsthand and who was driven by extreme religious and ideological fervor, scholarly protocol would normally relegate this secondary source, interesting as it may be, to the realm of the deeply problematic. (Indeed, this is where it long resided until Kenneth Porter noticed this work and later presented many of its claims without qualification.) Giddings's book should be seen as following the literary lead of Douglass, especially the latter's novella, *The Heroic Slave* (1853), in which a successful slave revolt onboard the ship *Creole* in 1841 is utilized to refute black stereotypes and to provide inspiration for future insurrections. (Giddings was censured by the House for his tenacious and heated defense of this particular insurgency, as it broke the "gag-rule" then in force.[32]) Despite *Exiles's* pretentions as legitimate history, replete with footnotes—although the most implausible assertions are left uncorroborated—the book is at least equal part fiction. Two of the book's leading events, for example, the supposed kidnapping of Osceola's "black" wife, an event that Giddings believed sparked the Seminole war, and the peace initiative at the Withlacoochee that was misattributed to John Caesar instead of the Seminoles themselves are both instances of fiction.[33] Yet Giddings confidently assumed the guise of a historian, interjected actual historical documents within the text—which lent the book a veneer of legitimacy—and focused his narrative on the fate of African Americans, whom he labeled "exiles" (maroons), during the first two Seminole wars. The primary purpose of these wars, according to the author, was not Indian removal, as the treaties and myriad documents attest and the government freely admitted, but rather the re-enslavement of African Americans. It should be stressed that what passed as history during the antebellum era differed from modern standards; the primary aim was to affirm a moral stance, a goal that often required mythicization of the past.[34] Giddings therefore adapted the literary conventions of his time not only to advance his agenda but to place his cause within the predominant framework of moral progress.

Black stereotypes are diligently subverted throughout Giddings's narrative, but he notably failed to apply this same impulse to Native people. Hence blacks exhibited "superior caution and provident care," "physical courage," and stood their ground "with coolness and firmness," whereas Native combatants are referred to as "savages" who lacked strategic thinking, gave in to their impulses, and were supposed to be cowardly. "Indians did not exhibit that undaunted firmness on the field that was manifested by their more dusky allies," Giddings declared.[35] Blacks are presented as exhorting Indians to heroic feats and are even pictured as taking control of the Seminole "general council" while enacting "decrees."[36] The author's ignorance of the Florida interior and of Seminole governance is often apparent, yet he consistently used the trope of black *control* over Seminoles—citing Jesup—and further insisted that stalwart blacks were not in any sense slave property. Following his penchant for overstatement, Giddings placed the African American population at fourteen hundred despite the fact that only five hundred were eventually transported west with the Seminoles.[37] The author also addressed the lack of recognition of the war's *true* character in the historical record: "In looking over the official reports of our officers, the action of Congress, and the tone of the public press, we are forcibly impressed with the constant and unceasing efforts to hide from the public mind of the nation the real questions involved in this war."[38] In other words, his explanation for the embarrassing historical lacuna was a massive cover-up, but he offered no proof to substantiate this charge. Dearth of evidence, rather than casting doubt on the legitimacy of this thesis, is instead taken as de facto proof of a conspiracy by Giddings as well as his current successors, a logical leap that further defines this view as primarily ideological rather than historical.[39]

The impact of *Exiles* on antebellum society during the few remaining years before the Civil War may be impossible to determine. The author certainly received his share of glowing reviews from the abolitionist press. The fact that "Giddings was a propagandist who mingled fact and fancy in his appeals to the emotions of Northerners," as historian Rembert Patrick astutely observed in the early 1960s, can hardly be denied in light of modern historical standards.[40] During the antebellum period, however, charges of distortion, other than outbursts from southerners—some of whom also placed a bounty on Giddings's head—were not forthcoming. What is certain, however, is that Giddings is routinely cited, without appropriate caution, by a growing cohort of nonacademic historians who have followed the lead of more established authors, such as Canter Brown Jr., who has praised Giddings's "well-researched documentation" and even deemed it "a classic."[41] Among those few who acknowledge Giddings's shortcomings, *Exiles* is nevertheless esteemed as an important "primary resource and historical artifact" wherein—it is proclaimed by one website author, "inaccuracies are as interesting as the facts."[42] Given the easy access of this book on the internet, Giddings's intermingling of "fact and fancy" continues to influence the present. Lacking essential context, some are left entirely convinced of Giddings's hypothesis: that the true, heroic story of black rebellion has been intentionally kept from public notice, a charge that has understandably provoked anger. Author Y. N. Kly, for example, has demanded that blacks reject history that has unjustly consigned them to the subservient role of playing "Tonto" to the Seminoles.[43]

AMERICAN RACIAL IMAGINATION

The presence of well-funded and professionally designed heritage websites has begun to influence not only public opinion but those in academic circles as well.[44]

Like the publications of Larry Rivers and Canter Brown, internet efforts make a similar case for a supposedly "hidden" history of slave rebellion. Joseph A. Opala, a white Africanist and anthropologist, has taken this interpretation to new extremes on a website operated by the Gilder Lehrman Center (Yale) and has re-imagined eighteenth- and nineteenth-century Florida in terms of a neo-African homeland.[45] Runaway slaves are presented as the only persons capable of harnessing the resources of what the author fancifully labels Florida "jungles." "The Gullahs [former slaves] were physically more suited to the tropical climate," he asserts, "and possessed an indispensable knowledge of tropical agriculture; and, without their assistance, the Indians would not have been able to cope effectively with the Florida environment." While Euro-American settlers expanded toward the West and other sections of the South, a neo-African frontier, Opala imagines, was developing in the Florida swamps. When the two collided, there was a series of conflicts resulting in a full-scale "Negro War." In effect, the author mythologizes the territory as a place where African Americans became more "indigenous" than the Seminoles themselves—a truly egregious stance, as ruthless in its rejection of Native autonomy as any envisioned in the nineteenth century. For inspiration, Opala relied on the same body of work that has been discussed here, a development that illustrates how a dearth of scholarly critique can have far-reaching effects.[46] A forceful response to such a flawed thesis should be considered mandatory. Even so, as the concept of black sovereignty began as a counterhegemonic response to the societal evils of slavery and racism (and thus linked to the African American freedom struggle), current advocates have assumed a moral posture, making criticism difficult, to say the least. What is most revealing, however, is that the treatment of Native American identity has retained much the same illusory and negative character of the nineteenth century, even among historians who may otherwise deem themselves socially conscious and progressive.

In this respect, the settler-colonial mentality, with its fundamental marginalization of Indians, endures to the present. Robert A. Williams—a noted Native American rights scholar—has aptly concluded: "It's that unthinking, unconscious, and unreflective state of mind and belief embedded in the American racial imagination that determines and defines what most Americans care to think about Indians."[47] Because of the contemporary elevation of heritage proclamations in cultures worldwide, such subliminal influences surely make the already-challenging task of the historian even more daunting. At the minimum, historians have a responsibility to treat all those who trace their traditions to the Florida war with a sense of equity. Few, however, are immune to cultural influences and historical truth, as imperfect a notion as it may be, and have often suffered as a result (for the claims of Larry Rivers and other like-minded historians who interpret the war in terms of black sovereignty and assign a secondary role to Seminoles, see chapter 2).[48] The fact that biases inevitably enter the equation, however, certainly does not preclude customary adherence to logic and evidence, as well as the obligation to cordon off propaganda as inherently problematic.[49] As we have seen, Florida has been subject to illusory excess and imaginative marketing ploys that long preceded Disney. The territorial backwoods has often been utilized as a blank slate on which a certain type of visionary politics has been projected and, given the lack of countervailing voices, has grown more daring in its heritage claims. Ironically, while Porter himself once cautioned that he did not intend, "in overreaction to previous disregard or minimization of the frontier Negro, to present Negroes as the most important ethnic element on the American frontier," some of his ideological successors have given in to this very tendency, all within the malleable context of the Florida peninsula.[50]

Epilogue

Although most of the Florida peninsula was indeed spared further conflict after William J. Worth's proclamation in August 1842, one outstanding band of Indians still remained in a state of war, a final postscript to this conflict that has often been overlooked. Entirely in keeping with the war's maladroit and "never-ending" character, Worth neglected to include Pascofa—the leader of a band of Creeks who fled Alabama for the Apalachicola district early in the war—in his dealings with the Indian leadership. This group thus continued to raid settlements in the area. Because of the proximity to the territorial capital, these attacks caused considerable alarm and posed a political liability for the newly reappointed Governor Call. The Florida militia combed the wilderness but failed to uncover any of the miscreants. Under immense pressure to truly terminate hostilities, General Worth reached out to Lieutenant Colonel Hitchcock in Washington to lead the Third Infantry Regiment—still stationed in the region—in a punitive expedition. Once back in Florida, Hitchcock, convinced of the ineffectiveness of military action, proceeded with a plan that evolved into one of the most unique chapters of the war. "I have been much with Indians," he noted in his diary, "and look upon them as a part of the great human family, capable of being reasoned with and susceptible of passions and affections which, rightly touched, will secure moral results with almost mechanical certainty."[1] From his headquarters at Fort Stansbury, twelve miles south of Tallahassee, Hitchcock was at last in a position to enact his convictions and placed offensive operations on hold, despite orders to reopen the war.

Soon after arriving in the country, Hitchcock sent out several Native scouts to contact Pascofa's band, and after considerable patience and prompting, a few warriors cautiously met with Hitchcock for informal talks. Hitchcock consistently greeted each individual with friendly gestures and studiously kept his word. Pas-cofa eventually came in and met the lieutenant colonel in a face-to-face meeting that took place just outside the camp, with both men casually sitting down on a log with a single interpreter. Hitchcock's unusual blend of diplomacy and candor proved effective, and the chief agreed in principle to move to the Indian Territory, but only after consulting his people. Pascofa returned the next day with ten of his warriors and, in a demonstration of peaceful resolve, the men discharged their rifles in the air before they entered the post. In a scene recalled by one of the of-ficers, Pascofa stood before the camp, now grandly adorned with black ostrich feath-ers and a red turban that Hitchcock gave him. The chief spoke of a long-standing tribal prophecy that foretold of bloody wars and great suffering. Their nation would be divided, with some selling their land and departing while others were hunted down by white men, until the remainder would be reduced to misery and starva-tion. "Such is our present condition," Pascofa declared. But when all seemed hopeless, it was also foreseen that "a man with a *white heart* (referring to purity and honesty), and a *white tongue*, would offer them peace, and make them happy." The chief turned to Hitchcock and affirmed that he was that very man, the "rul-ing spirit" who "brushed the clouds from before the sun."[2] Whether this stemmed from actual prophecy or was a rhetorical flourish intended to flatter may never be known. What is clear is that diplomacy, even among those ranked below the "civilized," could indeed accomplish what war could not. On January 9, 1843, the hitherto aggressive band, now laden with food, blankets, cloth, and other items, was headed on its way west via steamboat. For his efforts, Hitchcock was rewarded with a commendation by the governor and legislative council in which Call as-serted that the enterprise "has been attended with more complete and signal suc-cess than any other expedition conducted against the savage enemy."[3]

For the next thirteen years, with the exception of a few violent flare-ups that set off significant anxiety, an uneasy peace existed between the remnant bands of Seminoles within their Everglades reserve and modest numbers of encroaching settlers, most of whom angrily condemned the lingering presence of the Semi-noles. Moreover, land speculators expected significant profits by the draining of south Florida wetlands and selling this acreage on the open market; thus, political pressure began to be applied in both the federal and state legislatures to finally deport the Indians. In addition, white settlers often sowed fears of an imminent uprising and went so far as to plant "evidence" that the Indians had not confined themselves to the reserve. In 1854, the US Army greatly amplified tensions by sending land surveyors directly into the two-and-a-half-million-acre reservation as well as increasing reconnaissance patrols.[4] A direct result of this intrusive

Daguerreotype of Billy Bowlegs taken prior to the Third Seminole War. National Portrait Gallery.

stance was a Seminole attack on a detachment of army surveyors who had fool-ishly encamped in close proximity to Billy Bowlegs's village on December 20, 1855, an incident that resulted in the deaths of four soldiers.[5]

The scale of the ensuing conflict, subsequently dubbed the Third Seminole War, was certainly not equivalent to the previous war. Native forces comprised no more than one hundred warriors, and, given these circumstances, military involve-ment was never as extensive as the prior war. New emphasis was also given to the role of the Florida militia. Despite the absence of pitched battles, scattered Semi-nole attacks throughout the state (the territory gained statehood in 1845) neverthe-less generated significant panic during the conflict's two-and-a-half-year duration. US forces were given a boost when the infamous William Harney, at that time a brigadier general, entered the picture and implemented changes to army procedure that were better fitted to guerilla war. Harney was later recalled for service in the west, but his successor nevertheless pursued the small bands of Seminoles with vigor, and in the end a beleaguered Billy Bowlegs—the nephew of Micanopy and thus a hereditary chief—along with seventy-five of his followers, finally relented. His decision was influenced by the fact that a delegation of western Seminoles (brought in by the army) emphatically urged the band's departure. Extraordinary monetary awards were also part of negotiations: $7,500 was allotted to the chief, while $250,000 was destined for the tribe as a whole upon their arrival west. Each warrior was assured $500, with an additional $100 directed for every woman and child. The money, according to the negotiator on the scene, "shall be paid to you, cash in hand, before the wheel of a steamer is turned to take you from Florida," a promise that was actually kept.[6] Abiaka, though noticeably absent from the negotiations, nevertheless made it known that even "two wagon loads of money will not induce him to leave."[7] Since the end of the previous war, Billy Bowlegs and Abiaca had developed a contentious relationship, and a division formed between the remaining Alachua Seminoles and the Miccosukees.[8] Be that as it may, along with captured warriors held on Egmont Key (a small island at the mouth of Tampa Bay) and women and children, a total of 165 ultimately departed by sea for the Arkansas reservation. The war officially closed on May 8, 1858. "The agonizing struggle, extending through a period of twenty-three years," proclaimed the New York *Herald*, "has at last terminated in the ruin and destruction of the gallant Seminole."[9] According to the *Herald*'s reporter, however, easily twice the number of Bowleg's party (330) still remained in Florida, including the irascible Abiaca.[10] The survivors withdrew into the most inhospitable regions of the Everglades, the Ten Thousand Islands and the Big Cypress Swamp, but their presence continued to loom in the fear-laden imaginations of settlers for years to come.

THE SETTLER-COLONIAL PAST AND PRESENT

The Second Seminole War delivered a severe setback to Andrew Jackson's mission of Indian removal, conjured visions of pan-Indian rebellion, and contradicted the deep-rooted national conviction that the military would forever triumph over Native people. The success "of a civilized, strong, and abundantly provided nation," a genuinely puzzled writer for the *North American Review* noted in 1842, could no longer be assumed in such a contest, and, quite inexplicably, the government could not account for this mystifying performance.[11] As a result of the army's first operations under challenging subtropical conditions, the nation's settler-colonial framework, founded on ideas of racial dominance and providential destiny, had been undermined. Malaria epidemics and the wilderness terrain favored the Seminole to such a degree that the US military eventually relied on treachery and duplicitous dealings, as well as monetary inducements, to "rid" Florida—albeit incompletely—of its Native people.

The United States had, in essence, experienced what earlier colonial powers had discovered in similar regions of the world. In many cases, the diseases and physical hardships of the tropics rendered any attempt at settler-colonialism impossible—a concept that has now become axiomatic among many scholars.[12] Eighteenth-century Jamaica, for example, virtually embodied the kind of extravagant wealth that could be obtained in the New World, as slave-based sugar production created massive fortunes for a relative few. But, as recent demographic studies have revealed, British attempts at establishing a stable and productive settler population utterly failed, as the high mortality of white newcomers was so extensive that the birthrate could never surpass the death toll. Early Jamaica thus constituted a failed settler society, despite its status as a supremely affluent colony.[13] Unlike Jamaica, however, territorial East Florida did not possess the resources that could quickly fill government coffers. Instead, an ill-advised attempt was made to establish a full-fledged settler presence, with the United States blithely discounting Spain's centuries of experience in this region. As historian Alfred W. Crosby has stated, successful settler-colonial endeavors flourished in more moderate latitudes such as New Zealand, Australia, and South Africa, as well as the nontropical regions of North America. It was only within a temperate climate that these *Neo-Europes*, to use Crosby's term, were able to fully replicate European-styled and predominantly "white" states, not only by their reliance on a specific type of agriculture but on a sophisticated economic structure and myriad governmental and cultural attributes as well.[14] (As one may expect, the newly formed political and juridical institutions were skewed toward bolstering settler power while marginalizing the surviving Native people.[15]) In conjunction with these human invaders, a host of other biological entities arrived as well—animals, cultivars, myriad diseases, and so forth. Importation of Old World flora and fauna therefore transformed distinct regions throughout the world into Europeanized zones. But any successful metamorphosis was far more challenging in the tropics. While generations of horses and cattle adapted and thrived in Florida, endemic malaria was still the most powerful curb to non-Native human population growth.

Although only the extreme southern end of the Florida peninsula can be technically regarded as falling within the tropic zone, the bulk of East Florida is atypical in that it lies between two warm oceans (the Gulf of Mexico and the Atlantic) and rests on a karst typography that features an intricate system of subterranean freshwater caves that, in addition to a super-abundance of surface wetlands, helps generate the most humid region in the United States.[16] In addition to exotic native plants and animals, mosquitoes, as we have seen, proliferated under such conditions and became vectors of an especially lethal form of malaria. The soil was also quantifiably different, as the state contains the largest concentration of aquod (wet and sandy) soil in the nation.[17] The fertile lands that lured Georgian settlers in the early nineteenth century only existed because of the organic nutrients that were found in previous old-growth forests. The productiveness of the soil rapidly diminished after settlers cleared forests and employed intensive farming methods. Although the land perfectly suited Indigenous agropastoralists and teemed with fish and game, the Florida peninsula was certainly the most "un-European" of localities to be found anywhere along the eastern seaboard—as the negative reactions of various generals attest. Hence Jacksonian true-believers were thoroughly misguided in presuming that the settler-colonial model of Kentucky and Tennessee (along with their attendant folk heroes, such as Daniel Boone) could possibly be duplicated within this distinctive region. The United States discovered what Britain had long before experienced in its Caribbean colonies; settler-colonialism had intrinsic geographic limitations and European-style wars conducted in tropical areas were similarly problematic. In the long run, citing Crosby, "the humid tropics proved to be a mouthful for which Europeans had the teeth, but not the stomach."[18] In the case of the Second Seminole War, "stomaching" the situation meant dealing with recurrent epidemics and numerous unseen terrors that left many survivors physically and mentally traumatized.

As we have seen throughout this book, recognition of the war's settler-colonial origins is imperative if one truly desires to come to terms with this conflict, a basic assumption that has been lacking in the historiography. But as Lorenzo Veracini has demonstrated in *Settler Colonial Present* (2015), this task is made even more arduous by the retention of settler-colonial consciousness in the present day. The history of the war is not only subverted by the continued abnegation of Seminole sovereignty by advocates of black rebellion, but certain works such as John and Mary Lou Missall's *The Seminole Wars: America's Longest Indian Conflict* (2004) feature an interpretation of the war that so clearly upholds a settler-colonial bias that it serves a valuable heuristic function here.

The Missalls—a husband and wife team—initially rely on a "clash of cultures" thesis that assigns responsibility for the war to both whites and Seminoles, in supposedly equal measure. This view bypasses the essential point that the conflict was a straightforward attempt to subjugate and remove an exceedingly vulnerable ethnic minority. To assign equal fault to the dispossessed, merely because of their intrinsic cultural differences, thus seems off-kilter, to say the least. "As much as we might lament the fact from today's perspective," the authors claim, "there was simply no way the two cultures could coexist."[19] This same fatalistic lament echoed throughout the land, and on both sides of the political spectrum, during the early nineteenth century. Rather than consider the unequal power dynamic that under-girded such a posture, the authors evade this entirely and postulate a "that was then, this is now" argument. Only in the present times, we are informed, have more enlightened versions of both white and Native culture evolved. "Indians are no longer hunters who require vast hunting grounds and live by the warrior's code. Most Americans no longer seek to develop every square inch of the continent." "But in the early nineteenth-century," we are informed, "neither culture was will-ing to change."[20]

Based on the evidence that has unfolded in these pages, one hardly knows how to respond to such ethical evasions. The Missalls nevertheless reflect a certain folk belief that has endured in popular culture; that is, if viewed dispassionately, the Indians were just as culpable as whites for the Indian wars. And in case non-Natives are ever tempted to feel remorse, the Missalls offer a welcome respite: "White Americans should not feel guilty for placing the Indians in this situation; it was a natural occurrence." They then shift the burden entirely onto Indigenous people. Employing an unrepentant social Darwinism, the writers emphatically declare: "*Native Americans were faced with the classic evolutionary imperative: adapt or die.*" If one simply replaces "adapt" with "yield," such a slogan could just as well have been emblazoned on the settlers' wagons as they struggled to estab-lish dominion over the Seminole homeland. Hence a settler-colonial mentality continues to assert itself today, even among historians, just as forcefully as the frontier mind-set of almost two hundred years ago.[21]

The Missalls, as many others who study the war, still give credence to the au-thority of the treaties that were enacted in Florida. Indeed, they believe that "there could be no hope for peace" without these legal constructs. "Had *both parties* adhered to the stipulations they had made," the authors claim, "they might have established a mutual trust that would have turned enemies into good neighbors."[22] Given what we now know about the discredited circumstances of the treaty-making process, it is hardly necessary to provide a detailed rebuttal to such an assumption. But it is still instructive to note how much weight continues to be given to these coerced and fraudulent legal instruments. Their extraordinary power as legitimat-ing illusions continues in full force.

If past injustice continues to be repudiated or avoided in such a manner, his-tory is not only subverted, but any attempt at reconciliation with the present-day

Seminoles—certainly a desideratum—will surely face insurmountable challenges. The inability to admit the dispossession, violence, and loss of life inflicted upon Native people exhibit "psychological elements of a colonial mentality," as a social scientist observed in relation to these same leanings in her home country of Australia.[23] Repudiation of any sense of collective guilt is an obvious defense mechanism, for any admission of the appallingly unjust actions of the past could pose a threat to social identity. Early settlers similarly avoided guilt by attributing the passing of the "savage race" as inevitable, as Euro-Americans preferred to envision themselves as merely following God's plan. Subscribing to convenient notions of Divine Providence (invoking the sacred while pursuing the profane) was the preferred order of the day. Confronting the full force of the wrongs enacted against America's Indigenous people could very well constitute a threat of such magnitude as to erode an individual's core identity (a reason, as has been suggested, that so many junior officers lingered in depression or resigned their commissions). Expressions of mea culpa, needless to say, are very rarely articulated by either the political or military elite. And so the same line of evasions and denials endure. The descendants of settlers and Florida's Native people (perpetrator and victim) may live together in a modern state, but they do so in a milieu of avoidance or denial on the part of the majority. The startlingly successful Seminole casinos and business investments not only defy nineteenth-century narratives of an inferior, vanishing race but also project a robust message of empowerment. Be that as it may, the moral weight of past wrongs will linger until just recognition is awarded and white Euro-Americans extinguish the destructive reasoning and language of settler-colonialism. Oppression, it must be stressed, not only resides within formal institutions but, even more insidiously, thrives and perpetuates itself within group consciousness as well.

Of the approximately six thousand Seminoles who lived in Florida before the war, only half survived to be deported west—a demographic loss of stunning proportions. Of the few hundred who managed to retain a foothold in the Everglades, a population of nearly five thousand has endured to the present. Four thousand are enrolled citizens of the Seminole Tribe of Florida, more than six hundred constitute the Miccosukee Tribe of Indians of Florida, and a few hundred identify as "Independent Seminoles." All, of course, are descendants of the dedicated holdouts of 1858. Today, as one can readily understand, Abiaka has attained a legendary standing among tribal members, with two statues representing the leader in prime locations. One statue has Abiaka surrounded by representations of the surviving nine clans—Bear, Panther, Otter, Deer, Wind, Bird, Toad, Mole, and Snake—another has him directing a woman and child to safety. To be sure, the determination of their forebears has become an obvious point of pride. Willie Johns, chief justice of the Seminole Supreme Court, recently expressed this feeling by his somewhat lighthearted admission during a ceremony honoring the Seminole war dead that "I wake up every morning and give thanks that I am *not* in Oklahoma."[24]

Notes

Abbreviations

ASP:IA	*American State Papers, Indian Affairs*
ASP:MA	*American State Papers, Military Affairs*
GM	Gilcrease Museum, Tulsa, OK
GPO	Government Printing Office, Washington, DC
HRB	Hargrett Rare Book and Manuscript Library, University of Georgia Libraries, Athens, GA
LOC	Library of Congress, Washington, DC
LR	Letters Received by the Office of the Adjutant General, Main Series 1822–60
NARA	National Archives and Records Administration, Washington, DC
NPS	National Park Service, Washington, DC
NYPL	New York Public Library, New York, NY
PKY	P. K. Yonge Library of Florida History, University of Florida, Gainesville, FL
TP	*The Territorial Papers of the United States*
WLC	William L. Clements Library, University of Michigan, Ann Arbor, MI

Introduction

1. The Creek War (1836) in Alabama was directly inspired by the Seminole insurgence, and military leaders thereafter feared an even more threatening Seminole-Creek war; see Ellisor, *Second Creek War*, 158, 177, 210.

2. For reference to a supposed Indian and slave uprising, see Thomas Jesup to J. R. Poinsett (Fort Christmas, Powell's camp), January 2, 1838, LR, roll 0167, RG 94, NARA.

3. The British were similarly concerned about a hypothetical black and Indian alliance; see Braund, "Creek Indians, Blacks and Slavery," 611.

4. Quotations from Elderkin, *Biographical Sketches*, 17, 19.

5. See, for example, Porter, "Analysis of an 'Official Report,'" 296.

6. A few examples of the usual negligible mention given the war include Wilentz, *Rise of American Democracy*, and Sellers, *Market Revolution*.

7. Mahon, *Second Seminole War*.

8. For the $40 million figure, see Mahon, *Second Seminole War*, 326. For comparison

of the annual budgets, see "Government Spending in the US," usgovernmentspending.com, accessed September 11, 2016, http://www.usgovernmentspending.com/total_spending_1840USrn. For the myriad problems that plagued the army, see Watson, *Peacekeepers and Conquerors*, 180; Vandervort, *Indian Wars*, 131; Kennett, *Sherman*, 27.

9. G. Tompkins to Joel Poinsett, March 24, 1838, LR, roll 0176, RG 94, NARA. For more on the advantages afforded by these withdrawals, see Knetsch, *Fear and Anxiety*, 230.

10. For the amount of these losses, see David Levy, "Speech of Mr. David Levy of Florida, in the House of Representatives, June 12, 1842," *Florida Herald and Southern Democrat*, August 1, 1842.

11. "The Seminoles" (from the *Political Arena*), *National Intelligencer*, January 15, 1838.

12. For an apt discussion of similar circumstances across the world, see McNeill, *Mosquito Empires*, 9–10.

13. "For Whom Will You Vote?" *Lorain Standard*, October 6, 1840.

14. Walkiewicz, "Portraits and Politics," 109.

15. Unsigned review of "The Song of Hiawatha by H. W. Longfellow," *Athenaeum*, November 10, 1855, 1295.

16. For confirmation that Taylor only used a small number of tethered and muzzled dogs in a brief experiment, see Z[achary] Taylor to R[obert] R. Reid, March 23, 1840, and L. Thomas to John McLaughlin, March 7, 1840, both from LR, roll 0218, RG 94, NARA; see also chapter 11.

17. For a concise review of the literature on settler-colonialism, see Veracini, *Settler Colonialism*, 6–11. In addition, see Bateman and Pilkington, *Studies in Settler Colonialism*; Ford, *Settler Sovereignty*; Byrd, *Transit of Empire*; Goldstein, *United States Colonialism*; Krautwurst, "What Is Settler Colonialism?" 55–72; Denoon, "Understanding Settler Societies," 511–27; Mamdani, "Settler Colonialism," 596–614; Mamdani, "Beyond Settler and Native as Political Identities," 651–64; Wynn, "Settler Societies," 353–66; Wolfe, *Settler Colonialism*; Wolfe, "Settler Colonialism and the Elimination of the Native," 387–409; Wolfe, "Land, Labor, and Difference," 866–905; Wolfe, "Structure and Event," 102–32; Veracini, *Settler Colonial Present*; Veracini, "On Settlerness," 1–17; Veracini, "Colonialism and Genocides," 148–61; and Moses, ed., *Genocide and Settler Society*. Moreover, see issues of *Settler Colonial Studies*, *Critical Race and Whiteness Studies*, and *American Indian Quarterly*.

18. Wolfe, *Settler Colonialism*, 162–73; Wolfe, "Settler Colonialism and the Elimination of the Native," 387–409.

19. For the Xhosa Wars, see Storey, *Guns, Race, and Power*; Switzer, *Power and Resistance*; and Stapleton, *Maqoma*.

20. Baptist, *Creating an Old South*, 3.

CHAPTER 1: Treaties and Reservations

1. Henry Prince, "Account of Henry Prince of the 2nd Seminole War," March 21, 1891, Native American History Collection, WLC; see also "Indian Hostilities," *Jacksonville Courier*, December 17, 1835. On the distinctiveness of individual war whoops, I am indebted to ethnohistorian Patricia Wickman.

2. Joel W. Jones, extract from a letter dated February 24, 1836 (St. Augustine), in

Jones, "A Brief Narrative of Some of the Principal Events in the Life of Joel W. Jones," 1849, manuscript, 144, PKY.

3. For the role of the Alachua region during the war, see Monaco, "Alachua Settlers," 1–32. For Tierras de la Chua, see Crown Collection of Photographs of American Maps, Series 3, #129–30, PKY.

4. Bartram, *Travels*, 165.

5. Monaco, "Fort Mitchell," 8. Cattle production in this area actually dated to the mid-seventeenth century under the Spanish. The largest cattle ranch in Florida was located at Paynes Prairie; see Worth, *Timucuan Chiefdoms*, 199–202; Bushnell, "Marquez Cattle Barony," 408, 423; Arnade, "Cattle Raising," 116–24; and Wickman, *Tree that Bends*, 196.

6. Monaco, "Shadows and Pestilence," 565–88.

7. Monaco, "Alachua Settlers," 1–32. According to one contemporary, individual settlements ranged from five to fifteen families; see George G. Keen, October 9, 1899, in Denham and Brown, eds., *Cracker Times*, 29.

8. D. L. Clinch to R. Jones (Fort King), January 22, 1835, LR, roll 0105, M567, RG 94, NARA; emphasis original.

9. J. H. Eaton to L. Cass (Tallahassee), March 8, 1835, in Potter, *War in Florida*, 37.

10. D. L. Clinch to Lewis Cass, October 17, 1835, LR, roll 0106, M567, RG 94, NARA; Cass to Clinch, October 22, 1835, in ASP:MA 6:552; Patrick, *Aristocrat in Uniform*, 89; "Extract from a Letter of the Secretary of War, Dated War Department, February 18, 1836, to General Wiley Thompson, Superintendent of Indian Removal, Seminole Agency, Florida," in ASP:MA 6:522–23. For the number of men in the army, see Mahon, *Second Seminole War*, 116.

11. James D. Westcott in Mahon, *Second Seminole War*, 73.

12. "To the Editor of the Argus" (Tallahassee), February 6, 1836, in *Albany Argus*, February 23, 1836; see also "H" [pseud.], "Letters from Florida, No. 3," December 12, 1835, in *Atlas*, December 29, 1835.

13. J[ames] Gadsden to the Secretary of War, June 11, 1823, in TP, 22:696.

14. The Alachua planter elite included Duncan Clinch and John H. McIntosh Jr. as well as Moses E. Levy, a former West Indies merchant (who owned one hundred thousand acres in East Florida) and the father of future congressional delegate and US senator David L. Yulee; see Monaco, *Moses Levy of Florida*.

15. Schafer, "Swamp of an Investment," 29.

16. [Governor] James Grant to Henry Bouquet (St. Augustine), August 11, 1765, accessed June 27, 2017, https://www.unf.edu/floridahistoryonline/Projects/Grant/. On the failure of the British as colonists, see Braund, "Congress Held in a Pavilion," 95.

17. Weisman, "*Importance of the Seminole Wars*," 397.

18. Landers, "Introduction," in *Colonial Plantations*, 1–10.

19. Wolfe, "Settler Colonialism," 388.

20. Andrew Jackson to John C. Calhoun (Pensacola), September 17, 1821, in TP, 22:207.

21. "Florida Indians: Communicated to the House of Representatives, February 21, 1823," in ASP:IA 2:408–10. The benevolent tone of this document is quite remarkable for its time. Ultimately, however, Native rights were placed within the purview of appointed Indian agents and were subject to the discretion of the president.

22. These characteristics of reservations are noted in Veracini, *Settler Colonialism*, 28.

23. Mahon, *Second Seminole War*, 46–47.

24. "Government Spending in the U.S.," accessed July 28, 2015, http://www.usgov ernmentspending.com/total_spending_1823; Covington, *Seminoles of Florida*, 52. I have used Covington's figure of $1.25 per acre.

25. James Gadsden to the Secretary of War, May 17, 1826, in *TP*, 23, 545–46.

26. For reference to the Coweta Creek raids in June 1821, see Brown, "Runaway Negro Plantations," 15–19; Brown, "Florida Crisis," 421.

27. Lewis and Jordan, *Creek Indian Medicine*, 9; Wickman, *Tree that Bends*, 51; Woodward, *Woodward's Reminiscences*.

28. For the general strategy of accommodation, see Dueck, *Reluctant Crusaders*, 11–12. For an extensive look at contemporary accommodation strategies, see Werbner and Anwar, *Black and Ethnic Leaderships*.

29. William P. DuVal to Thomas L. McKenney, February 22, 1826, in *ASP:IA* 2:664. The Jackson administration eventually conceded that the reservation "does not contain a sufficiency of good tillable land"; see Thomas L. McKenney to Governor DuVal, May 22, 1826, in *TP*, 23, 557.

30. "Talk of the Florida Delegation of Indians, Delivered by Tuckasse Emathla, the Head Chief, in Reply to One from the Hon. James Barbour, Secretary of War," May 17, 1826, in *New York Spectator*, June 2, 1826.

31. "Petition to the President of the United States (Alachua County, Territory of Florida)," January 1834, in *ASP:MA* 6:465–66.

32. Joseph M. White, "Copy of a Letter to the Editor Dated Washington City, Feb'ry 5, 1826," *Pensacola Gazette and West Florida Advertiser*, March 11, 1826; emphasis original.

33. Friend, "Mutilated Bodies," 15.

34. Césaire, *Discourse on Colonialism*, 42.

35. Menges, "Ecology and Conservation of Florida Scrub," 7–20.

36. Williams, *Territory of Florida*, 72–73; emphasis original.

37. "Florida: Its Soil and Products," *Western Journal* 6 (June 1851): 181. The Alachua region had a centuries-old tradition of cattle production; see Bushnell, "Cattle Barony," 408, 423, and Weber, *Spanish Frontier*, 310; see also Knetsch, *Fear and Anxiety*, 1–11.

38. For contemporary recognition of sacred ground, see Sprague, journal entry, April 27, 1839, in White, "Macomb's Mission," 160, and Simmons, *Notices of East Florida*, 46.

39. "Florida Indians," *Connecticut Journal*, August 7, 1827; "Florida Indians," from the *Pensacola Gazette*, *Michigan Herald*, August 22, 1827.

40. This thesis is defined throughout Deloria, *God Is Red*.

41. "Talk by the Delegation of Florida Indians," May 17, 1826, in *TP* 23, 549; for the importance of the umbilical cord among the Seminoles, I am grateful to historian Pat Wickman.

42. Miller, *Coacoochee's Bones*, 31.

43. Simmons, "Recollections of the Late Campaign," 547.

44. Waters, "Ontology of Identity," 163.

45. For the ethical relationship to the land, see Schweninger, *Listening to the Land*, 1–15. For the relationship between Native people and the environment, see Peterson,

Being Human, 125–26. For the meaning of ceremonial ground, see Wickman, *Tree that Bends*, 95.

46. Thomas Jesup to Joel Poinsett, June 15, 1837, LR, roll 0146, M567, RG 94, NARA; emphasis added.

47. Ibid.

48. The incident regarding Coppinger was in response to his refusal, apparently under orders from his superior, the governor of Cuba, to surrender the official archives of Florida as stipulated in the Adams-Onís Treaty. For a formal protest against this affair, see Don Juan Joaquin de Anduaga to the Secretary of State [J. Q. Adams], November 22, 1821, in Hertslet, *British and Foreign State Papers*, 313–16. See also Coppinger, *Manifesto*. Reportedly, Coppinger's predecessor, Sebastián Kindelán, became so incensed during the Patriot War that he was prepared to engage in a duel with President James Madison; see Doherty, "Code Duello," 245.

49. Everett, *Speech of Horace Everett*, 6; emphasis original.

50. For an examination of Jefferson's goal of removal, see Abel, "History of Events," 244; Wallace, *Jefferson and the Indians*, 206–40; and Peterson, *Thomas Jefferson*, 771, 773–74, 776.

51. Lewis Cass, "Annual Report of the Secretary of War Showing the Condition of the Department in 1832," November 25, 1832, in ASP:MA, 22. Cass's view of Indians was rife with racism; see Fierst, "Rationalizing Removal," 1–35.

52. On ethnic cleansing, see Osterhammel, *Transformation of the World*, 342; Anderson, *Ethnic Cleansing and the Indian*; Howe, *What Hath God Wrought?* 423; Hall, *Earth into Property*, 311; Coates, *Trail of Tears*, 108; Hixson, *American Settler Colonialism*; Cave, "Abuse of Power," 1331; and Mamdani, "Settler Colonialism," 598.

53. For reference to the associated forts, see Remini, *Andrew Jackson*, 148.

54. Quotations from Joseph Kerr to Lewis Cass, June 14, 1832, in "Correspondence on the Subject of the Emigration of Indians, 1831–1833," 23rd Cong., 1st sess., 1833, S. Doc. 512, 1:719–20.

55. Kanstroom, *Deportation Nation*, 70; Banner, *How the Indians Lost Their Land*, 208–9; Mamdani, "Settler Colonialism," 596–614.

56. Cave, "Abuse of Power," 1331.

57. Quoted in Snow, *Question of Aborigines*, 77.

58. Rosen, *Indians and State Law*, 114–15; see also E. A. Hitchcock to J. S. Spencer (secretary of war), in "Message from the President of the United States, Transmitting the Report of Lieutenant Colonel Hitchcock, Respecting the Affairs of the Cherokee Indians, &c. January 31, 1843," 27th Congress, 3rd sess., 1843, H. Doc. 219, 15.

59. For the number of treaties under Jackson, see Remini, *Andrew Jackson*, 148. For the use of the term *legitimating illusion*, see Wolfe, *Settler Colonialism*, 173. Wolfe defines this term in relation to literary and artistic renderings of Native people that were deeply influenced by Romanticism. I have used it here to apply to Indian treaties as well.

60. Tocqueville, *Democracy in America*, 353.

61. Sprague, *Florida War*, 287.

62. Ibid.

63. Mahon, *Second Seminole War*. A revised edition was released in 1985, but the bulk of this study has remained unchanged since 1967.

64. Ibid., 78. See also Mahon, "Two Seminole Treaties," 1–21.

65. Hunter, "Captain Nathaniel Wyche Hunter," 74. For Mahon's notice of the prevalence of this attitude among officers, see Mahon, *Second Seminole War*, 77. See also Skelton, *Profession of Arms*, 323–24.

66. See especially Sprague, *Florida War*, 288–89.

67. "Debate in the Senate," *National Intelligencer*, June 2, 1838.

68. Prucha, *Indian Treaties*, 176, n. 48.

69. Hitchcock, *Fifty Years in Camp and Field*, 79–80. For the actual Treaty of Payne's Landing, see "Treaty with the Seminole, 1832," in Kappler, *Indian Affairs*, 344–45. Thruston is listed as a witness to an agreement with the Seminoles that supposedly recognized the legitimacy of Payne's Landing, dated April 23, 1835, at the Seminole Agency near Fort King; see Cohen, *Notices of Florida*, 55.

70. Ibid. For the refusal of Seminoles to accept the legitimacy of the treaty and the accusations of erroneous translations, see James Gadsden to Lewis Cass, November 1, 1834, in *ASP:MA* 6:507–8. For Hitchcock's letter to the assistant adjutant general of the army, see E. A. Hitchcock to Major S[amuel] Cooper (Fort Brooke), October 22, 1840, folder 7, Box 2 (1986 Acquisition), Ethan Allen Hitchcock Collection, Beinecke Rare Book and Manuscript Library, Yale University, New Haven, CT.

71. Two hundred dollars, a substantial sum at this time, was also awarded to Cudjo, another interpreter; see "Treaty with the Seminole, 1832," in Kappler, *Indian Affairs*, 344. For verification of Abraham's susceptibility to bribery and general "love of money," see Wiley Thompson to George Gibson (Seminole Agency), September 21, 1835, in *ASP:MA* 6:546. On the propensity of "Seminole negroes" who "possessed the confidence of the Chiefs" to accept payment to mislead and betray the Indians during the war, see Thomas S. Jesup, Letter to the Editor (draft), 1858, box 1, folder 7, Thomas S. Jesup Papers, WLC.

72. "Talk of the Seminole Chiefs," in Cohen, *Notices of Florida*, 58.

73. "Treaty with the Florida Tribes of Indians, 1823," in Kappler, *Indian Affairs*, 203.

74. "Treaty with the Seminole, 1832," in Kappler, *Indian Affairs*, 344–45.

75. Brown, "Runaway Negro Plantations," 9.

76. Hitchcock, *Fifty Years in Camp and Field*, 80.

77. For the signing date, see Mahon, *Second Seminole War*, 82. The winter conditions were reportedly mild for this time of year, but they would nevertheless have seemed severe by Florida natives; see Hickmon, "Weather and Crops," 448.

78. Cohen, *Notices of Florida*, 58.

79. McKenney, *Memoirs*, 280.

80. McCall, *Letters from the Frontier*, 301. For other negative interpretations of this treaty, see Satz, *American Indian Policy*, 102, and Foreman, *Indian Removal*, 321.

81. Potter, *War in Florida*, 67 [footnote].

82. Ross, *Letter from John Ross*, 8. Schermerhorn, a Dutch Reform minister, has been called, among other epithets, "a well-chosen tool for a mission of fraud and treachery"; see Baillou, introduction to *John Howard Payne*, 7.

83. Abel, *American Indian as Slaveholder*, 17.

84. "Delegate White to the Secretary of War, January 23, 1832," in *TP* 24:637.

85. Sprague, *Florida War*, 72; see also John Phagan to the Secretary of War, February 7, 1832, in *TP* 24:651–52.

86. Sprague, *Florida War*, 72–73. Phagan waited twenty years before being paid for

his services at Fort Gibson (a total of $450); see "An Act for the Relief of John Phagan," *Globe*, September 13, 1854.

87. Sprague, *Florida War*, 73.

88. Monaco, "Ethan Allen Hitchcock," 188–89; Hitchcock, journal entry, April 30, 1841, Diary #20, 25, 28, 36, Hitchcock Diaries, GM; Satz, *American Indian Policy*, 161, 193–94; Gibson, *Chickasaws*, 196, 213–14.

89. Hitchcock, *Fifty Years in Camp and Field*, 120.

CHAPTER 2: Seminoles, Slaves, and Maroons

1. Rivers, *Rebels and Runaways*, 142. Rivers is joined by Canter Brown Jr. in advancing the theory that the Second Seminole War should more properly be construed as a slave rebellion. See Rivers and Brown, "The Indispensable Man"; Rivers, *Slavery in Florida*, 189–209; Brown, "Persifor F. Smith," 407–10; Brown, *Florida's Peace River Frontier*, 41–59; Brown, "The Florida Crisis," 419–42; and Twyman, *Black Seminole Legacy*.

2. Rivers, *Rebels and Runaways*, 5.

3. Recent treatments by military historians follow in the tradition set by Mahon's *History of the Second Seminole War* and emphasize the ultimate authority of Seminole leaders. See Vandervort, *Indian Wars*; Missall and Missall, *Seminole Wars*; Samuel Watson, "Seminole Strategy"; Knetsch, "Strategy, Operations, and Tactics," 128–54; Watson, *Peacekeepers and Conquerors*; Knetsch, *Fear and Anxiety*; and Hall, "Reckless Waste of Blood and Treasure."

4. For documentation attesting to Spanish sovereignty over this region and the tribes who lived there, see Don Luis Rodrigo de Ortega, August 7, 1739, "List of Florida Provinces, 1736," in Worth, *Struggle for the Georgia Coast*, 184–85.

5. Frank, *Creeks and Southerners*, 14.

6. Kathryn E. Holland Braund supports the earlier time frame in *Deerskins and Duffels*, 4–5. Steven C. Hann comments on the divergence of opinion in *Invention of the Creek Nation*, 5.

7. Calloway, *American Revolution in Indian Country*, 249; Hann, *Creek Nation*, 182.

8. According to William Bartram's *Travels*, Cuscowilla's location is within the present limits of the town of Micanopy, about twelve miles south of Gainesville. But as yet, no archaeological survey has been conducted to determine its exact locale.

9. Weisman, *Like Beads on a String*, 41–43; Braund, "Congress Held in a Pavilion," 82; for Payne's record of killing Spaniards, see Patrick, *Florida Fiasco*, 180.

10. Weisman, "Plantation System," 138.

11. Stojanowski, *Bioarchaeology of Ethnogenesis*, 138–40; Weisman, *Unconquered People*, 25; Miller, *Coacoochee's Bones*, 8.

12. Fairbanks, "Ethno-Archaeology of the Florida Seminole," 166–69.

13. Yuchees (also Yuchis), according to Brent Weisman, joined the Seminoles during the Second Seminole War but remained in separate villages and retained their own identity; see Weisman, "Band of Outsiders," 221.

14. Ethridge, *Creek Country*, 32–53; Saunt, "Taking Account of Property," 733; Sattler, "Remnants, Renegades, and Runaways," 42–43.

15. For reference to merging with remnant Timucua and Apalache, see Fairbanks, "Ethno-Archaeology," 166.

16. In regard to 1765, see Weisman, *Unconquered People*, 17, 26, and Kevin Mulroy,

Freedom on the Border, 7; see also "A Grant of Indian Territory from the Upper Creek Indians as Also the Lower Creeks and Seminolies to Colonel Thomas Brown Superintendent of Indian Affairs for the Southern District of North America," March 1, 1783, World Digital Library, accessed October 21, 2015, http://www.wdl.org/en/item/14197/?utm_source=feed&utm_medium=rss&utm_campaign=feed.

17. Bartram, *Travels*, 164–65.

18. Veracini, *Settler Colonialism*, 78–79.

19. Veracini, *Settler Colonial Present*, 5–6.

20. "Speech of Mr. Levy, of Florida, in the House of Representatives, June 12, 1842," *Florida Herald and Southern Democrat*, August 1, 1842. For Levy's Caribbean origins, see Monaco, *Moses Levy of Florida*, 71.

21. "Speech of Mr. Levy," *Florida Herald and Southern Democrat*, August 1, 1842. The erroneous notion that Seminoles were not aboriginal but were exogenous "others" still remains problematic today.

22. Veracini, *Settler Colonialism*, 79.

23. Veracini, "On Settlerness," 2; see also Jodi A. Byrd, *Transit of Empire*, xv–xix, 222.

24. Grady, *Anglo-Spanish Rivalry*, 73.

25. Landers, "Bondsmen into Vassals," 125–26.

26. Saunt, *New Order of Things*, 125.

27. The practice of slavery by Native people in Florida may not have been as uniform as commonly accepted. One observer noted that Opauney's Town, a Seminole village located north of Tampa Bay, held twenty slaves who "performed the same labor that is generally expected on plantations in Florida" and lived in separate "Negro houses" adjacent to the fields; see Horatio S. Dexter to William P. Duval (St. Augustine), August 20, 1823, in Boyd, "Horatio S. Dexter," 91–92.

28. Th[omas] S. Jesup to J. C. Spencer, December 28, 1841, in "Seminole War—Slaves Captured," House Doc. 55, 27th Cong., 2nd Sess., January 29, 1842.

29. Dexter, "Observations on the Seminole Indians" [1823], in Boyd, "Horatio S. Dexter," 81.

30. Millett, *Maroons of Prospect Bluff*.

31. Wright, *Creeks and Seminoles*, 183.

32. Sayers, "Marronage Perspective," 136.

33. Landers, "Bondsmen into Vassals," 128–29.

34. For the Patriot War, see Cusick, *The Other War of 1812*, and Patrick, *Florida Fiasco*. For black reinforcements from Cuba, see [Colonel] Smith to [Major] Thomas Bourke, October 25, 1812, in Davis, "United States Troops," 261.

35. For the diplomatic nature of this interaction, see Landers, "Bondsmen into Vassals," 136.

36. Millett, *Prospect Bluff*, 232–35.

37. Dexter, "Observations," 84.

38. Brown, "Runaway Negro Plantations," 15–19; Landers, *Black Society*, 237; Millett, *Prospect Bluff*, 250–51.

39. Millett, *Prospect Bluff*, 251.

40. Dexter, "Observations," 81.

41. Thomas S. Jesup, February 3, 1837, "Diary Seminole Campaign," RG 900000, Series M86–12, State Archives of Florida, Tallahassee, 92.

42. Gould, "Entangled Histories," 771.

43. "Of Property," in Locke, *Works of John Locke*, 165–72. See also Arneil, *John Locke*.

44. "Petition for Admission into the Union" and "Resolution by the Legislative Council of the Elotchaway [Alachua] District," January 25, 1814, Patriot War Documents, Miscellaneous Documents, Alma Clyde Field Library of Florida History, Cocoa.

45. D. L. Clinch to R. Jones (Fort King), January 22, 1835, LR, roll 0105, M567, RG 94, NARA.

46. Such fears can be traced to the mid-eighteenth century, when the British were similarly concerned about a hypothetical black and Indian alliance; see Braund, "Creek Indians, Blacks and Slavery," 611.

47. Patrick, *Aristocrat in Uniform*, 66.

48. "Hayti and the Haytiens," *DeBow's Review* 16, no. 1 (January 1854): 35. For more on the impact of the Haitian Revolution, see Clavin, *Toussaint Louverture*; Hunt, *Haiti's Influence on Antebellum America*; and James, *The Black Jacobins*.

49. Frances Anne Kemble to Elizabeth Dwight Sedgwick, April 1839, in Kemble, *Journal of a Residence*, 295.

50. Kaplan, "Fanon, Trauma and Cinema," 153. See also Patrick, *Aristocrat*, 64–65; Walvin, *Questioning Slavery*, 122; Grant, *Way It Was in the South*, 49–51; and Cecil-Fronsman, *Common Whites*, 83–84.

51. On the use of power, see Harris, "How Did Colonialism Dispossess?" 165.

52. Simmons, *Notices of East Florida*, 76.

53. Deposition of Edward M. Wanton, January 14, 1835, ASP:MA 6:461. Since prime steers were rated at $20 each, full-grown slaves in excellent health could sell for the equivalent of $800 (circa 1812).

54. Simmons, *Notices of East Florida*, 75–76.

55. Statement of John Hicks, January 14, 1829, in Sprague, *The Florida War*, 66.

56. Quoted in Covington, *Seminoles of Florida*, 63; for the number of Micanopy's slaves, see Dexter, "Observations," 88.

57. Chang, *Color of the Land*, 22.

58. Weisman, "Plantation System," 137.

59. Simmons, *Notices of East Florida*, 81–85.

60. Braund, "Creek Indians," 608.

61. Osceola quotations in Sprague, *Florida War*, 86.

62. Simmons, *Notices of East Florida*, 84–85; Morse, *Report to the Secretary of War*, appendix, 309.

63. For reference to slave cowboys, see Saunt, *New Order of Things*, 134; for quote regarding cattle and wealth, see "Extract of a Letter from Captain Bell to the Secretary of War," January 22, 1822, in *Letter from the Secretary of War*, 17.

64. Dexter, "Observations," 81. For a detailed look at Seminole cattle production, see Parker, "Cattle Trade in East Florida," 150–67; in addition, see Fairbanks, "Ethno-Archaeology," 168. Commercial cattle ranches in this region dated to the mid-seventeenth century under the Spanish. Predating the Seminoles, the largest cattle ranch in Florida was located at Paynes Prairie; see Worth, *Timucuan Chiefdoms*, 199–202; Bushnell, "Menendez Marquez Cattle Barony," 408, 423; Baker, "Spanish Ranching," 82–100; and Arnade, "Cattle Raising in Spanish Florida," 116–24.

65. Parker, "Cattle Trade," 162.

66. Landers, *Black Society*, 91–92.

67. Simmons, *Notices of East Florida*, 75. Choctaw herds grew to 43,000 head during the 1820s, but Simmons was referring to an earlier time period; Carson, "Choctaw Cattle Economy," 11.

68. Covington, *Seminoles*, 29. Signs of affluence, including "an abundance of jewelry pieces," were discovered at an archaeological dig at the Paynes Town site; see Blakney-Bailey, "Paynes Town Seminole Site," 158, 164.

69. Slave cowboys would have followed a general pattern established in Latin America and the Caribbean (especially Santo Domingo, Cuba, and Puerto Rico); see Stinchcombe, *Sugar Island Slavery*, 52; Slatta, *Cowboys of the Americas*, 95–96; Andrews, *Afro-Latin America*, 15–16; and Brockington, *Leverage of Labor*, 135, 158.

70. The binary tendency of conceptualizing slavery is discussed in Snyder, *Slavery in Indian Country*, 5–6. For slave variability, see Thompson, "Between Slavery and Freedom," 414. For the antithesis of slavery within a Native context, see Saunt, "Creeks, Seminoles, and the Problem of Slavery," 161.

71. McLoughlin, "America's Slaveholding Indians," 370.

72. Porter, "Relations between Negroes and Indians," 326.

73. Porter, "Negro Abraham," 9.

74. Porter, "Three Fighters for Freedom," 54.

75. Porter, *Black Seminoles*, 73. Porter makes a similar unverified claim in "John Caesar," 197.

76. Jane Landers refers to "the important and pioneering work of Kenneth W. Porter, to whom we are all indebted," in Landers, *Black Society*, 368 n. 2. In a very brief sampling, Porter is cited no less than thirty-one times in Rivers, *Rebels and Runaways* and an equal number in Mulroy, *Freedom on the Border*, thirty-three in Mulroy's, *Seminole Freedmen*, and a startling sixty-seven instances in Dixon, "Black Seminole Involvement and Leadership," an unpublished dissertation that has often been cited by black sovereignty proponents.

77. Mamdani, "Settler Colonialism," 607; emphasis added.

78. Penieres quote from Porter, *Black Seminoles*, 25.

79. For reference to Penieres contracting "the cursed Negro fever" [malaria], see J. A. Penieres to [William Lee], July 2, 1821, PKY. For background on Penieres, see J. C. Calhoun to Andrew Jackson, March 31, 1821, in *TP* 22:24, and Mahon, "Treaty of Moultrie Creek," 351. Penieres was also accused of incompetency; see Boyd, "Horatio S. Dexter," 67, 69.

80. George M. Brooke to G. Humphries, May 6, 1828, in Sprague, *Florida War*, 52.

81. For St. Augustine slave sales, see Landers, *Black Society*, 174. For an example of manumission, see "Deed of Sale, Micanopy, Chief of the Seminole Tribe of Indians (Ft. King)," May 6, 1834, Ancient Records Deed Book B, Alachua County Clerk of the County Court, Gainesville, FL. This document describes a transaction by Micanopy wherein he sold "a certain negro girl named Catherine" to the girl's birth parents, John and Susan Paine, for $140 with the stipulation that the five-year-old would be awarded freedom when she reached the age of twenty-one. On the practice of *coartación* and manumission in Spanish Florida, see Landers, *Black Society*, 139–44.

82. Mulroy, *Seminole Freedmen*, 44.

83. Genovese, *Roll Jordon Roll*, 82; Genovese, *The World the Slaveholders Made*, 6;

Van Deburg, *Black Villains and Social Bandits*, 41. For the perception of Indian masters as too lenient, see Krauthamer, *Black Slaves, Indian Masters*, 6. The Seminole approach to slavery bore a resemblance to earlier Creek practice, a scenario that also drew criticism from whites; see Chang, *Color of the Land*, 22.

84. Kokomoor, "A Re-assessment of Seminoles," 215.

85. Bauman, "Making and Unmaking of Strangers," 1.

86. Wolfe, "Structure and Event," 103, 113–14; Altman, "Indigenous Rights," 52–53.

87. Quoted in Klos, "Blacks and the Seminole Removal Debate," 63.

88. As Weisman has noted: "Ultimately the prevailing political wisdom held that the Seminoles possessed two forms of property to which they were not entitled, and had no rights to: land and people"; see Weisman, "*Seminole Wars in Florida*," 393.

89. Veracini, *Settler Colonialism*, 86.

90. "Copy of a Letter from a Highly Respectable Gentleman of Florida," January 20, 1836, *ASP:MA* 6:20. For a review of this topic, see Clavin, "'It Is a Negro, Not an Indian War," 181–208.

91. Cohen, *Notices of Florida*, 239. See also Motte, *Journey into Wilderness*, 210.

92. For a discussion of stereotypes and ideology, see Deloria, *Indians in Unexpected Places*, 9–10.

93. Sattler, "Siminoli Italwa," 143, 209; Miller, "Seminoles and Africans," 35–36.

94. Motte, *Journey in Wilderness*, 210; emphasis added.

95. George Klos has placed this number at four hundred, of which eighty were identified as maroons; see Klos, "Blacks and the Seminole Removal," 58. Mulroy (*Seminole Freedmen*, 46) notes that five hundred blacks were eventually transported west with the Seminoles.

96. Kenneth Porter used Jesup's phrase throughout his work; see, for example, "Florida Slaves and Free Negroes in the Seminole War, 1835–1842," *Journal of Negro History* 28, no. 4 (October 1943): 390–421; "Three Fighters for Freedom," *Journal of Negro History* 28, no. 1 (January 1943): 51–72; "Notes Supplementary to 'Relations between Negroes and Indians,'" *Journal of Negro History* 18, no. 3 (July 1933): 282–321; and Porter, *Black Seminoles*, 66–67, 107.

97. Jesup's remark has become so ubiquitous that a full list of books that have referred to it would be pointless. A seldom acknowledged by-product of this mass acceptance has been the fact that scores of PhD students have also uncritically accepted this phrase. A limited sample of dissertations follow: Terrence M. Weik, "A Historical Archaeology of Black Seminole Maroons in Florida: Ethnogenesis and Culture Contact at Pilaklikaha" (PhD diss., University of Florida, 2002); Yvonne Tolagbe Ogunleye, "An African-Centered Historical Analysis of the Self-Emancipated Africans of Florida, 1738–1838" (PhD diss., Temple University, 1995); Dale Rosengarten, "Social Origins of the African-American Lowcountry Basket" (PhD diss., Harvard University, 1997); Anthony E. Dixon, "Black Seminole Involvement and Leadership during the Second Seminole War, 1835–1842" (PhD diss., Indiana University, 2007); Philip Matthew Smith, "Persistent Borderland: Freedom and Citizenship in Territorial Florida" (PhD diss., Texas A&M University, 2007).

98. Thomas S. Jesup to William Schley (Volusia), December 9, 1836, folder 13, box 50, HRB.

99. Jesup to B. F. Butler, December 9, 1836, *ASP:MA* 7:820.

100. Brown, *Looking for Angola.*

101. Jesup to [Captain] P. H. Galt (Garey's Ferry), August 13, 1837, LR, roll 106, RG 94, NARA.

102. Jesup to [Major] Whiting, June 4, 1837, LR, roll 0145, RG 94, NARA.

103. Jesup to Armistead, June 6, 1837, LR, roll 0145, RG 94, NARA.

104. Jesup, "The Capture of Osceola," *National Intelligencer*, October 13, 1858. Additional details are found in Thomas S. Jesup, undated draft letter [1858], folder 7, box 1, Thomas S. Jesup Papers, WLC.

105. Jesup to J. R. Poinsett, March 14, 1838, LR, roll 0167, RG 94, NARA.

106. Jesup to William Wilkins, May 22, 1844, folder 6, box 1, Jesup Papers, WLC.

107. Ibid.

108. On one occasion, Porter acknowledged Jesup was employing hyperbole but subsequently retreated to a more literalist approach; see Porter, "Negroes and the Seminole War," 427.

109. Rivers advances the theory of a vast conspiracy and cover-up in a videotaped lecture: "Dr. Larry Rivers at the University of Florida." Moreover, Y. N. Kly, although not a professional historian, goes into unusual depth about what he considers the deliberate suppression of information, including (unsubstantiated) claims of press censorship, in Kly, "The Gullah War," 50, n. 41, n. 42.

110. I have placed this ahistorical impulse into a specific "heritage" framework; see Monaco, "Whose War Was It?" See also chapter 11.

CHAPTER 3: "It Came with the Suddenness of the Whirlwind"

1. Mahon believed that this large assembly was solely in expectation of annuity payments; Mahon, *Second Seminole War*, 95.

2. Lewis Cass to Wiley Thompson, January 1, 1835, ASP:MA 7:522.

3. Simmons, "Recollections," 547.

4. A. Jackson to "The Chiefs and Warriors of the Seminole Indians in Florida," February 16, 1835, in ASP:MA 7:524; Remini, *Andrew Jackson*, 306.

5. "The Chiefs and Warriors," February 16, 1835, in ASP:MA 7:524.

6. For the relationship to William H. Simmons, see George E. Buker, "Introduction," in *Notices of East Florida*, xvii. For Simmons's article, see "Recollections," 542–57. This lengthy article was published earlier as a serial in *Atkinson's Saturday Evening Post* throughout August 1836. (Simmons's journalistic importance has previously been missed in the historiography.) See also "Recollections of the Late Campaign in East Florida," *National Intelligencer*, July 21 and 27, 1836; *Richmond Whig*, July 27, 1836; "Osceola," *Cincinnati Mirror* and *Western Gazette of Literature, Science, and the Arts*, August 27, 1836; "The Indian Chief—'Oceola,'" *Alexandria Gazette*, July 15, 1836. Joining Simmons was another onlooker named John Bemrose, who recorded his impression of the war dance many years after the event; see Bemrose, *Reminiscences*, 21–22. The Bemrose version differs significantly from Simmons, likely because of the length of time that elapsed after the author recalled the affair, many years after the fact.

7. Bemrose, *Reminiscences*, 22.

8. Simmons, "Recollections," 546.

9. Ibid.

10. Mahon, *Second Seminole War*, 96; Wickman, *Osceola's Legacy*, 65; for background on Abiaka, see West, "Abiaka," 366–410.

11. Sprague, *Florida War*, 84; Boyd, "The Seminole War," 52.

12. "Speech of Mr. Everett," June 3, 1836, in *Appendix to the Congressional Globe*, 24th Cong., 1st sess., June 1836, 543.

13. Ibid, 544.

14. Simmons, "Recollections," 548; Smith, *Sketch of the Seminole War*, 10; Mahon, *Second Seminole War*, 96.

15. For the composition of the war council, see Wickman, *Osceola's Legacy*, 15.

16. Grimsley, *Hard Hand of War*; Lee, *Barbarians and Brothers*.

17. Patrick, *Florida Fiasco*, 231–34; Cusick, *The Other War of 1812*, 256. It appears that Seminoles managed to leave with their slaves and most of their cattle before these forces struck.

18. For the importance of international borders, see Buhaug and Gaines, "Geography of Civil War," 422.

19. "Affairs in Florida," *National Intelligencer*, January 29, 1836.

20. Watson, "Seminole Strategy," 160.

21. "Petition to the President of the United States (Alachua County, Territory of Florida) January 1834," ASP:MA 6:465–66.

22. Boyd, "The Seminole War," 55; George Gillett Keen, October 14, 1899, in Denham and Brown, *Cracker Times and Pioneer Lives*, 27. This incident occurred near the Hogtown settlement; see Cohen, *Notices of Florida*, 65–66.

23. Weisman, "Cove of the Withlacoochee," 4.

24. Boyd, "The Seminole War," 56.

25. "Seminole War: First Campaign. Extracts from the Journal of a Private," *New Hampshire Gazette*, May 9, 1837.

26. Fanning to Clinch (Fort King), November 28, 1835, and D. L. Clinch to [Major General] A. Macomb (St. Augustine), December 1, 1835, LR, roll 0106, RG 94, NARA. For Charley Emathla's Apalachee origins, see Miller, *Coacoochee's Bones*, 30, 38; others in the proremoval factions are mentioned in Mahon, *Second Seminole War*, 93.

27. Dowd, *A Spirited Resistance*, 170–71.

28. Boyd, "The Seminole War," 56; Sprague, *Florida War*, 88.

29. Sprague, *Florida War*, 88.

30. Wickman believes Osceola was a member of the Bird Clan, a clan that entitled its members to be "lawgivers and law enforcers"; see Wickman, *Osceola's Legacy*, 74.

31. "Extract from a Letter Dated Jan. 1, 1836," *Mississippi Free Trader* and *Natchez Gazette*, January 15, 1836. Black Dirt may have been a kinsman of Charley Emathla; see Wright, *Creeks and Seminoles*, 299.

32. *Florida Herald and Southern Democrat*, May 12, 1836; for escalating tensions, see Fanning to Clinch (Fort King), November 28, 1835, and D. L. Clinch to [Major General] A. Macomb (St. Augustine), December 1, 1835, LR, roll 0106, RG 94, NARA. For reference to the attacks in Alachua during the first week in December, see D. L. Clinch to R. Jones (Fort Defiance), December 9, 1835, LR; R. K. Call to [Colonel] J. C. Love, December 6, 1835, Richard Keith Call Papers, accessed November 26, 2016, https://www.floridamemory.com/items/show/267432.

33. D. L. Clinch to R. Jones (Fort Defiance), December 9, 1835, LR, roll 0106, RG 94, NARA.

34. Quotations from Clinch to Jones (Fort Drane), December 26, 1835, LR.

35. Clinch to Jones (Fort Drane), December 16, 1835, LR.

36. Andrew Jackson to Secretary of War, December 11, 1835, "Pioneer Days in Florida: Diaries and Letters from the Settling of the Sunshine State, 1800–1900," PKY. The content of this letter was crossed out by pen sometime after it was received by the secretary of war but is still clearly legible.

37. Mahon, *Second Seminole War*, 101; Boyd, "Seminole War," 57; John Warren to D. L. Clinch, December 19, 1835, in *United States' Telegraph*, January 6, 1836; "KOCOA Map, Battle of Black Point" and "Battlefield Landscape Analysis," in Gary Ellis, C. S. Monaco, Ken Nash, J. Dean, and J. Principe, "Fort Defiance/Fort Micanopy and the Opening Battles of the Second Seminole War 1835–1836, Historic and Archeological Study," American Battlefield Protection Program, NPS, 2010–2011, 58–61.

38. For the number of cattle, see Potter, *The War in Florida*, 5.

39. Letter to the Editor, December 30, 1835, *New York Commercial Advertiser*, January 18, 1836; see also "Seminole War," *New York Spectator*, January 21, 1836.

40. Bartholomew Lynch, diary entries, October 25, 1838, and March 3, 1839, in McGaughy, "Lynch's Journal," 166, 187. Lynch was born in County Kerry, Ireland, and saw additional service in the war with Mexico. He left the service with the rank of sergeant and worked in Philadelphia as a watchman for the Navy Yard; see "Biography of Mrs. Shaw and Mrs. Lynch" (from the *Philadelphia Bulletin*), *Daily Scioto Gazette*, March 28, 1853.

41. Sprague, *Florida War*, 90–91; emphasis original. The most definitive record of the Dade ambush, at least from the perspective of the US Army, is Laumer, *Dade's Last Command*.

42. "Statement of Rawson [sic] Clarke," in Cohen, *Notices of Florida*, 71–72.

43. Sprague, *Florida War*, 91.

44. Vandervort, *Indian Wars*, 134; quote from "Affairs in Florida," *National Intelligencer*, January 29, 1836.

45. Clark alters his account later, emphasizing some points and ignoring others; see, for example, "Ransom Clark," *Army and Navy Chronicle*, June 15, 1837.

46. Sprague, *Florida War*, 90.

47. An important exception is Watson, "Seminole Strategy," 155–80.

48. Mahon, *Second Seminole War*, 121.

49. Sprague, *Florida War*, 98.

50. For example, Joseph Hernandez borrowed the extraordinary sum of $38,000 from the First Union Bank of Florida in 1835; see Siebert, "Sugar Industry in Florida," 314; Boyd, "The Seminole War"; for more on the indebtedness of these planters, see Wayne, *Sugar Works*, 42.

51. "Reminiscences of the Life of George Ormand, 1892" (typescript), 15–16, Ormand Family Papers, PKY.

52. For the Dunham attack, see Cohen, *Notices of Florida*, 87–88; for more on Dunham, see Motte, *Journey into Wilderness*, 152, 292 n. 6.

53. Sprague, *Florida War*, 216.

54. Ormand, "Reminiscences," 15, PKY.

55. Cohen, *Notices of Florida*, 96; Boyd, "The Seminole War," 65.

56. Quotations from "Extracts from a Letter Dated Fort George (Fl.), May 9, 1836" (from the *Charleston Courier*), *National Intelligencer*, May 24, 1836.

57. Quotation "From Our Correspondent" (Fort Brooke), April 13, 1836, in the *Maryland Gazette*, May 12, 1836.

58. Cohen, *Notices of Florida*, 81.

59. Jane Murray Sheldon, "Seminole Attacks near New Smyrna, 1836–1856," *Florida Historical Quarterly* 8, no. 4 (April 1930): 191–93. This narrative was dictated by Sheldon to her daughter in 1890.

60. Cohen, *Notices of Florida*, 78–79.

61. Humphreys, May 2, 1836 (Fort Drane), in "Field Journal," 215.

62. Humphreys, May 2, 1836, in "Field Journal," 215. After the war, Humphreys became a leading engineer and member of the American Philosophical Society.

63. "Seminole War," January 27, 1836, *Register of Debates*, 24th Cong., 1st Sess., 1836, 12, 2359; "Hostilities in Florida: Report of the Secretary of War," *Evening Post*, February 17, 1836; Lewis Cass to Winfield Scott, January 21, 1836, ASP:MA 6, 61.

64. "Affairs of Florida: In Senate, February 10," *Niles Weekly Register*, February 20, 1836; M. Dickerson to Lewis Cass, May 18, 1836, in ASP:MA 6, 440; Prince, diary entry, April 9, 1836, in Prince, *Storm of Bullets*, 39.

65. Bemrose, *Reminiscences*, 42.

66. Clinch to Jones (Fort Drane), January 4, 1836, LR, NARA; Mahon, *Second Seminole War*, 108.

67. R. K. Call to [Governor] John H. Eaton, January 8, 1836, in "Proceedings of Military Courts of Inquiry on the Operations of the Army under Command of Major General Scott and Major General Gaines, and on the Course Pursued by these Officers Respectively," ASP:MA 7:220.

68. Bemrose, *Reminiscences*, 49.

69. Ibid.

70. Ibid., 51; Mahon, *Second Seminole War*, 120. Bemrose remarked that the Seminoles' high-quality rifles, supplied from Cuba, were of a smaller bore; their shots were reputed to maim, often quite terribly, rather than kill. According to a recent archaeological investigation of the battlefield site, however, archaeologist Gary Ellis (Gulf Archaeology Research Institute) discovered a wide range of ball shot, none of which was particularly small; personal communication with Ellis, June 15, 2016. The most common firearm used by the army was the US musket, M1816, a .69 caliber, smoothbore flintlock; Ron G. Hickox, *U.S. Military Edged Weapons of the Second Seminole War, 1835–1842*, 54.

71. Mahon, *Second Seminole War*, 109–11; Missall and Missall, *The Seminole War*, 97–100; Patrick, *Aristocrat in Uniform*, 99–106; Knetsch, *Fear and Anxiety*, 89–92; for Clinch's official report of the battle, see Cohen, *Notices*, 83–86.

72. Bemrose, *Reminiscences*, 56.

73. Patrick, *Aristocrat*, 109–110.

74. Knetsch, "Strategy, Operations and Tactics," 130.

75. McReynolds, *The Seminoles*, 161.

76. Sprague, *Florida War*, 93.

CHAPTER 4: The United States Responds

1. "Indian Hostilities—The Massacre," *New York Commercial Advertiser*, January 27, 1836; see also Stone, *Joseph Brant-Thayendanega*.

2. Brown, "Persifor F. Smith," 396.

3. "Public Meeting in Charleston, Jan. 21," in Cohen, *Notices of Florida*, 111; on the ages of volunteers, see Lynch, March 17, 1836, in McGaughy, "Journal."

4. Baldwin, *Notices of the Campaigns*, 12–13.

5. Cohen, *Notices of Florida*, 116, 119.

6. Hitchcock, diary entry, January 30, 1836, Diary # 7, Ethan Allen Hitchcock Diaries, GM, 7–8.

7. "Captain Hitchcock's Testimony," January 14, 1837, Military Court of Inquiry, in *ASP:MA* 7:370; "Indian Hostilities," *Spectator*, February 8, 1836.

8. On the receipt of these orders, see Hitchcock, February 1836, Diary #7, 21–22; supporting the view that Gaines had not seen these orders, see Geo[rge] McCall, letter to the editor, *New Orleans Bulletin*, May 18, 1836, in "Proceedings of the Military Court," 382; for the antipathy that existed between Gaines and Scott, see Coffman, *Old Army*, 67–68; Skelton, *Profession of Arms*, 200; Peskin, *Winfield Scott*, 76–79, 91–96, 120–22.

9. Hitchcock, February 1836, Diary #7, 13–16.

10. Hitchcock, February 1836, Diary #7, 16–19.

11. "Official," *Globe*, March 10, 1836. Hitchcock's report, dated February 23, first appeared in the *Globe* and was then reprinted nationally.

12. Smith, *Sketch of the Seminole War*, 39; for another contemporary account, see Barr, *Correct and Authentic Narrative*.

13. Smith, *Sketch of the Seminole War*, 42.

14. Missall and Missall, *Seminole Wars*, 106. According to Lt. Henry Prince, the dirge was *Scots wha hae wi'Wallace bled*; see Prince, *Storm of Bullets*, 30.

15. For example, the *Virginia Free Press*, February 18, 1836, stated: "Fort King . . . is sacked and every human being—officers, men, women and children murdered; aye, murdered in cold blood."

16. Hitchcock, February 1836, Diary #7, 20; see also Barr, *Authentic Narrative*, 15.

17. "Deposition of General Clinch," January 6, 1837, Military Court of Inquiry, in *ASP:MA* 7:155.

18. Hitchcock, February 1836, Diary #7, 24; this engagement is also noted in Prince, February 27, 1836, *Diary*, 15.

19. Hitchcock, February 1836, Diary #7, 24; "Interrogation of Captain Thistle," January 17, 1837, in *ASP:MA* 7:375. This encampment was evidently at the same site that Clinch had occupied.

20. E. A. Hitchcock to [Hon.] Francis S. Lyon (Fort Drane), March 11, 1836, in "Proceedings of the Military Court," 378.

21. Hitchcock, February 1836, Diary #7, 26.

22. Hitchcock later determined the exact number of his opponents from Fuche Luste Hadjo; see "From Florida, Tampa March 20," *Niles' Weekly Register*, April 23, 1836.

23. Prince, *Diary*, 16

24. Spenser, "Veue of the Present State of Ireland," 89.

25. Prince, *Diary*, 16; for the "hideous" nature of "their yells, and painted, naked

figures," see "Letter from Fort Brooke, Tampa Bay, Florida, Dated Jan. 16" (from the *Baltimore Patriot*), *Schenectady Reflector*, February 19, 1836.

26. Hitchcock, February 1836, Diary #7, 28.

27. Ibid., 30; Mahon, *Second Seminole War*, 147.

28. Edmund P. Gaines to [Duncan] Clinch (Camp Izard), February 28, 1836, Military Court of Inquiry, in *ASP:MA* 7:427.

29. "Testimony of Captain Hitchcock," January 13, 1837, Military Court of Inquiry, in *ASP:MA* 7, 368.

30. Gaines to Clinch (Camp Izard), February 29, 1836, in *ASP:MA* 7, 427; see also Prince, *Diary*, 17; Mahon, *Seminole War*, 147; Missall and Missall, *Seminole Wars*, 107.

31. Gaines to Clinch (Camp Izard), February 29, 1836, in *ASP:MA* 7:427.

32. Hitchcock, February 1836, Diary #7, 30–31.

33. "Defense of Major General E. P. Gaines before the Court of Inquiry," February 1837, in *ASP:MA* 7:399.

34. On the challenge to a duel, see Coffman, *The Old Army*, 69; Eisenhower, *Agent of Destiny*, 120; Peskin, *Winfield Scott*, 77–78.

35. Coffman, *The Old Army*, 66–69.

36. Prince, diary entry, March 5, 1838, *Diary*, 22.

37. Bemrose, *Reminiscences*, 77. An estimated one hundred men could not continue active duty; see "Testimony of Charles M. Thruston," December 9, 1836, in *ASP:MA* 7:144.

38. Hitchcock, March 1836, Diary #7, 32.

39. George E. Harral to E. A. Hitchcock (New Orleans), October 9, 1836, in *ASP:MA* 7:435

40. Hitchcock, March 1836, Diary #7, 34.

41. In Sprague's version of events (Sprague, *Florida War*, 111–12), the interpreter was identified as John Caesar. While the author was never present at the Withlacoochee, he nevertheless relied on "intelligent Indians and negroes" who were supposedly on the scene when Sprague wrote his history twelve years after the event. According to this rendition, Caesar reached out on his own accord and did not consult the Seminoles—a most improbable scenario. This claim is contrary to the documentary evidence, including Hitchcock's diary, wherein no mention of Caesar (or any controversy) is given. Because of Hitchcock's principal role during the proceedings, I defer to his account. The voluminous testimony of the 1836–37 Military Court of Inquiry (cited herein), including depositions from all the officers who were present, also fails to identify or mention Caesar.

42. Hitchcock, March 1836, Diary #7, 35.

43. Harral to Hitchcock, October 9, 1836, in *ASP:MA* 7:435.

44. Mahon, *Second Seminole War*, 127.

45. Hitchcock, March 1836, Diary #7, 35.

46. Silver, "A Counter-Proposal," 207–15.

47. Hitchcock, March 1836, Diary #7, 35.

48. Joel W. Jones, extract from a letter dated February 24, 1836 (St. Augustine), in Jones, "A Brief Narrative of Some of the Principal Events in the Life of Joel W. Jones," 1849, typescript, 59, PKY. For the amount of damages, see "Speech of Mr. Levy of Florida, in the House of Representatives, June 12, 1842," *Florida Herald and Southern Democrat*, August 1, 1842; see also Monaco, "Alachua Settlers," 1–32.

49. Harral to Hitchcock, October 9, 1836, Military Court of Inquiry, in *ASP:MA* 7, 435.

50. Hitchcock, March 1836, Diary #7, 39–43.

51. "Testimony of Captain Thistle," January 18, 1837, in *ASP:MA* 7:539.

52. "Military Court of Inquiry," in *ASP:MA* 7:52–53, 146–47, 306, 379–80, 389–90, 520–21, 529–30, 532–33, 557–58.

53. Ibid., 53, 557–58.

54. Hitchcock, March and April, 1836, Diary #7, 48–53.

55. "Indian Hostilities—The Massacre," *New York Commercial Advertiser*, January 27, 1836.

56. "Deposition of Colonel James Gadsden," Military Court of Inquiry, in *ASP:MA* 7:134; for the reaction of Jackson to the Gaines's affair, see Gadsden to Jackson, July 24, 1836, series 1, general correspondence, Andrew Jackson Papers, LOC.

57. For reference to the War of 1812, see Missall and Missall, *Seminole War*, 113. For reference to the grand army, see Prince, *Diary*, March 26, 1836, 34.

58. Francis Marion Robertson to Henrietta Robertson (Fort Drane), March 17, 1836, in Robertson, "The Richmond Blues," 57.

59. "Major General Scott's Address or Summary of Evidence Taken in His Case," in *ASP:MA* 7:185; "Defense of Major Gen. Scott," *National Intelligencer*, January 27, 1837.

60. Bemrose, *Reminiscences*, 78.

61. Edmund P. Gaines to "Officers of the Light Brigade," March 11, 1836, in Missall and Missall, *This Miserable Pride*, 25.

62. "Indian Hostilities—The Massacre," *New York Spectator*, January 28, 1836.

63. James Gadsden to General Eustis (Fort Drane), March 16, 1837, in *ASP:MA* 7:262.

64. Joel W. Jones, entry from March 29, 1836, in Jones, "A Brief Narrative," 1849, typescript, 63, PKY.

65. Ibid., April 5, 1836, 64.

66. For mention of the measles outbreak at this time, see "From Our Correspondent" (Fort Brooke), April 13, 1836, in *Maryland Gazette*, May 12, 1836; "General Scott, Baffled," *Floridian*, April 30, 1836.

67. "General Scott" (from the Washington *Globe* of this morning), *Baltimore Gazette and Daily Advertiser*, July 29, 1836.

68. "General Scott, Baffled," *Floridian*, April 30, 1836.

69. Klunder, *Lewis Cass*, 92.

70. Augustus Crawford to [Governor] William Schley, June 20, 1836, folder 9, box 50, HRB.

71. "Dismal News from Florida" (from the Tallahassee *Floridian*), *National Banner and Nashville Whig*, May 25, 1836; see also "Indian Hostilities," *Niles' Weekly Register*, May 28, 1836. For Scott's maligning comments and the consequences in Florida, see Jos[eph] M. White to Andrew Jackson (Washington, DC), May 28, 1836, in "Petition of Thomas S. Jesup," 7–8.

72. Jos[eph] M. White to Andrew Jackson, May 28, 1836, *Niles' Weekly Register*, July 2, 1836.

73. "25th Congress, 1st Session," September 19, 1837, *Globe*, September 19, 1837.

74. "Opinion of the Court in Reference to the Failure of the Campaign in Florida,

Conducted by Major General Scott, in 1836," Military Court of Inquiry, in *ASP:MA* 7:463.

75. Ibid., "Opinion of the Court in Reference to the Failure of the Campaign in Florida, Conducted by Major General Gaines, in 1836," in *ASP:MA* 7:464–65.

76. Peskin, *Winfield Scott*, 100; Andrew Jackson, "Opinion of the President," February 14, 1837, in *United States' Telegraph*, February 16, 1837; Andrew Jackson to the President of the Court of Inquiry (Washington, DC), February 18, 1837, in *ASP:MA* 7:160.

77. Mahon, *Second Seminole War*, 164.

78. Colonel Lane to T. T. Webb, September 30, 1836, in *Army and Navy Chronicle*, November 24, 1836.

79. "Documentary Testimony," February 22, [1836], in *ASP:MA* 7:160.

80. "Extract of a Letter to the Editor of the *Savannah Georgian*," September 4, 1836, in *Army and Navy Chronicle*, September 22, 1836; "Florida," *New York Spectator*, June 30, 1836; "Proceeding of Congress, House of Representatives, January 30, 1836," in *National Intelligencer*, February 3, 1836; Mahon, *Second Seminole War*, 175.

81. Andrew A. Humphreys, "Proposition to Abandon Fort King," May 17, 1836, roll 0122, NARA.

82. Humphreys, journal entry, May 23, 1836 (Fort Drane), in "Field Journal," 219; "Petition of Gad Humphreys"; "From Florida" (from the *Savannah Georgian*), *Eastern Argus* (Portland, ME), June 14, 1836.

83. Humphreys, June 19, 1836 (Fort Drane), in "Field Journal," 221–22.

84. "The Battle of Micanopy" (from the Washington *Globe*), in the *St. Augustine Herald*, August 31, 1836. This lengthy version of the battle was authored by Captain R. B. Lee. Heileman's brief report was published earlier; see J. F. Heileman, "Battle of Micanopy—Official," June 10, 1836, in *National Intelligencer* (Washington, DC), June 28, 1836. The battle was also briefly noted in the *Times* (London), July 13, 1836.

85. Humphreys, who was present at Heileman's death, wrote that he died from jaundice, one of the side effects of severe malaria infection; Humphreys, July 23, 1836, in "Field Journal," 230.

86. "Lt. Colonel Heileman," *Army and Navy Chronical*, August 11, 1836.

87. *Florida Herald* (St. Augustine), June 25, 1836.

88. Letter to the Editor, "A Citizen of Middle Florida," *National Intelligencer* (Washington, DC), August 27, 1836; Bemrose, *Reminiscences*, 99.

89. *Christian Intelligencer and Eastern Chronicle* (Gardiner, ME), September 16, 1836.

90. Bemrose, *Reminiscences*, 104.

91. "Welika Pond" (from the Washington *Globe*), *Boston Courier*, August 15, 1836; Humphreys, July 23, 1836, in "Field Journal," 229; see also Gary Ellis et al., "Battlefield Landscape Analysis," in *Opening Battles of the Second Seminole War*, 61–70.

92. "Military Correspondence" (Frederick, MD), December 26, 1836, *Connecticut Herald* (New Haven), January 10, 1837; "Distressing Intelligence," *St. Louis Commercial Bulletin* (St. Louis, MO), June 1, 1836.

CHAPTER 5: "Sacrifice of National Honor"

1. Skelton, *Profession of Arms*, 115.

2. *Sylvanus Thayer*, 4; Morrison, *The Best School*, 151; Skelton, *Profession of Arms*, 115; Watson, "How the Army Became Accepted," 234.

3. Morrison, *West Point*, 151; Higgenbotham, "Military Education," 45.

4. Watson, "This Thankless . . . Unholy War," 17 n. 9.

5. "Deposition of James Gadsden," Military Court of Inquiry, in *ASP:MA* 7:135.

6. "The Florida War," *St. Louis Commercial Bulletin*, November 16, 1836.

7. For the attitude of instructors toward southerners, see Hunter, "Nathaniel Wyche Hunter," 64.

8. Hitchcock, *Fifty Years in Camp and Field*, 165.

9. The concept of moral nobility is found throughout Aristotle's *Nicomachean Ethics*; Aristotelian ethics remains at the core of academy training; see Brinsfield, "Army Values and Ethics," 69–84; Oh, "Relevance of Virtue Ethics," accessed November 20, 2016, http://isme.tamu.edu/ISME07/Oh07.html.

10. "Moliere" [pseud.], *Morning Herald*, September 26, 1837; see also "Florida Campaign—1837: Extract from a Journal of a Late Field Officer," *Army and Navy Chronicle*, February 7, 1839; Skelton, *Profession of Arms*, 315; Vandervort, *Indian Wars*, 130–31.

11. de Vattel, *The Law of Nations*, 302–03. This publication had a profound impact on jurists, politicians, and military officers throughout nineteenth-century America; see Solis, *The Law of Armed Conflict*, 18; Rolfs, *No Peace for the Wicked*, 61–62. Vattel reduced key aspects of lawful war to a simple premise: "1. To recover what belongs or is due us. 2. To provide for our future safety by punishing the aggressor or offender. 3. To defend ourselves, or protect ourselves from injury, by repelling unjust violence." Since the treaties were fraudulent and coerced, then it certainly followed—especially in the face of actions to remove the Indians by armed force—that their refusal to emigrate and their defense of reservation lands would constitute a just war. It is also clear that former cadets at West Point did not group Indians under Vattel's category of "savage nations," as exemplified by such figures as Attila, Genghis Khan, and Tamerlane: "lawless robbers" who acted without mercy and made war "from inclination purely, and not from love to their country." In such cases, the author, a Swiss jurist, encouraged severe punishment, even extermination.

12. Hunter, "Nathaniel Wyche Hunter," 74.

13. William T. Sherman to Ellen B. Ewing, September 7, 1841, in Sherman, *Home Letters*, 14.

14. For the number of resignations, see Mahon, *Second Seminole War*, 188.

15. Vandervort, *Indian Wars*, 128.

16. Ellis, "Battlefield Landscape Analysis—The Battles of Black Point, Welika Pond and Black Point," in Ellis et al., "Fort Defiance/Fort Micanopy," 56–70. In this study, archaeologist Ellis provides the most detailed battlefield analysis of the Second Seminole War yet undertaken. This investigation includes KOCOA (key terrain, observation/fields of fire, cover and concealment, obstacles, and avenues of approach) maps, a standardized method of conducting a forensic review of military actions. It should also be noted that the Seminoles were keen observers of the US Army before hostilities commenced; see Bemrose, *Reminiscences*, 25. For an ethnohistorical analysis of earlier forms of warfare among the Maskókî, see Patricia Riles Wickman, *Tree That Bends*, 95–102.

17. John W. Phelps, February 26, 1838, Diary—1838–1839, Series III Diaries, John Wolcott Phelps Papers, Archives and Manuscripts, NYPL.

18. This last characteristic became fuel for scathing satire in such newspapers as

James Gordon Bennett's *New York Herald*; see especially "Florida War," *New York Herald*, November 29, 1837.

19. Mahon, *Second Seminole War*, 183; Knetsch, *Seminole Wars*, 93.

20. Doherty, "Richard K. Call," 170; M. Dickerson to Lewis Cass, May 18, 1836, in *ASP:MA* 6:440.

21. William S. Foster, journal entry, November 20, 1836, William S. Foster Journals (1836-37), PKY; "Late from Florida," *Evening Star*, December 19, 1836; Mahon, *Second Seminole War*, 184; R. K. Call to the Secretary of War, November 27, 1836 (Volusia), *Globe*, December 12, 1836; "Late and Important from Florida" (from the *Savannah Georgian*), December 5, 1836, in *Daily Commercial Bulletin*, January 5, 1837.

22. "Extract from a Letter from 'an Officer of the Army of Florida,' Dated Volusia, 1st December" (the *Alexandria Gazette*), in *Enquirer*, December 15, 1836; for reference to "noxious vapours," see Motte, *Journey into Wilderness*, 144.

23. Moniac was of mixed Creek and Euro-American ancestry; see Hauptman, "Cadet David Moniac," 322-48; "David Moniac," Encyclopedia of Alabama, accessed November 21, 2016, http://www.encyclopediaofalabama.org/article/h-1159.

24. J. W. Phelps to John Phelps (Fort Heileman), July 10, 1837, in Phelps, "Letters," 73-74.

25. Mahon, *Second Seminole War*, 185.

26. "Extract from a Letter from 'an Officer of the Army of Florida,' Dated Volusia, 1st December" (the *Alexandria Gazette*), in *Enquirer*, December 15, 1836. Call noted three dead but did not include the Creek fatalities; R. K. Call to the Secretary of War (Volusia), November 27, 1836, in *Enquirer*, December 15, 1836.

27. Andrew Jackson to James Gadsden (Washington, DC), November 1836, series 6, additional correspondence, Andrew Jackson Papers, LOC.

28. Kieffer, *Maligned General*, 4.

29. Jesup to [General] James Taylor, December 28, 1812, in Kieffer, *Maligned General*, 14-15.

30. Phelps, February 26, 1838, and April 24, 1838, Phelps Papers, NYPL.

31. Jesup to Poinsett (Volusia), November 21, 1837, LR, roll 0146, NARA.

32. Hunter, "Captain Nathaniel Wyche Hunter," 74.

33. For the ill-health of the Creeks, volunteers, and regulars, see T[homas] Jesup to R. Jones (Tampa Bay), January 1, 1837, LR, roll 0144, NARA.

34. Ibid.; Mahon, *Second Seminole War*, 196.

35. Jesup to Butler (Fort Armstrong), January 19, 1837, LR, NARA.

36. Jesup to Joel Poinsett (Tampa Bay), June 15, 1837, roll 0146, NARA.

37. Jesup to Jones, January 12, 1837, roll 0146, NARA.

38. Thomas Childs to [Mrs. Childs], January 24, 1837, in "Major Childs, U.S.A.," 372. Childs's version differs from Jesup's correspondence to the adjutant general. Jesup failed to mention the ad hoc nature of the Creeks' encounter with Osuchee and instead describes the event as a fully planned operation; see Jesup to Jones (Fort Armstrong), February 7, 1837, LR, NARA.

39. "Florida Campaign—1837: Extract from the Journal of a Late Field Officer," *Army and Navy Chronicle*, February 7, 1839.

40. Mahon, *Second Seminole War*, 197; Porter, "John Caesar," 200.

41. Childs to [Mrs. Childs], January 29, 1837, in "Major Childs, U.S.A.," 373-74.

42. Jesup to Jones (Fort Armstrong), February 7, 1837, *Globe*, February 24, 1837.

43. Childs to [Mrs. Childs], February 2, 1837, in "Major Childs, U.S.A.," 374. For reference to the capture of Abraham's wife, see Childs, April 3, 1837, "Major Childs," no. 4 (April 1875): 283.

44. Howard, *Oklahoma Seminoles*, 97–103, 243; Grantham, *Creation Myths*, 36, 43.

45. Du Bois, *Souls of Black Folk*, 2–3.

46. Sounaffee Tustenukke to [Coe Hadjo] (Tampa Bay), September 11, 1837, in Porter, "Negro Abraham," 39.

47. Childs to [Mrs. Childs], February 3, 1837, in "Major Childs, U.S.A.," 169.

48. Ibid. For reference to the loss of Jumper's command, see Foster, journal entry, November 20, 1836, William S. Foster Journals, PKY.

49. "Restoration of Certain Negroes to the Seminoles."

50. "From Florida," *Niles' Weekly Register*, March 25, 1837.

51. Childs, March 14, 1837, "Major Childs," no. 4 (April 1875): 280–81.

52. For reference to Jumper's illness, see "From Florida" (from the *New York Gazette*), *Rhode Island Republican*, April 12, 1837.

53. Childs, March 14, 1837, "Major Childs," 280–81.

54. Ibid. Childs referred to Alligator as Micanopy's spokesman, and Jumper indeed played a lesser role in the proceedings because of his illness. Childs also identified Abraham as Micanopy's new sense-bearer, the post formerly held by Jumper and then held by Abraham for a few months during the "Capitulation."

55. Mahon, *Second Seminole War*, 203.

56. "Later from Florida—The Indian War Ended. Oseola Surrendered," *New York Commercial Advertiser*, February 21, 1837; emphasis original.

57. Ibid.; see also "The Seminoles Subdued—Oceola Prisoner of War," *Globe*, February 21, 1837.

58. "Another Campaign," *Floridian*, June 17, 1837; emphasis added.

59. "Late from Florida—Osceola Not Captured," *Evening Star*, February 24, 1837; emphasis original. Northeastern Whigs were far more dubious about these claims; see "The Florida War Not Ended," *Atlas*, February 24, 1837; for Jesup's report, see "Th. S. Jesup, Major General Commanding, February 7, 1837," in *Maryland Gazette*, March 2, 1837; for the *Globe's* reaction, see "The War Not Ended Yet," *Globe*, March 8, 1837.

60. "Latter from Florida," *Evening Star*, January 28, 1837.

61. "The Great Oseola Surrendered," *Evening Post*, February 21, 1837.

62. "The Close of the Campaign," *Richmond Enquirer*, February 21, 1837.

63. Mahon, *Second Seminole War*, 203–4.

64. Jesup to Poinsett, June 7, 1837, roll 0146, NARA; Kiefer, *Maligned General*, 170.

65. Jesup to Poinsett, June 7, 1837, NARA.

66. Ibid. A visiting delegation of Cherokees later affirmed that the majority "stood in open hostility [to the treaty], and disavowed all moral obligations to acknowledge its binding force." John Ross, February 17, 1838, in Foreman, "Report of Cherokee Deputation," 434.

67. Jesup to Jones (Fort Heileman), July 25, 1837, roll 0147, NARA.

68. Mahon, *Second Seminole War*, 205.

69. "Another Campaign," *Floridian*, June 17, 1837.

70. Thomas Jesup to [Captain] J. A. Lagnel (St. Augustine), July 14, 1837, roll 0145, NARA.

71. Jesup to Poinsett, June 15, 1837 (Tampa Bay), roll 0145, NARA.

72. Jesup to C. A. Harris (St. Augustine), September 24, 1837, in "Negroes &c, Captured from Indians in Florida"; Jesup to [Col.] Miller (St. Augustine), July 8, 1837, roll 0145, NARA.

73. Wickman, *Osceola's Legacy*, 25.

74. Mahon, *Second Seminole War*, 205.

75. "Orders No. 175," September 6, 1837, in "Negroes &c, Captured from Indians in Florida."

76. According to the abolitionist Joshua Giddings, the people of the free states were thereby forced to become "involved in the guilt of enslaving our fellow men"; see Giddings, *Pacificus: Rights and Privileges*, 10.

77. Mahon, *Second Seminole War*, 206.

78. Motte, *Journey into Wilderness*, 120.

79. Ibid.

80. Jesup to Jones (St. Augustine), October 2, 1837, roll 0145, NARA; information regarding Osceola's capture, as related by him to a visiting Cherokee delegation, is contained in "William Penn" [pseud.], "The Cherokee Mediation," *National Intelligencer*, April 29, 1841.

81. Wickman, *Osceola's Legacy*, 100–101. According to a source cited by this author, Osceola supposedly knew that his capture was imminent.

82. Jarvis, "Army Surgeon's Notes," 278.

83. Sprague, *Florida War*, 216–19; Mahon, *Second Seminole War*, 214–16; Wickman, *Osceola's Legacy*.

84. Jesup to Poinsett (St. Augustine), October 22, 1837, roll 0145, RG 94, NARA; Sprague, *Florida War*, 216–18; Mahon, *Second Seminole War*, 211–17; Missall and Missall, *Seminole Wars*, 134.

85. "General Jesup's Account of Oseola's Capture," *Atlas*, December 22, 1837.

86. "The Florida War," *Albany Evening Journal*, October 1, 1841.

87. "Orders, No. 203" (St. Augustine), October 24, 1837, in Sprague, *Florida War*, 182.

88. "Speech of Mr. Benton of Missouri," 353–57.

CHAPTER 6: The Last Pitched Battles

1. Moulton, "Cherokees and the Second Seminole War," 297; Foreman, "Report of Cherokee Deputation," 434.

2. Kooweskowe [John Ross], "To the Chiefs, Headmen and Warriors of the Seminoles" (Washington City), October 18, 1837, in "Indian Mediation," *Niles' National Register*, November 25, 1837.

3. Ibid.

4. Foreman, "Report," 427; "William Penn" [pseud.], "The Cherokee Mediation," *Daily National Intelligencer*, April 29, 1841. Fowl Creek was also known as the Chickasawhatchee; see "Florida War," *Army and Navy Chronicle*, January 18, 1838.

5. For Scott's orders, see Purdue and Green, *The Cherokee Nation*, 123.

6. John Pickrell, journal entry, December 14, 1837, in White, "Journals of Lieutenant John Pickrell," 169.

7. Unidentified source in Foreman, "Report," 431.

8. John Sherburne to Joel Poinsett (Augusta, GA), September 22, 1837, Poinsett Papers, Historical Society of Pennsylvania, Philadelphia; for more on Bushyhead, see *Missions to the Heathen*, 500.

9. Pickrell, journal entry, December 14, 1837, in White, "Journals," 169; Mahon, *Second Seminole War*, 222–23.

10. Jno. Ross to Joel R. Poinsett (Washington, DC), January 2, 1838, in "Memorial of the Cherokee Mediators," 11–12.

11. Jesup to Poinsett (Fort Christmas, Powell's camp), January 2, 1838, roll 0167, LR.

12. Quotation by Young, "The Cherokee Nation," 502; see also Duffield, "Cherokee Emigration," 339–40. A slightly lower death rate was given at the time; see "Indian Missions: Cherokees," 10.

13. Poinsett, *An Inquiry*, 43.

14. Frazer and Hutchings, "Drawing the Line," 51.

15. Henry A. Wise, "Debate in the House of Representatives, on the Seminole War," January 24, 1838, *National Intelligencer*, January 25, 1838.

16. "Speech of Rep. Churchill Cambreleng," January 24, 1838, *National Intelligencer*, January 25, 1838.

17. Mahon, *Second Seminole War*, 225–26.

18. "Recollections of a Campaign in Florida," 72.

19. Lynch, diary entry, February 8, 1837, in "Journal," 51.

20. Zachary Taylor to John J. Crittenden (Fort Gardiner), January 12, 1838, in Kersey and Petersen, "Was I a Member of Congress. . . ," 453; Knetsch, *Seminole Wars*, 101.

21. Taylor to Crittenden, January 12, 1838, in Kersey and Petersen, "Was I a Member of Congress. . . ," 449.

22. The name was taken from a popular song, "Sam Jones, the Fisherman," and was inspired by Abiaka's former trade as provider of fish to the army garrisons—evidently a ruse to garner intelligence: "The Oklawaha," *Harper's New Monthly Magazine* 308, no. 52 (January 1876): 172.

23. West, "Abiaka," 366–68, 378.

24. Mahon, *Second Seminole War*, 224; Wickman, *Osceola's Legacy*, 102–5.

25. Ibid., 105–6.

26. Foreman, "Report of Cherokee Deputation," 435.

27. Taylor to Crittenden, January 12, 1838, in Kersey and Petersen, "Was I a Member of Congress. . . ," 450.

28. Ibid., 449.

29. Mahon, *Second Seminole War*, 227; for notice of Jumper's death, see *Army and Navy Chronicle*, May 10, 1838.

30. The number of Seminole warriors is taken from Sprague, who drew his information from Alligator; see Sprague, *Florida War*, 213. An unnamed officer who fought at Okeechobee estimated that two hundred was "nearest to fact"; see "Fort Gardner on the Kissimmee," December 30, 1837 (from the *Army and Navy Chronicle*), *Enquirer*, January 27, 1838.

31. William S. Foster, journal entry, December 25, 1837, in Foster, *Miserable Pride*, 126.

32. Robert C. Buchanan, journal entry, December 25, 1837, in White, "A Journal," 146.

33. For Taylor's limitations as a tactician, see Bauer, *Zachary Taylor*, 80–81.

34. Mahon, "Missouri Volunteers," 166–76.

35. "Fort Gardner on the Kissimmee," December 30, 1837 (from the *Army and Navy Chronicle*), *Enquirer*, January 27, 1838.

36. Mahon, "Missouri Volunteers," 166–76.

37. Z. Taylor to R. Jones (Fort Gardner), January 4, 1838, in "Report of the Battle of Lake Okeechobee," *Niles' National Register*, February 10, 1838.

38. Sprague, *Florida War*, 213.

39. William Foster to Betty Foster (Fort Fraser, Peace Creek), January 2, 1838, in *Miserable Pride*, 128.

40. Sprague, *Florida War*, 214.

41. "The Late Battle in Florida," *Daily Picayune*, January 10, 1838; see also "Disastrous News from Florida," *National Intelligencer*, January 11, 1838; "From Florida—Disastrous Intelligence," *Albany Argus*, January 16, 1838; "Disastrous News from Florida," *Centinel of Freedom*, January 16, 1838.

42. Taylor to Jesup, December 26, 1837, *Globe*, January 27, 1838.

43. "From Florida" (from the *Mobile Mercantile Advertiser*), *National Aegis*, January 24, 1838.

44. Eisenhower, *Zachary Taylor*, 28.

45. Bauer, *Zachary Taylor*, 94–95; Mahon, *Second Seminole War*, 247.

46. *Daily Commercial Bulletin*, March 20, 1838.

47. Thomas H. Benton, "Missouri Volunteers in Florida," *Globe*, February 15, 1838.

48. Colonel James Chiles et al., Letter to the Editor, *Daily Commercial Bulletin*, March 20, 1838.

49. Z. Taylor to T. S. Jesup, *Globe*, January 27, 1838.

50. Mahon, "Missouri Volunteers," 167, n. 4; Mahon, *Second Seminole War*, 221.

51. Monk, "Christmas Day in Florida," 9.

52. Missall and Missall, *Miserable Pride*, 129.

53. Foster to [Mrs. Foster] (Camp Rest, near Fort Fraser), January 13, 1838, in *Miserable Pride*, 138; emphasis original.

54. Ibid., 139.

55. For a contemporary description of this area, see Motte, *Journey into Wilderness*, 186.

56. Jesup to Jones (camp on Jupiter River), January 26, 1838, in *New York Commercial Advertiser*, February 20, 1838. According to the on-scene remarks of Dr. Nathan Jarvis, there were four hundred artillery, six hundred dragoons, four hundred Tennesseans, and thirty-five Delaware Indians present; see "Interesting from Florida," *Philadelphia Inquirer*, February 23, 1838; see also "Extract of a Letter by an Officer of the U.S. Artillery in Florida" (Jupiter River), January 27, 1838, *Vermont Phoenix*, February 23, 1838; Jarvis, journal entry, January 27, 1838, in "Army Surgeon's Notes," 452.

57. "Extract from an Anonymous Officer" (Camp Locha-Hatchee), January 25, 1838, *Enquirer*, February 20, 1838.

58. "Extract of a Letter by an Officer of the U.S. Artillery in Florida" (Jupiter River), January 27, 1838, *Vermont Phoenix*, February 23, 1838, LR.

59. For Tuskegee's command, see John W. Phelps, February 23, 1838, Diary—1838–1839, Phelps Papers, NYPL; "Letter from Fort Pierce," February 15, 1838, *Niles' National Register*, March 17, 1838; "The Indian War" (from the Richmond Whig), *Fayetteville Observer*, March 7, 1838.

60. "Another Battle in Florida," *Daily Picayune*, February 13, 1838.

61. "The Florida War (from a Letter of an Officer in the Army . . . under the Date of January 25)," *Albany Evening Journal*, February 19, 1838; see also Motte, *Journey into Wilderness*, 194.

62. C. A. Finley, MD, to J. A. Chambers (camp on the Locha Hatchee), January 25, 1838, LR; Motte, *Journey into Wilderness*, 195.

63. For the number of warriors, see Jesup to Jones (camp on Jupiter River), January 26, 1838, LR.

64. Foster to [Mrs. Foster], February 15, 1838, in *Miserable Pride*, 147.

65. Jesup to Colonel W. Mills (Fort Jupiter), February 4, 1838, LR.

66. For the number without shoes, see Jesup to Jones (camp on Jupiter River), January 31, 1838, LR; see also Jarvis, journal entry, January 27, 1838, in "Surgeon's Notes," 452; "The Florida War," *Albany Evening Journal*, February 19, 1838.

67. "Interesting from Florida," *Philadelphia Inquirer*, February 23, 1838; Jarvis, journal entry, January 27, 1838, in "Surgeon's Notes," 452.

68. Jesup to Poinsett (six miles north of Fort McNeil), January 5, 1838, LR.

69. Jesup to Jones (camp on Jupiter River), February 4, 1838, LR.

70. Jesup to Jones (Fort Floyd), January 18, 1838, LR.

71. Mahon, *Second Seminole War*, 235–36.

72. Jesup to Jones (camp twenty-eight miles south of Jupiter), February 9, 1838, LR.

73. C. A. Finley, MD, to J. A. Chambers (camp on the Locha Hatchee), January 25, 1838, LR.

74. Kieffer, *Maligned General*, 202.

75. Phelps, February 24, 1838, Diary—1838–1839, Phelps Papers, NYPL.

76. Ibid.

77. Ibid.

78. Motte, *Journey into Wilderness*, 209.

79. Phelps, February 24, 1838, Phelps Papers, NYPL.

80. Motte, *Journey into Wilderness*, 209; see also Mahon, *Second Seminole War*, 236.

81. Motte, *Journey into Wilderness*, 209.

82. Phelps, February 27, 1838, Phelps Papers.

83. Jesup to Z. Taylor (Camp Jupiter, "Confidential"), March 7, 1838, LR.

84. Phelps, February 26, 1838, Phelps Papers.

85. Phelps, March 6, 1838, Phelps Papers.

86. Motte, *Journey into Wilderness*, 219–20, 235; for the price of each rifle, see Phelps, March 6, 1838, Phelps Papers. The review board's initial decision was unfavorable, but on Colt's request another seven-member board was ordered to set up an additional review; see Jesup to Samuel Colt (Camp Jupiter), March 11, 1838, LR. The following day, Jesup approved the sale; Jesup to Colt, March 12, 1838. For reference to Abiaka's long familiarity with this part of the Everglades, see West, "Abiaka," 374–75.

87. Jesup to Z. Taylor (Camp Jupiter), March 15, 1838, LR.

88. Poinsett to Jesup, March 1, 1838, in *National Intelligencer*, March 19, 1838; Mahon, *Second Seminole War*, 237.

89. Poinsett to Jesup, March 1, 1838, in *National Intelligencer*.

90. Jesup to Poinsett (Fort Jupiter), March 23, 1838, LR.

91. Ibid.

92. Jesup to [Governor] R. K. Call (Fort Jupiter), March 15, 1838, LR.

93. Mahon, *Second Seminole War*, 238.

94. Jesup to Poinsett (undated), in *Niles' National Register*, September 8, 1838.

95. Kieffer, *Maligned General*, 214.

CHAPTER 7: "Never-Ending, Still-Beginning War"

1. "The Seminoles" (from the *Political Arena*), *National Intelligencer*, January 15, 1838.

2. *United States' Telegraph*, February 22, 1836; "Termination of the Florida War," *North American and Daily Advertiser*, May 13, 1842. This phrase was adapted from a famous line by the poet John Dryden and was popular at the time.

3. "The Seminoles" (from the *Political Arena*), *National Intelligencer*, January 15, 1838.

4. Rumors predominated, but the administration never provided a complete accounting of war expenditures, presumably to avoid damaging the interests of the Democratic Party.

5. "General Taylor and His Policy," *Army and Navy Chronicle*, January 3, 1839.

6. Taylor to Call (Camp Gilmer), July 14, 1838, roll 0177, LR.

7. Taylor to Jones (Fort Brooke), August 4, 1838, LR.

8. Ibid.

9. R. K. Call to Taylor, August 21, 1838, LR.

10. Monaco, "Alachua Settlers," 16–17; Watson, "Thomas Sidney Jesup," 109.

11. Brown, "Back Country Rebellions," 73–99.

12. Taylor to Twiggs (Tampa Bay), February 16, 1839, roll 0197, LR. Hospitals were also supposed to be placed at each of these central garrisons; see Taylor to Twiggs (Fort Micanopy), March 15, 1839, LR; Sprague, journal entry, April 28, 1839, in White, "Macomb's Mission," 160.

13. Unfortunately, modern historians have ignored the primacy of settler-colonialism to Taylor's strategy and have instead focused on the military alone, an interpretation that has skewed understanding of this phase of the war. See, for example, Mahon, *Second Seminole War*, 248–51; Missall and Missall, *Seminole Wars*, 158–60.

14. Pearce, "Torment of Pestilence," 448–53; Doherty, "Ante-bellum Pensacola," 343–45.

15. "Debate in the House of Representatives, February 1, 1837," *National Intelligencer*, February 8, 1837; see also Cushing, *An Oration*.

16. "Debate in the House of Representatives," *National Intelligencer*, February 8, 1837.

17. Taylor to Lawson (Fort Brooke), September 7, 1838, LR.

18. Taylor to Jones, July 5, 1838, LR.

19. Mahon, *Second Seminole War*, 249.

20. Taylor to Call (Fort Brooke), December 18, 1838, LR.

21. [Captain] La Motte to [Colonel] Twiggs (Fort Brooke), September 21, 1838; for reference to settlers erecting their own picket fortifications, see Taylor to Twiggs (Fort Clinch), December 4, 1838, LR.

22. Taylor to Jones (Fort Brooke), January 22, 1839, roll 0196, LR.

23. "Extract of a Letter Dated, Fort King, April 27, 1839" (from the *St. Augustine News*), *Army and Navy Chronicle*, May 16, 1839.

24. "Governor Reid to the Legislative Council of Florida," December 10, 1839, in Sprague, *Florida War*, 239.

25. Mahon, *Second Seminole War*, 247.

26. Taylor to Jones (Tampa), July 20, 1839, in Sprague, *Florida War*, 226.

27. Benton, "A Bill to Provide for the Armed Occupation."

28. Covington, "Armed Occupation Act of 1842," 42.

29. "Kit-Cats from the Capitol," *New York Spectator*, August 13, 1842.

30. Henry Clay, "Draft of Speech in the Senate," February 18, 1839, in *Papers of Henry Clay*, 288.

31. Benton, "Florida Armed Occupation Bill," 170–71.

32. Covington, "Armed Occupation," 42. Tension between settlers and land speculators was a constant feature of early America; see Sachs, *Home Rule*, 5–11, 29–39.

33. For background on political realignment and Whig gains, see Holt, *American Whig Party*, 64, 87; Formisano, "History and the Election of 1840," 662.

34. Horace Everett, "House of Representatives, February 27, 1839," *Congressional Globe*, March 4, 1839.

35. Benton, "Florida Armed Occupation Bill," 169.

36. "Military Costumes," *Army and Navy Chronicle*, November 7, 1839.

37. Alexander Macomb, "General Orders," May 18, 1839, in Sprague, *Florida War*, 229; Mahon, *Second Seminole War*, 255–56.

38. For example, see Henry Clay to Robert Swartwout (Washington, DC), April 2, 1838, in *Papers of Henry Clay*, 168; see also "Florida War" (correspondence of the *Army and Navy Chronicle*), Fort King, May 27, 1839, *New York Spectator*, June 20, 1839.

39. Sprague, journal entries, April 5, 1839, and April 30, 1839, in "Macomb's Mission," 144, 162; Anonymous letter dated Garey's Ferry, May, 1, 1839, *National Intelligencer*, May 18, 1839.

40. Macomb to Poinsett (Fort King), May 22, 1839, in *National Intelligencer*, June 1, 1839; Sprague, April 6, 1839, "Macomb's Mission," 145–46.

41. Macomb to Poinsett (Fort King), May 22, 1839, in *National Intelligencer*, June 1, 1839.

42. Sprague, May 2, 1839, "Macomb's Mission," 163. For reference to Taylor's assumption that he was about to be relieved, see George Griffin to Lieutenant Colonel John Green (camp on the Ocilla), April 17, 1839, roll 0197, LR.

43. Mahon, *Second Seminole War*, 259; Taylor to Poinsett (Tampa), August 1, 1839, roll 0198, LR.

44. Sprague, May 5, 1839, "Macomb's Mission," 165.

45. Sprague, May 9, 1839, 168.

46. Sprague, *Florida War*, 95; Mahon, *Second Seminole War*, 270.

47. Macomb to Poinsett (Fort King), May 22, 1839, in *National Intelligencer*, June 1, 1839.

48. Sprague, May 21, 1839, "Macomb's Mission," 183; see also Mahon, *Second Seminole War*, 256–57. For reference to the $1,000, see Sprague, April 22 and April 23, 1839, 156.

49. Sprague, May 19, 1839, 181–82; Alexander Macomb, "General Orders" (Fort King), May 18, 1839, in *Weekly Messenger*, June 5, 1839.

50. "Letter from the Citizens of Alachua and Columbia Counties," *Florida Herald and Southern Democrat*, August 22, 1839.

51. "More of the Florida War," *Weekly Messenger*, June 26, 1839.

52. Sturtevant, "Chaikaka," 45.

53. Ibid., 44–45; this same assertion was made by Harney's early biographer in Reavis, *William Selby Harney*, 134.

54. "Copy of a Letter from a Young Officer of the Army to a Friend in This City, Dated Fort Lauderdale, E.F., June 20, 1839," in *Army and Navy Chronicle*, August 8, 1838; on Abiaka's acceptance, see C. Tompkins to G. Griffin (camp near Fort Lauderdale), June 22, 1839, roll 0198, LR.

55. "Correspondence of the *National Gazette*," Garey's Ferry, E. Florida, August 7, 1839, *National Gazette*, August 20, 1839; Sprague, *Florida War* [Samson's Narrative], 316.

56. "Correspondence of the *National Gazette*," Garey's Ferry, E. Florida, August 7, 1839, *National Gazette*, August 20, 1839.

57. "Extract of a Letter from a Gentleman at Key Biscayne, Dated August 7, 1839," in *Army and Navy Chronicle*, August 29, 1839.

58. Letter to the Editor (from the Philadelphia *North American*), Sanibel, July 22, 1839, in *Commercial Advertiser*, August 17, 1839.

59. "The Late Indian Massacre: Correspondence of the National Gazette," Garey's Ferry, East Florida, August 7, 1839, in *Alexandria Gazette*, August 20, 1839.

60. Sturtevant, "Chaikaka," 47.

61. Neill, "Spanish Indians," 43–58.

62. Ibid., 44. For more on this lucrative trade, see Dodd, "Tampa Bay Fisheries," 246–56.

63. Sprague, *Florida War* [Sampson's Narrative], 316. The direct participation of the war council is also revealed in another ploy by Abiaka and Chitto in September, whereby soldiers were enticed to participate in a "dance," and then were waylaid and shot. A firsthand narrative, once again by an escaped interpreter, was published in the *Army and Navy Chronicle*, November 14, 1839.

64. Sprague, *Florida War* [Sampson's Narrative], 316. On the propensity of "Seminole negroes" who "possessed the confidence of the Chiefs to accept payment to mislead and betray the Indians during the war, see Thomas S. Jesup, draft letter [1858], folder 7, box 1, Jesup Papers, WLC.

65. Preston, *The Texture of Contact*, 156–57; Stiggins, *Creek Indian History*, 95; Drake, *Indians of North America*, 68; Knowles, "The Torture of Captives," 151–225.

66. Tompkins to Harney (Fort Lauderdale), August 30, 1839, LR.

67. "Correspondence of the *National Gazette*," Garey's Ferry, E. Florida, August 7, 1839, *National Gazette*, August 20, 1839.

68. "Copy of a Letter from a Young Officer of the Army to a Friend in This City, Dated Fort Lauderdale, E.F., June 20, 1839," *Army and Navy Chronicle*, August 8, 1838.

69. Taylor to Jones (Tampa), June 25, 1839, roll 0197, LR; Taylor to Poinsett (Tampa), August 1, 1839, roll 0198, NARA.

70. Taylor to Jones (Tampa), November 27, 1839, roll 0198, LR.

71. Bauer, *Zachary Taylor*, 93.

72. Ibid.

73. Taylor to Jones (Fort Gadsden), February 26, 1840, roll 0218, LR.

74. Armistead to Jones (Fort Heileman), May 11, 1840, roll 0201, LR.

75. Armistead to Jones (Fort Heileman), May 19, 1840, roll 0201, LR.

76. "From Florida," *Sun*, May 27, 1840.

77. Mahon, *Second Seminole War*, 278; Captain Bonneville to Lieutenant Asheton (Fort King), May 30, 1840, roll 0201, NARA.

78. Armistead to Poinsett, June 18, 1840, roll 0201, NARA.

79. W. W. Bliss to [Dr.] Brush (Fort King), June 10, 1840, roll 0201, NARA.

80. "Order No. 21" (Fort King), June 22, 1840, roll 0201, NARA.

81. Armistead to Poinsett (Fort King), November 15, 1840, roll 0202, NARA.

82. "Order No. 57," November 15, 1840, roll 0202, NARA.

83. Hitchcock, November 22, 1840, Diary #16, Hitchcock Diaries, GM, 75; Secretary of War to Walker K. Armistead, November 2, 1840, in *TP*, 26:224.

84. Later, Armistead did his best to bribe Seminole leaders, going so far as showing them a chest filled with Treasury notes, a scene that failed to please, as they were expecting payment in silver; Hitchcock, March 18, 1841, Diary #19, 9–10.

85. Hitchcock, November 15, 1840, Diary #16, 68.

86. Ibid., December 8, 1840, 107–108.

87. Ibid., November 21, 1840, 73.

88. Bell's sister-in-law was married to Hitchcock's brother. For additional mention of Hitchcock's friendship with Bell, see Satz, *American Indian Policy*, 160, 172–73, n. 24. Bell married Jane Erwin, a prominent socialite and sister of Ann Erwin; see Robinson, "General Ethan Allen Hitchcock," 174; "Descendants of Andrew Erwin," accessed November 22, 2015, http://www.wikitree.com/genealogy/Erwin-Descendants-146.

89. Hitchcock, December 7, 1840, Diary #16, 105–106; Hitchcock, December 16, 1840, Diary #17, 3.

90. Ibid., January 13, 1841, 63–68; Hitchcock, April 15, 1841, Diary #20, 10.

91. Buker, *Swamp Sailors*, 110.

92. Watson, *Peacekeepers and Conquerors*, 224; for a contemporary (and critical) description of this incident, see Hitchcock, December 29, 1840, Diary #17, 25–26; see also Vandervort, *Indian Wars*, 135. Andrew Jackson famously declared during the First Seminole War that "the laws of war did not apply to conflicts with savages"; quoted in Witt, *Lincoln's Code*, 99.

93. "Message of Governor Reid to the Legislative Council," February 28, 1841, in *TP*, 26:112–13; "Secretary of War to Walker K. Armistead," February 1, 1841, in *TP*, 26:250.

94. Hitchcock, May 15, 1841, 63–66, 75. Armistead's letter of resignation arrived just at this time. The general mistakenly believed that he was going to be replaced by Gaines and wished to make the transition that much easier; see Hitchcock, May 17, 1841, 76. See also Monaco, "Wishing that Right May Prevail," 188–89.

95. "Mr. Ogle's Speech," *Log Cabin*, August 1, 1840; Borchard, *Abraham Lincoln*, 21–22.

96. W. T. Sherman to John Sherman (Fort Pierce), March 30, 1841, in *The Sherman Letters*, 13. For a tally of payments to individual Seminoles, see "Payments Made to Seminole Chiefs and Warriors on Their Emigrating West of the Mississippi River by Order Col. Worth," June 6, 1842, roll 0262, LR. Hitchcock maintained a particular rapport with Coacoochee and proved instrumental in gaining the latter's subsequent concession to emigrate; see Monaco, "Wishing that Right May Prevail," 189.

97. Hall, "A Reckless Waste," 74.

98. Monaco, "Wishing that Right May Prevail," 189.

99. Hall, "A Reckless Waste," 74.

100. Knetsch, *Florida's Seminole Wars*, 134–35.

101. Buker, *Swamp Sailors*, 6, 134.

102. John Spencer, "Memorandum to the Commanding General," May 10, 1842, roll 0262, LR.

103. Monaco, "Wishing that Right May Prevail," 190.

104. Watson, *Peacekeepers and Conquerors*, 186.

105. John Tyler, "Termination of the Florida War, May 11, 1842," *Madisonian*, May 12, 1842.

106. "Speech of Senator Preston, Twenty-Seventh Congress, Second Session, May 10, 1842," *Madisonian*, May 12, 1842.

107. West, "Abiaka," 404.

108. *Boston Traveler*, April 11, 1843.

109. Covington, "The Agreement of 1842," 10.

110. A full account of the 60 officers and 105 enlisted men is given in "Address of the Rev. Richard Watters," *North American and Daily Advertiser*, December 2, 1842. Ninety-eight of the enlisted men were members of Dade's command and seven were from General Clinch's force.

111. "Order No. 25," July 25, 1842, *Florida Herald and Southern Democrat*, August 8, 1842.

112. "Address of the Rev. Richard Watters," *North American and Daily Advertiser*, December 2, 1842.

113. "Honors to the Dead" (from the *St. Augustine News*), *Niles' National Register*, September 10, 1842.

114. Ibid.

115. "Major Dade and his Command," *Evening Post*, August 30, 1842.

116. Ibid.

117. "Address of the Rev. Richard Watters."

118. Denham, *Rogue's Paradise*, 48.

119. Wickman, *Tree that Bends*, 71.

120. West, "Abiaka," 393–94.

CHAPTER 8: Malarial Sword and Shield

1. *Christian Intelligencer and Eastern Chronicle*, September 16, 1836; "Late from Florida," *Saratoga Sentinel*, August 3, 1836; "Florida," *Alexandria Gazette*, August 30, 1836; *New Bedford Mercury*, September 2, 1836; "Florida" (from the *New York Journal of Commerce*), *Vermont Gazette*, August 30, 1836; "Florida," *Albany Argus*, August 30, 1836; "Physician Second" [pseudo.], *National Intelligencer*, November 24, 1843.

2. Mahon, *Second Seminole War*, 325; Sprague, *Florida War*, 526–48. The number of individuals who died after their discharge from the service may never be known.

3. The proportion of deaths to the actual numbers on the field was emphasized by "Physician Second" [pseudo.] "Florida," *National Intelligencer*, August, 15 and 26, 1843.

4. During the war's final year, expectations of finally resolving the war were so intense that President Tyler declared that "a summer campaign was resolved upon, as the best mode of bringing it [the war] to a close"; see Tyler, "Message from the President," 8.

5. For reference to the synergy of malaria with other diseases, see Snow and Omumbo, "Malaria," 204; Van Geertruyden, "Malaria and Human Immunodeficiency Virus," 278–85; Singer, *Introduction to Syndemics*, 129, 146, 160, 172–73.

6. Harney, "Report of Surgeon Benjamin F. Harney," 637, 645.

7. "Marsh Fevers: Quinine in High Doses," *Boston Medical and Surgical Journal* 12 (August 5, 1835): 419; Van Buren, "Report on the Use of Quinine Sulphate," 78; Etemad, *Possessing the World*, 33.

8. Coolidge, *Statistical Report*, 1839–1855, 637. While quinine sulphate was in use in the United States at this time, the usual dose was far lower than that given during the Seminole war.

9. Curtain, *Death by Migration*, 63; McCormick, "Report of Assistant Surgeon James McCormick," 639. McCormick noted that "nearly all the authors whom I have read, and whom I was taught to regard as standard authorities — condemned in the most unqualified terms the use of Peruvian bark, and all its preparations."

10. Forry and Lawson, *Statistical Report*, 286–313. Malaria is listed here either as intermittent or remittent fever. See also Sternberg, *Etiology and Prevention of Yellow Fever*, 45; Humphreys, *Yellow Fever and the South*, 49; Dupré, "On the Yellow Fever," 380.

11. Thomas Lawson to John Bell, June 19, 1841, roll 0233, LR. Some with serious complications from malaria who also happened to have excellent political connections would be allowed as much as two years' leave; see Thomas Childs to Alexander Macomb, July 7, 1840, roll 0205, LR; for the effect of officer absences on the Florida campaign, see "The Army," *Army and Navy Chronicle*, October 12, 1837. A large number of officer resignations also contributed to the shortage; see Denham, "Some Prefer the Seminoles," 39.

12. For the heritable component of resistance and tolerance, see Raberg et al., "Decomposing Health," 38.

13. Thomas Jesup to Major Gross, July 25, 1837, roll 0167, LR. For a local community's immunity to such diseases as malaria and yellow fever, see Bell, *Mosquito Soldiers*, 14–15, 18, 61–62, 81–82. For African immunity from certain strains of malaria, see Kiple, *The Caribbean Slave*, 164. On the comparative health of the Seminole population in Florida, albeit at a much later date, see Covington, "Florida Seminoles," 195–96.

14. Bartholomew M. Lynch, May 2, 1837, in McGaughy, "Lynch's Journal," 66.

15. McNeill, *Mosquito Empires*, 9–10.

16. Daniel Schafer, "Malaria in Florida," email correspondence with author, June 8, 2014; [John] Harries to [Jeffery] Amherst, December 14, 1763, in Boyd, "From a Remote Frontier," 405–6. Conditions were similar for West Florida as well, with most fatalities stemming from "malignant and bilious fevers"; see Coker, "Pensacola's Medical History," 184–86; Rea, "Graveyard for Britons," 345–64.

17. Grob, *Deadly Truth*, 67.

18. Manuel de Montiano to Diego de Penalosa, January 19, 1747, in Manucy, "Some Military Affairs," 207; for the large number of deaths and the prevalence of disease in Spanish Florida, see Coker, "Pensacola's Medical History," 181–82, 188–92.

19. Gillett, *Army Medical Department*, 58.

20. Meier, *Nature's Civil War*, 17–18; Rosenberg, "The Therapeutic Revolution," in *Explaining Epidemics*, 12–13.

21. "Report of Assistant Surgeon J. J. B. Wright," *Statistical Report, 1839–1855*, 653.

22. Rosenberg, "Therapeutic Revolution," 13.

23. Warner and Tighe, eds., "Jacob Bigelow, a Harvard Medical Professor," 95.

24. On the decline of heroic medicine during the Civil War, see Hawk, "An Ambulating Hospital," 197; see also Rothstein, *American Physicians*, 177–83; Starr, *Transformation of American Medicine*, 56.

25. "A Review of *Statistical Report on the Sickness and Mortality*," 142.

26. Among those who managed to pass the initial screening process and were then invited to stand before a board of examiners, only six were approved out of twenty-six candidates in 1841. The following year, a mere two succeeded from a field of seventeen; see Brown, *The Medical Department*, 166.

27. Starr, *American Medicine*, 56. The army also demanded periodic examinations of surgeons as essential for future promotion; see Lawson to R. Jones, October 15, 1839, and Lawson to J. R. Poinsett, September 16, 1839, roll 0119, LR.

28. Thomas Lawson to S. Cooper, July 5, 1839, in Brown, *Medical Department*, 165–66; see also Gillett, *Army Medical Department*, 79–80; for a description of the newly designed uniform, see *General Regulations for the Army*, 371–72.

29. For conditions of the War of 1812, see Mann, *Medical Sketches of the Campaigns*; for the rotation of surgeons in Florida, see Gillett, *Army Medical Department*, 60, 68.

30. L. Thomas to [Colonel] Twiggs, March 5, 1840, roll 0122, LR.

31. Motte, *Journey into Wilderness*, 106–8.

32. For the size and dimensions of general hospitals in Florida, see Gillette, *Army Medical Department*, 63.

33. "From the Army in Florida," *Pennsylvania Inquirer and Daily Courier*, August 18, 1837. The Fort Brooke facility was considered the "principal general hospital" in Florida; see A. N. McLaren, "Fort Brooke," in Lawson and Coolidge, *Statistical Report, 1839–1855*, 329–30. After Armistead's command, this facility was transferred to Cedar Key.

34. Secretary Poinsett eventually ordered that stewards be allotted the pay, clothing, and rations of army sergeants; see J. R. Poinsett, "Regulations Governing the Pay of Hospital Stewards," March 28, 1840, roll 0214, LR. Hospital matrons and female attendants were in service in the North at this time, but male staff was the rule in Florida and the southeast region in general; see Sarnecky, *Army Nurse Corps*, 10–12.

35. The cost for food and forage during the war amounted to more than one million dollars. See Risch, *Quartermaster Support*, 223–26. For more on rations, see Potter, *War in Florida*, 135.

36. Gillett, *Army Medical Department*, 65.

37. Bemrose, *Reminiscences*, 55, 58. Various skin ointments and herbal poultices likewise proved beneficial; ibid., 126 n. 14, 127 n. 15. For a list of medicines and herbs used at this time, see *General Regulations*, 311–12, 314.

38. Sigmond, "Lectures on Materia Medica," 446–51.

39. For a detailed description of an amputation at a small post hospital, see Samuel Forry to J. W. Phelps (Fort King), August 1, 1837, in Forry, "Letters of Samuel Forry," 138–39.

40. Gillett, *Army Medical Department*, 64, 87.

41. "JRP" [Joel R. Poinsett] to Walker K. Armistead, December 3, 1840, in TP, 26: 230–31. Hospitals at Cedar Key, Tampa, St. Augustine, and Pilatka were specifically noted.

42. Baird and Hoffman, "Primaquine Therapy," 1336–345; Baird, "Acute *Plasmodium Vivax* Malaria," 36–57.

43. J. P. Russell to [General] Jones, December 5, 1839, and J. P. Russell, "List of Non-Commissioned Officers and Soldiers of the 3rd Artillery of the 1st, 2nd, and 7th Infantry Remaining at Fort Columbus, N.Y. December 5, 1839, and Who Came from Florida as Invalids," both in roll 0194, LR. Recruitment quotas resulted in the enlistment of men "from 16 to 60," according to one contemporary—although officially no one older than thirty-five should have been recruited for duty. See Lynch, October 2, 1836, in McGaughy, "Lynch's Journal," 13.

44. Muhlberger et al., "Age as a Risk Factor," 990–95; Wilson, "Population Mobility and the Geography," 31–32.

45. George Watson to Thomas Jesup (Garey's Ferry), July 27, 1837, roll 0145, LR.

46. "War in Florida," *Niles' Weekly Register*, September 3, 1836.

47. Particulars regarding the Garey's Ferry encampment are taken from Thomas Childs, July 29, 1836, in "General Childs, U.S.A.: Extracts from his Correspondence with his Family," *The Historical Magazine* (November 1873): 299; "From Florida," *Niles' Weekly Register*, September 24, 1836; Rhodes, *Censuses of Florida*, 78–80, 148.

48. "War in Florida," *Niles' Weekly Register*, September 3, 1836.

49. A similar situation occurred in the village of Newnansville (Fort Gilleland), where six hundred women and children along with sixty men constituted the next largest refugee encampment; see Andrew A. Humphreys, "Proposition to Abandon Fort King," May 17, 1836, roll 0122, LR. For another (more condescending) look at this settler encampment, which was apparently healthier than Black Creek, see Motte, *Journey into Wilderness*, 90–91.

50. Pearce, "Torment of Pestilence," 450; Humphreys, *Yellow Fever*, 49; Dupre, "On the Yellow Fever," 380.

51. Only fifty men were recorded to have perished from yellow fever during the course of the war; see the death tables in Sprague, *Florida War*, 526–48. These low numbers should not be taken as definitive since causes of death were often marked "unknown." Even so, it appears that yellow fever never reached epidemic proportions within the army.

52. Bemrose, *Reminiscences*, 99.

53. Andrew A. Humphreys, journal entry, June 19, 1836 (Fort Drane), in Humphreys, "Field Journal," 224.

54. Bemrose, *Reminiscences*, 133. For another example of "malady turned to madness," see Barr, *Authentic Narrative*, 7.

55. Mishra and Newton, "Diagnosis and Management," 189–98.

56. Rowles, "Incidents and Observations," 159.

57. *Florida Herald*, October 27, 1836; see also "News from Florida," *New York Spectator*, November 3, 1836; "From Florida," *Scioto Gazette*, November 9, 1836; "Extract

from a Letter from One of the Tennessee Volunteers in Florida," *Globe*, November 30, 1836.

58. Andrew Jackson to James Gadsden (Washington, DC), November, 1836, Andrew Jackson Papers, series 6, additional correspondence, LOC.

59. [Lieutenant] Temple to [Major] Heileman (Micanopy), June 15, 1836, roll 0133, LR.

60. "From Florida," *Albany Argus*, August 29, 1837; *National Gazette*, August 26, 1837.

61. Lee to Jesup (St. Augustine), July 10, 1837, roll 0146, LR.

62. The psychological effects of the battlefield can be traced to the Sumerian text the *Epic of Gilgamesh*; see Young, *Harmony of Illusions*, 3–4.

63. Berrios, *History of Mental Symptoms*, 238–41; Hooper, *Inaugural Essay on Phrenitis*; Petersen, "Brain Fever," 445–64. See also Wood, "Inflammation and Brain Fever," 438–40. In a rare study of suicide in Paris (1836), "brain fever" ranked lower in incidence than such causes as "disgust of life" or "disappointed love"; see "Statistical Report from the Morgue," 191–92.

64. Hunt, *Memory, War, and Trauma*, 17–18. Bemrose, *Reminiscences*, 134.

65. "Mr. Carmichael on Inflammatory Affections," 459–65; Weiner, "Madman in the Light of Reason," 290.

66. Rush, *Medical Inquiries and Observations*, 19–29.

67. Reiss, *Theatres of Madness*, 4; Gob, *Mental Institutions in America*, 80–83.

68. Duffy, *History of American Medicine*, 78–79; Mintz, *Moralists and Modernizers*, 96–101.

69. Henderson, *Medical Examination of Recruits for the Army*, 41–42. For the contemporary understanding of insanity, see Prichard, *Treatise on Insanity*.

70. Hunter, "Captain Nathaniel Wyche Hunter," 67, 71, 74.

71. "Speech of Hon. T. A. Howard."

72. Ibid. No actual antiwar movement emerged, at least in the sociological sense. Rather, Whigs engaged in partisan politics and utilized the theme of moral superiority to distinguish themselves from Democrats; see chapter 10.

73. Ibid.

74. "Fort Fanning, E.F., March 14, 1840," in "Correspondence of the *Army and Navy Chronicle*," *Boston Courier*, April 30, 1840.

75. Joseph R. Smith to [Mrs. Smith], March 6, 1838, in Mahon, "Letters," 340.

76. Watson, *Peacekeepers and Conquerors*, 180; Vandervort, *Indian Wars*, 131; Kennett, *Sherman*, 27. The incidence of PTSD, even among Vietnam veterans, also remains difficult to determine with accuracy; see Dean, *Shook over Hell*, 15. For the problem of alcoholism, see Lynch, January 8, 1839, and March 1, 1839, in McGaughy, "Lynch's Journal," 179, 182; for self-inflicted injuries and attempted suicide, see Hunter, "Nathaniel Wyche Hunter," 73, and Reynold M. Kirby, September 14, 1837, Kirby Diary, PKY.

77. Coolidge, *Statistical Report*, 637.

78. Scudder, "Eclectic Medicine," 298.

79. In the South, quinine was considered the "*Sampson* of the *Materia Medica*" by 1844; Duffy, *American Medicine*, 75. For the role of the Florida war in the proliferation of quinine, see Ockenhouse et al., "Military Contributions," 12–16. Ill-effects also led to

deep-seated antipathy to the drug in certain regions; see Rothstein, *American Physicians*, 189.

80. Ucko, *New Counterinsurgency Era*, 27–28; Hall, "Reckless Waste of Blood and Treasure," 83; Vandervort, *Indian Wars*, 136.

81. For the ascendance of the Medical Department, see Gillett, *Army Medical Department*, 72. For the reaction of the American Medical Association, see "Review of Statistical Report," 142. For the rise in the statistical approach throughout the world, see Arnold, *Colonizing the Body*, 66. On the social significance of statistical evidence during this period, see Rosen, *Public Health*, 215–18.

CHAPTER 9: Land of Darkness and Shadows

1. "Speech of Mr. Reynolds of Illinois," 141. For background on Reynolds, see *Reynolds' History of Illinois*.

2. Elderkin, *Biographical Sketches*, 19–20.

3. Ibid., 19.

4. Cole, *Myth of Evil*, 97, 230.

5. "The Florida Train," *Floridian and Advocate*, July 17, 1841. For further description of these hammocks, see Sprague, April 28, 1839, in "Macomb's Mission," 161.

6. Similar ecological change occurred in such settler habitats as New Zealand, where—in the course of one hundred years—the ecology shifted from predominant rainforest to mostly grassland. See Dominy, "Hearing Grass, Thinking Grass," 54.

7. Davis, "Alligators and Plume Birds," 237–54.

8. Tropical old-growth stands can only be seen in select areas of South Florida; see Tanner and Hamel, "Old-Growth Deciduous Forests," 106–08.

9. Simon, "Mind and Madness," 182.

10. Nash, *Inescapable Ecologies*, 5; Valencius, *Health of the Country*, 160.

11. Henry Hollingsworth, October 4, 1836, Hollingsworth diary, 1836–37, Tennessee State Library and Archives, Nashville, TN.

12. Holmes, "Use of Quinine in Florida," 297.

13. "Copy of a Letter from a Young Officer of the Army to a Friend in this City, Dated Fort Lauderdale, E.F., June 20, 1839," in *Army and Navy Chronicle*, August 8, 1838.

14. Meindl, "Water, Water, Everywhere," 122.

15. Simmons, "Recollections of the Late Campaign," 547.

16. Nash, *Wilderness and the American Mind*, 9.

17. Hollingsworth, October 4, 1836, Hollingsworth diary.

18. Rodenbough, *From Everglades to Canyon*, 33.

19. "Testimony of Colonel William Lindsay," December 7, 1836, in *ASP:MA* 7:137. For mention of the unparalleled "verdure" of these "primeval groves of nature," specifically in the Micanopy area, see Simmons, *Notices of East Florida*, 48.

20. "Major General Scott's Address or Summary of Evidence Taken in his Case," January 19, 1836, in *ASP:MA* 7:198.

21. Winfield Scott to Lewis Cass, June 14, 1836, in *ASP:MA* 7:279.

22. The method of girdling or stripping off the bark at the base of trees (thus killing them) escalated during the citrus and vegetable boom of the 1880s, a cheap method of clearing hammock land. See Webber, *Eden of the South*, 26. For an earlier account of

the advantages of agricultural production in the interior, with reference to the 1830s, see "Florida: Its Soil and Products," 178–83.

23. The region's farming potential only came into its own after the arrival of the railroad in the latter part of the nineteenth century.

24. Sprague, May 6, 1839, in "Macomb's Mission," 166.

25. Veracini, *Settler Colonialism*, 18–20.

26. Denham, "Some Prefer the Seminoles," 40.

27. Weber, *Spanish Frontier*, 245–47. Rembert Patrick's use of "white trash" in reference to an entire group of Georgian settlers (*Florida Fiasco*, 195–210) certainly exemplifies this bent.

28. Weber, *Spanish Frontier*, 245–47.

29. Phelps diary, April 2, 1839, NYPL.

30. Ibid., April 9, 1839.

31. Frazier, *Slavery and Crime in Missouri*, 135–37; *American Slavery as It Is*, 89.

32. Vandervort, *Indian Wars*, 53; Ostler, *The Plains Sioux*, 41–43; Neely, *The Civil War*, 157; Adams, *Prince of Dragoons*, 132–33.

33. Eisenhower, *Agent of Destiny*, 425 n. 7.

34. Hitchcock, *Fifty Years in Camp and Field*, 420.

35. Some Florida politicians, particularly David Levy, also wanted increased population in order to qualify the territory for statehood.

36. This tendency is also noted in Pearce, "Torment of Pestilence," 450.

37. D[avid] Levy, Letter to the Editor, *National Intelligencer*, October 1, 1842.

38. Ibid.; see also Lawson, *Statistical Report, 1819–1839*, 311.

39. "Physician Second," "Florida—No. III," *National Intelligencer*, September 19, 1843; Lawson, *Statistical Report, 1819–1839*, 311. Coffman notes the obvious discrepancy in *The Old Army*, 51.

40. The first in this series was identified as "Florida—No. 1," *National Intelligencer*, May 18, 1843, and concluded with "Florida—No. IX," December 25, 1843.

41. Ibid., December 9, 1843.

42. Carter and Mendis, "Burden of Malaria," 564–94; for the importance of relative humidity, see Yazoume Ye et al., *Malaria Transmission Risk*, 103.

43. "Physician Second," "Florida—No. IV," *National Intelligencer*, October 11, 1843.

44. *Tropical Plant*, September 4, 1843, quoted in "Physician Second—No. IV," *National Intelligencer*, October 11, 1843.

45. Ibid.

46. "Florida Emigrants," *Sun*, February 13, 1844.

47. Patterson, *Mosquito Crusades*, 97, 99; McNeill, *Mosquito Empires*, 204–7; Brady, *War Upon the Land*, 47; Bell, *Mosquito Soldiers*, 11.

48. Carter and Mendis, "Burden of Malaria," 564–94.

49. "The New El Dorado," *New Bedford Mercury*, May 26, 1843.

50. Knetsch, *Fear and Anxiety*, 241. The number of new arrivals—based on a study by Knetsch and Paul S. George ("A Problematical Law," 63–80)—is considerably less than earlier estimates. For reference to ten thousand new settlers, see "Speech of the Hon. T. H. Benton." For additional insight regarding the Armed Occupation Act, see Jensen, *Origins of American Social Policy*, 181–84.

51. Quote regarding settlers from "Florida" (from the *Ancient City*, St. Augustine),

Mississippi Free Trader, December 13, 1853; see also DeBow, *Census of the United States,* ix; an influx of winter tourists in such locales as St. Augustine nevertheless took place post–Civil War; see Hillyer, *Designing Dixie,* 44–87.

52. Lawson to David L. Yulee, October 1, 1855, in "The Florida Peninsula: Its Climate and Superior Salubrity," *National Intelligencer,* March 25, 1858.

53. *Vital Statistics of the United States,* xxii. Malaria is listed under remittent and intermittent fever. Florida's ranking could have presented problems for tourism and immigration, but this result was not widely publicized; the few exceptions included Russell, "Malaria," 417, and "Malaria," *American Journal of Dental Science,* 336.

54. Eagan, *Florida Settler,* 11.

55. Billings, *Report on the Mortality and Vital Statistics,* 23.

56. Patterson, "Trials and Tribulations of Amos Quito," 164, 167; for the definition of holoendemic (rate of more than 75 percent), see Hay, Smith, and Snow, "Measuring Malaria Endemicity," 369–78.

57. Crosby, *Ecological Imperialism,* 67.

58. Baird, "Vivax Malaria," 36–57; Dauer and Faust, "Malaria Mortality," 942.

59. Dauer and Faust, "Malaria Mortality," 941.

60. "US Population by State," accessed June 6, 2014, http://www.demographia.com/db-state1900.htm.

61. Patterson, "Trials and Tribulations," 162–65.

62. For reference to the embittered feelings of officers and enlisted men, see Watson, "Thankless . . . Unholy War," 9–50.

63. For the number of militia, see Robertson, *Soldiers of Florida,* 9; Mahon, *Second Seminole War,* 325.

64. "Analysis of an 'Official Report,'" 296.

CHAPTER 10: Osceola as Settler-Colonial Icon

1. Wickman, *Osceola's Legacy,* 75. As a yahola, Osceola manifested a special connection to the spirit realm: see Wright, *Creeks and Seminoles,* 249–50. For the importance of a yahola as a male deity, see Swanton, *Creek Religion,* 485.

2. "G" [pseud.], letter to the editor, *Daily Commercial Bulletin,* March 5, 1838.

3. "For Whom Will You Vote?" *Lorain Standard,* October 6, 1840.

4. "Speech of Mr. Benton of Missouri" (June 8, 1838), *Globe,* June 12, 1838.

5. A short selection of newspapers that published Catlin's description include "Osceola," *Daily Commercial Bulletin and Missouri Literary Register,* February 14, 1838; "Osceola" (from the *New York Evening Star*), *Cincinnati Daily Gazette,* February 8, 1838; "Graphic Portrait of Osceola," *Newark Daily Advertiser,* February 2, 1838; "Portrait of Osceola," *Centinel of Freedom,* February 6, 1838; "Osceola—The Victim of Jesup's Treachery" (from the *New York Star*), *National Aegis,* February 14, 1838; "Osceola," *Native American,* February 10, 1838. For Catlin's Whig affiliations and his Osceola commission, see Dippie, *Catlin,* 64, 88–91.

6. Wickman, *Osceola's Legacy,* 67–106. The author eschews "myth" in favor of verifiable facts regarding Osceola—an understandable priority for a biography. In doing so, however, Wickman fails to consider the wider implications of the myth-making process and ignores the role of the Whig Party in the development of Osceola's tragic hero persona as well as the Democratic focus on the Red Devil stereotype.

7. Steven Smith, in Haiman, *Best Practices*, 58. See also Hanggli, Bernhard, and Kriesi, "Construction of the Frames"; Hanggli, "Key Factors in Frame Building," in *Political Communication*, 69–81, 125–42; and Carragee and Roefs, "Recent Frame Research," 214–33.

8. For the emergence of the Whig Party, see Wilentz, *American Democracy*, 482–518; see also Holt, *Jacksonian Politics*, and Howe, *American Whigs*.

9. Wiener, *Americanization of the British Press*, 4; North, *Newspaper and Periodical Press*, 90–91; Couch, *Information Technologies*, 152–53; for the need for melodramatic content, see Copeland, *Antebellum Era*, 14, 163–66.

10. For the newspaper exchange, see Coward, *Newspaper Indian*, 14–15, 62, and Kielbowicz, "Newsgathering," 42–48. For the number and volume of newspapers and periodicals, see Tucher, "Newspapers and Periodicals," 400, and North, *Newspaper and Periodical Press*, 47.

11. Coward, *Newspaper Indian*, 57–62. Popular history has stressed one-dimensional accounts, but this general tendency also includes more serious authors, including John Mahon.

12. [Representative] Waddy Thompson, "House of Representatives, Debate on the President's Message," December 30, 1839, *Daily National Intelligencer*, January 8, 1840.

13. Wolfe, *Settler Colonialism*, 173; Tankard, "Empirical Approach," 97.

14. Wolfe, *Settler Colonialism*, 162–73.

15. Hobbes, *Leviathan*, 65. Hobbes's "natural men" in effect acted as wolves and not men; see Berlin, "Hobbes, Locke, and Professor Macpherson," 58.

16. Golway, *Machine Made*; Allen, *Rise and Fall of Tammany Hall*; MacGregor, "Tammany," 391–407.

17. This appears to be a fairly universal phenomenon within settler-colonial societies; see, for example, Stafford, "Going Native," 162–73.

18. LeFevre, "Logics of Difference," 137. Slotkin utilized the "Indianized" terminology throughout his *Regeneration through Violence*.

19. Veracini, *Settler Colonialism*, 47.

20. Wolfe, *Settler Colonialism*, 389; for "self-othering," see During, "Rousseau's Patrimony," 47–71.

21. "Song of Hiawatha," 1295.

22. Wickman, *Osceola's Legacy*, 68.

23. Ibid., 25, 71.

24. For a discussion of kitsch in the history of mass culture, see Macdonald's classic essay "A Theory of Mass Culture," 59–73.

25. "Seminole War," *New York Commercial Advertiser*, January 18, 1836; see also *New York Spectator*, January 21, 1836; *Enquirer*, January 19, 1836; and *Mercury*, January 21, 1836. For scalping among soldiers, see "Major Childs, U.S.A.," 371; Strang, "Skulls, Scalps and Seminoles"; James Ormand, "Reminiscences of the Life of James Ormond," February 3, 1892, typescript, 15, Ormand Papers, PKY.

26. "Latest from Florida," *National Intelligencer*, February 25, 1836.

27. Sprague, journal entry, April 27, 1839, in "Macomb's Mission," 160. For additional references to the sacred character of the peninsular interior, see Sprague, *Florida War*, 251, 273. See also Simmons, *Notices of East Florida*, 46–47. The sacredness of this land was undoubtedly related to the burial sites and to locations once used for the annual

busk ceremony and sacred fires. For reference to the busk ceremony and dance grounds as representing "the spiritual core of Seminole life," see Weisman, *Beads on a String*, 152. For the Seminoles' reverence for burial land, see Strang, "Violence, Ethnicity, and Human Remains," 979, 982, 985. Seminoles also revered the ancient burial mounds of earlier Indigenous people. The most conservative faction of present-day Florida Seminoles maintains an all-inclusive view of the sacred, including "Sacred Burial Grounds, Sacred Sunlight, Sacred Waters, [and] Sacred Air"; see Peter B. Gallagher, "Bobby C. Billie Takes on National Park Service," *Seminole Tribune*, November 22, 2011.

28. Colonel John Warren to Colonel Ab[raham] Eustis (Jacksonville), January 14, 1836, roll 0122, LR.

29. Abraham Eustis to Secretary of War, January 7, 1836, and Eustis to [Winfield] Scott, April 10, 1836, roll 0122, LR.

30. Simmons, "Recollections," 542.

31. Trask, *Black Hawk*, 64.

32. Simmons, "Recollections," 543.

33. Ibid.

34. Parkin and Philips, *Laughter and Power*, 7, 11–12; Bhabha, "Of Mimicry and Man," 121–31.

35. Simmons, "Recollections," *Atkinson's Casket*.

36. Cohen, *Notices of Florida*, 233–37.

37. Martin, "Interpreting Metamora," 84–85; Lott, *Love and Theft*, 55–56.

38. Cohen, *Notices of Florida*, 235. Osceola's mother was a Creek who also had partial white ancestry. Osceola nonetheless assumed membership in the Bird Clan by virtue of his mother's affiliation and self-identified as Indian; see Wickman, *Osceola's Legacy*, 72, 143.

39. Cohen, *Notices of Florida*, 235.

40. Mason, "Politics of Metamora," 92, 105.

41. Cohen, *Notices of Florida*, 237.

42. Cohen, *Notices of Florida*, 237.

43. Drinnon, *Facing West*, 123–30.

44. "Speech of Mr. Levy, of Florida, in the House of Representatives, June 12, 1842," *Florida Herald and Southern Democrat*, August 1, 1842.

45. "The Florida War: Mr. Underwood's (of Kentucky) Late Speech in Congress," *New Hampshire Sentinel*, January 25, 1838.

46. "Private Correspondence," *Herald*, March 21, 1836.

47. This quote appeared in various papers, including "Important from Florida— Oceola Taken," *Morning Herald*, November 1, 1837; "St. Augustine," *Maryland Gazette*, November 2, 1837; *Daily Ohio Statesmen*, November 3, 1837; *Daily Commercial Bulletin and Missouri Literary Messenger*, November 11, 1837.

48. R. B. Lee, "Fort Defiance, Micanopy, East Florida, July 12, 1836," *Army and Navy Chronicle*, August 25, 1836. For mention of Jumper, see R. B. Lee to [Lieutenant Colonel] Bankhead (Fort Defiance), May 23, 1836, roll 0122, LR.

49. Vandervort, *Indian Wars*, 128.

50. "Description of Osceola, by One of the Cherokee Delegation—in a Letter to His Children in New Hampshire, St. Augustine, Nov. 10, 1837," in *Connecticut Herald*, January 23, 1838.

51. Monaco, "Opening Battles of the Second Seminole War."

52. For reference to Tecumseh's admonition against indiscriminate killing, see Halbert and Hall, *Creek War*, 44.

53. For a rare account of the torture of a militia soldier by Coacoochee's band, see Ormond, "Reminiscences," 17.

54. *Pensacola Gazette*, April 23, 1836; see also "From the South," *Herald*, May 17, 1837; "The Indian War," *Fayetteville Observer*, February 23, 1837. For reference to saving the lives of military prisoners, see "Important from Florida," *New Hampshire Sentinel*, March 30, 1837. A black man named Sampson, a member of Osceola's band, claimed that Osceola directed warriors to spare the lives of settler women and children; see John K. Mahon, "Typescript Containing Information on Seminole Chiefs," Mahon Papers, PKY.

55. Darby and Dwight, *New Gazetteer*, 165.

56. Shire, *Threshold of Manifest Destiny*, 58–59.

57. "Latest from Florida," *Camden Commercial Courier*, November 4, 1837.

58. John Hatheway to Samuel Hatheway (Charleston Harbor), January 6, 1838, in *Letters of Maj. John S. Hatheway*, 37–38.

59. According to one account, Osceola contracted malaria in 1836 while in the vicinity of Fort Drane; see Mahon, *Second Seminole War*, 218.

60. George Catlin, "Graphic Portrait of Osceola," *Newark Daily Advertiser*, February 2, 1838.

61. For contemporary reference to Weedon's "pickling" of the head, see "3rd Artillery" [pseud.], *Herald*, June 19, 1842. For the outrage that erupted after plans for exhibiting the head in New York City came to light, see "Domestic News" (from the *Sunday Morning News*), *Alexandria Gazette*, June 14, 1838; "Shameful—if True," *Public Ledger*, June 14, 1838; "An Outrage" (from the *Ohio Transcript*), *Daily Commercial Bulletin*, December 18, 1838; and "An Outrage," *Hudson River Chronicle*, June 19, 1838. Wickman believes that Frederick Weedon was primarily influenced by a legitimate interest in phrenology and natural history rather than by the more typical desire to attain "dark trophies" (*Osceola's Legacy*, 181–82). But I certainly concur with others who see such actions as reflecting more complex motives, including revenge for the army dead. See Strang, "Violence, Ethnicity, and Human Remains," 986, and Grounds, "American Place Names," 287–322; see also Harrison, *Dark Trophies*, 85–86.

62. "Death of Osceola," *New York Commercial Advertiser*, February 10, 1838.

63. "Death of Osceola, or Powell" (from the *New York Star*), *Rhode Island Republican*, February 14, 1838. The *Star* was owned and edited by Mordecai Noah, a former Jackson advocate turned conservative Whig. Noah was never on the party payroll, however, and described his paper as an "independent Whig Journal." For more on the *Star*, see Sarna, *Jacksonian Jew*, 98–100, 102.

64. Halttunen, "Pornography of Pain," 303–34. For the central role of emotion, see Blauvelt, *Work of the Heart*.

65. "The Wife of Osceola" (from the *Nashville Whig*), *Daily Commercial Bulletin*, May 24, 1838. This story was also reprinted in the *Alexandria Gazette*, July 1, 1838—a quintessential Whig organ—and the mass circulation *Morning Herald*, June 16, 1838.

66. Schantz, *Awaiting the Heavenly Country*, 4, 34–35; Watson, *Liberty and Power*, 221.

67. *Morning Herald*, February 23, 1838.

68. "Then Burst a Noble Heart," *New York Spectator*, February 8, 1838.

69. On the "coupling of Christianity and government" among Whig leaders, see Portnoy, *Their Right to Speak*, 23; see also Wilentz, *American Democracy*, 490–91.

70. For examples of the "dying Indian" motif, see Flint, *Transatlantic Indian*, 26–52.

71. "Portrait of Osceola," *Evening Post*, May 30, 1838. This portrait was by William Laning, a relatively unknown artist from Charleston. It should also be noted that William Cullen Bryant's *Evening Post* aligned itself with the Democratic Party. For other examples of the political use of the heroic Indian motif, see Martin, "Interpreting Metamora," 73–101.

72. Johnson, "George Catlin's Picturesque," 72.

73. "Death of Osceola" (from the *New York Star*), *Adams Sentinel*, February 26, 1838.

74. For the significance of urban regions in promulgating the romantic genre, see Wolfe, *Settler Colonialism*, 173. On the rising and waning of the Romantic genre in America as it related to white culture's treatment of Native people, see Berkhofer, *White Man's Indian*.

75. Walkiewicz, "Portraits and Politics," 109.

76. For a list of towns and counties, see Hellmann, *Historical Gazetteer*, 57, 69, 197, 204, 214, 356, 358, 556, 635, 676. Almost half of the states eventually incorporated the name of Osceola into some sort of public commemoration; see Missal and Missal, *Seminole Wars*, 137; see also Grounds, "American Place Names," 287–322; Coe, *Red Patriots*, 113.

77. Veracini, *Settler Colonialism*, 47. According to Linda Tuhiwai Smith, "Renaming the land was probably as powerful ideologically as changing the land" (Smith, *Decolonizing Methodologies*, 51).

78. George Catlin, "Portrait of Osceola," *Centinel of Freedom*, February 6, 1838; "Osceola—the Victim of Jesup's Treachery" (from the *New York Star*), *National Aegis*, February 14, 1838.

79. Although the composition of the Whig Party was heterogeneous, certain generalities can be made as far as its appeal among the professional and learned classes; see Howe, *American Whigs*, 13; Holt, *Whig Party*, 85–87.

80. Street, "Original Poetry: Osceola," 324.

81. "Death of Osceola," *Niles' Weekly Register*, February 17, 1838. On the Whig tendency to assume that "their efforts ultimately benefited others," see Kohl, *Politics of Individualism*, 89; see also Egerton, "Jacksonian Historiography," 129.

82. *New York Spectator*, September 2, 1840.

83. "G." [pseud.], Letter to the Editor, *Daily Commercial Bulletin and Missouri Literary Register*, March 5, 1838.

84. Grimes, "Phenomenology of Exteriorization," 509.

85. "G." [pseud.], Letter to the Editor, *Daily Commercial Bulletin and Missouri Literary Register*, March 5, 1838.

86. "For Whom Will You Vote?" *Lorain Standard*, October 6, 1840; emphasis original.

87. See, for example, "Speeches at the Great Whig Convention" (from the *Claremont Eagle*), *Vermont Phoenix*, February 28, 1840. During the 1840 presidential campaign, Whigs charged Van Buren with effeminacy, and for their part Democrats claimed that

frontier women sent Harrison petticoats in order to shame him; see Stevens, "William Henry Harrison," 33–34; see also Casper, *Constructing American Lives*, 99–100.

88. Thomas Hart Benton, "Florida Indian War," 72, 80.

89. "Speech of Mr. Benton, of Missouri."

90. "Major Childs, U.S.A.," 280; Motte, *Journey into Wilderness*, 143; Cohen, *Notices of Florida*, 236.

91. "From Florida" (from the *New York Gazette*), *Rhode Island Republican*, April 22, 1837; emphasis added.

92. "Removal of the Indians," 70. For the tendency of settler-colonialism to view Indigenous persons as phantoms, see Veracini, *Settler Colonialism*, 84–86.

93. Douglass, *Frederick Douglass: Selected Speeches*, 485. Contemporary notions of the superior "industry and foresight" of black slaves vis-a-vis Indian masters was quite common; see Doran, "Negro Slaves," 335.

94. Taylor, *Contesting Constructed Indian-ness*, 13. In contrast, earlier examinations of Osceola's celebrity presumed that such distinctions never elicited any "practical benefit" to the public at large; see Boyd, "Asi-Yaholo or Osceola," 249.

95. Walkiewicz, "Portraits and Politics," 109.

96. Simmons, "Recollections," 542; emphasis original.

97. For an examination of the importance of theater within the colonial mind-set, see J. S. Bratton, *Acts of Supremacy*; see also Martin, "Interpreting 'Metamora,'" 73–101.

98. Fort Moultrie is now managed by the NPS. For discussion of the geographical and spatial elements of settler-colonialism, see Harris, "How Did Colonialism Dispossess?" 167–68. See also Bauman, "Making and Unmaking of Strangers," 12.

CHAPTER 11: **Bloodhounds, Abolitionists, and Freedom Fighters**

1. "The Florida War" (from the *N.Y. Whig*), in the *Emancipator*, March 12, 1840.

2. "The Elections," *Extra Globe*, September 1, 1840; see also Watson, *Liberty and Power*, 217.

3. Campbell, "Seminoles, the 'Bloodhound War,' and Abolitionism," 259–302.

4. J. R. Poinsett to Thomas Benton, February 17, 1840, and Poinsett to Z[achary] Taylor, January 26, 1840, in *Richmond Enquirer*, February 22, 1840; "Bloodhounds in Florida," February 11, 1840, in *New York Commercial Advertiser*, February 14, 1840.

5. "From the *Montreal Courier*," *New York Spectator*, September 2, 1840; see also "Sketch of Democracy," *Age*, March 8, 1840; *Colonial Gazette*, November 27, 1839; *Courier*, November 21, 1839.

6. "E.L.A.," Letter to the Editor, *National Gazette*, February 13, 1840. One of the most detailed descriptions regarding the supposed vicious training given to these dogs appeared in the *American Masonic Register*, February 1, 1840.

7. A few examples of such outcries include: "Twenty-sixth Congress—First Session, February 11, 1840," *Albany Argus*, February 21, 1840; "The Bloodhounds—Value of Explanations in the Official Organ," *Madisonian*, February 13, 1840; "The Dogs of War," *Illinois Weekly State Journal*, May 22, 1840; "The Standing Army: A Parody," *Richmond Whig*, June 5, 1840; *Boston Traveler*, April 7, 1840; "The Excitement of Composition," *National Intelligencer*, May 22, 1840.

8. Jesup to Call (camp near Jupiter Inlet), February 18, 1838, LR.

9. Campbell, "Bloodhound War," 264.

10. Z[achary] Taylor to R[obert] R. Reid, March 23, 1840, and L. Thomas to John McLaughlin, March 7, 1840, both from roll 0218, LR.

11. Ibid.; see also Covington, "Cuban Bloodhounds," 119.

12. For the number of petitions, see Campbell, "Bloodhound War," 275. See also "Bloodhounds," *Gloucester Telegraph*, January 18, 1840; "Florida—The Blood-Hounds," *Portland Weekly Adviser*, January 21, 1840; "The Bloodhound Expedient and the Press," *Philadelphia Inquirer*, January 31, 1840; and "Division of Florida," *Pennsylvania Freeman*, January 16, 1840.

13. For background on the ascendant culture of individual rights at this time, see Clark, "Sacred Rights of the Weak," 463–93.

14. For Southard's abolitionist standing, see "American Anti-Slavery Society," *New York Spectator*, May 21, 1840.

15. "The Bloodhound War," *Liberator*, March 20, 1840.

16. Ibid.

17. "Washington," *North American and Daily Advertiser*, January 27, 1840.

18. Covington, "Bloodhounds," 115.

19. "The Florida Service" (from the *New York Commercial Advertiser*), *New Bedford Mercury*, February 28, 1840; "The Bloodhound War," *National Gazette*, February 5, 1840; "The Bloodhound War" (from the *Tallahassee Star*), *New York Commercial Advertiser*, January 25, 1840; "The Bloodhound Humbug," *Norwich Courier*, February 12, 1840; "The Bloodhound Humbug," *Portsmouth Journal of Literature and Politics*, June 20, 1840; "The Bloodhound Expedition," *Tennessee Whig*, February 27, 1840.

20. Caricatures also remain as one of the few visual records of this prephotographic era and serve as good social barometers of the period; see Hunt, *Political Caricature*, 2.

21. *Morning Herald*, February 27, 1840.

22. "Indian and Negro War," *Liberator*, March 18, 1837.

23. Ibid.

24. Harrold, "Romanticizing Slave Revolt," and Stewart, "Joshua Giddings," in *Antislavery Violence*, 93–95, 167–88. Despite his position within the mainstream political system, Giddings was still esteemed by Garrisonian abolitionists; see Washington, *Sojourner Truth's America*, 237.

25. Stewart, *Holy Warriors*, 163; Stewart, "Christian Statesmanship," 51.

26. Stauffer, *Black Hearts of Men*, 183.

27. Ibid.

28. Stauffer, "Advent among the Indians," 245; see also Douglass, *Selected Speeches*, 148.

29. Slotkin, *Regeneration through Violence*.

30. Social scientists consider the acceptance of the dominant virtues within society as crucial to minority acceptance; see Yancey, *Who is White?* 45; Khan, *Theory of Universal Democracy*, 102; and Forst, "Toleration, Justice and Reason," 73–78.

31. Thompson, "Introduction," xxi.

32. Stewart, *Abolitionist Politics*, 113.

33. The most definitive description of this peace initiative can be found in the daily journal entries of Ethan Allen Hitchcock. Hitchcock noted that Seminole leaders were in command while a few black translators were necessarily present, remaining on the sidelines. There is no reference at all to John Caesar; see Ethan Allen Hitchcock Diaries,

February and March 1836, Diary #7, GM. Osceola biographer Patricia Riles Wickman (*Osceola's Legacy*, 58) described the chronology of the story of Osceola's supposed black wife as "unlikely" and other essential details as either questionable or suspect and concludes by dismissing this story as unreliable. The first reference to such an event in the contemporary press was contained in a congressional speech published in the *National Intelligencer*, December 24, 1836. This unverified claim was later utilized by the abolitionist press to stir passionate outcry.

34. Kammen, *Mystic Chords of Memory*, 70.

35. Giddings, *Exiles of Florida*, 117.

36. Ibid., 99.

37. Ibid., 97.

38. Ibid., 58.

39. Y. N. Kly, an activist and self-taught historian, goes into unusual depth about what he considers the deliberate suppression of information, including claims of press censorship, in "Gullah War," 50 n. 41, n. 42.

40. Patrick, preface to *The Exiles of Florida*, xii.

41. Brown, "Tales of Angola," 5–21.

42. Bird, "Rebellion."

43. Kly, "Gullah War," 29.

44. Sarah E. Johnson, a literature professor, cites J. B. Bird's website in her article "You Should Give Them Blacks to Eat," 73–74, 90 n. 22.

45. Opala, "Black Seminoles" and "Conclusion."

46. For all quotations, see endnote 45.

47. Williams, *Like a Loaded Weapon*, xxvi.

48. For an extensive critique of "black sovereignty" champions, see Monaco, "Whose War Was It?" 31–66.

49. Haskell, *Objectivity is Not Neutrality*, 169.

50. Porter, *The Negro on the American Frontier*, 4.

Epilogue

1. Hitchcock, *Fifty Years in Camp and Field*, 165.

2. "Scraps from my Florida Journal.—No. 6," *Spirit of the Times*, January 4, 1845; emphasis added.

3. Call, "Gentlemen of the Senate and House," 33. Hitchcock's proceedings with Pascofa are also briefly mentioned in McReynolds, *The Seminoles*, 236–37.

4. Knetsch, *Seminole Wars*, 149; for the size of the Seminole reserve, see Jennings, "Fort Denaud," 27.

5. Missall and Missall, *Seminole Wars*, 213.

6. "Speech of Colonel Rector," *Herald*, April 4, 1858. See, in addition, "The Indian Delegation in Florida," *National Intelligencer*, February 27, 1858, and Covington, *Seminoles*, 143.

7. "The Final Departure of Billy Bowlegs and his Tribe to Arkansas," May 12, 1858, *Herald*, May 27, 1858.

8. West, "Abiaka," 407–8.

9. "Our Special Tampa Correspondence," *Herald*, May 27, 1858.

10. "Final Departure," *Herald*, May 27, 1858.

11. "The Florida War," *North American Review* 54 (January 1842): 33.

12. Veracini, *Settler Colonial Present*, 17.

13. Burnard, "A Failed Settler Society," 63–82.

14. Crosby, *Ecological Imperialism*. See also Acemoglu et al., "Colonial Origins," 1370. Crosby also notes that "disease was the most important factor in dictating that hot, wet America would be a land of racial mixture"; Crosby, *Ecological Imperialism*, 141.

15. Ahluwalia, "When Does a Settler Become a Native?" 63–73.

16. Florida Climate Center, Office of the State Climatologist, accessed October 10, 2016, https://climatecenter.fsu.edu/topics/humidity; Miller, *Environmental History*.

17. "Soils," Natural Resources Conservation Services Florida (USDA), accessed October 10, 2016, http://www.nrcs.usda.gov/wps/portal/nrcs/main/fl/soils/.

18. Crosby, *Ecological Imperialism*, 135.

19. Missall and Missall, *Seminole Wars*, 225.

20. Ibid.

21. Ibid.; emphasis added.

22. Ibid.; emphasis original.

23. Maddison, "Postcolonial Guilt and National Identity," 696.

24. Willie Johns, "Memorial Day Commemoration, Second Seminole War," Micanopy, May 25, 2015.

Bibliography

Manuscript Sources

Alachua County Clerk of the Court, Gainesville, FL
  Ancient Records (Deed Books)
Alma Clyde Field Library of Florida History, Cocoa, FL
  Patriot War Documents
Augusta Museum of History, Augusta, GA
  Documents and Manuscript Collection
Beinecke Rare Book and Manuscript Library, Yale University, New Haven, CT
  Ethan Allen Hitchcock Collection (Yale Collection of Western Americana)
Gilcrease Museum, Tulsa, OK
  Ethan Allen Hitchcock Diaries
Hargrett Rare Book and Manuscript Library, University of Georgia Libraries, Athens, GA
  Seminole War Collection
Historical Society of Pennsylvania, Philadelphia, PA
  Joel R. Poinsett Papers
  Henry D. Gilpin Collection
Library of Congress, Manuscript Division, Washington, DC
  Andrew Jackson Papers
  Zachary Taylor Papers
National Archives and Records Administration, Washington, DC
  Letters Received by the Office of the Adjutant General, Main Series 1822–60, Record Group 94
New York Public Library, New York, NY
  John Wolcott Phelps Papers
P. K. Yonge Library of Florida History, University of Florida, Gainesville, FL
  Crown Collection of Photographs of American Maps
  Joel W. Jones Manuscript
  John K. Mahon Papers
  Ormand Family Papers
  Reynold M. Kirby Diary (1837–38)
  William S. Foster Journals (1836–37)
  Miscellaneous Manuscript Collection
State Archives of Florida, Tallahassee, FL
  Richard Keith Call Papers

Thomas S. Jesup, Seminole Campaign Diary
Tennessee State Library and Archives, Nashville, TN
    Henry Hollingsworth Diary (1836–37)
University of South Florida Library, Tampa, FL
    Rare Maps Collection
William L. Clements Library, University of Michigan, Ann Arbor, MI
    Native American History Collection
    Thomas S. Jesup Papers

Newspapers

Adams Sentinel (Gettysburg, PA)
Age (London, UK)
Albany Argus (Albany, NY)
Albany Evening Journal (Albany, NY)
Alexandria Gazette (Alexandria, VA)
American Masonic Register (Albany, NY)
Army and Navy Chronicle (Washington, DC)
Atlas (Boston, MA)
Baltimore Gazette and Daily Advertiser (Baltimore, MD)
Boston Courier (Boston, MA)
Boston Traveler (Boston, MA)
Camden Commercial Courier (Camden, SC)
Centinel of Freedom (Newark, NJ)
Christian Intelligencer and Eastern Chronicle (Gardiner, ME)
Cincinnati Mirror (Cincinnati, OH)
Colonial Gazette (London, UK)
Connecticut Herald (New Haven, CT)
Connecticut Journal (New Haven, CT)
Courier (London, UK)
Daily Commercial Bulletin (St. Louis, MO)
Daily Ohio Statesmen (Columbus, OH)
Daily Picayune (New Orleans, LA)
Daily Scioto Gazette (Chillicothe, OH)
Eastern Argus (Portland, ME)
Emancipator (New York, NY)
Enquirer (Richmond, VA)
Evening Post (New York, NY)
Evening Star (New York, NY)
Extra Globe (Washington, DC)
Fayetteville Observer (Fayetteville, NC)
Florida Herald and Southern Democrat (St. Augustine, FL)
Floridian (Tallahassee, FL)
Floridian and Advocate (Tallahassee, FL)
Globe (Washington, DC)
Gloucester Telegraph (Gloucester, MA)
Harper's New Monthly Magazine (New York, NY)

Herald (New York, NY)
Hudson River Chronicle (Sing Sing, NY)
Illinois Weekly State Journal (Springfield, IL)
Liberator (Boston, MA)
Log Cabin (New York, NY)
Lorain Standard (Elyria, OH)
Madisonian (Washington, DC)
Maryland Gazette (Annapolis, MD)
Mercury (New York, NY)
Mississippi Free Trader and Natchez Gazette (Natchez, MS)
Morning Herald (New York, NY)
National Aegis (Worcester, MA)
National Banner and Nashville Whig (Nashville, TN)
National Gazette (Philadelphia, PA)
National Intelligencer (Washington, DC)
Native American (Washington, DC)
New Bedford Mercury (New Bedford, MA)
New Hampshire Gazette (Portsmouth, NH)
New Hampshire Sentinel (Keene, NH)
New York Commercial Advertiser (New York, NY)
New York Spectator (New York, NY)
New York Whig (New York, NY)
Newark Daily Advertiser (Newark, NJ)
Niles' Weekly Register (Baltimore, MD)
North American and Daily Advertiser (Philadelphia, PA)
Norwich Courier (Norwich, CT)
Pennsylvania Freeman (Philadelphia, PA)
Pennsylvania Inquirer and Daily Courier (Philadelphia, PA)
Pensacola Gazette and West Florida Advertiser (Pensacola, FL)
Philadelphia Inquirer (Philadelphia, PA)
Portland Weekly Adviser (Portland, ME)
Portsmouth Journal of Literature and Politics (Portsmouth, NH)
Public Ledger (Philadelphia, PA)
Rhode Island Republican (Newport, RI)
Richmond Whig (Richmond, VA)
Saratoga Sentinel (Saratoga Springs, NY)
Schenectady Reflector (New York, NY)
Spirit of the Times (New York, NY)
St. Louis Commercial Bulletin (St. Louis, MO)
Sun (Baltimore, MD)
Tennessee Whig (Jonesborough, TN)
Times (London, UK)
Tropical Plant (Jacksonville, FL)
United States' Telegraph (Washington, DC)
Vermont Gazette (Bennington, VT)
Vermont Phoenix (Brattleboro, VT)

Virginia Free Press (Charlestown, VA)
Weekly Messenger (Boston, MA)

Published Primary Sources

American Slavery As It Is: Testimony of a Thousand Witnesses. New York: American Anti-Slavery Society, 1839.

"Analysis of an 'Official Report to the Surgeon General, U.S. Army on the Use of Large Doses of Sulphate of Quinine in Diseases of the South, with Notices of the Climate and Diseases of Florida, &c,' by John B. Porter, M.D., Assistant Surgeon, U.S. Army." *American Journal of the Medical Sciences* 20 (October 1845): 296–316.

"An Army Surgeon's Notes on Frontier Service, 1833–1838." *Journal of the Military Services Institution of the United States* 39 (September/October 1906): 451–60.

Baldwin, Benjamin Franklin. *Notices of the Campaigns of the Tennessee Volunteers, under General Robert Armstrong, in the Years 1836–7.* Nashville: N.p., 1843.

Barr, James. *A Correct and Authentic Narrative of the Indian War in Florida, with a Description of Maj. Dade's Massacre, and an Account of the Extreme Suffering, for Want of Provision, of the Army—Having Been Obliged to Eat Horse's and Dog's Flesh, Etc.* New York: J. Narine, 1836.

Bartram, William. *Travels of William Bartram.* Edited by Mark Doren Van. New York: Dover Publications, 1955.

Bemrose, John. *Reminiscences of the Second Seminole War.* Edited by John K. Mahon. Tampa, FL: University of Tampa Press, 2001.

Benton, Thomas Hart. "Florida Armed Occupation Bill: Mr. Benton's Speech." In *Thirty Years' View; Or, a History of the Working of the American Government for Thirty Years from 1820 to 1850: Chiefly Taken from the Congress Debates, the Private Papers of General Jackson, and the Speeches of Ex-Senator Benton, with His Actual View of Men and Affairs: With Historical Notes and Illustrations and Some Notices of Eminent Deceased Contemporaries.* New York: D. Appleton, 1858.

———. "Florida Indian War: Its Origin and Conduct." In *Thirty Years' View; Or, a History of the Working of the American Government for Thirty Years from 1820 to 1850: Chiefly Taken from the Congress Debates, the Private Papers of General Jackson, and the Speeches of Ex-Senator Benton, with His Actual View of Men and Affairs: With Historical Notes and Illustrations and Some Notices of Eminent Deceased Contemporaries.* New York: D. Appleton, 1858.

Bigelow, Jacob. "Jacob Bigelow, a Harvard Medical Professor, Challenges the Physician's Power to Cure, 1835." In *Major Problems in the History of American Medicine and Public Health: Documents and Essays.* Edited by John Harley Warner and Janet Ann Tighe, 94–96. Boston: Cengage, 2001.

Billings, John S., ed. *Report on the Mortality and Vital Statistics of the United States as Returned at the Tenth Census (June 1, 1880).* Washington, DC: GPO, 1885.

Call, R. K. "Gentlemen of the Senate and House of Representatives, January 13, 1843." In *A Journal of the Proceedings of the Legislative Council of the Territory of Florida.* Tallahassee: S. S. Sibley, 1843.

Carter, Clarence Edwin, ed. *The Territorial Papers of the United States.* 28 vols. Washington, DC: United States Government Printing Office, 1934–1975.

Childs, Thomas. "Major Childs, U.S.A.—Extracts from His Correspondence with His Family." *Historical Magazine* 3rd ser. 2:299–304, 371–74; 3rd ser. 3:169–71, 280–84.

Clay, Henry. *The Papers of Henry Clay. January 1, 1837-December 31, 1843.* Edited by Robert Seager and Melba Hay Porter. Vol. 9. Lexington: University Press of Kentucky, 1988.

Cohen, M. M. *Notices of Florida and the Campaigns.* Charleston, SC: Burges and Honour, 1836.

Congressional Globe. Vol. 7. Washington, DC: Blair and Rives, 1839.

Coolidge, Richard H., ed. *Statistical Report on the Sickness and Mortality in the Army of the United States: Compiled from the Records of the Surgeon General's Office: Embracing a Period of Sixteen Years, from January, 1839 to January, 1855.* Washington, DC: A. O. P. Nicholson, 1856.

Copeland, David A. *The Antebellum Era: Primary Documents on Events from 1820 to 1860.* Westport, CT: Greenwood, 2003.

Coppinger, José. *Manifesto, Que Hace el Coronel Español Don José Coppinger Demostrando el Injusto y Violento Proceder Que Se Há Observado en San Augustin de Florida.* Philadelphia: Hurtel, 1821.

Correspondence on the Subject of the Emigration of Indians, 1831–1833. Washington, DC: Duff Green, 1834.

Cushing, Caleb. *An Oration, on the Material Growth and Territorial Progress of the United States: Delivered at Springfield, Mass., on the Fourth of July, 1839.* Springfield, MA: Merriam, Wood and Company, 1839.

DeBow, J. D. B., ed. *Seventh Census of the United States, 1850.* Washington, DC: U.S. Census Office, 1853.

Denham, James M., and Canter Brown Jr., eds. *Cracker Times and Pioneer Lives: The Florida Reminiscences of George Gillett Keen and Sarah Pamela Williams.* Edited by James M. Denham and Canter Brown. Columbia: University of South Carolina Press, 2000.

De Tocqueville, Alexis. *Democracy in America.* Translated by Henry Reeve. 3rd ed. New York: George Adlard, 1839.

De Vattel, Emmerick. *The Law of Nations: Or, Principles on the Law of Nature Applied to the Conduct and Affairs of Nations and Sovereigns.* Rev. ed. London: G. G. and J. Robinson, 1797.

Dexter, Horatio S. "Observations on the Seminole Indians [1823]." Edited by Mark F. Boyd. *Florida Anthropologist* 11, no. 3 (September 1958): 81–85.

Dickens, Asbury, ed. *American State Papers, Documents, Legislative and Executive, of the Congress of the United States, for the Second Session of the Twenty-Fourth, and the First and Second Sessions of the Twenty-Fifth Congress. Military Affairs.* Vol. 7. Washington, DC: Gales and Seaton, 1861.

Douglass, Frederick. *Frederick Douglass: Selected Speeches and Writings.* Edited by Philip S. Foner. Chicago: Lawrence Hill, 1999.

Drake, Samuel G. *The Book of the Indians of North America: Comprising Details in the Lives of about Five Hundred Indian Chiefs and Others.* Boston: Josiah Drake, 1833.

Dupré, C. C. "On the Yellow Fever at Key West, East Florida." *American Journal of the Medical Sciences* 4 (1841): 380–84.

Eagan, D. *The Florida Settler or Immigrants' Guide: A Complete Manual of Information concerning the Climate, Soil, Products and Resources of the State.* Tallahassee: Commission of Lands and Immigration, 1873.

Elderkin, James D. *Biographical Sketches and Anecdotes of a Soldier of Three Wars, as Written by Himself: The Florida, the Mexican War and the Great Rebellion, Together with Sketches of Travel, also of Service in a Militia Company and a Member of the Detroit Light Guard Band for over Thirty Years.* Detroit, MI: Author, 1899.

Everett, Horace. *Speech of Horace Everett, of Vermont: Delivered in the House of Representatives, in Committee of the Whole on the Indian Annuity Bill, Friday, June 3, 1836.* Washington, DC: National Intelligencer Office, 1836.

Florida History Online: The Indian Frontier in British East Florida; Letters to Governor James Grant from British Soldiers and Indian Traders. Accessed September 13, 2016. http://www.unf.edu/floridahistoryonline/Projects/Grant/letters.html#oo8.

"Florida: Its Soil and Products." *Western Journal* 6, no. 3 (June 1851): 178–83.

Foreman, Grant, ed. "Report of Cherokee Deputation into Florida." *Chronicles of Oklahoma* 9, no. 4 (December 1931): 423–38.

Forry, Samuel. "Letters of Samuel Forry, Surgeon U.S. Army, 1837–1838: Part I." *Florida Historical Society Quarterly* 6, no. 3 (1928): 133–48.

Forry, Samuel, and Thomas Lawson, eds. *Statistical Report on the Sickness and Mortality in the Army of the United States: Compiled from the Records of the Surgeon General's and Adjutant General's Offices: Embracing a Period of Twenty Years, from January, 1819, to January, 1839.* Washington, DC: Jacob Gideon, Jr., 1840.

Foster, William S. *This Miserable Pride of a Soldier: The Letters and Journals of Col. William S. Foster in the Second Seminole War.* Edited by John Missall and Mary Lou Missall. Tampa, FL: University of Tampa Press, 2005.

Frank, Andrew K. *Creeks and Southerners: Biculturalism on the Early American Frontier.* Lincoln: University of Nebraska Press, 2005.

General Regulations for the Army of the United States, 1841. Washington, DC: J. and G. S. Gideon, 1841.

Giddings, Joshua. *The Exiles of Florida: Or, the Crimes Committed by Our Government against the Maroons, Who Fled from South Carolina and Other Slave States, Seeking Protection under Spanish Laws.* Columbus, OH: Follett, Foster and Co., 1858.

——. *Pacificus, the Rights and Privileges of the Several States in Regard to Slavery Being a Series of Essays, Published in the Western Reserve Chronicle, (Ohio,) after the Election of 1842.* Warren, OH: N.p., 1842.

"A Grant of Indian Territory from the Upper Creek Indians as Also the Lower Creeks and Seminoles to Colonel Thomas Brown Superintendent of Indian Affairs for the Southern District of North America." *World Digital Library.* Accessed September 15, 2016. http://www.wdl.org/en/item/14197/?utm_source=feed&utm_medium=rss&utm _campaign=feed%2C.

Harney, Benjamin F. "Report of Surgeon Benjamin F. Harney." *Statistical Report on the Sickness and Mortality in the Army of the United States: Compiled from the Records of the Surgeon General's Office: Embracing a Period of Sixteen Years, from January, 1839 to January, 1855.* Edited by Thomas Lawson and Richard H. Coolidge. Washington, DC: A. O. P. Nicholson, 1856.

Hatheway, John Shadrach. *Frontier Soldier: The Letters of Maj. John S. Hatheway, 1833–1853*. Vancouver, WA: Vancouver National Historic Reserve Trust, 1999.

"Hayti and the Haytiens." *DeBow's Review* 16, no. 1 (January 1854): 32–38.

Henderson, Thomas. *Hints on the Medical Examination of Recruits for the Army: And on the Discharge of Soldiers from the Service on Surgeon's Certificate: Adapted to the Service of the United States*. Philadelphia: Haswell, Barrington, and Haswell, 1840.

Hertslet, Lewis, ed. *British and Foreign State Papers, 1821–1822*. London: J. Harrison and Son, 1829.

History of American Missions to the Heathen, from Their Commencement to the Present Time. Worcester, MA: Spooner and Howard, 1840.

Hitchcock, Ethan Allen. *Fifty Years in Camp and Field, Diary of Major-General Ethan Allen Hitchcock, U.S.A.* Edited by W. A. Croffut. New York: G. P. Putnam's Sons, 1909.

Hobbes, Thomas. *Leviathan; Or, the Matter, Form and Power of a Commonwealth, Ecclesiastical and Civil*. London: George Routledge and Sons, 1886.

Holmes, R. S. "Remarks on the Use of Quinine in Florida, and on Malaria and Its Influence in that State." *American Journal of the Medical Sciences* 24 (October 1846): 297–309.

Hooper, John H. *An Inaugural Essay on Phrenitis, for the Degree of Doctor of Physick: Submitted to the Consideration of the Hon. Robert Smith, Provost, and of the Regents, of the University of Maryland*. Baltimore: Ralph W. Pomeroy and Co., 1815.

Humphreys, Andrew A. "Andrew Atkinson Humphreys' Seminole War Field Journal." Edited by Matthew T. Pearcy. *Florida Historical Quarterly* 85, no. 2 (Fall 2006): 204–30.

Hunter, Nathaniel Wyche. "Captain Nathaniel Wyche Hunter and the Florida Indian Campaigns, 1837–1841." Edited by Reynold Wik. *Florida Historical Quarterly* 39, no. 1 (July 1960): 62–75.

"Indian Missions: Cherokees." *Foreign Missionary Chronicle* 8, no. 1 (January 1840): 10.

Jarvis, N. S. "An Army Surgeon's Notes on Frontier Service, 1833–1838." *Journal of the Military Services Institution of the United States* 39 (1906): 275–86.

Kemble, Francis A. *Journal of a Residence on a Georgian Plantation in 1838–1839*. New York: Harper Brothers, 1864.

Kersey, Harry A., Jr., and Michael Petersen, eds. "'Was I a Member of Congress . . .': Zachary Taylor's Letter to John J. Crittenden, January 12, 1838, concerning the Second Seminole War." *Florida Historical Quarterly* 75, no. 4 (Spring 1997): 447–61.

Letter from the Secretary of War to the Chairman of the Committee on Indian Affairs, Transmitting Sundry Documents and Correspondences in Relation to the Indians of Florida. Washington, DC: n.p., 1823.

Locke, John. "Of Property." In *The Works of John Locke, Esq.*, 165–72. Vol. 2. London, 1714.

Mahon, John K., ed. "Letters from the Second Seminole War." *Florida Historical Quarterly* 36, no. 4 (1958): 331–52.

"Malaria." *American Journal of Dental Science* 11, no. 7 (November 1877): 336.

Mann, James. "Medical Sketches of the Campaigns of 1812, 13, 14: To Which Are Added, Surgical Cases, Observations on Military Hospitals, and Flying Hospitals Attached to a Moving Army: Also, an Appendix Comprising a Dissertation on Dysentery Which Obtained the Boylstonian Prize Medal for the Year 1806 and Observations on the Winter Epidemic of 1815–16, Denominated Peripneumonia Notha, as It Appeared at Sharon and Rochester, State of Massachusetts: Mann, James, 1759–1832: Internet Archive." Accessed September 19, 2016. https://archive.org/details/medicalsketches 000mannuoft.

"Marsh Fevers: Quinine in High Doses." *Boston Medical and Surgical Journal* 12 (August 5, 1835): 419–20.

McCall, George A. *Letters from the Frontier*. Philadelphia: J. B. Lippincott, 1868.

McCormick, James. "Report of Assistant Surgeon James McCormick." In *Statistical Report on the Sickness and Mortality in the Army of the United States: Compiled from the Records of the Surgeon General's Office: Embracing a Period of Sixteen Years, from January, 1839 to January, 1855*. Edited by Thomas Lawson and Richard H. Coolidge. Washington, DC: A. O. P. Nicholson, 1856.

McGaughy, Jr., Felix P. "The Squaw Kissing War: Bartholomew M. Lynch's Journal of the Second Seminole War, 1836–1839." Master's thesis, Florida State University, 1965.

McKenney, Thomas L. *Memoirs, Official and Personal: With Sketches of Travels among the Northern and Southern Indians*. New York: Paine and Burgess, 1846.

Morse, Jedidiah. *A Report to the Secretary of War of the United States on Indian Affairs: Comprising a Narrative of a Tour Performed in the Summer of 1820 under a Commission from the President of the United States for the Purpose of Ascertaining, for the Use of the Government, the Actual State of the Indian Tribes in Our Country*. New Haven, CT: S. Converse, 1822.

Motte, Jacob Rhett. *Journey into Wilderness: An Army Surgeon's Account of Life in Camp and Field during the Creek and Seminole Wars, 1836–1838*. Edited by James F. Sunderman. Gainesville: University of Florida Press, 1953.

"Mr. Carmichael on Inflammatory Affections of the Brain and Its Membranes." *Medico-Chirurgical Review* 38 (1833): 459–65.

Penieres, Jean Augustin. "Letter from Jean Augustin Penieres, July 2, 1821." PKY: University of Florida. Accessed September 15, 2016. http://web.uflib.ufl.edu/spec/pkyonge /newax4.html.

"Petition of Gad Humphreys." February 10, 1846. H. Rpt. 203, 29th Cong., 1st Sess., 1846.

"Petition of Thomas S. Jesup, Stating That He Has Sustained an Injury in Consequence of an Omission in a Document Printed by Order of the Senate, and Praying Redress." Sen. Doc. 231, 26th Cong., 2nd Sess., 1841.

Phelps, John W. "Letters of Lieutenant John W. Phelps, U.S.A., 1837–1838." *Florida Historical Society Quarterly* 6, no. 2 (1927): 67–84.

Poinsett, Joel Roberts. *An Inquiry into the Received Opinions of Philosophers and Historians: On the Natural Progress of the Human Race from Barbarism to Civilization*. Charleston, SC: J. S. Burges, 1834.

Porter, John B. "ART. IV.—Analysis of an 'Official Report to the Surgeon-General, U.S. Army, on the Use of Large Doses of Sulphate of Quinine in Diseases of the South, with Notices of the Climate and Diseases of Florida, &c. &c.'" *American Journal of the Medical Sciences* 20 (October 1845): 296–315.

Potter, Woodburne. *The War in Florida: Being an Exposition of Its Causes, and an Accu-*

rate History of the Campaigns of Generals Clinch, Gaines, and Scott. Baltimore: Lewis and Coleman, 1836.

Prichard, James Cowles. A Treatise on Insanity and Other Disorders Affecting the Mind. London: Sherwood, 1835.

Prince, Henry. Amidst a Storm of Bullets: The Diary of Lt. Henry Prince in Florida. Edited by Frank Laumer. Tampa, FL: University of Tampa Press, 1998.

"Proceedings of the Military Court of Inquiry, in the Case of Major General Scott and Major General Gaines." In Public Documents Printed by Order of the Senate of the United States, Second Session of the Twenty-Fourth Congress. Washington, DC: Gales and Sutton, 1837.

"Recollections of a Campaign in Florida." Yale Literary Magazine 11, no. 2 (December 1845): 72–80.

"Removal of the Indians." North American Review 30 (January 1830): 62–121.

"Restoration of Certain Negroes to the Seminoles." June 28, 1848. House Doc. 55, Executive Documents, 31st Cong., 2nd Sess., 1947.

"Review of Statistical Report on the Sickness and Mortality in the Army of the United States, Compiled from the Records of the Surgeon General's Office; Embracing a Period of Sixteen Years, From January, 1839 to January, 1855." American Journal of the Medical Sciences 67 (1857).

Right of President to Withhold Papers—Frauds to Indians. Message from the President of the United States, Transmitting the Report of Lieutenant Colonel Hitchcock, Respecting the Affairs of the Cherokee Indians, &c. January 31, 1843. Referred to the Committee on Indian Affairs. February 25, 1843. Report Made by Committee, and Ordered to Be Printed. Washington, DC, 1843.

Robertson, Francis Marion. "The Richmond Blues in the Second Seminole War: Letters of Captain Francis Marion Robertson, M.D." Edited by Thomas H. Robertson Jr. Military Collector and Historian 54, no. 2 (Summer 2002): 51–63.

Rodenbough, Theophilus F. From Everglade to Canyon with the Second United States Cavalry: An Authentic Account of Service in Florida, Mexico, Virginia, and the Indian Country: Including the Personal Recollections of Prominent Officers: With an Appendix Containing Orders, Reports and Correspondence, Military Records . . . 1836–1875. Norman: University of Oklahoma, 2000.

Ross, John. Letter from John Ross, the Principal Chief of the Cherokee Nation, to a Gentleman of Philadelphia. Philadelphia, 1838.

Rowles, W. P. "Incidents and Observations in Florida in 1836." The Southron, or Lily of the Valley (1841): 157–61.

Rush, Benjamin. Medical Inquiries and Observations upon the Diseases of the Mind. Philadelphia: Kimber and Richardson, 1812.

Russell, Charles P. "Malaria." Popular Science Monthly 9 (August 1876): 416–26.

Scudder, J. M. "A Brief History of Eclectic Medicine." Eclectic Medical Journal 39 (1879): 297–308.

"Seminole War—Slaves Captured. Message from the President of the United States Transmitting the Information Called for by a Resolution of the House of Representatives of August 9, 1841, in Relation to the Origin of the Seminole War, of Slaves Captured, &c." Accessed September 15, 2016. https://vtext.valdosta.edu/xmlui/bitstream/handle/10428 /1062/ms146–028_spencer_seminole-slaves_1841.pdf?sequence=3&isAllowed=y.

Sheldon, Jane Murray. "Seminole Attacks near New Smyrna, 1836–1856." *Florida His-torical Quarterly* 8, no. 4 (April 1930): 188–96.

Sherman, William T. *Home Letters of General Sherman.* Edited by M. A. DeWolfe Howe. New York: C. Scribner's Sons, 1909.

———. *The Sherman Letters: Correspondence between General and Senator Sherman from 1837 to 1891.* Edited by Rachel Thorndike. New York: C. Scribner's Sons, 1894.

Sigmond, George. "Lectures on Materia Medica and Therapeutics, Now in Course of Delivery at the Windmill-Street School of Medicine: On Cinchona." *The Lancet* 1 (1837): 446–51.

Simmons, James W. "Recollections of the Late Campaign in East Florida." *Atkinson's Casket: Gems of Literature, Wit and Sentiment* 11 (November 1836): 542–57.

Simmons, William H. *Notices of East Florida.* 1822; Reprint ed. Gainesville: University of Florida Press, 1973.

Smith, W. W. *Sketch of the Seminole War and Sketches during a Campaign.* Charleston: Dan J. Dowling, 1836.

"Speech of Hon. T. A. Howard, of Indiana, in the House of Representatives, February 12, 1840," *Appendix to the Congressional Globe,* 26th Cong., 1st Sess., 1840.

"Speech of the Hon. T. H. Benton, of Missouri, in Senate, January 12, 1840." *Appendix to the Congressional Globe,* 26th Cong., 1st Sess., 1840.

"Speech of Mr. Benton of Missouri, June 8, 1838." *Congressional Globe.* 25th Cong., 2nd Sess., 1838, 353–57.

"Speech of Mr. Everett of Vermont, June 3, 1836." *Appendix to the Congressional Globe,* 24th Cong., 1st Sess., June 1836, 543.

"Speech of Mr. Reynolds of Illinois, in the House of Representatives February 5, 1841." *Appendix to the Congressional Globe,* 26th Cong., 2nd Sess., 1841.

Spenser, Edmund. "A Veue of the Present State of Ireland." In *The Complete Works in Verse and Prose of Edmund Spenser,* edited by Alexander B. Grosart, 13–256. Vol. 9. Manchester: Spenser Society, 1882–1884.

Sprague, J. T. *The Origin, Progress, and Conclusion of the Florida War.* New York: D. Appleton and Company, 1848.

Street, Alfred B. "Original Poetry: Osceola." *New-York Mirror: A Weekly Gazette of Literature and the Fine Arts* 15, no. 41 (1838): 324.

"Substance of a Statistical Report from the Morgue, Paris, 1836." *The Medico-Chirurgical Review* 13 (1837): 191–92.

"Treaty with the Seminole, 1832." In *Indian Affairs: Laws and Treaties,* edited by Charles J. Kappler, 394–95. Vol. 2. Washington, DC: GPO, 1904.

Tyler, John. "Message from the President of the United States to the Two Houses of Congress, at the Commencement of the Second Session of the Twenty-Seventh Congress, December 7, 1841." 27th Cong., 2nd Sess., 1841.

United States. Cong. House. *Memorial of the Cherokee Mediators, March 26, 1838.* 25th Cong., 2nd Sess. H. Doc. 285, 1838.

United States. Cong. House. *Negroes &c, Captured from Indians in Florida.* 25th Cong., 3rd Sess. H. Doc. 225, 1839.

United States. Cong. Senate. *A Bill to Provide for the Armed Occupation of That Part of Florida Which Is Now Overrun and Infested by Marauding Bands of Hostile Indians.* By Thomas H. Benton. 25th Cong., 3rd Sess., 1839.

Unsigned Review. "The Song of Hiawatha by H. W. Longfellow." *Athenaeum*, November 10, 1855, 1295.

Van Buren, W. H. "Report on the Use of Quinine Sulphate, in Miasmatic Diseases of the South." *New York Journal of Medicine* 6 (1846): 77–83.

The Vital Statistics of the United States: Embracing the Tables of Deaths, Births, Sex and Age, to Which Are Added the Statistics of the Blind, the Deaf and Dumb, the Insane, and the Idiotic, Compiled from the Original Returns of the Ninth Census, (June 1, 1870) under the Direction of the Secretary of the Interior. Washington: G.P.O., 1872.

White, Frank F., ed. "A Journal by Lt. Robert C. Buchanan during the Seminole War." *Florida Historical Quarterly* 29, no. 2 (October 1950): 132–51.

———. "The Journals of Lieutenant John Pickrell, 1836–1837." *Florida Historical Quarterly* 38, no. 2 (October 1959): 142–71.

———. "Macomb's Mission to the Seminoles: John T. Sprague's Journal Kept during April and May, 1839." *Florida Historical Quarterly* 35, no. 2 (October 1956): 130–93.

Williams, John Lee. *The Territory of Florida: Or Sketches of the Topography, Civil and Natural History of the Country, the Climate and the Indian Tribes, from the First Discovery to the Present Time, with a Map, Views & Etc.* New York: A. T. Goodrich, 1837.

Wood, James. "Observations on Inflammation and Brain Fever." *Edinburgh Medical and Surgical Journal* 13 (October 1817): 438–40.

Woodward, Thomas S. *Woodward's Reminiscences of the Creek or Muscogee Indians, Contained in Letters to Friends in Georgia and Alabama.* Montgomery, AL: Barrett and Wimbish, 1859.

Secondary Sources

Abel, Annie H. *The American Indian as Slaveholder and Secessionist: An Omitted Chapter in the Diplomatic History of the Southern Confederacy.* Cleveland: Arthur H. Clark, 1915.

———. "The History of Events Resulting in Indian Consolidation West of the Mississippi River." In *Annual Report of the American Historical Association for the Year 1906: In Two Volumes.* Vol. 1. Washington, D.C.: G.P.O., 1908.

Acemoglu, Daron, et al. "The Colonial Origins of Colonial Comparative Development: An Empirical Investigation." *American Economic Review* 91, no. 5 (December 2001): 1369–1401.

Adams, George Rollie. *General William S. Harney: Prince of Dragoons.* Lincoln: University of Nebraska, 2001.

Ahluwalia, Pal. "When Does a Settler Become a Native? Citizenship and Identity in a Settler Society." *Pretexts: Literary and Cultural Studies* 10, no. 1 (2001): 63–73.

Allen, Oliver E. *The Tiger: The Rise and Fall of Tammany Hall.* Reading, MA: Addison-Wesley, 1993.

Altman, John. "Indigenous Rights, Mining Corporations, and the Australian State." In *The Politics of Resource Extraction: Indigenous Peoples, Multinational Corporations, and the State*, edited by Suzana Sawyer and Edmund Terence Gomez, 46–74. Houndmills, Basingstoke: Palgrave Macmillan, 2012.

Anderson, Gary Clayton. *Ethnic Cleansing and the Indian: The Crime That Should Haunt America.* Norman: University of Oklahoma Press, 2014.

Andrews, George Reid. *Afro-Latin America, 1800–2000*. Oxford: Oxford University Press, 2004.

Arnade, Charles W. "Cattle Raising in Spanish Florida, 1513–1763." *Agricultural History* 35, no. 3 (July 1961): 116–24.

Arneil, Barbara. *John Locke and America: The Defense of English Colonialism*. New York: Oxford University Press, 1996.

Arnold, David. *Colonizing the Body: State Medicine and Epidemic Disease in Nineteenth-Century India*. Berkeley: University of California Press, 1993.

Baird, J. Kevin. "Evidence and Implications of Mortality Associated with Acute Plasmodium Vivax Malaria." *Clinical Microbiology Reviews* 26, no. 1 (2013): 36–57.

Baird, J. K., and S. L. Hoffman. "Primaquine Therapy for Malaria." *Clinical Infectious Diseases* 39, no. 9 (2004): 1336–345.

Baker, Henry. "Spanish Ranching and the Alachua Sink: A Preliminary Report." *Florida Anthropologist* 46, no. 2 (June 1993): 82–100.

Banner, Stuart. *How the Indians Lost Their Land: Law and Power on the Frontier*. Cambridge, MA: Belknap Press of Harvard University Press, 2005.

Baptist, Edward E. *Creating an Old South: Middle Florida's Plantation Frontier before the Civil War*. Chapel Hill: University of North Carolina Press, 2002.

Bateman, Fiona, and Lionel Pilkington, eds. *Studies in Settler Colonialism: Politics, Identity and Culture*. Houndmills, Basingstoke: Palgrave Macmillan, 2011.

Bauer, K. Jack. *Zachary Taylor: Soldier, Planter, Statesman of the Old Southwest*. Baton Rouge: Louisiana State University Press, 1985.

Bauman, Z. "Making and Unmaking of Strangers." *Thesis Eleven* 43, no. 1 (November 1995): 1–16.

Bell, Andrew McIlwaine. *Mosquito Soldiers: Malaria, Yellow Fever, and the Course of the American Civil War*. Baton Rouge: Louisiana State University Press, 2010.

Berkhofer, Robert F. *The White Man's Indian: Images of the American Indian from Columbus to the Present*. New York: Random House, 1978.

Berlin, Isaiah. "Hobbes, Locke, and Professor Macpherson." In *Thomas Hobbes: Critical Assessments*, edited by Preston T. King, 55–58. London: Routledge, 2000.

Bernhard, Laurent, Hanspeter Kriesi, and Regula Hanggli. "Construction of the Frames." In *Political Communication in Direct Democratic Campaigns: Enlightening or Manipulating?* edited by Hanspeter Kriesi, 69–81. Houndmills, Basingstoke: Palgrave Macmillan, 2011.

Berrios, G. E. *The History of Mental Symptoms: Descriptive Psychopathology since the Nineteenth Century*. Cambridge: Cambridge University Press, 1996.

Bhabha, Homi K. "Of Mimicry and Man: The Ambivalence of Colonial Discourse." In *The Location of Culture*, 121–31. London: Routledge, 1994.

Bird, J. B. "Rebellion: John Horse and the Black Seminoles, First Black Rebels to Beat American Slavery." Accessed September 22, 2016. http://www.johnhorse.com.

Blakney-Bailey, Jane Anne. "An Analysis of Historic Creek and Seminole Settlement Patterns, Town Design, and Architecture the Paynes Town Seminole Site (8Al366): A Case Study." Ph.D. diss., University of Florida, 2007.

Blauvelt, Martha T. *The Work of the Heart: Young Women and Emotion, 1780–1830*. Charlottesville: University of Virginia Press, 2007.

Borchard, Gregory A. *Abraham Lincoln and Horace Greeley*. Carbondale: Southern Illinois University Press, 2011.

Bourdieu, Pierre. *Language and Symbolic Power*. Cambridge, UK: Polity, 1992.

Boyd, Mark F. "Asi-Yaholo or Osceola." *Florida Historical Quarterly* 33, no. 3/4 (1955): 249–305.

———. "From a Remote Frontier: Letters Passing between Captain Harries in Command at Apalache (St. Marks) in 1764 and His Commander-in-Chief, General Gage, in New York." *Florida Historical Quarterly* 20, no. 1 (1941): 82–92.

———. "Horatio S. Dexter and Events Leading to the Treaty of Moultrie Creek with the Seminole Indians." *Florida Anthropologist* 11, no. 1 (September 1958): 65–95.

———. "The Seminole War: Its Background and Onset." *Florida Historical Quarterly* 30, no. 1 (July 1951): 3–115.

Brady, Lisa M. *War upon the Land: Military Strategy and the Transformation of Southern Landscapes during the American Civil War*. Athens: University of Georgia, 2012.

Bratton, J. S. *Acts of Supremacy: The British Empire and the Stage, 1790–1930*. Manchester: Manchester University Press, 1991.

Braund, Kathryn E. Holland. "The Congress Held in a Pavilion: John Bartram and the Indian Congress at Fort Picolata, East Florida." In *America's Curious Botanist: A Tercentennial Reappraisal of John Bartram, 1699–1777*, edited by Nancy Hoffmann and John Van Horne, 79–96. Philadelphia: American Philosophical Society, 2004.

———. "The Creek Indians, Blacks and Slavery." *Journal of Southern History* 57, no. 4 (November 1991): 601–36.

———. *Deerskins and Duffles: Creek Indian Trade with Anglo-America, 1685–1815*. Lincoln: University of Nebraska Press, 1993.

Brinsfield, John W. "Army Values and Ethics: A Search for Consistency and Relevance." *Parameters* 28, no. 3 (Autumn 1998): 69–84.

Brockington, Lolita Gutiérrez. *The Leverage of Labor: Managing the Cortés Haciendas in Tehuantepec, 1588–1688*. Durham, NC: Duke University Press, 1989.

Brown, Jr., Canter. "The Florida Crisis of 1826–1827 and the Second Seminole War." *Florida Historical Quarterly* 73, no. 4 (April 1995): 419–42.

———. *Florida's Peace River Frontier*. Orlando: University of Central Florida Press, 1991.

———. "Looking for Angola: Interview with Canter Brown, Jr." Accessed September 15, 2016. http://archive.today/YKWX.

———. "Persifor F. Smith, the Louisiana Volunteers, and Florida's Second Seminole War." *Louisiana History* 34, no. 4 (Autumn 1993): 389–410.

———. "The 'Sarrazota or Runaway Negro Plantations': Tampa Bay's First Black Community, 1812–1821." *Tampa Bay History* 12, no. 2 (Fall 1990): 5–19.

———. "Tales of Angola: Free Blacks, Red Stick Creeks, and International Intrigue in Spanish Southwest Florida, 1812–1821." In *Go Sound the Trumpet! Selections in Florida's African American History*, edited by David H. Jackson and Canter Brown Jr., 5–21. Tampa, FL: University of Tampa Press, 2005.

Brown, Harvey E., ed. *The Medical Department of the United States Army from 1775–1873*. Washington, DC: Surgeon General's Office, 1873.

Brown, Richard Maxwell. "Back Country Rebellions and the Homestead Ethic in America, 1740–1799." In *Tradition, Conflict, and Modernization: Perspectives on the Amer-*

ican Revolution, edited by Don Fehrenbacher and Richard Maxwell Brown. New York: Academic Press, 1977.

Buhaug, Halvard, and Scott Gaines. "The Geography of Civil War." *Journal of Peace Research* 39, no. 4 (July 2002): 417–33.

Buker, George E. "Introduction." In *Notices of East Florida*, by William H. Simmons. Facsimile Ed. Gainesville: University of Florida Press, 1973.

——. *Swamp Sailors in the Second Seminole War*. Gainesville: University Press of Florida, 1997.

Burnard, Trevor. "A Failed Settler Society: Marriage and Demographic Failure in Early Jamaica." *Journal of Social History* 26, no. 1 (Autumn 1994): 63–82.

Bushnell, Amy. "The Menendez Marquez Cattle Barony at La Chua and the Determinants of Economic Expansion in Seventeenth-Century Florida." *Florida Historical Quarterly* 56, no. 4 (April 1978): 408–32.

Byrd, Jodi A. *The Transit of Empire: Indigenous Critiques of Colonialism*. Minneapolis: University of Minnesota Press, 2011.

Calloway, Colin G. *The American Revolution in Indian Country: Crisis and Diversity in Native American Communities*. Cambridge: Cambridge University Press, 1995.

Campbell, John. "The Seminoles, the 'Bloodhound War,' and Abolitionism, 1796–1865." *Journal of Southern History* 72, no. 2 (2006): 259–302.

Carragee, K. M., and Wim Roefs. "The Neglect of Power in Recent Framing Research." *Journal of Communication* 54, no. 2 (2004): 214–33.

Carson, James Taylor. "Native Americans, the Market Revolution and Culture Change: The Choctaw Cattle Economy, 1690–1830." *Agricultural History* 35, no. 3 (July 1961): 1–18.

Carter, R., and K. N. Mendis. "Evolutionary and Historical Aspects of the Burden of Malaria." *Clinical Microbiology Reviews* 15, no. 4 (2002): 564–94.

Casper, Scott E. *Constructing American Lives: Biography and Culture in Nineteenth-Century America*. Chapel Hill: University of North Carolina Press, 1999.

Cave, Alfred A. "Abuse of Power: Andrew Jackson and the Indian Removal Act of 1830." *The Historian* 65, no. 6 (December 2003): 1330–353.

Cecil-Fronsman, Bill. *Common Whites: Class and Culture in Antebellum North Carolina*. Lexington: University Press of Kentucky, 1992.

Césaire, Aimé. *Discourse on Colonialism*. Translated by Joan Pinkham. New York: Monthly Review Foundation Incorporated, 2000.

Chang, David A. *The Color of the Land: Race, Nation, and the Politics of Landownership in Oklahoma, 1832–1929*. Chapel Hill: University of North Carolina Press, 2010.

Clark, Elizabeth B. "'The Sacred Rights of the Weak': Pain, Sympathy, and the Culture of Individual Rights in Antebellum America." *Journal of American History* 82, no. 2 (1995): 463–93.

Clavin, Matthew. "'It Is a Negro, Not an Indian War': Southampton, St. Domingo, and the Second Seminole War." In *America's Hundred Years' War: U.S. Expansion to the Gulf Coast and the Fate of the Seminole, 1763–1858*, edited by Stephen W. Belko, 181–208. Gainesville: University Press of Florida, 2011.

——. *Toussaint Louverture and the American Civil War: The Promise and Peril of a Second Haitian Revolution*. Philadelphia: University of Pennsylvania Press, 2010.

Coates, Julia. *Trail of Tears*. Santa Barbara, CA: ABC-CLIO, 2014.

Coe, Charles H. *Red Patriots: The Story of the Seminoles*. Cincinnati: Editor Publishing Company, 1898.

Coffman, Edward M. *The Old Army: A Portrait of the American Army in Peacetime, 1784–1898*. New York: Oxford University Press, 1986.

Coker, William S. "Pensacola's Medical History: The Colonial Era, 1559–1821." *Florida Historical Quarterly* 77, no. 2 (1998): 181–92.

Cole, Phillip. *The Myth of Evil: Demonizing the Enemy*. Westport, CT: Praeger, 2006.

Couch, Carl J. *Information Technologies and Social Order*. New Brunswick, NJ: Transaction, 1996.

Covington, James W. "The Agreement of 1842 and Its Effect upon Seminole History." *Florida Anthropologist* 31, no. 1 (March 1978): 8–11.

——. "The Armed Occupation Act of 1842." *Florida Historical Quarterly* 40, no. 1 (July 1961): 41–52.

——. "Cuban Bloodhounds and the Seminoles." *Florida Historical Quarterly* 33, no. 2 (1954): 111–19.

——. "Florida Seminoles: 1900–1920." *Florida Historical Quarterly* 53, no. 2 (1974): 181–97.

——. *The Seminoles of Florida*. Gainesville: University Press of Florida, 1993.

Coward, John M. *The Newspaper Indian: Native American Identity in the Press, 1820–90*. Urbana: University of Illinois, 1999.

Crosby, Alfred W. *Ecological Imperialism: The Biological Expansion of Europe, 900–1900*. 2nd ed. Cambridge: Cambridge University Press, 2004.

Curtin, Philip D. *Death by Migration: Europe's Encounter with the Tropical World in the Nineteenth Century*. Cambridge: Cambridge University Press, 1989.

Cusick, James G. *The Other War of 1812: The Patriot War and the American Invasion of Spanish East Florida*. Gainesville: University Press of Florida, 2003.

Darby, William, and Theodore Dwight Jr. *A New Gazetteer of the United States of America*. Hartford, CT: Edward Hopkins, 1833.

Dauer, C. C., and E. C. Faust. "Malaria Mortality in the United States, with Especial Reference to the Southeastern States." *Southern Medical Journal* 30, no. 9 (September 1937): 939–43.

Davis, Jack E. "Alligators and Plume Birds: The Despoliation of Florida's Living Aesthetic." In *Paradise Lost? The Environmental History of Florida*, edited by Jack E. Davis and Raymond Arsenault, 235–59. Gainesville: University Press of Florida, 2005.

Davis, T. Frederick. "United States Troops in Spanish East Florida, 1812–13." *Florida Historical Quarterly* 9, no. 4 (April 1931): 3–23.

Dean, Eric T. *Shook over Hell: Post-Traumatic Stress, Vietnam, and the Civil War*. Cambridge, MA: Harvard University Press, 1997.

De Baillou, Clemens. "Introduction." In *John Howard Payne to His Countrymen*, edited by Clemens De Baillou, by John Howard Payne. Athens: University of Georgia Press, 1961.

Deloria, Philip Joseph. *Indians in Unexpected Places*. Lawrence: University Press of Kansas, 2004.

Deloria, Vine. *God Is Red: A Native View of Religion*. New York: Grosset and Dunlop, 1973.

Denham, James M. *A Rogue's Paradise: Crime and Punishment in Antebellum Florida, 1821–1861*. Tuscaloosa: University of Alabama Press, 1997.

———. "'Some Prefer the Seminoles': Violence and Disorder among Soldiers and Settlers in the Second Seminole War, 1835–1842." *Florida Historical Quarterly* 70, no. 1 (July 1991): 38–54.

Denoon, Donald. "Understanding Settler Societies." *Historical Studies* 18, no. 73 (1979): 511–27.

Dippie, Brian W. *Catlin and His Contemporaries: The Politics of Patronage.* Lincoln: University of Nebraska, 1990.

Dixson, Anthony. "Black Seminole Involvement and Leadership during the Second Seminole War, 1835–1842." PhD diss., Indiana University, 2007.

Dodd, Dorothy. "Captain Bunce's Tampa Bay Fisheries, 1835–1840." *Florida Historical Quarterly* 25, no. 3 (January 1947): 246–56.

Doherty, Herbert J., Jr. "Ante-Bellum Pensacola, 1821–1860." *Florida Historical Quarterly* 37, no. 3–4 (January 1959): 337–56.

———. "Code Duello in Florida." *Florida Historical Quarterly* 29, no. 4 (April 1951): 243–52.

———. "Richard K. Call vs. the Federal Government on the Seminole War." *Florida Historical Quarterly* 31, no. 3 (January 1953): 163–80.

Dominy, Michele D. "Hearing Grass, Thinking Grass: Postcolonialism and Ecology in Aotearoa-New Zealand." In *Disputed Territories: Land, Culture and Identity in Settler Societies*, edited by David S. Trigger and Gareth Griffiths. Hong Kong: Hong Kong University Press, 2003.

Doran, Michael F. "Negro Slaves of the Five Civilized Tribes." *Annals of the Association of American Geographers* 68, no. 3 (1978): 335–50.

Dowd, Gregory Evans. *A Spirited Resistance: The North American Indian Struggle for Unity, 1745–1815.* Baltimore: Johns Hopkins University Press, 1992.

Drinnon, Richard. *Facing West: The Metaphysics of Indian-hating and Empire-building.* Minneapolis: University of Minnesota Press, 1980.

Du Bois, W. E. B. *The Souls of Black Folk.* New York: Dover Publications, 1903.

Dueck, Colin. *Reluctant Crusaders: Power, Culture, and Change in American Grand Strategy.* Princeton, NJ: Princeton University Press, 2006.

Duffield, Lathel F. "Cherokee Emigration: Reconstructing Reality." *Chronicles of Oklahoma* 80, no. 3 (Fall 2002): 314–47.

Duffy, John. *From Humors to Medical Science: A History of American Medicine.* Urbana: University of Illinois Press, 1993.

During, Simon. "Rousseau's Patrimony: Primitivism, Romance and Becoming Other." In *Colonial Discourse, Postcolonial Theory*, edited by Francis Barker, Peter Hulme, and Margaret Iversen. Manchester: Manchester University Press, 1994.

Egerton, Douglas R. "An Update on Jacksonian Historiography: The Biographies." In *Rebels, Reformers, and Revolutionaries: Collected Essays and Second Thoughts*, 121–34. New York: Routledge, 2002.

Eisenhower, John S. D. *Agent of Destiny: The Life and Times of General Winfield Scott.* Norman: University of Oklahoma Press, 1997.

———. *Zachary Taylor.* New York: Henry Holt, 2009.

Ellis, Gary, C. S. Monaco, Ken Nash, Jill Principe, Jonathan Dean. "Fort Defiance / Fort Micanopy and the Opening Battles of the Second Seminole War 1835–1836, Historic and Archeological Study." American Battlefield Protection Program, NPS, 2010–2011.

Ellisor, John T. *The Second Creek War: Interethnic Conflict and Collusion on a Collapsing Frontier.* Lincoln: University of Nebraska Press, 2010.

Etemad, Bouda. *Possessing the World: Taking the Measurements of Colonization from the 18th to the 20th Century.* New York: Berghahn, 2007.

Ethridge, Robbie. *Creek Country: The Creek Indians and Their World.* Chapel Hill: University of North Carolina Press, 2003.

Fairbanks, Charles H. "The Ethno-Archaeology of the Florida Seminole." In *Tacachale: Essays on the Indians of Florida and Southeastern Georgia during the Historic Period,* edited by Samuel Proctor and Jerald T. Milanich, 163–93. Gainesville: University Press of Florida, 1994.

Fierst, John T. "Rationalizing Removal: Anti-Indianism in Lewis Cass's North American Review Articles." *Michigan Historical Review* 36, no. 2 (Fall 2010): 1–35.

Flint, Kate. *The Transatlantic Indian, 1776–1930.* Princeton, NJ: Princeton University Press, 2008.

Ford, Lisa. *Settler Sovereignty: Jurisdiction and Indigenous People in America and Australia, 1788–1836.* Cambridge, MA: Harvard University Press, 2010.

Foreman, Grant. *Indian Removal: The Emigration of the Five Civilized Tribes of Indians.* Norman: University of Oklahoma Press, 1953.

Formisano, Ronald P. "The New Political History and the Election of 1840." *Journal of Interdisciplinary History* 23, no. 4 (1993): 661–82.

Forst, Rainer. "Toleration, Justice and Reason." In *The Culture of Toleration in Diverse Societies: Reasonable Toleration,* edited by Catriona McKinnon and Dario Castiglione, 71–85. Manchester: Manchester University Press, 2003.

Frank, Andrew K. *Creeks and Southerners: Biculturalism on the Early American Frontier.* Lincoln: University of Nebraska Press, 2005.

Frazer, Elizabeth, and Kimberly Hutchings. "Drawing the Line between Violence and Non-violence: Deceits and Conceits." In *Masquerades of War,* edited by Christine Sylvester, 43–57. London: Routledge, 2015.

Frazier, Harriet C. *Slavery and Crime in Missouri, 1773–1865.* Jefferson, NC: McFarland, 2001.

Friend, Craig Thompson. "Mutilated Bodies, Living Specters: Scalpings and Beheadings in the Early South." In *Death and the American South,* edited by Lorri Glover, 15–35. New York: Cambridge University Press, 2015.

Genovese, Eugene D. *Roll, Jordan, Roll: The World Slaves Made.* New York: Random House, 1976.

———. *The World the Slaveholders Made: Two Essays in Interpretation.* Hanover, NH: University Press of New England, 1988.

Gibson, Arrell M. *The Chickasaws.* Norman: University of Oklahoma Press, 1971.

Gillett, Mary C. *The Army Medical Department, 1818–1865.* Washington, DC: Center of Military History, U.S. Army, 1987.

Goldstein, Alyosha, ed. *Formations of United States Colonialism.* Durham, NC: Duke University Press, 2014.

Golway, Terry. *Machine Made: Tammany Hall and the Creation of Modern American Politics.* New York: Norton, 2014.

Gould, Eliga H. "Entangled Histories, Entangled Worlds: The English-Speaking Atlantic as a Spanish Periphery." *American Historical Review* 112, no. 3 (June 2007): 764–86.

Grady, Timothy Paul. *Anglo-Spanish Rivalry in Colonial South-East America, 1650–1725.* London: Pickering and Chatto, 2010.

Graham, Brian, G. J. Ashworth, and J. E. Tunbridge. *Pluralising Pasts: Heritage, Identity and Place in Multicultural Societies.* London: Pluto, 2007.

Grant, Donald L. *The Way It Was in the South: The Black Experience in Georgia.* Athens: University of Georgia Press, 1993.

Grantham, Bill. *Creation Myths and Legends of the Creek Indians.* Gainesville: University Press of Florida, 2002.

Grimes, Ronald L. "Masking: Toward a Phenomenology of Exteriorization." *Journal of the American Academy of Religion* 43, no. 3 (September 1975): 508–16.

Grimsley, Mark. *The Hard Hand of War: Union Military Policy toward Southern Civilians, 1861–1865.* Cambridge: Cambridge University Press, 1995.

Grob, Gerald N. *The Deadly Truth: A History of Disease in America.* Cambridge, MA: Harvard University Press, 2002.

———. *Mental Institutions in America: Social Policy to 1875.* New Brunswick, NJ: Transaction Publishers, 2009.

Grounds, R. A. "Tallahassee, Osceola, and the Hermeneutics of American Place-Names." *Journal of the American Academy of Religion* 69, no. 2 (2001): 287–322.

Hahn, Steven C. *The Invention of the Creek Nation, 1670–1763.* Lincoln: University of Nebraska Press, 2004.

Haiman, Robert J. *Best Practices for Newspaper Journalists: A Handbook for Reporters, Editors, Photographers and Other Newspaper Professionals on How to Be Fair to the Public.* Arlington, VA: Freedom Forum, 2000.

Halbert, H. S., and T. H. Ball. *The Creek War of 1813 and 1815.* Edited by Frank L. Owsley Jr. Tuscaloosa: University of Alabama Press, 1995.

Hall, Anthony. *Earth into Property: Colonization, Decolonization, and Capitalism.* Montreal: McGill-Queen's University Press, 2010.

Hall, John W. "'A Reckless Waste of Blood and Treasure': The Last Campaign of the Second Seminole War." In *Between War and Peace: How America Ends Its Wars,* edited by Matthew Moten, 64–84. New York: Free Press, 2011.

Halttunen, Karen. "Humanitarianism and the Pornography of Pain in Anglo-American Culture." *American Historical Review* 100, no. 2 (1995): 303.

Harris, Cole. "How Did Colonialism Dispossess? Comments from an Edge of Empire." *Annals of the Association of American Geographers* 94, no. 1 (March 2004): 165–82.

Harrison, Simon. *Dark Trophies: Hunting and the Enemy Body in Modern War.* New York: Berghahn, 2012.

Haskell, Thomas L. *Objectivity Is Not Neutrality: Explanatory Schemes in History.* Baltimore: Johns Hopkins University Press, 1998.

Hauptman, Laurence M. "Cadet David Moniac: A Creek Indian's Schooling at West Point, 1817–1822." *Proceedings of the American Philosophical Society* 152, no. 3 (2008): 322–48.

Hawke, Allan. "An Ambulating Hospital: Or, How the Hospital Train Transformed Army Medicine." *Civil War History* 48, no. 3 (2002): 197–219.

Hay, Simon I., David L. Smith, and Robert W. Snow. "Measuring Malaria Endemicity from Intense to Interrupted Transmission." *The Lancet Infectious Diseases* 8, no. 6 (2008): 369–78.

Hellmann, Paul T. *Historical Gazetteer of the United States*. New York: Routledge, 2005.

Hickmon, W. C. "Weather and Crops in Arkansas, 1819–1879." *Monthly Weather Review* 48, no. 8 (August 1920): 448.

Hickox, Ron G. *U.S. Military Edged Weapons of the Second Seminole War, 1835–1842: A Study of U.S. Military Edged Weapons from 1818 to 1842*. Tampa, FL: R. G. Hickox, 1984.

Higgenbotham, Don. "Military Education before West Point." In *Thomas Jefferson's Military Academy: Founding West Point*, edited by Robert M. S. McDonald, 23–53. Charlottesville: University of Virginia Press, 2004.

Hillyer, Reiko. *Designing Dixie: Tourism, Memory, and Urban Space in the New South*. Charlottesville: University of Virginia Press, 2014.

Hixson, Walter L. *American Settler Colonialism: A History*. New York: Palgrave Macmillan, 2013.

Holt, Michael F. *The Rise and Fall of the American Whig Party: Jacksonian Politics and the Onset of the Civil War*. New York: Oxford University Press, 1999.

Howard, James H. *Oklahoma Seminoles: Medicines, Magic, and Religion*. Norman: University of Oklahoma Press, 1984.

Howe, Daniel Walker. *What Hath God Wrought: The Transformation of America, 1815–1848*. New York: Oxford University Press, 2007.

Humphreys, Margaret. *Yellow Fever and the South*. Baltimore: Johns Hopkins University Press, 1999.

Hunt, Alfred N. *Haiti's Influence on Antebellum America: Slumbering Volcano in the Caribbean*. Baton Rouge: Louisiana State University Press, 1988.

Hunt, Nigel C. *Memory, War, and Trauma*. Cambridge: Cambridge University Press, 2010.

Hunt, Tamara L. *Defining John Bull: Political Caricature and National Identity in Late Georgian England*. Aldershot: Ashgate, 2003.

James, Cyril L. *The Black Jacobins: Toussaint L'Ouverture and the San Domingo Revolution*. New York: Vintage Books, 1989.

Jennings, Jay. "Fort Denaud: Logistics Hub of the Third Seminole War." *Florida Historical Quarterly* 80, no. 1 (Summer 2001): 24–42.

Jensen, Laura. *Patriots, Settlers, and the Origins of American Social Policy*. Cambridge: Cambridge University Press, 2003.

Johnson, Kendall. "'Rising from the Stain on a Painter's Palette': George Catlin's Picturesque and the Legibility of Seminole Removal." *Nineteenth Century Prose* 29, no. 2 (2002): 69–93.

Johnson, Sara E. "'You Should Give Them Blacks to Eat': Waging Inter-American Wars of Torture and Terror." *American Quarterly* 61, no. 1 (2009): 65–92.

Kammen, Michael G. *Mystic Chords of Memory: The Transformation of Tradition in American Culture*. New York: Vintage, 1991.

Kanstroom, Dan. *Deportation Nation: Outsiders in American History*. Cambridge, MA: Harvard University Press, 2007.

Kaplan, E. Ann. "Fanon, Trauma and Cinema." In *Frantz Fanon: Critical Perspectives*, edited by Anthony Alessandrini, 146–58. New York: Routledge, 1999.

Kennett, Lee B. *Sherman: A Soldier's Life*. New York: HarperCollins, 2001.

Khan, L. Ali. *A Theory of Universal Democracy: Beyond the End of History*. The Hague: Kluwer Law International, 2003.

Kieffer, Chester L. *Maligned General: The Biography of Thomas Sidney Jesup*. San Rafael, CA: Presidio Press, 1979.

Kielbowicz, Richard B. "Newsgathering by Printers Exchanges before the Telegraph." *Journalism History* 9, no. 2 (1982): 42–48.

Kiple, Kenneth F. *The Caribbean Slave: A Biological History*. Cambridge: Cambridge University Press, 1984.

Klos, George. "Blacks and the Seminole Removal Debate, 1821–1835." *Florida Historical Quarterly* 68, no. 1 (July 1989): 55–78.

Klunder, Willard Carl. *Lewis Cass and the Politics of Moderation*. Kent, OH: Kent State University Press, 1996.

Kly, Y. N. "The Gullah War, 1739–1858." In *The Legacy of Ibo Landing: Gullah Roots of African American Culture*, edited by Marquetta L. Goodwine, 19–53. Atlanta, GA: Clarity Press, 1998.

Knetsch, Joe. *Fear and Anxiety on the Florida Frontier: Articles on the Second Seminole War, 1835–1842*. Dade City, FL: Seminole Wars Foundation, 2008.

——. *Florida's Seminole Wars, 1817–1858*. Charleston, SC: Arcadia Publishing, 2003.

——. "Strategy, Operations and Tactics in the Second Seminole War, 1835–1842." In *America's Hundred Years' War: U.S. Expansion to the Gulf Coast and the Fate of the Seminole, 1763–1858*, edited by Stephen W. Belko, 128–54. Gainesville: University Press of Florida, 2011.

Knetsch, Joe, and Paul S. George. "A Problematical Law: The Armed Occupation of 1842 and Its Impact on Southeast Florida." *Tequesta* 53 (1993): 63–80.

Knowles, Nathaniel. "The Torture of Captives by the Indians of Eastern North America." *Proceedings of the American Philosophical Society* 84, no. 2 (March 1940): 151–225.

Kohl, Lawrence Frederick. *The Politics of Individualism: Parties and the American Character in the Jacksonian Era*. New York: Oxford University Press, 1989.

Kokomoor, Kevin D. "A Re-assessment of Seminoles, Africans, and Slavery on the Florida Frontier." *Florida Historical Quarterly* 88, no. 2 (Fall 2009): 209–36.

Krauthamer, Barbara. *Black Slaves, Indian Masters: Slavery, Emancipation, and Citizenship in the Native American South*. Chapel Hill: University of North Carolina Press, 2013.

Krautwurst, Udo. "What Is Settler Colonialism? An Anthropological Meditation on Frantz Fanon's 'concerning Violence.'" *History and Anthropology* 14, no. 1 (2003): 55–72.

Landers, Jane. *Black Society in Spanish Florida*. Urbana: University of Illinois Press, 1999.

——. "Introduction." In *Colonial Plantations and Economy in Florida*, edited by Jane Landers, 1–10. Gainesville: University Press of Florida, 2000.

——. "Transforming Bondsmen into Vassals: Arming Slaves in Colonial Spanish America." In *Arming Slaves: From Classical Times to the Modern Age*, edited by Christopher Leslie Brown and Philip D. Morgan, 120–45. New Haven: Yale University Press, 2006.

Laumer, Frank. *Dade's Last Command*. Gainesville: University Press of Florida, 1995.

Lee, Wayne E. *Barbarians and Brothers: Anglo-American Warfare, 1500–1865*. Oxford: Oxford University Press, 2011.

Lefevre, Tate A. "Representation, Resistance and the Logics of Difference: Indigenous Culture as Political Resource in the Settler-state." *Settler Colonial Studies* 3, no. 2 (2013): 136–40.

Lewis, David, and Ann Jordan. *Creek Indian Medicine Ways: The Enduring Power of Mvskoke Religion*. Albuquerque: University of New Mexico Press, 2002.

Lott, Eric. *Love and Theft: Blackface Minstrelsy and the American Working Class*. New York: Oxford University Press, 1995.

Lowenthal, David. *The Heritage Crusade and the Spoils of History*. Cambridge: Cambridge University Press, 1998.

Macdonald, Dwight. "A Theory of Mass Culture." In *Mass Culture: The Popular Arts in America*, edited by Bernard Rosenberg and David Manning White, 59–73. New York: Free Press, 1957.

Macgregor, Alan Leander. "Tammany: The Indian as Rhetorical Surrogate." *American Quarterly* 35, no. 4 (1983): 391–407.

Maddison, Sarah. "Postcolonial Guilt and National Identity: Historical Injustice and the Australian Settler State." *Social Identities* 18, no. 6 (November 2012): 695–709.

Mahon, John K. *History of the Second Seminole War, 1835–1842*. Gainesville: University Press of Florida, 1985.

———. "Letters from the Second Seminole War." *Florida Historical Quarterly* 36, no. 4 (April 1958): 331–52.

———. "Missouri Volunteers at the Battle of Okeechobee: Christmas Day 1837." *Florida Historical Quarterly* 70, no. 2 (October 1991): 166–76.

———. "Two Seminole Treaties: Payne's Landing, 1832, and Ft. Gibson, 1833." *Florida Historical Quarterly* 41, no. 1 (July 1962): 1–21.

Mamdani, Mahmood. "Beyond Settler and Native as Political Identities: Overcoming the Political Legacy of Colonialism." *Comparative Studies in Society and History* 43, no. 4 (October 2001): 651–64.

———. "Settler Colonialism: Then and Now." *Critical Inquiry* 41, no. 3 (Spring 2015): 596–614.

Manucy, Albert C. "Some Military Affairs in Territorial Florida." *Florida Historical Quarterly* 25, no. 2 (1946): 202–11.

Martin, Scott C. "Interpreting 'Metamora': Nationalism, Theater, and Jacksonian Indian Policy." *Journal of the Early Republic* 19, no. 1 (1999): 73–101.

Mason, Jeffrey D. "The Politics of Metamora." In *The Performance of Power: Theatrical Discourse and Politics*, edited by Sue-Ellen Case and Janelle G. Reinelt, 92–110. Iowa City: University of Iowa Press, 1991.

McDonald, Robert M. S. "Military Education before West Point." In *Thomas Jefferson's Military Academy: Founding West Point*. Charlottesville: University of Virginia Press, 2004.

McLoughlin, William G. "Red Indians, Black Slavery and White Racism: America's Slaveholding Indians." *American Quarterly* 26, no. 4 (October 1974): 367–85.

McNeill, J. R. *Mosquito Empires: Ecology and War in the Greater Caribbean, 1620–1914*. Cambridge: Cambridge University Press, 2010.

McReynolds, Edwin C. *The Seminoles*. Norman: University of Oklahoma Press, 1957.

Meier, Kathryn Shively. *Nature's Civil War: Common Soldiers and the Environment in 1862 Virginia*. Chapel Hill: University of North Carolina Press, 2013.

Meindl, Christopher F. "Water, Water, Everywhere." In *Paradise Lost: The Environmental History of Florida*, edited by Jack E. Davis and Raymond Arsenault, 113–37. Gainesville: University Press of Florida, 2005.

Menges, Eric S. "Ecology and Conservation of Florida Scrub." In *Savannas, Barrens, and Rock Outcrop Plant Communities of North America*, edited by Roger Anderson, James Fralish, and Jerry Baskin, 7–22. Cambridge: Cambridge University Press, 1999.

Miller, James J. *An Environmental History of Northeast Florida*. Gainesville: University Press of Florida, 1998.

Miller, Susan A. *Coacoochee's Bones: A Seminole Saga*. Lawrence: University Press of Kansas, 2003.

———. "Seminoles and Africans under Seminole Law: Sources and Discourses of Tribal Sovereignty and 'Black Indian' Entitlement." *Wicazo Sa Review* (Spring 2005): 23–47.

Millett, Nathaniel. *The Maroons of Prospect Bluff and Their Quest for Freedom in the Atlantic World*. Gainesville: University Press of Florida, 2013.

Mintz, Steven. *Moralists and Modernizers: America's Pre-Civil War Reformers*. Baltimore: Johns Hopkins University Press, 1995.

Mishra, Saroj K., and Charles R. J. C. Newton. "Diagnosis and Management of the Neurological Complications of Falciparum Malaria." *Nature Reviews Neurology* 5, no. 4 (2009): 189–98.

Missall, John, and Mary Missall Lou. *The Seminole Wars: America's Longest Indian Conflict*. Gainesville: University Press of Florida, 2004.

Monaco, C. S. "Alachua Settlers and the Second Seminole War." *Florida Historical Quarterly* 91, no. 1 (Summer 2012): 1–32.

———. "Fort Mitchell and the Settlement of the Alachua Country." *Florida Historical Quarterly* 79, no. 1 (2000): 1–25.

———. *Moses Levy of Florida: Jewish Utopian and Antebellum Reformer*. Baton Rouge: Louisiana State University Press, 2005.

———. "Opening Battles of the Second Seminole War." In "Fort Defiance / Fort Micanopy and the Opening Battles of the Second Seminole War 1835–1836, Historic and Archeological Study," by Gary Ellis, et al. American Battlefield Protection Program, NPS, 2010–11.

———. "Red Devil or Tragic Hero?: Osceola as Settler-Colonial Icon." *American Indian Quarterly* 39.2 (2015): 180–212.

———. "Shadows and Pestilence: Health and Medicine during the Second Seminole War." *Journal of Social History* 48, no. 3 (2015): 565–88.

———. "Whose War Was It? African American Heritage Claims and the Second Seminole War," *American Indian Quarterly* 41, no. 1 (Winter 2017).

———. "Wishing That Right May Prevail: Ethan Allen Hitchcock and the Second Seminole War." *Florida Historical Quarterly* 93, no. 2 (Fall 2014): 167–94.

Monk, J. Floyd. "Christmas Day in Florida, 1837." *Tequesta* 38 (1978): 5–38.

Morrison, James L. *The Best School: West Point, 1833–1866*. Kent, OH: Kent State University Press, 1998.

Moses, A. Dirk, ed. *Genocide and Settler Society: Frontier Violence and Stolen Indigenous Children in Australian History*. New York: Berghahn Books, 2004.

Moulton, Gary E. "Cherokees and the Second Seminole War." *Florida Historical Quarterly* 53, no. 3 (January 1975): 296–305.

Muhlberger, N., et al. "Age as a Risk Factor for Severe Manifestations and Fatal Outcome of Falciparum Malaria in European Patients: Observations from TropNetEurop and

SIMPID Surveillance Data." *Clinical Infectious Diseases* 36, no. 8 (April 2003): 990–95.

Mulroy, Kevin. *Freedom on the Border: The Seminole Maroons in Florida, the Indian Territory, Coahuila, and Texas*. Lubbock: Texas Tech University Press, 1993.

———. *The Seminole Freedmen: A History*. Norman: University of Oklahoma Press, 2007.

Nash, Roderick. *Wilderness and the American Mind*. 5th ed. New Haven, CT: Yale University Press, 2014.

Neely, Mark E. *The Civil War and the Limits of Destruction*. Cambridge, MA: Harvard University Press, 2007.

Neill, Wilfred T. "The Identity of Florida's 'Spanish Indians.'" *Florida Anthropologist* 8, no. 2 (June 1955): 43–58.

North, S. N. D. *History and Present Condition of the Newspaper and Periodical Press of the United States with a Catalogue of the Publications of the Census Year*. Washington, DC: GPO, 1884.

Ockenhouse, Christian F. et al. "History of U.S. Military Contributions to the Study of Malaria." *Military Medicine* 170, no. 4 (April 2005): 12–16.

Oh, Daniel. "The Relevance of Virtue Ethics and Application to the Formation of Character Development in Warriors." International Society for Military Ethics. Accessed September 11, 2016. http://isme.tamu.edu/ISME07/Oh07.html.

Opala, Joseph A. "Black Seminoles—Gullahs Who Escaped from Slavery" and "Conclusion." In *The Gullah: Rice, Slavery and the Sierra Leone-American Connection*. Accessed September 22, 2016. http://glc.yale.edu/sites/default/files/files/Black%20Seminoles%20.pdf and http://glc.yale.edu/sites/default/files/files/Conclusion.pdf.

Osterhammel, Jürgen. *The Transformation of the World: A Global History of the Nineteenth Century*. Translated by Patrick Camiller. Princeton, NJ: Princeton University Press, 2014.

Ostler, Jeffrey. *The Plains Sioux and U.S. Colonialism from Lewis and Clark to Wounded Knee*. Cambridge: Cambridge University Press, 2004.

Parker, Susan R. "The Cattle Trade in East Florida, 1784–1821." In *Colonial Plantations and Economy in Florida*, edited by Jane G. Landers, 150–67. Gainesville: University Press of Florida, 2000.

Parkin, John, and John Phillips. "Foreword." In *Laughter and Power*, edited by John Parkin and John Phillips, 7–10. Bern: Peter Lang, 2006.

Patrick, Rembert W. *Aristocrat in Uniform: General Duncan L. Clinch*. Gainesville: University Press of Florida, 1963.

———. "Editorial Preface." In *The Exiles of Florida: Or, the Crimes Committed by Our Government against the Maroons, Who Fled from South Carolina and Other Slave States, Seeking Protection under Spanish Laws*, by Joshua R. Giddings, xi–xii. 1858; reprint, Gainesville: University Press of Florida, 1964.

———. *Florida Fiasco: Rampant Rebels on the Georgia-Florida Border, 1810–1815*. Athens: University of Georgia Press, 1954.

Patterson, Gordon M. *The Mosquito Crusades: A History of the American Anti-Mosquito Movement from the Reed Commission to the First Earth Day*. New Brunswick, NJ: Rutgers University Press, 2009.

———. "The Trials and Tribulations of Amos Quito: The Creation of the Florida Anti-Mosquito Association." In *Paradise Lost? The Environmental History of Florida*, edited by Jack E. Davis and Raymond Arsenault, 160–76. Gainesville: University of Florida, 2005.

Pearce, George F. "Torment of Pestilence: Yellow Fever Epidemics in Pensacola." *Florida Historical Quarterly* 56, no. 4 (April 1978): 448–72.

Peckham, Robert Shannan. "Mourning Heritage: Memory, Trauma and Restitution." In *Rethinking Heritage: Cultures and Politics in Europe*, 205–14. New York: Palgrave Macmillan, 2003.

Perdue, Theda, and Michael Green D. *The Cherokee Nation and the Trail of Tears*. New York: Viking, 2007.

Peskin, Allan. *Winfield Scott and the Profession of Arms*. Kent, OH: Kent State University Press, 2003.

Peterson, Anna Lisa. *Being Human: Ethics, Environment, and Our Place in the World*. Berkeley: University of California Press, 2001.

Peterson, Audrey C. "Brain Fever in Nineteenth-Century Literature: Fact and Fiction." *Victorian Studies* 19, no. 4 (1976): 445–64.

Peterson, Merrill D. *Thomas Jefferson and the New Nation: A Biography*. New York: Oxford University Press, 1970.

Porter, Kenneth W. *Black Seminoles: History of a Freedom-Seeking People*. Edited by Alcione M. Amos and Thomas P. Senter. Gainesville: University Press of Florida, 1996.

——. "Florida Slaves and Free Negroes in the Seminole War, 1835–1842." *Journal of Negro History* 28, no. 4 (October 1943): 390–421.

——. "John Caesar: Seminole Negro Partisan." *Journal of Negro History* 31, no. 2 (April 1946): 190–207.

——. "The Negro Abraham." *Florida Historical Quarterly* 25, no. 1 (July 1946): 1–43.

——. *The Negro on the American Frontier*. New York: Arno, 1971.

——. "Negroes and the Seminole War, 1835–1842." *Journal of Southern History* 30, no. 4 (November 1964): 427–50.

——. "Relations between Negroes and Indians within the Present Limits of the United States." *Journal of Negro History* 17, no. 3 (July 1932): 287–367.

——. "Three Fighters for Freedom." *Journal of Negro History* 28, no. 1 (January 1943): 51–72.

Portnoy, Alisse. *Their Right to Speak: Women's Activism in the Indian and Slave Debates*. Cambridge, MA: Harvard University Press, 2005.

Preston, David L. *The Texture of Contact: European and Indian Settler Communities on the Frontiers of Iroquoia, 1667–1783*. Lincoln: University of Nebraska Press, 2009.

Prucha, Francis Paul. *American Indian Treaties: The History of a Political Anomaly*. Berkeley: University of California Press, 1994.

Råberg, Lars, Andrea L. Graham, and Andrew F. Read. "Decomposing Health: Tolerance and Resistance to Parasites in Animals." *Philosophical Transactions of the Royal Society B: Biological Sciences* 364, no. 1513 (2009): 37–49.

Rea, Robert R. "'Graveyard for Britons,' West Florida, 1763–1781." *Florida Historical Quarterly* 47, no. 4 (1969): 345–64.

Reavis, L. U. *The Life and Military Services of General William Selby Harney*. St. Louis, MO: Bryan, Brand, 1878.

Reiss, Benjamin. *Theatres of Madness: Insane Asylums and Nineteenth-Century American Culture*. Chicago: University of Chicago Press, 2008.

Remini, Robert V. *Andrew Jackson*. New York: Harper Perennial, 1999.

Reynolds, John. *Reynolds' History of Illinois: My Own Times: Embracing Also the History of My Life*. Chicago: Chicago Historical Society, 1879.

Rhodes, Karen Packard. *Non-Federal Censuses of Florida, 1784–1945: A Guide to Sources*. Jefferson, NC: McFarland, 2010.

Risch, Erna. *Quartermaster Support of the Army: A History of the Corps, 1775–1939*. Washington, DC: Center of Military History, U.S. Army, 1989.

Rivers, Larry. "Dr. Larry Rivers at the University of Florida." YouTube. November 19, 2012. 1:11:20. https://www.youtube.com/watch?v=E_JOfjgT6q8.

——. *Rebels and Runaways: Slave Resistance in Nineteenth-Century Florida*. Urbana: University of Illinois Press, 2012.

——. *Slavery in Florida: Territorial Days to Emancipation*. Gainesville: University Press of Florida, 2000.

Rivers, Larry E., and Canter Brown Jr. "'The Indispensable Man': John Horse and Florida's Second Seminole War." *Journal of the Georgia Association of Historians* 18 (1997): 1–23.

Robertson, Fred L. *Soldiers of Florida in the Seminole Indian, Civil, and Spanish-American Wars*. Live Oak, FL: Board of State Institutions, 1903.

Robinson, H. E. "General Ethan Allen Hitchcock: Some Account of a Missouri Author Somewhat Neglected but Whose Writings Will Live When More Popular Writers Are Forgotten." *Missouri Historical Review* 2, no. 3 (April 1908): 173–87.

Rolfs, David. *No Peace for the Wicked: Northern Protestant Soldiers and the American Civil War*. Knoxville: University of Tennessee Press, 2009.

Rosen, Deborah A. *American Indians and State Law: Sovereignty, Race, and Citizenship, 1790–1880*. Lincoln: University of Nebraska Press, 2007.

Rosen, George. *A History of Public Health*. Baltimore: Johns Hopkins University Press, 1993.

Rosenberg, Charles E. *Explaining Epidemics and Other Studies in the History of Medicine*. Cambridge: Cambridge University Press, 1992.

Rothstein, William G. *American Physicians in the Nineteenth Century: From Sects to Science*. Baltimore: Johns Hopkins University Press, 1985.

Sachs, Honor. *Home Rule: Households, Manhood, and National Expansion on the Eighteenth-Century Kentucky Frontier*. New Haven, CT: Yale University Press, 2016.

Sarna, Jonathan D. *Jacksonian Jew: The Two Worlds of Mordecai Noah*. New York: Holmes and Meier, 1981.

Sarnecky, Mary T. *A History of the U.S. Army Nurse Corps*. Philadelphia: University of Pennsylvania, 1999.

Sattler, Richard A. "Remnants, Renegades, and Runaways: Seminole Ethnogenesis Reconsidered." In *History, Power, and Identity: Ethnogenesis in the Americas, 1492–1992*, edited by Jonathan Hill, 36–69. Iowa City: University of Iowa Press, 1996.

——. *Siminoli Italwa: Socio-Political Change among the Oklahoma Seminoles between Removal and Allotment, 1836–1905*. Ph.D. diss., University of Oklahoma, 1987.

Satz, Ronald N. *American Indian Policy in the Jacksonian Era*. Lincoln: University of Nebraska Press, 1974.

Saunt, Claudio. "'The English Has Now a Mind to Make Slaves of Them All': Creeks, Seminoles, and the Problem of Slavery." *American Indian Quarterly* 22, no. 1–2 (Winter-Spring 1998): 157–80.

——. *A New Order of Things: Property, Power, and the Transformation of the Creek Indians, 1733–1816*. Cambridge: Cambridge University Press, 1999.

——. "Taking Account of Property: Stratification among the Creek Indians in the Early Nineteenth Century." *William and Mary Quarterly* 57, no. 4 (October 2000): 733–60.

Sayers, Daniel O. "Marronage Perspective for Historical Archaeology in the United States." *Historical Archaeology* 46, no. 4 (2013): 135–61.

Schafer, Daniel L. "'A Swamp of an Investment'? Richard Oswald's British East Florida Plantation Experiment." In *Colonial Plantations and Economy in Florida*, edited by Jane Landers, 11–38. Gainesville: University Press of Florida, 2000.

Schantz, Mark S. *Awaiting the Heavenly Country: The Civil War and America's Culture of Death*. Ithaca, NY: Cornell University Press, 2008.

Schweninger, Lee. *Listening to the Land: Native American Literary Responses to the Landscape*. Athens: University of Georgia Press, 2008.

Sellers, Charles. *The Market Revolution: Jacksonian America, 1815–1846*. New York: Oxford University Press, 1994.

Shire, Laurel Clark. *The Threshold of Manifest Destiny: Gender and National Expansion in Florida*. Philadelphia: University of Pennsylvania Press, 2016.

Siebert, Wilber. "The Early Sugar Industry in Florida." *Florida Historical Quarterly* 35, no. 4 (April 1957): 312–19.

Silver, James W. "A Counter-Proposal to the Indian Removal Policy of Andrew Jackson." *Journal of Mississippi History* 4 (October 1942): 207–15.

Simmon, Bennett. "Mind and Madness in Classical Antiquity." In *History of Psychiatry and Medical Psychology: With an Epilogue on Psychiatry and the Mind-body Relation*, edited by Edwin R. Wallace and John Gach, 175–97. New York: Springer, 2008.

Singer, Merrill. *Introduction to Syndemics: A Critical Systems Approach to Public and Community Health*. San Francisco: Jossey-Bass, 2009.

Skelton, William B. *An American Profession of Arms: The Army Officer Corps, 1784–1861*. Lawrence: University Press of Kansas, 1992.

Slatta, Richard W. *Cowboys of the Americas*. New Haven, CT: Yale University Press, 1990.

Slotkin, Richard. *Regeneration through Violence: The Mythology of the American Frontier, 1600–1860*. Norman: University of Oklahoma Press, 1973.

Smith, Linda Tuhiwai. *Decolonizing Methodologies: Research and Indigenous Peoples*. London: Zed, 1999.

Snow, Alpheus Henry. *The Question of Aborigines in the Law and Practice of Nations, including a Collection of Authorities and Documents Written at the Request of the Department of State*. Washington, DC: GPO, 1919.

Snow, Robert W., and Judy A. Omumbo. "Malaria." In *Disease and Mortality in Sub-Saharan Africa*, edited by Dean T. Jamison et al., 195–213. Washington, DC: World Bank, 2006.

Snyder, Christina. *Slavery in Indian Country: The Changing Face of Captivity in Early America*. Cambridge, MA: Harvard University Press, 2010.

Solis, Gary D. *The Law of Armed Conflict: International Humanitarian Law in War*. Cambridge: Cambridge University Press, 2010.

Stafford, Jane. "Going Native: How the New Zealand Settler Became Indigenous." *Journal of New Zealand Literature* 23, part 1, Special Issue (January 2005): 162–73.

Stapleton, Timothy J. *Maqoma: Xhosa Resistance to Colonial Advance, 1798–1873.* Johannesburg: J. Ball, 1994.

Starr, Paul. *The Social Transformation of American Medicine: The Rise of a Sovereign Profession and the Making of a Vast Industry.* New York: Basic Books, 1982.

Stauffer, John. "Advent among the Indians: The Revolutionary Ethos of Gerrit Smith, James McCune Smith, Frederick Douglass, and John Brown." In *Antislavery Violence: Sectional, Racial, and Cultural Conflict in Antebellum America*, edited by John R. McKivigan and Stanley Harrold, 236–73. Knoxville: University of Tennessee Press, 1999.

———. *The Black Hearts of Men: Radical Abolitionists and the Transformation of Race.* Cambridge, MA: Harvard University Press, 2002.

Sternberg, George. *Report on the Etiology and Prevention of Yellow Fever.* Washington, DC: GPO, 1890.

Stevens, Kenneth R. "William Henry Harrison." In *Buckeye Presidents: Ohioans in the White House*, edited by Philip Weeks, 9–39. Kent, OH: Kent State University Press, 2003.

Stewart, James Brewer. *Abolitionist Politics and the Coming of the Civil War.* Amherst: University of Massachusetts Press, 2008.

———. "Christian Statesmanship, Codes of Honor, and Congressional Violence: The Antislavery Travails and Triumphs of Joshua Giddings." In *In the Shadow of Freedom: The Politics of Slavery in the National Capital*, edited by Paul Finkelman and Donald R. Kennon, 36–57. Athens: Ohio University Press, 2011.

———. *Holy Warriors: The Abolitionists and American Slavery.* Revised ed. New York: Hill and Wang, 1997.

———. "Joshua Giddings, Antislavery Violence, and Congressional Politics of Honor." In *Antislavery Violence: Sectional, Racial, and Cultural Conflict in Antebellum America*, edited by John R. McKivigan and Stanley Harrold, 167–92. Knoxville: University of Tennessee Press, 1999.

Stiggins, George. *Creek Indian History: A Historical Narrative of the Genealogy, Traditions, and Downfall of the Ispocoga or Creek Indian Tribe of Indians.* Edited by Virginia Brown Pounds. Birmingham, AL: Birmingham Public Library Press, 1989.

Stinchcombe, Arthur L. *Sugar Island Slavery in the Age of Enlightenment: The Political Economy of the Caribbean World.* Princeton, NJ: Princeton University Press, 1995.

Stojanowski, Christopher M. *Bioarchaeology of Ethnogenesis in the Colonial Southeast.* Gainesville: University Press of Florida, 2010.

Stone, William L. *Life of Joseph Brant-Thayendanega: Including the Border Wars of the American Revolution, and Sketches of the Indian Campaigns of Generals Harmar, St. Clair and Wayne, and Other Matters Connected with the Indian Relations of the United States and Great Britain, from the Peace of 1783 to the Indian Peace of 1795.* New York: Alexander V. Blake, 1838.

Storey, William Kelleher. *Guns, Race, and Power in Colonial South Africa.* Cambridge: Cambridge University Press, 2008.

Strang, Cameron B. "Skulls, Scalps and Seminoles: Science and Violence in Florida, 1800–1842." Library of Congress Webcast. Accessed September 21, 2016. https://www.loc.gov/today/cyberlc/feature_wdesc.php?rec=5237.

———. "Violence, Ethnicity, and Human Remains during the Second Seminole War." *Journal of American History* 100, no. 4 (2014): 973–94.

Sturtevant, William C. "Chaikaka and the 'Spanish Indians': Documentary Sources Compared with Seminole Tradition." *Tequesta* 13 (1953): 35–73.

Swanton, John R. *Creek Religion and Medicine*. Lincoln: University of Nebraska Press, 2000.

Switzer, Les. *Power and Resistance in an African Society: The Ciskei Xhosa and the Making of South Africa*. Madison: University of Wisconsin Press, 1993.

Sylvanus Thayer, Founder of Technical Education in the United States. West Point, NY: Association of Graduates, United States Military Academy, 1965.

Tankard, James W., Jr. "The Empirical Approach to the Study of Media Framing." In *Framing Public Life: Perspectives on Media and Our Understanding of the Social World*, edited by Stephen D. Reese, Oscar H. Gandy, and August E. Grant, 95–106. Mahwah, NJ: Lawrence Erlbaum Associates, 2001.

Tanner, James T., and Paul B. Hamel. "A Long-Term View of Old-Growth Deciduous Forests." In *Bottomland Hardwoods of the Mississippi Alluvial Valley*. Fayetteville, AR: U.S. Department of Agriculture, 1995.

Taylor, Michael. *Contesting Constructed Indian-ness: The Intersection of the Frontier, Masculinity, and Whiteness in Native American Mascot Representations*. Lanham, MD: Lexington Books, 2013.

Thompson, Arthur W. "Introduction." In *The Exiles of Florida: Or, the Crimes Committed by Our Government against the Maroons, Who Fled from South Carolina and Other Slave States, Seeking Protection under Spanish Laws*, by Joshua R. Giddings, xiii–xxvii. 1858; reprint, Gainesville: University Press of Florida, 1964.

Thompson, Doug. "Between Slavery and Freedom on the Atlantic Coast of Honduras." *Slavery and Abolition* 33, no. 3 (September 2012): 403–16.

"Total 1840 Government Spending." Government Spending in United States: Federal State Local for 1840. Accessed September 11, 2016. http://www.usgovernmentspend ing.com/total_spending_1840USrn.

Trask, Kerry A. *Black Hawk: The Battle for the Heart of America*. New York: Henry Holt, 2007.

Tucher, Andie. "Newspapers and Periodicals." In *A History of the Book in America—An Extensive Republic: Print, Culture, and Society in the New Nation, 1790–1840*, edited by Robert A. Gross and Mary Kelly, 389–415. Chapel Hill: University of North Carolina, 2010.

Twyman, Bruce Edward. *The Black Seminole Legacy and North American Politics, 1693–1845*. Washington, DC: Howard University Press, 1999.

Ucko, David H. *The New Counterinsurgency Era: Transforming the U.S. Military for Modern Wars*. Washington, DC: Georgetown University Press, 2009.

Valenčius, Conevery Bolton. *The Health of the Country: How American Settlers Understood Themselves and Their Land*. New York: Basic Books, 2002.

Van Deburg, William. *Hoodlums: Black Villains and Social Bandits in American Life*. Chicago: University of Chicago Press, 2004.

Vandervort, Bruce. *Indian Wars of Mexico, Canada and the United States, 1812–1900*. New York: Routledge, 2006.

Van Geertruyden, J. P. "Interactions between Malaria and Human Immunodeficiency Virus Anno 2014." *Clinical Microbiology and Infection* 20, no. 4 (2014): 278–85.

Veracini, Lorenzo. "Colonialism and Genocides: Towards an Analysis of the Settler Archive of the European Imagination." In *Empire, Colony, Genocide: Conquest, Occupation and Subaltern Resistance in World History*, edited by A. Dirk Moses, 148–61. New York: Berghahn Books, 2008.

——. "On Settlerness." *Borderlands* 10, no. 1 (2011): 1–17. Accessed September 15, 2016. http://www.borderlands.net.au/vol10no1_2011/veracini_settlerness.pdf.

——. *Settler Colonialism: A Theoretical Overview*. Houndmills, Basingstoke: Palgrave Macmillan, 2010.

——. *The Settler Colonial Present*. Houndmills, Basingstoke: Palgrave Macmillan, 2015.

Walkiewicz, Kathryn. "Portraits and Politics: The Specter of Osceola in Leaves of Grass." *Walt Whitman Quarterly Review* 25, no. 3 (2008): 108–15.

Wallace, Anthony F. C. *Jefferson and the Indians: The Tragic Fate of the First Americans*. Cambridge, MA: Belknap Press of Harvard University Press, 1999.

Walvin, James. *Questioning Slavery*. London: Routledge, 1996.

Washington, Margaret. *Sojourner Truth's America*. Urbana: University of Illinois Press, 2009.

Waters, Anne. "Ontology of Identity and Interstitial Being." In *American Indian Thought: Philosophical Essays*, edited by Anne Waters, 153–70. Malden, MA: Wiley-Blackwell, 2003.

Watson, Harry L. *Liberty and Power: The Politics of Jacksonian America*. New York: Hill and Wang, 1990.

Watson, Samuel J. "How the Army Became Accepted: West Point Socialization, Military Accountability, and the Nation-State during the Jacksonian Era." *American Nineteenth Century History* 7, no. 2 (June 2006): 219–51.

——. *Peacekeepers and Conquerors: The Army Officer Corps on the American Frontier, 1821–1846*. Lawrence: University Press of Kansas, 2013.

——. "Seminole Strategy, 1812–1858: A Prospectus for Further Research." In *America's Hundred Years' War: U.S. Expansion to the Gulf Coast and the Fate of the Seminole, 1763–1858*, edited by Stephen W. Belko, 155–80. Gainesville: University Press of Florida, 2011.

——. "'This Thankless . . . Unholy War': Army Officers and Civil–Military Relations in the Second Seminole War." In *The Southern Albatross: Race and Ethnicity in the American South*, edited by Philip D. Dillard and Randal L. Hall, 9–49. Macon, GA: Mercer University Press, 1999.

——. "Thomas Sidney Jesup: Soldier, Bureaucrat, Gentleman Democrat." In *The Human Tradition in Antebellum America*, edited by Michael A. Morrison, 99–114. Lanham, MD: Rowman and Littlefield, 2000.

Wayne, Lucy B. *Sweet Cane: The Architecture of the Sugar Works of East Florida*. Tuscaloosa: University of Alabama Press, 2010.

Webber, Carl. *The Eden of the South, Descriptive of the Orange Groves, Vegetable Farms, Strawberry Fields, Peach Orchards, Soil, Climate, Natural Peculiarities, and the People of Alachua County, Florida, Together with Other Valuable Information for Tourists, Invalids, or Those Seeking a Home in Florida*. New York: Leve and Alden, 1883.

Weber, David J. *The Spanish Frontier in North America*. New Haven, CT: Yale University Press, 1992.

Weiner, Dora B. "The Madman in the Light of Reason: Enlightenment Psychiatry." In *History of Psychiatry and Medical Psychology: With an Epilogue on Psychiatry and the*

Mind-Body Relation, edited by Edwin R. Wallace and John Gach, 255–312. New York: Springer, 2008.

Weisman, Brent R. "The Background and Continued Cultural and Historical Importance of the Seminole Wars in Florida." *FIU Law Review* 9, no. 2 (2014): 391–404. http://ecollections.law.fiu.edu/lawreview/vol9/iss2/14/.

———. "A Band of Outsiders: Yuchi Identity among the Nineteenth-Century Seminoles." In *Yuchi Indian Histories before the Removal Era*, edited by Jason Jackson Baird, 215–31. Lincoln: University of Nebraska Press, 2012.

———. "The Cove of the Withlacoochee: A First Look at the Archaeology of an Interior Florida Wetland." *Florida Anthropologist* 39, no. 1–2 (March-June 1986): 4–23.

———. *Like Beads on a String: A Culture History of the Seminole Indians in North Peninsular Florida*. Tuscaloosa: University of Alabama Press, 1989.

———. "The Plantation System of the Florida Seminole Indians and Black Seminoles during the Colonial Era." In *Colonial Plantations and Economy in Florida*, edited by Jane Landers, 136–49. Gainesville: University Press of Florida, 2000.

———. *Unconquered People: Florida's Seminole and Miccosukee Indians*. Gainesville: University Press of Florida, 1999.

Werbner, Pnina, and Muhammad Anwar, eds. *Black and Ethnic Leaderships in Britain: The Cultural Dimensions of Political Action*. London: Routledge, 1991.

West, Patsy. "Abiaka or Sam Jones, in Context: The Mikasuki Ethnogenesis through the Third Seminole War." *Florida Historical Quarterly* 94, no. 3 (2016): 366–410.

Wickman, Patricia R. *Osceola's Legacy*. Tuscaloosa: University of Alabama Press, 2006.

———. *The Tree that Bends: Discourse, Power, and the Survival of the Maskókî People*. Tuscaloosa: University of Alabama Press, 1999.

Wiener, Joel H. *The Americanization of the British Press, 1830s-1914: Speed in the Age of Transatlantic Journalism*. Houndmills, Basingstoke: Palgrave Macmillan, 2011.

Wilentz, Sean. *The Rise of American Democracy*. New York: W. W. Norton, 2007.

Williams, Robert A. *Like a Loaded Weapon: The Rehnquist Court, Indian Rights, and the Legal History of Racism in America*. Minneapolis: University of Minnesota Press, 2005.

Wilson, Mary E. "Population Mobility and the Geography of Microbial Threats." In *Population Mobility and Infectious Disease*, edited by Yiorgos Apostolopoulos and Sevil F. Sönmez, 21–28. New York: Springer, 2007.

Witt, John Fabian. *Lincoln's Code: The Laws of War in American History*. New York: Free Press, 2012.

Wolfe, Patrick. "Land, Labor, and Difference: Elementary Structures of Race." *American Historical Review* 106, no. 3 (2001): 866–905.

———. "Settler Colonialism and the Elimination of the Native." *Journal of Genocide Research* 8, no. 4 (2006): 387–409.

———. *Settler Colonialism and the Transformation of Anthropology: The Politics and Poetics of an Ethnographic Event*. London: Cassell, 1999.

———. "Structure and Event: Settler Colonialism, Time, and the Question of Genocide." In *Empire, Colony, Genocide: Conquest, Occupation, and Subaltern Resistance in World History*, edited by A. Dirk Moses, 102–32. New York: Berghahn Books, 2008.

Worth, John E. *The Struggle for the Georgia Coast*. Gainesville: University Press of Florida, 1998.

———. *Timucuan Chiefdoms of Spanish Florida. Assimilation*. Gainesville: University Press of Florida, 1998.

Wright, J. Leitch, Jr. *Creeks and Seminoles: The Destruction and Regeneration of the Muscogulge People*. Lincoln: University of Nebraska Press, 1986.

Wynn, Graeme. "Settler Societies in Geographical Focus." *Historical Studies* 20, no. 80 (1983): 353–66.

Yancey, George A. *Who Is White? Latinos, Asians, and the New Black/Nonblack Divide*. Boulder, CO: Lynne Rienner, 2003.

Ye, Yazoume, et al. *Environmental Factors and Malaria Transmission Risk: Modeling the Risk in the Holoendemic Area of Burkina Faso*. Fanham, UK: Ashgate, 2008.

Young, Allan. *The Harmony of Illusions: Inventing Post-Traumatic Stress Disorder*. Princeton, NJ: Princeton University Press, 1995.

Young, Mary. "The Cherokee Nation: Mirror of the Republic." *American Quarterly* 33, no. 5 (Winter 1981): 502–24.

Index

Page numbers in italics signify photos, drawings, or maps.

CPSIA information can be obtained
at www.ICGtesting.com
Printed in the USA
FSHW012147070120
65859FS